THE COMPLETE WORKS OF ROBERT BROWNING, VOLUME VI

Robert Browning in 1865; an engraving based on a photograph by Jeffrey. Courtesy of the Armstrong Browning Library.

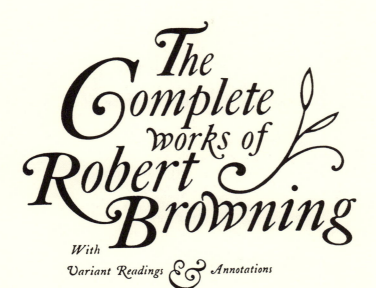

The Complete works of Robert Browning

With Variant Readings & Annotations

Volume VI

EDITED BY

JOHN C. BERKEY

ALLAN C. DOOLEY

SUSAN E. DOOLEY

BAYLOR UNIVERSITY

WACO, TEXAS

OHIO UNIVERSITY PRESS

ATHENS, OHIO

1996

THE COMPLETE WORKS OF ROBERT BROWNING

Ohio University Press, Athens, Ohio 45701

Printed in the United States of America

99 98 97 96 5 4 3 2 1

Ohio University Press books are printed on acid-free paper ∞

Library of Congress Cataloging—Publication Data
(Revised for vol. 6)

Browning, Robert, 1812-1889.
The complete works of Robert Browning, with variant readings & annotations. Editorial board.

Vol. 6 edited by John C. Berkey, Allan C. Dooley and Susan E. Dooley.
Includes bibliographical references and indexes.
I. King, Roma A. (Roma Alvah), 1914- ed.
II. Herring, Jack W., 1925- . III. Crowder, A. B.
IV. Title.
PR4201.K5 1969 821′.8 68-18389
ISBN 0-8214-1137-3 (v. 6)

CONTENTS

	Page Number
PREFACE	ix
TABLES	xxii
ACKNOWLEDGMENTS	xxvi
MEN AND WOMEN, VOLUME II	3
Andrea del Sarto (Called "The Faultless Painter")	7
Before	16
After	18
In Three Days	19
In a Year	21
Old Pictures in Florence	24
In a Balcony	37
Saul	72
"De Gustibus—"	90
Women and Roses	92
Protus	94
Holy-Cross Day	96
The Guardian-Angel	102

Cleon 105
The Twins 117
Popularity 119
The Heretic's Tragedy 122
Two in the Campagna 127
A Grammarian's Funeral 130
One Way of Love 135
Another Way of Love 136
"Transcendentalism: a Poem in Twelve Books" 138
Misconceptions 140
One Word More 141

BEN KARSHOOK'S WISDOM 151

LAST POEMS BY ELIZABETH BARRETT BROWNING (1862)
Dedication 155
Advertisement 156

THE GREEK CHRISTIAN POETS AND THE ENGLISH POETS BY ELIZABETH BARRET BROWNING (1863)
Advertisement 157

POETICAL WORKS (1863 and 1865)
Title Page 159
Dedication 160
Contents 161
Notes 165

EURYDICE TO ORPHEUS; A PICTURE BY LEIGHTON 167

DRAMATIS PERSONÆ 171
James Lee's Wife 175
Gold Hair: a Story of Pornic 193
The Worst of It 201
Dîs Aliter Visum; or, Le Byron de Nos Jours 206
Too Late 214
Abt Vogler 220
Rabbi Ben Ezra 226
A Death in the Desert 235
Caliban upon Setebos; or, Natural Theology in the Island 259
Confessions 271
May and Death 273
Prospice 275
Youth and Art 276
A Face 280
A Likeness 282
Mr. Sludge, "The Medium" 285
Apparent Failure 352
Epilogue 355

A SELECTION FROM THE WORKS OF ROBERT BROWNING (1865)
Preface 361

A SELECTION FROM THE POETRY OF ELIZABETH BARRETT BROWNING (1866)
Preface 363

POETICAL WORKS (1868 and 1870)
Title page 365
Notes 367
Contents 369

DEAF AND DUMB 373

EDITORIAL NOTES
Men and Women, Volume II 377
Ben Karshook's Wisdom 422
Eurydice to Orpheus 425
Dramatis Personæ 426
Deaf and Dumb 466

CUMULATIVE INDEX OF TITLES 469

Preface

I contents

This edition of the works of Robert Browning is intended to be complete. It will comprise at least seventeen volumes and will contain:

1. The entire contents of the first editions of Browning's works, arranged in their chronological order of publication. (The poems included in *Dramatic Lyrics, Dramatic Romances and Lyrics,* and *Men and Women,* for example, appear in the order of their first publication rather than in the order in which Browning rearranged them for later publication.)
2. All prefaces and dedications which Browning is known to have written for his own works and for those of Elizabeth Barrett Browning.
3. The two prose essays that Browning is known to have published: the review of a book on Tasso, generally referred to as the "Essay on Chatterton," and the preface for a collection of letters supposed to have been written by Percy Bysshe Shelley, generally referred to as the "Essay on Shelley."
4. The front matter and the table of contents of each of the collected editions (1849, 1863, 1865, 1868 [70, 75], 1888-1889) which Browning himself saw through the press.
5. Poems published during Browning's lifetime but not collected by him.
6. Poems not published during Browning's lifetime which have come to light since his death.
7. John Forster's *Thomas Wentworth, Earl of Strafford,* to which Browning contributed significantly, though the precise extent of his contribution has not been determined.
8. Variants appearing in primary and secondary materials as defined in Section II below.
9. Textual emendations.
10. Informational and explanatory notes for each work.

II primary and secondary materials

Aside from a handful of uncollected short works, all of Browning's works but *Asolando* (1889) went through two or more editions during his lifetime. Except for *Pauline* (1833), *Strafford* (1837), and *Sordello* (1840), all the works published before 1849 were revised and corrected for the 1849 collection. *Strafford* and *Sordello* were revised and corrected for the collection of 1863, as were all the other works in that edition. Though no further poems were added in the collection of 1865, all the works were once again corrected and revised. The 1868 collection added a revised *Pauline* and *Dramatis Personae* (1864) to the other works, which were themselves again revised and corrected. A new edition of this collection in 1870 contained further revisions and Browning corrected his text again for an 1875 reimpression. The printing of the last edition of the *Poetical Works* over which Browning exercised control began in 1888, and the first eight volumes are dated thus on their title-pages. Volumes 9 through 16 of this first impression are dated 1889, and we have designated them 1889a to distinguish them from the second impression of all 16 volumes, which was begun and completed in 1889. Some of the earlier volumes of the first impression sold out almost immediately, and in preparation for a second impression, Browning revised and corrected the first ten volumes before he left for Italy in late August, 1889. The second impression, in which all sixteen volumes bear the date 1889 on their title-pages, consisted of a revised and corrected second impression of volumes 1-10, plus a second impression of volumes 11-16 altered by Browning in one instance. This impression we term 1889 (see section III below).

Existing manuscripts and editions are classified as either primary or secondary material. The primary materials include the following:

1. The manuscript of a work when such is known to exist.

2. Proof sheets, when known to exist, that contain authorial corrections and revisions.

3. The first and subsequent editions of a work that preserve evidence of Browning's intentions and were under his control.

4. The collected editions over which Browning exercised control:

1849—*Poems*. Two Volumes. London: Chapman and Hall.

1863—*The Poetical Works*. Three Volumes. London: Chapman and Hall.

1865—*The Poetical Works*. Three Volumes. London: Chapman and Hall.

1868—*The Poetical Works*. Six Volumes. London: Smith, Elder and Company.

1870—*The Poetical Works*. Six Volumes. London: Smith, Elder and Company. This resetting constituted a new edition, which was stereotyped and reimpressed several times; the 1875 impression contains revisions by Browning.

1888-1889—*The Poetical Works*. Sixteen Volumes. London: Smith, Elder and Company. Exists in numerous stereotype impressions, of which two are primary material:

1888-1889a—The first impression, in which volumes 1-8 are dated 1888 and volumes 9-16 are dated 1889.

1889—The corrected second impression of volumes 1-10 and a second impression of volumes 11-16 altered by Browning only as stated in section III below; all dated 1889 on the title pages.

5. The corrections in Browning's hand in the Dykes Campbell copy of 1888-1889a, and the manuscript list of corrections to that impression in the Brown University Library (see section III below).

Other materials (including some in the poet's handwriting) that affected the text are secondary. Examples are: the copy of the first edition of *Pauline* which contains annotations by Browning and John Stuart Mill; the copies of the first edition of *Paracelsus* which contain corrections in Browning's hand; a very early manuscript of *A Blot in the 'Scutcheon* which Browning presented to William Macready, but not the one from which the first edition was printed; informal lists of corrections that Browning included in letters to friends, such as the corrections to *Men and Women* he sent to D. G. Rossetti; verbal and punctuational changes Browning essayed in presentation copies of his works or in his own copies, if not used by his printers; Elizabeth Barrett's suggestions for revisions in *A Soul's Tragedy* and certain poems in *Dramatic Romances and Lyrics;* and the edition of *Strafford* by Emily Hickey for which Browning made suggestions.

The text and variant readings of this edition derive from collation of primary materials as defined above. Secondary materials are occasionally discussed in the notes and sometimes play a part when emendation is required.

III COPY-TEXT

The copy-text for this edition is Browning's final text: the first ten volumes of 1889 and the last six volumes of 1888-1889a, as described above. For this choice we offer the following explanation.

Manuscripts used as printer's copy for twenty of Browning's thirty-four book publications are known to exist; others may yet become available. These manuscripts, or, in their absence, the first editions of the works, might be considered as the most desirable copy-text. And this would be the case for an author who exercised little control over his text after the manuscript or first edition stage, or whose text clearly became corrupted in a succession of editions. To preserve the intention of such an author, one would have to choose an early text and emend it as evidence and judgment demanded.

With Browning, however, the situation is different, and our copy-text choice results from that difference. Throughout his life Browning continually revised his poetry. He did more than correct printer's errors and clarify previously intended meanings; his texts themselves remained fluid, subject to continuous alteration. As the manuscript which he submitted to his publisher was no doubt already a product of revision, so each subsequent edition under his control reflects the results of an ongoing process of creating, revising, and correcting. If we were to choose the manuscript (where extant) or first edition as copy-text, preserving Browning's intention would require extensive emendation to capture the additions, revisions, and alterations which Browning demonstrably made in later editions. By selecting Browning's final corrected text as our copy-text, emending it only to eliminate errors and the consequences of changing house-styling, we present his works in the form closest to that which he intended after years of revision and polishing.

But this is true only if Browning in fact exercised extensive control over the printing of his various editions. That he intended and attempted to do so is apparent in his comments and his practice. In 1855, demanding accuracy from the printers, he pointed out to his publisher Chapman, "I attach importance to the mere stops . . ." (DeVane and Knickerbocker, p. 83). There is evidence of his desire to control the details of his text as early as 1835, in the case of *Paracelsus*. The *Paracelsus* manuscript, now in the Forster and Dyce collection in the Victoria and Albert Museum Library, demonstrates a highly unconventional system of punctuation. Of particular note is Browning's unrestrained use of dashes, often in strings of two or three, instead of more precise or orthodox punctuation marks. It appears that this was done for its rhetorical effect. One sheet of Part 1 of the manuscript and all but the first and last sheets of Part 3 have had punctuation revised in pencil by someone other than Browning, perhaps J. Riggs, whose name appears three times in the margins of Part 3. In addition to these revisions, there are analogous punctuation revisions (in both pencil and ink) which appear to be in Browning's hand, and a few verbal alterations obviously in the poet's script.

A collation of the first edition (1835) with the manuscript reveals that a major restyling of punctuation was carried out before *Paracelsus* was published. However, the revisions incorporated into the first edition by no means slavishly follow the example set by the pencilled revisions of Parts 1 and 3 of the manuscript. Apparently the surviving manuscript was not used as printer's copy for the first edition. Browning may have submitted a second manuscript, or he may have revised extensively in proof. The printers may have carried out the revisions to punctuation, with or without the poet's point by point involvement. With the present evidence, we cannot be conclusive about the extent of Browning's control over the first edition of *Paracelsus*. It can be stated, however, in the light of the incompleteness of the pencilled revisions and the frequent lack or correspondence between the pencilled revisions and the lines as printed in 1835, that Browning himself may have been responsible for the punctuation of the first edition of *Paracelsus.* Certainly he was responsible for the frequent instances in the first and subsequent editions where the punctuation defies conventional rules, as in the following examples:

> What though
> It be so?—if indeed the strong desire
> Eclipse the aim in me—if splendour break
> (Part I, 11. 329-331)
>
> I surely loved them—that last night, at least,
> When we . . . gone! gone! the better: I am saved
> (Part II, 11. 132-133)
>
> Of the body, even,)—what God is, what we are,
> (Part V, 1. 642, 1849 reading)

The manuscripts of *Colombe's Birthday* (1844) and *Christmas-Eve and Easter-Day* (1850) were followed very carefully in the printing of the first editions. There are slight indications of minor house-styling, such as the spellings *colour* and *honour* for the manuscripts' *color* and *honor.* But the unorthodox punctuation, used to indicate elocutionary and rhetorical subtleties as well as syntactical relationships, is carried over almost unaltered from the manuscripts to the first editions. Similar evidence of Browning's painstaking attention to the smallest details in the printing of his poems can be seen in the manuscript and proof sheets of *The Ring and the Book* (1868-69). These materials reveal an interesting and significant pattern. It appears that Browning wrote swiftly, giving primary attention to wording and less to punctuation, being satisfied to use dashes to indicate almost any break in thought, syntax, or rhythm. Later, in the proof sheets for Books 1-6 of the poem and in the manuscript itself for Books 7-12, he changed the dashes to more specific and purposeful punctuation marks. The revised punctuation is what was printed, for the most part, in the first edition of *The Ring and the Book;* what further revisions there are conform to Browning's practice, though hardly to standard rules. Clearly Browning was in control of nearly every aspect of the published form of his works, even to the "mere stops."

Of still greater importance in our choice of copy-text is the substantial evidence that Browning took similar care with his collected editions. Though he characterized his changes for later editions as trivial and few in number, collations reveal thousands of revisions and corrections in each successive text. *Paracelsus,* for example, was extensively revised for the 1849 *Poems;* it was again reworked for the *Poetical Works* of 1863. *Sordello,* omitted in 1849, reappeared in 1863 with 181 new lines and short marginal glosses; Browning admitted only that it was "corrected *throughout*" (DeVane and Knickerbocker, p. 157). The poems of *Men and Women* (1855) were altered in numerous small but meaningful ways for both the 1863 and 1865 editions of the *Poetical Works* (See Allan C. Dooley, "The Textual Significance of Robert Browning's 1865 *Poetical Works,*" *PBSA* 71 [1977], 212-18). Michael Hancher cites evidence of the poet's close supervision of the 1868 collected edition ("Browning and the *Poetical Works* of 1888-1889," *Browning Newsletter,* Spring, 1971, 25-27), and Michael Meredith has traced Browning's attentions to his text in the 1870 edition and an 1875 reimpression of it ("Learning's Crabbed Text," *SBHC* 13 [1985], 97-107); another perspective is offered in Allan C. Dooley's *Author and Printer in Victorian England* (1992), Ch. 4-5. Mrs. Orr, writing of the same period in Browning's life, reports his resentment of those who garbled his text by misplacing his stops (*Life,* pp. 357-58).

There is plentiful and irrefutable evidence that Browning controlled, in the same meticulous way, the text of his last collected edition, that which we term 1888-1889. Hancher has summarized the relevant information:

> The evidence is clear that Browning undertook the 1888-1889 edition of his *Poetical Works* intent on controlling even the smallest minutiae of the text. Though he at one time considered supplying biographical and explanatory notes to the poems, he finally decided against such a scheme, concluding, in his letter to Smith of 12 November 1887, "I am correcting them carefully, and *that* must suffice." On 13 January 1888, he wrote, regarding the six-volume edition of his collected works published in 1868 which was to serve as the printer's copy for the final edition:
> "I have thoroughly corrected the six volumes of the Works, and can let you have them at once." . . . Browning evidently kept a sharp eye on the production of all sixteen of the volumes, including those later volumes. . . . Browning returned proof for Volume 3 on 6 May 1888, commenting, "I have had, as usual, to congratulate myself on the scrupulous accuracy of the Printers"; on 31 December he returned proofs of Volume 11, "corrected carefully"; and he returned "the corrected Proofs of Vol. XV" on 1 May 1889.

Throughout his long career, then, Browning continuously revised and corrected his works. Furthermore, his publishers took care to follow his directions exactly, accepting his changes and incorporating them into each successive edition. This is not to say that no one else had any effect whatsoever on Browning's text: Elizabeth Barrett made suggestions for revisions to *A Soul's Tragedy* and *Dramatic Romances and Lyrics.* Browning accepted some suggestions and rejected others, and those which he accepted we regard as his own. Mrs. Orr reports that Browning sent proof sheets to Joseph Milsand, a friend in France, for corrections (*Life,* p. 183), and that Browning accepted suggestions from friends and readers for the corrections of errors in his printed works. In some of the editions, there are slight evidences of minor house-styling in capitalization and the indication of quotations. But the evidence of Browning's own careful attention to revisions and corrections in both his manuscripts and proof sheets assures us that other persons played only a very minor role in the development of his text. We conclude that the vast majority of the alterations in the texts listed above as Primary Materials are Browning's own, and that only Browning's final corrected text, the result of years of careful work by the poet himself, reflects his full intentions.

The first impression of Browning's final collected edition (i.e., 1888-1889a) is not in and of itself the poet's final corrected text. By the spring or 1889 some of the early volumes of the first impression were already sold out, and by mid-August it was evident that a new one would be required. About this time James Dykes Campbell, Honorary Secretary of the London Browning Society, was informed by Browning that he was making further corrections to be incorporated into the new impression. According to Dykes Campbell, Browning had corrected the first ten volumes and offered to transcribe the corrections into Dykes Campbell's copy of 1888-1889a before leaving for Italy. The volumes altered in Browning's hand are now in the British Library and contain on the flyleaf of Volume I Dykes Campbell's note explaining precisely what happened. Of course, Dykes Campbell's copy was not the one used by the printer for the second impression. Nevertheless, these changes are indisputably Browning's and are those which, according to his own statement, he proposed to make in the new impression. This set of corrections carries, therefore, great authority.

Equally authoritative is a second set of corrections, also in Browning's hand, for part of 1888-1889a. In the poet's possession at the time of his death, this handwritten list was included in lot 179 of Sotheby, Wilkinson, and Hodge's auction of Browning materials in 1913; it is today located in the Brown University Library. The list contains corrections only for Volumes 4-10 of 1888-1889a. We know that Browning, on 26 July 1889, had completed and sent to Smith "the corrections for Vol. III in readiness for whenever you need them." By the latter part of August, according to Dykes Campbell, the poet had finished corrections for Volumes 1-10. Browning left for Italy on 29 August. The condition of the Brown University list does not indicate that it was ever used by the printer. Thus we surmise that the Brown list (completing the corrections through volume 10) may be the poet's copy of another list sent to his publisher. Whatever the case, the actual documents used by the printers—a set of marked volumes or handwritten lists—are not known to exist. A possible exception is a marked copy of *Red Cotton Night-Cap Country* (now in the Berg Collection of the New York Public Library) which seems to have been used by printers. Further materials used in preparing Browning's final edition may yet appear.

The matter is complicated further because neither set of corrections of 1888-1889a corresponds exactly to each other nor to the 1889 second impression. Each set contains corrections the other omits, and in a few cases the sets present alternative corrections of the same error. Our study of the Dykes Campbell copy of 1888-1889a reveals fifteen discrepancies between its corrections and the 1889 second impression. The Brown University list, which contains far fewer corrections, varies from the second impression in thirteen instances. Though neither of these sets of corrections was used by the printers, both are authoritative; we consider them legitimate textual variants, and record them as such. The lists are, of course, useful when emendation of the copy-text is required.

The value of the Dykes Campbell copy of 1888-1889a and the Brown University list is not that they render Browning's text perfect. The corrections to 1888-1889a must have existed in at least one other, still more authoritative form: the documents which Browning sent to his publisher. That this is so is indicated by the presence of required corrections in the second impression which neither the Dykes Campbell copy nor the Brown University list calls for. The significance of the existing sets of corrections is that they clearly indicate two important points: Browning's direct and active interest in the preparation of a corrected second impression of his final collected edition; and, given the high degree of correspondence between the two sets of corrections and the affected lines of the second impression, the concern of the printers to follow the poet's directives.

The second impression of 1888-1889 incorporated most of Browning's corrections to the first ten volumes of the first impression. There is no evidence whatever that any corrections beyond those which Browning sent to his publisher in the summer of 1889 were ever made. We choose, therefore, the 1889 corrected second impression of volumes 1-10 as copy-text for the works in those volumes. Corrections to the first impression were achieved by cutting the affected letters of punctuation out of the stereotype plates and pressing or soldering in the correct pieces of type. The corrected plates were then used for many copies, without changing the date on the title pages (except, of course, in volumes 17 [*Asolando*] and 18 [*New Poems*], added to the set by the publishers in 1894 and 1914 respectively). External evidence from publishers' catalogues and the advertisements bound into some volumes of 1889 indicate that copies of this impression were produced as late as 1913, although the dates on the title pages of volumes 1-16 remained 1889. Extensive plate deterioration is characteristic of the later copies, and use of the Hinman collator on early and late examples of 1889 reveals that the inserted corrections were somewhat fragile, some of them having decayed or disappeared entirely as the plates aged. (See Allan C. Dooley, "Browning's *Poetical Works* of 1888-1889," *SBHC* 7:1 [1978], 43-69.)

We do not use as copy-text volumes 11-16 of 1889, because there is no present evidence indicating that Browning exercised substantial control over this part of the second impression of 1888-1889. We do know that he made one correction, which he requested in a letter to Smith quoted by Hancher:

> I have just had pointed out to [me] that an error, I supposed corrected, still is to be found in the 13th Volume—(Aristophanes' Apology) page 143, line 9, where the word should be Opora—without an i. I should like it altered, if that may be possible.

This correction was indeed made in the second impression. Our collations of copies of volumes 11-16 of 1889a and 1889 show no other intentional changes. The later copies do show, however, extensive type batter, numerous scratches, and irregular inking. Therefore our copy-text for the works in the last six volumes of 1888-1889 is volumes 11-16 of 1888-1889a.

IV VARIANTS

In this edition we record, with a very few exceptions discussed below, all variants from the copy-text appearing in the manuscripts and in the editions under Browning's control. Our purpose in doing this is two-fold.

1. We enable the reader to reconstruct the text of a work as it stood at the various stages of its development.

2. We provide the materials necessary to an understanding of how Browning's growth and development as an artist are reflected in his successive revisions to his works.

As a consequence of this policy our variant listings inevitably contain some variants that were not created by Browning; printer's errors and readings that may result from house-styling will appear occasionally. But the evidence that Browning assumed responsibility for what was printed, and that he considered and used unorthodox punctuation as part of his meaning, is so persuasive that we must record even the smallest and oddest variants. The following examples, characteristic of Browning's revisions, illustrate the point:

Pauline, l. 700:

1833: I am prepared—I have made life my own—

1868: I am prepared: I have made life my own.

"Evelyn Hope," l. 41:

1855: I have lived, I shall say, so much since then,
1865: I have lived (I shall say) so much since then,

"Bishop Blougram's Apology," l. 267:

1855: That's the first cabin-comfort I secure—
1865: That's the first-cabin comfort I secure:

The Ring and the Book, Book 11 ("Guido"), l. 1064:

1869: What if you give up boys' and girls' fools'-play
1872: What if you give up boy and girl fools'-play
1889a: What if you give up boy-and-girl-fools' play

We have concluded that Browning himself is nearly always responsible for such changes. But even if he only accepted these changes (rather than originating them), their effect on syntax, rhythm, and meaning is so significant that they must be recorded in our variant listings.

The only variants we do not record are those which strongly appear to result from systematic house-styling. For example, Browning nowhere indicated that he wished to use typography to influence meaning, and our inference is that any changes in line-spacing, depth of paragraph indentation, and the like, were the responsibility of the printers of the various editions, not the poet himself. House-styling was also very probably the cause of certain variants in the apparatus of Browning's plays, including variants in stage directions which involve a change only in manner of statement, such as *Enter Hampden* instead of *Hampden enters;* variants in the printing of stage directions, such as *Aside* instead of *aside,* or [*Aside.*] instead of [*Aside*], or [*Strafford.*] instead of [*Strafford*]; variants in character designations, such as *Lady Carlisle* instead of *Car* or *Carlisle.* Browning also accepted current convention for indicating quotations (see section V below). Neither do we list changes in type face (except when used for emphasis), nor the presence or absence of a period at the end of the title of a work.

V ALTERATIONS TO THE COPY-TEXT

We have rearranged the sequence of works in the copy-text, so that they appear in the order of their first publication. This process involves the restoration to the original order of the poems included in *Dramatic Lyrics, Dramatic Romances and Lyrics,* and *Men and Women.* We realize, of course, that Browning himself was responsible for the rearrangement of these poems in the various collected editions; in his prefatory note for the 1888-1889 edition, however, he indicates that he desired a chronological presentation:

> The poems that follow are again, as before, printed in chronological order; but only so far as proves compatible with the prescribed size of each volume, which necessitates an occasional change in the distribution of its contents.

We would like both to indicate Browning's stated intentions about the placement of his poems and to present the poems in the order which suggests Browning's development as a poet. We have chosen, therefore, to present the poems in order of their first publication, with an indication in the notes as to their respective subsequent placement. We also include the tables of contents of the editions listed as Primary Materials above.

We have regularized or modernized the copy-text in the following minor ways:

1. We do not place a period at the end of the title of a work, though the copy-text does.

2. In some of Browning's editions, including the copy-text, the first word of each work is printed in capital letters. We have used the modern practice of capitalizing only the first letter.

3. The inconsistent use of both an ampersand and the word *and* has been regularized to the use of *and*.

4. We have eliminated the space between the two parts of a contraction; thus the copy-text's *it 's* is printed as *it's*, for example.

5. We uniformly place periods and commas within closing quotation marks.

6. We have employed throughout the modern practice of indicating quoted passages with quotation marks only at the beginning and end of the quotation. Throughout Browning's career, no matter which publisher or printer was handling his works, this matter was treated very inconsistently. In some of the poet's manuscripts and in most of his first editions, quotations are indicated by quotation marks only at the beginning and end. In the collected editions of 1863 and 1865, issued by Chapman and Hall, some quoted passages have quotation marks at the beginning of each line of the quotation, while others follow modern practice. In Smith, Elder's collected editions of 1868 and 1888-1889, quotation marks usually appear at the beginning of each line of a quotation. We have regularized and modernized what seems a matter of house-styling in both copy-text and variants.

The remaining way in which the copy-text is altered is by emendation. Our policy is to emend the copy-text to eliminate apparent errors of either Browning or his printers. It is evident that Browning did make errors and overlook mistakes, as shown by the following example from "One Word More," the last poem in *Men and Women*. Stanza sixteen of the copy-text opens with the following lines:

What, there's nothing in the moon noteworthy?
Nay: for if that moon could love a mortal,
Use, to charm him (so to fit a fancy,
All her magic ('tis the old sweet mythos)
She . . .

Clearly the end punctuation in the third line is incorrect. A study of the various texts is illuminating. Following are the readings of the line in each of the editions for which Browning was responsible:

MS:	fancy)	1855:	fancy)	1865:	fancy)	1888:	fancy
P:	fancy)	1863:	fancy)	1868:	fancy)	1889:	fancy,

The omission of one parenthesis in 1888 was almost certainly a printers error. Browning, in the Dykes Campbell copy corrections to 1888-1889a, missed or ignored the error. However, in the Brown University list of corrections, he indicated that *fancy* should be followed by a comma. This is the way the line appears in the corrected second impression of Volume 4, but the correction at best satisfies the demands of syntax only partially. Browning might have written the line:

Use, to charm him, so to fit a fancy,

or, to maintain parallelism between the third and fourth lines:

Use, to charm him (so to fit a fancy),

or he might simply have restored the earlier reading. Oversights of this nature demand emendation, and our choice would be to restore the punctuation of the manuscript through 1868. All of our emendations will be based, as far as possible, on the historical collation of the passage involved, the grammatical demands of the passage in context, and the poet's treatment of other similar passages. Fortunately, the multiple editions of most of the works provide the editor with ample textual evidence to make an informed and useful emendation.

All emendations to the copy-text are listed at the beginning of the Editorial Notes for each work. The variant listings for the copy-text also incorporate the emendations, which are preceded and followed there by the symbol indicating an editor's note.

VI APPARATUS

1. *Variants.* In presenting the variants from the copy-text, we list at the bottom of each page readings from the known manuscripts,

proof sheets of the editions when we have located them, and the first and subsequent editions.

A variant is generally preceded and followed by a pickup and a drop word (example a). No note terminates with a punctuation mark unless the punctuation mark comes at the end of the line; if a variant drops or adds a punctuation mark, the next word is added (example b). If the normal pickup word has appeared previously in the same line, the note begins with the word preceding it. If the normal drop word appears subsequently in the line, the next word is added (example c). If a capitalized pickup word occurs within the line, it is accompanied by the preceding word (example d). No pickup or drop words, however, are used for any variant consisting of an internal change, for example a hyphen in a compounded word, an apostrophe, a tense change or a spelling change (example e). A change in capilalization within a line of poetry will be preceded by a pickup word, for which, within an entry containing other variants, the <> is suitable (example f). No drop word is used when the variant comes at the end of a line (example g). Examples from *Sordello* (all from Book I except c[2] which is from Book 4):

a. 611| *1840:*but that appeared *1863:*but this appeared

b. variant at end of line: 109| *1840:*intrigue:" *1863:*intrigue.
variant within line: 82| *1840:*forests like *1863:*forests, like

c. 132| *1840:*too sleeps; but *1863:*too sleeps: but 77| *1840:*that night by *1863:*that, night by night, *1888:*by night

d. 295| *1840:*at Padua to repulse the *1863:*at Padua who repulsed the

e. 284| *1840:*are *1863:*were
344| *1840:*dying-day, *1863:*dying day,

f. capitalization change with no other variants: 741| *1840:* retaining Will, *1863:*will,
with other variants: 843| *1840:*Was <> Him back! Why *1863:* Is <> back!" Why *1865:*him

g. 427| *1840:*dregs: *1863:*dregs.

Each recorded variant will be assumed to be incorporated in the next edition if there is no indication otherwise. This rule applies even in cases where the only change occurs in 1888-1889, although it means that the variant note duplicates the copy-test. A variant listing, then, traces the history of a line and brings it forward to the point where it matches the copy-text.

An editor's note always refers to the single word or mark of punctuation immediately preceding or following the comment, unless otherwise specified.

In Browning's plays, all character designations which happen to occur in variant listings are standardized to the copy-text reading. In listing variants in the plays, we ignore character designations unless the designation comes within a numbered line. In such a case, the variant is treated as any other word, and can be used as a pickup or drop word. When a character designation is used as a pickup word, however, the rule excluding capitalized pickup words (except at the beginning of a line) does not apply, and we do not revert to the next earliest uncapitalized pickup word.

2. *Line numbers.* Poetic lines are numbered in the traditional manner, taking one complete poetic line as one unit of counting. In prose passages the unit of counting is the type line of this edition.

3. *Table of signs in variant listings.* We have avoided all symbols and signs used by Browning himself. The following is a table of the signs used in the variant notes:

§ . . . §	Editor's note
< >	Words omitted
/	Line break
/ / , / / / , . . .	Line break plus one or more lines without internal variants

4. *Annotations.* In general principle, we have annotated proper names, phrases that function as proper names, and words or groups of words the full meaning of which requires factual, historical, or literary background. Thus we have attempted to hold interpretation to a minimum, although we realize that the act of selection itself is to some extent interpretive.

Notes, particularly on historical figures and events, tend to fullness and even to the tangential and unessential. As a result, some of the information provided may seem unnecessary to the scholar. On the other hand, it is not possible to assume that all who use this edition are fully equipped to assimilate unaided all of Browning's copious literary, historical, and mythological allusions. Thus we have directed our efforts toward a diverse audience.

Tables

1. *Manuscripts.* We have located manuscripts for the following of Browning's works; the list is chronological.

Paracelsus
Forster and Dyce Collection,
Victoria and Albert Museum, London

Colombe's Birthday
New York Public Library

Christmas-Eve and Easter-Day
  Forster and Dyce Collection,
  Victoria and Albert Museum, London
"Love Among the Ruins"
  Lowell Collection,
  Houghton Library, Harvard University
"The Twins"
  Pierpont Morgan Library, New York
"One Word More"
  Pierpont Morgan Library, New York
"James Lee's Wife," ll. 244-69
  Armstrong Browning Library, Baylor University
"May and Death"
  Armstrong Browning Library, Baylor University
"A Face"
  Armstrong Browning Library, Baylor University
Dramatis Personae
  Pierpont Morgan Library, New York
The Ring and the Book
  British Library, London
Balaustion's Adventure
  Balliol College Library, Oxford
Prince Hohenstiel-Schwangau
  Balliol College Library, Oxford
Fifine at the Fair
  Balliol College Library, Oxford
Red Cotton Night-Cap Country
  Balliol College Library, Oxford
Aristophanes' Apology
  Balliol College Library, Oxford
The Inn Album
  Balliol College Library, Oxford
Of Pacchiarotto, and How He Worked in Distemper
  Balliol College Library, Oxford
"Hervé Riel"
  Pierpont Morgan Library, New York
The Agamemnon of Aeschylus
  Balliol College Library, Oxford
La Saisaiz and The Two Poets of Croisic
  Balliol College Library, Oxford
Dramatic Idylls
  Balliol College Library, Oxford
Dramatic Idylls, Second Series
  Balliol College Library, Oxford

Jocoseria
Balliol College Library, Oxford
Ferishtah's Fancies
Balliol College Library, Oxford
Parleyings With Certain People of Importance in Their Day
Balliol College Library, Oxford
Asolando
Pierpont Morgan Library, New York

We have been unable to locate manuscripts for the following works, and request that persons with information about any of them communicate with us.

Pauline
Strafford
Sordello
Pippa Passes
King Victor and King Charles
"Essay on Chatterton"
Dramatic Lyrics
The Return of the Druses
A Blot in the 'Scutcheon
Dramatic Romances and Lyrics
Luria
A Soul's Tragedy
"Essay on Shelley"
Men and Women

2. *Editions referred to in Volume VI.* The following editions have been used in preparing the text and variants presented in this volume. The dates given below are used as symbols in the variant listings at the bottom of each page.

1855 *Men and Women.*
London: Chapman and Hall.

1863 *The Poetical Works.*
Three Volumes. London: Chapman and Hall.

1864a *Dramatis Personæ.*
First Edition. London: Chapman and Hall.

1864b *Dramatis Personæ.*
Second Edition. London: Chapman and Hall.

1865 *The Poetical Works.*
Three Volumes. London: Chapman and Hall.

1868 *The Poetical Works.*
Six Volumes. London: Smith, Elder and Company.

1870 *The Poetical Works.*
Six Volumes. London: Smith, Elder and Company.

1875 *The Poetical Works.*
Six Volumes. London: Smith, Elder and Company.
(corrected impression of 1870)

1888 *The Poetical Works.*
Volumes 1-8. London: Smith, Elder and Company.

1889a *The Poetical Works.*
Volumes 9-16. London: Smith, Elder and Company.

1889 *The Poetical Works.*
Sixteen Volumes. London: Smith, Elder and Company.
(corrected impression of 1888-89a)

3. *Short titles and abbreviations.* The following short forms of reference have been used in notes for this edition:

ABL	Armstrong Browning Library
B	Browning
BrU	Browning's list of corrections located at Brown University.
C1870	Browning's corrections in a copy of *Poetical Works* (1870) in the Pierpont Morgan Library.
Correspondence	*The Brownings' Correspondence,* ed. P. Kelley and R. Hudson. Winfield, KS, 1984-.
DC	Browning's corrections in James Dykes Campbell's copy of 1888-89a.
DeVane, *Hbk.*	W. C. DeVane. *A Browning Handbook.* New York, 1955.
DeVane and Knickerbocker	*New Letters of Robert Browning,* ed. W. C. DeVane and K. L. Knickerbocker. New Haven, 1950.
EBB	Elizabeth Barrett Browning
Hood	*Letters of Robert Browning Collected by Thomas J. Wise,* ed. T. L. Hood. New Haven, CT, 1933.
Hudson	*Browning to His American Friends,* ed. G. R. Hudson. New York, 1965.
Irvine and Honan	W. Irvine and P. Honan. *The Book, the Ring, and the Poet.* New York, 1974.
Kintner	*The Letters of Robert Browning and Elizabeth Barrett Barrett, 1845-1846,* ed. E. Kintner. Cambridge, MA, 1969.
Korg	J. Korg. *Browning and Italy.* Athens, OH, 1983.
Letters of EBB	*The Letters of Elizabeth Barrett Browning,* ed. F. G. Kenyon. New York, 1897.
Landis and Freeman	*Letters of the Brownings to George Barrett,* ed. P. Landis and R. E. Freeman. Urbana, IL, 1958.

Markus	J. Markus. *Dared and Done: the Marriage of Elizabeth Barrett and Robert Browning.* New York, 1995.
McAleer	*Dearest Isa: Robert Browning's Letters to Isabella Blagden,* ed. E. C. McAleer. Austin, TX, 1951.
New Poems	*New Poems by Robert Browning and Elizabeth Barrett Browning,* ed. F. G. Kenyon. New York, 1915.
OED	*The Oxford English Dictionary,* 2nd ed. Oxford, 1989.
Orr	Mrs. Sutherland Orr. *A Handbook to the Works of Robert Browning,* 6th ed. London, 1892.
P-C	*The Works of Robert Browning,* ed. C. Porter and H. A. Clarke. New York, 1910, 1912.
P1855	Proofs of the first edition of *Men and Women.*
P1864a	Proofs of the first edition of *Dramatis Personæ.*
Reconstruction	*The Browning Collections, a Reconstruction, with Other Memorabilia,* comp. P. Kelley and B. A. Coley. Waco, TX; New York; Winfield, KS; and London, 1984.
Vasari	Giorgio Vasari. *Lives of the Painters, Sculptors and Architects,* ed. and tr. A. B. Hinds. London, 1963.

Citations and quotations from the Bible refer to the King James Version.

Citations and quotations from Shakespeare refer to *The Riverside Shakespeare,* ed. G. B. Evans, et al. Boston: Houghton Mifflin, 1974.

ACKNOWLEDGMENTS

For providing money and services which have made it possible for us to assemble the materials used in preparing this volume, the following institutions have our sincere gratitude: the Ohio University Press; the Ohio University Library; Baylor University; the Armstrong Library of Baylor University; Kent State University's University Library, Institute for Bibliography and Editing, Research Council, and English Department; the Bibliographical Society of America; the Newberry Library; the Rutgers University Research Council.

We also thank the following for making available to us materials under their care: the Armstrong Browning Library, Baylor University;

the Tinker Collection, Yale University Library; the Berg Collection, New York Public Library; the British Library; the John Hay Library, Brown University; the Henry E. Huntington Library; the Department of Special Collections, Kent State University Library; Mr. Philip Kelley; the Department of Special Collections, Miami University of Ohio; Mr. John Murray; the Department of Special Collections, Ohio University Library; the Pierpont Morgan Library; the Humanities Research Center, University of Texas at Austin.

Of the many scholars who have assisted the editors of the present volume, the following deserve our special gratitude: Radd Ehrmann, Betty Coley Fredeman, Philip Kelley, Rick Newton, David Powell.

The frontispiece is reproduced by permission of the Armstrong Browning Library of Baylor University.

MEN AND WOMEN, VOLUME II

BEN KARSHOOK'S WISDOM

Edited by Allan C. Dooley and Susan E. Dooley

EURYDICE TO ORPHEUS

DRAMATIS PERSONÆ

DEAF AND DUMB

Text by John C. Berkey
Annotations by Allan C. Dooley and Susan E. Dooley

MEN AND WOMEN. Volume II

Edited by Allan C. Dooley and Susan E. Dooley

MEN AND WOMEN
Volume II

MEN AND WOMEN—VOLUME II

1855

ANDREA DEL SARTO

(CALLED "THE FAULTLESS PAINTER")

But do not let us quarrel any more,
No, my Lucrezia; bear with me for once:
Sit down and all shall happen as you wish.
You turn your face, but does it bring your heart?
I'll work then for your friend's friend, never fear,
Treat his own subject after his own way,
Fix his own time, accept too his own price,
And shut the money into this small hand
When next it takes mine. Will it? tenderly?
Oh, I'll content him,—but to-morrow, Love!
I often am much wearier than you think,
This evening more than usual, and it seems
As if—forgive now—should you let me sit
Here by the window with your hand in mine
And look a half-hour forth on Fiesole,
Both of one mind, as married people use,
Quietly, quietly the evening through,
I might get up to-morrow to my work
Cheerful and fresh as ever. Let us try.
To-morrow, how you shall be glad for this!
Your soft hand is a woman of itself,
And mine the man's bared breast she curls inside.
Don't count the time lost, neither; you must serve

---

§P: Proof of 1855. Ed. 1855, 1863, 1865, 1868, 1870, C1870, 1875, 1888, 1889. No full MS known to be extant. For discussion of MSS of individual poems, see Editorial Notes§
ANDREA DEL SARTO §Subsequent placement: *1863:* MW§ *Subtitle*| P: (CALLED THE "FAULTLESS.") *1855:* (CALLED "THE FAULTLESS PAINTER.") [2]| my Lucrezia: bear <> once, *1855:* my Lucrezia; bear <> once: [15]| P: half hour *1888:* half-hour [16]| P: mind as *1855:* mind, as [17]| *1855:* quietly, the *1865:* quietly the [20]| P: To-morrow how *1865:* To-morrow, how [23]| P: either

For each of the five pictures we require:
It saves a model. So! keep looking so—
My serpentining beauty, rounds on rounds!
—How could you ever prick those perfect ears,
Even to put the pearl there! oh, so sweet—
My face, my moon, my everybody's moon,
Which everybody looks on and calls his,
And, I suppose, is looked on by in turn,
While she looks—no one's: very dear, no less.
You smile? why, there's my picture ready made,
There's what we painters call our harmony!
A common greyness silvers everything,—
All in a twilight, you and I alike
—You, at the point of your first pride in me
(That's gone you know),—but I, at every point;
My youth, my hope, my art, being all toned down
To yonder sober pleasant Fiesole.
There's the bell clinking from the chapel-top;
That length of convent-wall across the way
Holds the trees safer, huddled more inside;
The last monk leaves the garden; days decrease,
And autumn grows, autumn in everything.
Eh? the whole seems to fall into a shape
As if I saw alike my work and self
And all that I was born to be and do,
A twilight-piece. Love, we are in God's hand.
How strange now, looks the life he makes us lead;
So free we seem, so fettered fast we are!
I feel he laid the fetter: let it lie!
This chamber for example—turn your head—
All that's behind us! You don't understand
Nor care to understand about my art,
But you can hear at least when people speak:
And that cartoon, the second from the door

1865: neither 24| P:require— *1865:* require: 26| P:on rounds *1855:* on rounds! 27| P:ears *1855:* ears, 32| P:less! *1865:* less. 33| P:made. *1865:* made, 38| P:That's <> know,—but *1855:* (That's <> know),—but 39| P:hopes *1855:* hope 41| P:chapel top; *1855:* chapel-top; 44| P:decrease *1865:* decrease, 50| P:lead! *1863:* life He *1868:* he <> lead; 51| P:are: *1863:* are! 52| *1863:* feel He *1868:* he 54| P:you *1868:* us! You 56| P:speak; *1868:* speak:

—It is the thing, Love! so such things should be—
Behold Madonna!—I am bold to say.
I can do with my pencil what I know,
What I see, what at bottom of my heart
I wish for, if I ever wish so deep—
Do easily, too—when I say, perfectly,
I do not boast, perhaps: yourself are judge,
Who listened to the Legate's talk last week,
And just as much they used to say in France.
At any rate 'tis easy, all of it!
No sketches first, no studies, that's long past:
I do what many dream of, all their lives,
—Dream? strive to do, and agonize to do,
And fail in doing. I could count twenty such
On twice your fingers, and not leave this town,
Who strive—you don't know how the others strive
To paint a little thing like that you smeared
Carelessly passing with your robes afloat,—
Yet do much less, so much less, Someone says,
(I know his name, no matter)—so much less!
Well, less is more, Lucrezia: I am judged.
There burns a truer light of God in them,
In their vexed beating stuffed and stopped-up brain,
Heart, or whate'er else, than goes on to prompt
This low-pulsed forthright craftsman's hand of mine.
Their works drop groundward, but themselves, I know,
Reach many a time a heaven that's shut to me,
Enter and take their place there sure enough,
Though they come back and cannot tell the world.

59| P:Behold Madonna, I *1865:* Behold Madonna! I *1868:* Behold Madonna!—I
63| P:say perfectly *1868:* say, perfectly, *1888:* too—what I DC,BrU:too—when I *1889:* too—when I 64| P:judge *1888:* judge, 67| P:it, *1865:* it; *1870:* it!
68| P:past— *1865:* past: 69| P:of all <> lives *1888:* of, all <> lives,
70| P:agonise *1888:* agonize 75| P:afloat, *1863:* afloat,— 76| P:some one *1863:* less, Someone 77| P:I <> matter—so *1855:* (I <> matter) so *1868:* matter)—so
78| P:Well, it is <> Lucrezia! I *1855:* Well, less is *1868:* more, Lucrezia: I
80| P:vexed, beating, stuffed *1868:* vexed beating stuffed *C1870:* brain,— *1875:* brain,
81| *C1870:* else,—than §change not made in subsequent texts§ 82| P:mine! *1855:* mine. 84| P:a Heaven *1855:* heaven *1865:* a Heaven *1868:* heaven

My works are nearer heaven, but I sit here.
The sudden blood of these men! at a word—
Praise them, it boils, or blame them, it boils too.
I, painting from myself and to myself,
Know what I do, am unmoved by men's blame
Or their praise either. Somebody remarks
Morello's outline there is wrongly traced,
His hue mistaken; what of that? or else,
Rightly traced and well ordered; what of that?
Speak as they please, what does the mountain care?
Ah, but a man's reach should exceed his grasp,
Or what's a heaven for? All is silver-grey
Placid and perfect with my art: the worse!
I know both what I want and what might gain,
And yet how profitless to know, to sigh
"Had I been two, another and myself,
Our head would have o'erlooked the world!" No doubt.
Yonder's a work now, of that famous youth
The Urbinate who died five years ago.
('Tis copied, George Vasari sent it me.)
Well, I can fancy how he did it all,
Pouring his soul, with kings and popes to see,
Reaching, that heaven might so replenish him,
Above and through his art—for it gives way;
That arm is wrongly put—and there again—
A fault to pardon in the drawing's lines,
Its body, so to speak: its soul is right,
He means right—that, a child may understand.
Still, what an arm! and I could alter it:
But all the play, the insight and the stretch—
Out of me, out of me! And wherefore out?
Had you enjoined them on me, given me soul,
We might have risen to Rafael, I and you!

87| *1865:* nearer Heaven *1868:* heaven 94| P:mistaken—what *1868:* mistaken; what 95–97| P:ordered—what of that? / Ah *1863:* that? / Speak as they please, what does the mountain care? / Ah *1868:* ordered; what 98| P:a Heaven for? all *1868:* heaven for? All 99| P:art—the *1868:* art: the 100| P:gain— *1868:* gain; *1888:* gain, 104| P:work, now *1865:* work now 106| P:me). *1863:* me.) 108| P:soul with *1855:* soul, with 109| P:that Heaven *1868:* heaven 110| P:way, *1855:* way; 113| P:speak! its *1863:* speak: its 115| P:it. *1865:* it: 117| P:me! out *1868:* me, out 119| P:you. *1870:* you, *C1870:* you!

Nay, Love, you did give all I asked, I think—
More than I merit, yes, by many times.
But had you—oh, with the same perfect brow,
And perfect eyes, and more than perfect mouth,
And the low voice my soul hears, as a bird
The fowler's pipe, and follows to the snare—
Had you, with these the same, but brought a mind!
Some women do so. Had the mouth there urged
"God and the glory! never care for gain.
The present by the future, what is that?
Live for fame, side by side with Agnolo!
Rafael is waiting: up to God, all three!"
I might have done it for you. So it seems:
Perhaps not. All is as God over-rules.
Beside, incentives come from the soul's self;
The rest avail not. Why do I need you?
What wife had Rafael, or has Agnolo?
In this world, who can do a thing, will not;
And who would do it, cannot, I perceive:
Yet the will's somewhat—somewhat, too, the power—
And thus we half-men struggle. At the end,
God, I conclude, compensates, punishes.
'Tis safer for me, if the award be strict,
That I am something underrated here,
Poor this long while, despised, to speak the truth.
I dared not, do you know, leave home all day,
For fear of chancing on the Paris lords.
The best is when they pass and look aside;
But they speak sometimes; I must bear it all.
Well may they speak! That Francis, that first time,
And that long festal year at Fontainebleau!
I surely then could sometimes leave the ground,
Put on the glory, Rafael's daily wear,
In that humane great monarch's golden look,—
One finger in his beard or twisted curl

124| P:hears as *1855:* hears, as 125| P:pipe and *1855:* pipe, and 129| *1863:* The Present <> Future *1868:* present <> future 130| P:with Angelo— *1865:* with Angelo: *1868:* with Agnolo! 131| P:waiting. Up to God all *1868:* waiting: up to God, all 132| P:seems— *1865:* seems: 136| P:had Rafael or has Angelo? *1855:* had Rafael, or *1868:* has Agnolo? 137| P:not— *1865:* not;

Over his mouth's good mark that made the smile,
One arm about my shoulder, round my neck,
The jingle of his gold chain in my ear,
I painting proudly with his breath on me,
All his court round him, seeing with his eyes,
Such frank French eyes, and such a fire of souls
Profuse, my hand kept plying by those hearts,—
And, best of all, this, this, this face beyond,
This in the background, waiting on my work,
To crown the issue with a last reward!
A good time, was it not, my kingly days?
And had you not grown restless . . . but I know—
'Tis done and past; 'twas right, my instinct said;
Too live the life grew, golden and not grey,
And I'm the weak-eyed bat no sun should tempt
Out of the grange whose four walls make his world.
How could it end in any other way?
You called me, and I came home to your heart.
The triumph was—to reach and stay there; since
I reached it ere the triumph, what is lost?
Let my hands frame your face in your hair's gold,
You beautiful Lucrezia that are mine!
"Rafael did this, Andrea painted that;
The Roman's is the better when you pray,
But still the other's Virgin was his wife—"
Men will excuse me. I am glad to judge
Both pictures in your presence; clearer grows
My better fortune, I resolve to think.
For, do you know, Lucrezia, as God lives,
Said one day Agnolo, his very self,
To Rafael . . . I have known it all these years . . .

156| P:about your shoulder, round your neck, *1855:*about my shoulder, round my neck, 157| P:in your ear, *1855:*in my ear, 158| P:You painting <> on you, *1855:*on me, *1863:*I painting 159| P:him seeing *1855:*him, seeing 161| P:Profuse, your hand *1855:*Profuse, my hand 163| P:back-ground *1863:*background 166| P:restless—but *1868:*restless . . . but 168| P:grey— *1863:*grey, 173| P:was to have ended there—if then *1855:*there—then if *1863:*was, to <> there; then *1865:*then, if *1888:*was—to reach and stay there; since 177| P:that— *1865:*that; 180| P:me! I *1855:*me. I 184| P:day Angelo, his *1868:*day Agnolo, his

(When the young man was flaming out his thoughts
Upon a palace-wall for Rome to see,
Too lifted up in heart because of it)
"Friend, there's a certain sorry little scrub
Goes up and down our Florence, none cares how,
Who, were he set to plan and execute
As you are, pricked on by your popes and kings,
Would bring the sweat into that brow of yours!"
To Rafael's!—And indeed the arm is wrong.
I hardly dare . . . yet, only you to see,
Give the chalk here—quick, thus the line should go!
Ay, but the soul! he's Rafael! rub it out!
Still, all I care for, if he spoke the truth,
(What he? why, who but Michel Agnolo?
Do you forget already words like those?)
If really there was such a chance, so lost,—
Is, whether you're—not grateful—but more pleased.
Well, let me think so. And you smile indeed!
This hour has been an hour! Another smile?
If you would sit thus by me every night
I should work better, do you comprehend?
I mean that I should earn more, give you more.
See, it is settled dusk now; there's a star;
Morello's gone, the watch-lights show the wall,
The cue-owls speak the name we call them by.
Come from the window, love,—come in, at last,
Inside the melancholy little house
We built to be so gay with. God is just.
King Francis may forgive me: oft at nights
When I look up from painting, eyes tired out,
The walls become illumined, brick from brick

186| P:When *1855:*(When 188| P:it, *1855:*it) 191| P:Who were *1855:*Who, were 192| P:you, pricked forward by *1855:*you are pricked on by *1863:*are, pricked 194| P:To Rafael's! and *1855:*To Rafael's!—And 195| P:dare—yet *1868:*dare . . . yet 199| P:but Michael Angelo? *1868:*but Michel Agnolo? 200-201| *C1870:*§mark directing the insertion of an altered repetition of line 198, written in margin§ Yes, all I care for if he spoke the truth, §change not made in subsequent texts§ 201| P:lost, *1863:*lost,— 203| P:so! And *1855:*so. And 207| P:Lucrezia—I should *1855:*I mean that I should 209| P:shew *1863:*show 211| P:window, Love *1868:*love 214| P:me. Oft *1868:*me: oft

Distinct, instead of mortar, fierce bright gold,
That gold of his I did cement them with!
Let us but love each other. Must you go?
That Cousin here again? he waits outside?
Must see you—you, and not with me? Those loans?
More gaming debts to pay? you smiled for that?
Well, let smiles buy me! have you more to spend?
While hand and eye and something of a heart
Are left me, work's my ware, and what's it worth?
I'll pay my fancy. Only let me sit
The grey remainder of the evening out,
Idle, you call it, and muse perfectly
How I could paint, were I but back in France,
One picture, just one more—the Virgin's face,
Not yours this time! I want you at my side
To hear them—that is, Michel Agnolo—
Judge all I do and tell you of its worth.
Will you? To-morrow, satisfy your friend.
I take the subjects for his corridor,
Finish the portrait out of hand—there, there,
And throw him in another thing or two
If he demurs; the whole should prove enough
To pay for this same Cousin's freak. Beside,
What's better and what's all I care about,
Get you the thirteen scudi for the ruff!
Love, does that please you? Ah, but what does he,
The Cousin! what does he to please you more?

I am grown peaceful as old age to-night.
I regret little, I would change still less.
Since there my past life lies, why alter it?
The very wrong to Francis!—it is true
I took his coin, was tempted and complied,
And built this house and sinned, and all is said.

217| P:mortar with bright *1855:* mortar fierce bright *1863:* mortar, fierce
219| *1865:* other, Must *1868:* other. Must 221| P:loans! *1863:* loans?
229| P:paint were *1863:* paint, were 231| P:your's *1888:* yours 232| P:is, Michael Angelo— *1868:* is, Michel Agnolo— 234| P:friend— *1855:* friend.
241| P:ruff. *1868:* ruff! 247| P:to Francis! it *1863:* to Francis!—it

My father and my mother died of want.
Well, had I riches of my own? you see
How one gets rich! Let each one bear his lot.
They were born poor, lived poor, and poor they died:
And I have laboured somewhat in my time
And not been paid profusely. Some good son
Paint my two hundred pictures—let him try!
No doubt, there's something strikes a balance. Yes,
You loved me quite enough, it seems to-night.
This must suffice me here. What would one have?
In heaven, perhaps, new chances, one more chance—
Four great walls in the New Jerusalem,
Meted on each side by the angel's reed,
For Leonard, Rafael, Agnolo and me
To cover—the three first without a wife,
While I have mine! So—still they overcome
Because there's still Lucrezia,—as I choose.

Again the Cousin's whistle! Go, my Love.

260| *1863:* In Heaven *1868:* heaven 261| P:the New Jerusalem *1888:* the New Jerusalem, 263| P:For <> Angelo *1868:* For <> Agnolo 267| P:whistle! go my *1855:* whistle! Go, my

BEFORE

I

Let them fight it out, friend! things have gone too far.
God must judge the couple: leave them as they are
—Whichever one's the guiltless, to his glory,
And whichever one the guilt's with, to my story!

II

Why, you would not bid men, sunk in such a slough,
Strike no arm out further, stick and stink as now,
Leaving right and wrong to settle the embroilment,
Heaven with snaky hell, in torture and entoilment?

III

Who's the culprit of them? How must he conceive
God—the queen he caps to, laughing in his sleeve,
"'Tis but decent to profess oneself beneath her:
Still, one must not be too much in earnest, either!"

IV

Better sin the whole sin, sure that God observes;
Then go live his life out! Life will try his nerves,
When the sky, which noticed all, makes no disclosure,
And the earth keeps up her terrible composure.

V

Let him pace at pleasure, past the walls of rose,
Pluck their fruits when grape-trees graze him as he goes!
For he 'gins to guess the purpose of the garden,

BEFORE §Subsequent placement: *1863:*DL§ 2| P:couple! leave *1868:*couple: leave 4| P:story. *1863:*with to *1865:*with, to *1868:*story! 8| P:snaky Hell *1868:*hell 9| P:Which of them's the culprit, how *1863:*Who's the culprit of them? How 10| P:God's the <> sleeve! *1863:*God—the <> sleeve, 11| P:'Tis <> her. *1863:*"'Tis <> her: 12| P:earnest either. *1863:*earnest, either!" *1888:*either! §emended to§ either!" §see Editorial Notes§ 13| P:observes, *1865:*observes; 14| P:out! life *1863:*Than *1865:*Then *1868:*out! Life 15| P:sky which *1865:*sky, which 17| P:pleasure past *1855:*pleasure, past 18| P:goes. *1868:*goes!

With the sly mute thing, beside there, for a warden.

VI

What's the leopard-dog-thing, constant at his side,
A leer and lie in every eye of its obsequious hide?
When will come an end to all the mock obeisance,
And the price appear that pays for the misfeasance?

VII

So much for the culprit. Who's the martyred man?
Let him bear one stroke more, for be sure he can!
He that strove thus evil's lump with good to leaven,
Let him give his blood at last and get his heaven!

VIII

All or nothing, stake it! Trusts he God or no?
Thus far and no farther? farther? be it so!
Now, enough of your chicane of prudent pauses,
Sage provisos, sub-intents and saving-clauses!

IX

Ah, "forgive" you bid him? While God's champion lives,
Wrong shall be resisted: dead, why, he forgives.
But you must not end my friend ere you begin him;
Evil stands not crowned on earth, while breath is in him.

X

Once more—Will the wronger, at this last of all,
Dare to say, "I did wrong," rising in his fall?
No?—Let go, then! Both the fighters to their places!
While I count three, step you back as many paces!

20| P:thing beside there for *1863:* beside, there, for *1865:* thing, beside there, for 21| P:constant to his *1863:* constant at his 22| P:eye on its *1863:* eye of its 23| P:end of all *1863:* end to all 26| P:can. *1863:* can! 28| P:heaven. *1863:* his Heaven! *1868:* heaven! 29| P:it! trusts *1868:* it! Trusts 30| P:so. *1863:* so! 32| P:saving-clauses. *1855:* sub-intents, and *1863:* sub-intents and saving-clauses! 34| P:why he *1863:* why, he 36| *1863:* him! *1868:* him. 37| P:more, will *1855:* more—Will 38| P:say "I *1863:* say, "I 39| P:then—both <> places— *1863:* then! both <> places! *1868:* then! Both 40| P:paces. *1863:* paces!

AFTER

Take the cloak from his face, and at first
Let the corpse do its worst!

How he lies in his rights of a man!
Death has done all death can.
And, absorbed in the new life he leads,
He recks not, he heeds
Nor his wrong nor my vengeance; both strike
On his senses alike,
And are lost in the solemn and strange
Surprise of the change.

Ha, what avails death to erase
His offence, my disgrace?
I would we were boys as of old
In the field, by the fold:
His outrage, God's patience, man's scorn
Were so easily borne!

I stand here now, he lies in his place:
Cover the face!

AFTER §Subsequent placement: *1863:* DL§ 2| P:worst. *1868:* worst! 5| P:And absorbed *1863:* And, absorbed 7| P:vengeance—both *1865:* vengeance; both 8| P:alike; *1855:* alike, 14| P:fold— *1863:* fold: 16| P:borne. *1868:* borne! 17| P:place— *1863:* place: 18| P:face. *1868:* face!

IN THREE DAYS

I

So, I shall see her in three days
And just one night, but nights are short,
Then two long hours, and that is morn.
See how I come, unchanged, unworn!
Feel, where my life broke off from thine,
How fresh the splinters keep and fine,—
Only a touch and we combine!

II

Too long, this time of year, the days!
But nights, at least the nights are short.
As night shows where her one moon is,
A hand's-breadth of pure light and bliss,
So life's night gives my lady birth
And my eyes hold her! What is worth
The rest of heaven, the rest of earth?

III

O loaded curls, release your store
Of warmth and scent, as once before
The tingling hair did, lights and darks
Outbreaking into fairy sparks,
When under curl and curl I pried
After the warmth and scent inside,
Thro' lights and darks how manifold—
The dark inspired, the light controlled!
As early Art embrowns the gold.

IN THREE DAYS §Subsequent placement: *1863:* DL§ 4| P:unworn— *1863:* unworn! 9| P:nights—at *1865:* nights, at 12| P:So, life's *1863:* So life's 13| P:what *1868:* her! What 16| P:scent as *1865:* scent, as 18| P:Out-breaking <> sparks *1863:* Outbreaking <> sparks, 20| P:inside *1863:* inside, 23| P:So early art embrowned *1855:* As early Art *1865:* embrowns

IV

What great fear, should one say, "Three days
That change the world might change as well
Your fortune; and if joy delays,
Be happy that no worse befell!"
What small fear, if another says,
"Three days and one short night beside
May throw no shadow on your ways;
But years must teem with change untried,
With chance not easily defied,
With an end somewhere undescried."
No fear!—or if a fear be born
This minute, it dies out in scorn.
Fear? I shall see her in three days
And one night, now the nights are short,
Then just two hours, and that is morn.

24| P:fear—should *1863:* fear, should 25| P:world, might *1868:* world might 26| P:delays *1855:* delays, 27| P:befell." *1868:* befell!" 28| P:fear—if *1863:* fear, if 38| P:hours and *1855:* hours, and

IN A YEAR

I

Never any more,
While I live,
Need I hope to see his face
As before.
Once his love grown chill,
Mine may strive:
Bitterly we re-embrace,
Single still.

II

Was it something said,
Something done,
Vexed him? was it touch of hand,
Turn of head?
Strange! that very way
Love begun:
I as little understand
Love's decay.

III

When I sewed or drew,
I recall
How he looked as if I sung,
—Sweetly too.
If I spoke a word,
First of all
Up his cheek the colour sprung,
Then he heard.

IV

Sitting by my side,
At my feet,

IN A YEAR §Subsequent placement: *1863:* DL§ [1]| P:more *1865:* more, [6]| P:strive— *1865:* strive: [14]| P:begun. *1863:* begun: [19]| P:sang, *1863:* sung, [23]| P:color sprang, *1863:* colour sprung,

So he breathed but air I breathed,
Satisfied!
I, too, at love's brim
Touched the sweet:
I would die if death bequeathed
Sweet to him.

V

"Speak, I love thee best!"
He exclaimed:
"Let thy love my own foretell!"
I confessed:
"Clasp my heart on thine
Now unblamed,
Since upon thy soul as well
Hangeth mine!"

VI

Was it wrong to own,
Being truth?
Why should all the giving prove
His alone?
I had wealth and ease,
Beauty, youth:
Since my lover gave me love,
I gave these.

VII

That was all I meant,
—To be just,
And the passion I had raised,
To content.
Since he chose to change
Gold for dust,

27| P:breathed the air *1865:* breathed but air 34| P:exclaimed. *1865:* exclaimed: 35| P:foretell,—" *1863:* foretell," *1865:* foretell!" 46| P:youth— *1865:* youth: 51| P:raised *1863:* raised,

If I gave him what he praised
Was it strange?

VIII

Would he loved me yet,
On and on,
While I found some way undreamed
—Paid my debt!
Gave more life and more,
Till, all gone,
He should smile "She never seemed
Mine before.

IX

"What, she felt the while,
Must I think?
Love's so different with us men!"
He should smile:
"Dying for my sake—
White and pink!
Can't we touch these bubbles then
But they break?"

X

Dear, the pang is brief,
Do thy part,
Have thy pleasure! How perplexed
Grows belief!
Well, this cold clay clod
Was man's heart:
Crumble it, and what comes next?
Is it God?

58| *1863:* and on. *1865:* and on, 65| P:"What—she *1868:* "What, she 67| P:men," *1868:* men!" 68| P:smile. *1865:* smile: 73| P:brief. *1863:* brief, 75| P:pleasure. How perplext *1868:* pleasure! How perplexed 78| P:heart. *1865:* heart: 79| P:it—and *1865:* it, and

OLD PICTURES IN FLORENCE

I

The morn when first it thunders in March,
The eel in the pond gives a leap, they say:
As I leaned and looked over the aloed arch
Of the villa-gate this warm March day,
No flash snapped, no dumb thunder rolled
In the valley beneath where, white and wide
And washed by the morning water-gold,
Florence lay out on the mountain-side.

II

River and bridge and street and square
Lay mine, as much at my beck and call,
Through the live translucent bath of air,
As the sights in a magic crystal ball.
And of all I saw and of all I praised,
The most to praise and the best to see
Was the startling bell-tower Giotto raised:
But why did it more than startle me?

III

Giotto, how, with that soul of yours,
Could you play me false who loved you so?
Some slights if a certain heart endures
Yet it feels, I would have your fellows know!
I' faith, I perceive not why I should care
To break a silence that suits them best,
But the thing grows somewhat hard to bear
When I find a Giotto join the rest.

OLD PICTURES IN FLORENCE §Subsequent placement: *1863:* DL§ *Title*| P:*OPUS MAGISTRI JOCTI* *1855: OLD PICTURES IN FLORENCE* 2| P:say. *1863:* say: 4| P:villa-gate, this *1868:* villa-gate this 5| P:snapt *1868:* snapped 6| P:beneath, where white and wide, *1855:* where, white *1863:* beneath where <> wide 7| P:Washed <> morning's *1863:* And washed *1868:* morning 14| P:see, DC,BrU:see *1889:* see 19| P:There be slights *1855:* Some slights 20| *1855:* It *1863:* Yet it 21| P:'Faith—I *1863:* I' faith, I

IV

On the arch where olives overhead
Print the blue sky with twig and leaf,
(That sharp-curled leaf which they never shed)
'Twixt the aloes, I used to lean in chief,
And mark through the winter afternoons,
By a gift God grants me now and then,
In the mild decline of those suns like moons,
Who walked in Florence, besides her men.

V

They might chirp and chaffer, come and go
For pleasure or profit, her men alive—
My business was hardly with them, I trow,
But with empty cells of the human hive;
—With the chapter-room, the cloister-porch,
The church's apsis, aisle or nave,
Its crypt, one fingers along with a torch,
Its face set full for the sun to shave.

VI

Wherever a fresco peels and drops,
Wherever an outline weakens and wanes
Till the latest life in the painting stops,
Stands One whom each fainter pulse-tick pains;
One, wishful each scrap should clutch the brick,
Each tinge not wholly escape the plaster,
—A lion who dies of an ass's kick,
The wronged great soul of an ancient Master.

VII

For oh, this world and the wrong it does!
They are safe in heaven with their backs to it,

27| P:leaf they *1863:* leaf which they 28| P:aloes I *1863:* aloes, I 32| P:in Florence besides *1855:* in Florence, besides 39| P:torch— *1863:* torch, 40| P:face, set *1868:* face set 43| P:in its system stops, *1855:* in the painting stops, 44| P:pains! *1865:* pains: 45| P:clutch its brick, *1863:* clutch the brick, 50| *1863:* in Heaven *1868:* heaven

The Michaels and Rafaels, you hum and buzz
    Round the works of, you of the little wit!
Do their eyes contract to the earth's old scope,
    Now that they see God face to face,
And have all attained to be poets, I hope?
    'Tis their holiday now, in any case.

VIII

Much they reck of your praise and you!
    But the wronged great souls—can they be quit
Of a world where their work is all to do,
    Where you style them, you of the little wit,
Old Master This and Early the Other,
    Not dreaming that Old and New are fellows:
A younger succeeds to an elder brother,
    Da Vincis derive in good time from Dellos.

IX

And here where your praise might yield returns,
    And a handsome word or two give help,
Here, after your kind, the mastiff girns
    And the puppy pack of poodles yelp.
What, not a word for Stefano there,
    Of brow once prominent and starry,
Called Nature's Ape and the world's despair
    For his peerless painting? (See Vasari.)

X

There stands the Master. Study, my friends,
    What a man's work comes to! So he plans it,

51| P:and Rafaels you *1855:*and Rafaels, you 53| P:scope *1855:*scope, 59| P:where all their work is to *1863:*where their work is all to 61| P:this <> other, *1863:*Old Master This <> Other, 62| P:fellows, *1863:*fellows: 63| P:That a *1863:*A 65| P:praise would yield returns *1863:*praise might yield returns, 67| P:Why, after *1855:*Here, after 69| P:there *1863:*there, 70| P:—Of *1863:*Of 71| P:ape *1863:*Called Nature's Ape 72| P:painting (see Vasari)? *1863:*painting? (see Vasari.) *1888:*painting? (See 73| P:There he stands now. Study *1863:*There stands the Master. Study 74| P:so *1868:*to! So

Performs it, perfects it, makes amends
For the toiling and moiling, and then, *sic transit!*
Happier the thrifty blind-fold labour,
With upturned eye while the hand is busy,
Not sidling a glance at the coin of their neighbour!
'Tis looking downward that makes one dizzy.

XI

"If you knew their work you would deal your dole."
May I take upon me to instruct you?
When Greek Art ran and reached the goal,
Thus much had the world to boast *in fructu*—
The Truth of Man, as by God first spoken,
Which the actual generations garble,
Was re-uttered, and Soul (which Limbs betoken)
And Limbs (Soul informs) made new in marble.

XII

So, you saw yourself as you wished you were,
As you might have been, as you cannot be;
Earth here, rebuked by Olympus there:
And grew content in your poor degree
With your little power, by those statues' godhead,
And your little scope, by their eyes' full sway,
And your little grace, by their grace embodied,
And your little date, by their forms that stay.

76| P:and there's its transit! *1863:*and then, *sic transit!* 80| P:'Tis the looking downward makes *1855:*'Tis looking *1863:*downward that makes 81| P:If <> dole. *1863:*"If <> dole." 83| P:When in Greece Art *1855:*When Greek Art 85| P:truth <> spoken *1855:*spoken, *1868:*The Truth 86| P:garble *1855:*garble, 87| P:re-uttered,—and Soul, which <> betoken, *1855:*and Soul (which <> betoken) *1863:*re-uttered, and 88| P:And Limbs, Soul informs, were made *1855:*And Limbs (Soul informs) were *1863:*informs) made 89| P:So you *1863:*So, you 91| P:And bringing your own shortcomings there, *1863:*Earth here, rebuked by Olympus there: 92| P:You grew *1863:*And grew 95| P:by such grace *1855:*by their grace

XIII

You would fain be kinglier, say, than I am?
    Even so, you will not sit like Theseus.
You would prove a model? The Son of Priam
    Has yet the advantage in arms' and knees' use.
You're wroth—can you slay your snake like Apollo?
    You're grieved—still Niobe's the grander!
You live—there's the Racers' frieze to follow:
    You die—there's the dying Alexander.

XIV

So, testing your weakness by their strength,
    Your meagre charms by their rounded beauty,
Measured by Art in your breadth and length,
    You learned—to submit is a mortal's duty.
—When I say "you" 'tis the common soul,
    The collective, I mean: the race of Man
That receives life in parts to live in a whole,
    And grow here according to God's clear plan.

XV

Growth came when, looking your last on them all,
    You turned your eyes inwardly one fine day
And cried with a start—What if we so small
    Be greater and grander the while than they?
Are they perfect of lineament, perfect of stature?
    In both, of such lower types are we
Precisely because of our wider nature;
    For time, theirs—ours, for eternity.

97| P:say than *1863:* say, than 98| P:so you *1855:* so, you 99| P:would fain be a <> the *1855:* You'd fain *1868:* You would prove a <> The 101| P:You are wroth *1855:* You're wroth 102| P:You are grieved *1855:* You're grieved 103| P:follow— *1863:* follow: 108| P:learn <> is the worsted's duty. *1863:* learned <> is a mortal's duty. 110| P:mean—the *1863:* mean: the 112| P:to God's own plan. *1863:* to God's clear plan. 116| P:Are greater, ay, greater the *1855:* they! *1863:* Be greater and grander the *1870:* they *1875:* they? 117| P:stature, *1855:* stature? 118| P:And in *1855:* In 119| P:nature— *1855:* nature; 120| P:eternity? *1855:* eternity.

XVI

To-day's brief passion limits their range;
  It seethes with the morrow for us and more.
They are perfect—how else? they shall never change:
  We are faulty—why not? we have time in store.
The Artificer's hand is not arrested
  With us; we are rough-hewn, nowise polished:
They stand for our copy, and, once invested
  With all they can teach, we shall see them abolished.

XVII

'Tis a life-long toil till our lump be leaven—
  The better! What's come to perfection perishes.
Things learned on earth, we shall practise in heaven:
  Works done least rapidly, Art most cherishes.
Thyself shalt afford the example, Giotto!
  Thy one work, not to decrease or diminish,
Done at a stroke, was just (was it not?) "O!"
  Thy great Campanile is still to finish.

XVIII

Is it true that we are now, and shall be hereafter,
  But what and where depend on life's minute?
Hails heavenly cheer or infernal laughter
  Our first step out of the gulf or in it?
Shall Man, such step within his endeavour,
  Man's face, have no more play and action
Than joy which is crystallized for ever,
  Or grief, an eternal petrifaction?

121| P:range, *1863:* range; 123| *1863:* change; *1865:* change *1868:* change: 126| P:us—we <> no-wise *1868:* us; we *1888:* nowise 127| P:They are set for *1855:* They stand for 130| P:what's *1868:* better! What's 131| P:Things half-learned <> heaven. *1855:* Things learned *1863:* in Heaven. *1868:* heaven: 135| P:just—was it not? "O!" *1855:* just (was it not?) "O!" 136| P:While thy *1855:* Thy 137| P:true, we *1863:* true that we 138| P:And what—is depending on life's one minute? *1863:* But what and where depend on life's minute? 139| P:Waits celestial cheer *1855:* Hails heavenly cheer 141| P:And Man, this step *1863:* Shall Man, such step 142| P:Has his face, do you think, no *1855:* His face, have no *1863:* Man's face 143| P:Than a joy *1855:* Than joy 144| *1855:* petrifaction! *1863:* petrifaction?

XIX

On which I conclude, that the early painters,
    To cries of "Greek Art and what more wish you?"—
Replied, "To become now self-acquainters,
    And paint man man, whatever the issue!
Make new hopes shine through the flesh they fray,
    New fears aggrandize the rags and tatters:
To bring the invisible full into play!
    Let the visible go to the dogs—what matters?"

XX

Give these, I exhort you, their guerdon and glory
    For daring so much, before they well did it.
The first of the new, in our race's story,
    Beats the last of the old; 'tis no idle quiddit.
The worthies began a revolution,
    Which if on earth you intend to acknowledge,
Why, honour them now! (ends my allocution)
    Nor confer your degree when the folk leave college.

XXI

There's a fancy some lean to and others hate—
    That, when this life is ended, begins
New work for the soul in another state,
    Where it strives and gets weary, loses and wins:
Where the strong and the weak, this world's congeries,
    Repeat in large what they practised in small,

146| P:To the cry *1855:* To cries 147| P:self-acquainters! *1855:* Replied, "Become now self-acquainters, *1863:* Replied, "To become 148| P:To paint man, man,—whatever *1855:* And paint *1863:* man, man, whatever *1888:* man man 149| P:Make the new *1855:* Make the hopes *1863:* Make new hopes 150| P:aggrandise <> tatters. *1863:* tatters: *1888:* aggrandize 151| P:So we bring <> play, *1855:* So bring *1863:* To bring <> play! 153| P:these, I say, full honour and *1863:* these, I exhort you, their guerdon and 155| P:new in <> story *1855:* new, in <> story, 156| P:old, 'tis *1865:* old 'tis 157| P:revolution *1863:* revolution, 158| P:if we on the earth intend to acknowledge *1855:* if on the earth we intend *1863:* on earth you intend to acknowledge, 159| P:Let us honour <> now—(ends *1855:* Honour *1863:* Why, honour *1868:* now! (ends 160| P:confer our degree <> folks *1863:* confer your degree *1888:* folk 164| P:wins— *1863:* wins; *1870:* wins:

Through life after life in unlimited series;
        Only the scale's to be changed, that's all.

XXII

Yet I hardly know. When a soul has seen
        By the means of Evil that Good is best,
And, through earth and its noise, what is heaven's serene,—
        When our faith in the same has stood the test—
Why, the child grown man, you burn the rod,
        The uses of labour are surely done;
There remaineth a rest for the people of God:
        And I have had troubles enough, for one.

XXIII

But at any rate I have loved the season
        Of Art's spring-birth so dim and dewy;
My sculptor is Nicolo the Pisan,
        My painter—who but Cimabue?
Nor ever was man of them all indeed,
        From these to Ghiberti and Ghirlandajo,
Could say that he missed my critic-meed.
        So, now to my special grievance—heigh ho!

XXIV

Their ghosts still stand, as I said before,
        Watching each fresco flaked and rasped,
Blocked up, knocked out, or whitewashed o'er:
        —No getting again what the church has grasped!
The works on the wall must take their chance;
        "Works never conceded to England's thick clime!"

171| P:And through *1863:* is Heaven's *1865:* And, through *1868:* heaven's 172| P:When its faith *1865:* When our faith 174| P:done. *1863:* done: *1865:* done; 175| P:of God— *1855:* of God, *1865:* of God: 176| P:enough for *1865:* enough, for 178| P:dewy, *1868:* dewy; 179| P:And my *1855:* My <> Pisan; *1863:* the Pisan, 180| P:And my *1855:* My *1863:* And painter *1865:* My painter 184| P:So now *1865:* So, now 185| P:ghosts would stand *1855:* ghosts now stand *1865:* ghosts still stand 187| P:o'er *1865:* o'er: 189| P:chance, *1863:* chance;

(I hope they prefer their inheritance
Of a bucketful of Italian quick-lime.)

XXV

When they go at length, with such a shaking
Of heads o'er the old delusion, sadly
Each master his way through the black streets taking,
Where many a lost work breathes though badly—
Why don't they bethink them of who has merited?
Why not reveal, while their pictures dree
Such doom, how a captive might be out-ferreted?
Why is it they never remember me?

XXVI

Not that I expect the great Bigordi,
Nor Sandro to hear me, chivalric, bellicose;
Nor the wronged Lippino; and not a word I
Say of a scrap of Frà Angelico's:
But are you too fine, Taddeo Gaddi,
To grant me a taste of your intonaco,
Some Jerome that seeks the heaven with a sad eye?
Not a churlish saint, Lorenzo Monaco?

XXVII

Could not the ghost with the close red cap,
My Pollajolo, the twice a craftsman,
Save me a sample, give me the hap
Of a muscular Christ that shows the draughtsman?
No Virgin by him the somewhat petty,
Of finical touch and tempera crumbly—

194| P:delusions *1865:*delusion 198| P:Why won't they reveal *1855:*Why not reveal 199| P:doom, that a captive's to be *1865:*doom, how a captive might be 200| *1855:*Why do they *1863:*Why is it they 201| P:great Bigordi *1870:*great Bigordi, 203| P:Nor wronged Lippino—and *1863:*Nor the wronged Lippino; and 204| P:of Fra Angelico's. *1863:*of Fra Angelico's: *1865:*of Frà 206| P:To afford me <> intonaco— *1855:*To grant me *1865:*intonaco, 207| *1863:*the Heaven *1868:*heaven 208| *1855:*No churlish *1863:*Not a churlish 213| P:Not a Virgin by him, the *1855:*No Virgin *1865:*him the

Could not Alesso Baldovinetti
    Contribute so much, I ask him humbly?

XXVIII

Margheritone of Arezzo,
    With the grave-clothes garb and swaddling barret
(Why purse up mouth and beak in a pet so,
    You bald old saturnine poll-clawed parrot?)
Not a poor glimmering Crucifixion,
    Where in the foreground kneels the donor?
If such remain, as is my conviction,
    The hoarding it does you but little honour.

XXIX

They pass; for them the panels may thrill,
    The tempera grow alive and tinglish;
Their pictures are left to the mercies still
    Of dealers and stealers, Jews and the English,
Who, seeing mere money's worth in their prize,
    Will sell it to somebody calm as Zeno
At naked High Art, and in ecstasies
    Before some clay-cold vile Carlino!

XXX

No matter for these! But Giotto, you,
    Have you allowed, as the town-tongues babble it,—

218| P:With grave-clothes <> barret, *1855:* With the grave-clothes *1865:* barret
220| P:Like a bald, saturnine, poll-clawed *1855:* You bald *1863:* bald, old, saturnine *1865:* bald old saturnine poll-clawed 221| *1855:* No poor *1863:* Not a poor
222| P:Where dim in *1855:* Where in 223| P:such still remain *1855:* such remain
224| P:hoarding does *1863:* hoarding it does 225| P:pass: for *1865:* pass; for
226| P:tinglish— *1865:* tinglish: *1868:* tinglish; 227| P:Works rot or are *1855:* Rot or are *1863:* Their pictures are 228| P:the English! *1863:* the English, *1870:* the English *1888:* the English, 229| P:—Who see mere *1855:* Seeing mere *1863:* Who, seeing 230| P:And sell <> some one calm *1855:* Who sell *1863:* Will sell <> somebody calm 231| P:At the naked Art <> ecstacies *1855:* At naked *1863:* naked High Art <> ecstasies
232| P:clay-cold, vile *1868:* clay-cold vile 234| P:it, *1863:* it,—

Oh, never! it shall not be counted true—
That a certain precious little tablet
Which Buonarroti eyed like a lover,—
Was buried so long in oblivion's womb
And, left for another than I to discover,
Turns up at last! and to whom?—to whom?

XXXI

I, that have haunted the dim San Spirito,
(Or was it rather the Ognissanti?)
Patient on altar-step planting a weary toe!
Nay, I shall have it yet! *Detur amanti!*
My Koh-i-noor—or (if that's a platitude)
Jewel of Giamschid, the Persian Sofi's eye;
So, in anticipative gratitude,
What if I take up my hope and prophesy?

XXXII

When the hour grows ripe, and a certain dotard
Is pitched, no parcel that needs invoicing,
To the worse side of the Mont Saint Gothard,
We shall begin by way of rejoicing;
None of that shooting the sky (blank cartridge),
Nor a civic guard, all plumes and lacquer,
Hunting Radetzky's soul like a partridge
Over Morello with squib and cracker.

235| *1855:*Never *1863:*Oh, never 238| P:Swallowed so <> womb, *1855:*Buried so *1863:*Was buried <> womb 239| P:Was left <> discover,— *1863:*And, left <> discover, 240| P:last, and *1863:*last! and 242| P:it not rather *1855:*it rather 243| P:Stood on the altar-steps, patient and weary too! *1863:*Patient on altar-steps planting a weary toe! *1865:*altar-step 244| P:yet, *detur* *1863:*yet! *detur* *1868:*yet! *Detur* 245| P:or, if <> platitude, *1855:*or (if <> platitude) 246| P:eye! *1870:*eye; 247| P:And so in <> gratitude *1855:*So, in <> gratitude, 249| P:hour is ripe *1863:*hour grows ripe 250| P:Pitched *1863:*Is pitched 251| P:worser <> St. *1855:*worse *1863:*of the Mont Saint *1870:*of the Mont St. *1888:*of the Mont Saint 252| P:We'll have, to begin <> rejoicing, *1855:*Have *1863:*We shall begin <> rejoicing; 253| P:of our shooting <> cartridge) *1855:*of that shooting <> cartridge), 254| P:As when civic guards *1855:*No civic guards *1863:*Nor a civic guard *1888:*lacquer DC,BrU:lacquer, *1889:*lacquer, 255| P:We hunted *1855:*Hunting 256| P:Over Mount Morello *1855:*Over Morello

XXXIII

This time we'll shoot better game and bag 'em hot—
No mere display at the stone of Dante,
But a kind of sober Witanagemot
(Ex: "Casa Guidi," *quod videas ante*)
Shall ponder, once Freedom restored to Florence,
How Art may return that departed with her.
Go, hated house, go each trace of the Loraine's,
And bring us the days of Orgagna hither!

XXXIV

How we shall prologize, how we shall perorate,
Utter fit things upon art and history,
Feel truth at blood-heat and falsehood at zero rate,
Make of the want of the age no mystery;
Contrast the fructuous and sterile eras,
Show—monarchy ever its uncouth cub licks
Out of the bear's shape into Chimæra's,
While Pure Art's birth is still the republic's.

XXXV

Then one shall propose in a speech (curt Tuscan,
Expurgate and sober, with scarcely an *"issimo,"*)

257| P:We'll shoot this time better *1863:*This time we'll shoot better 258| P:No stupid display *1855:*No display *1863:*No mere display 259| P:a sober kind of Witan-agemot *1855:*a kind *1863:*of sober Witana-gemot *1868:*sober Witanagemot 260| P:("Casa <> quod videas ante) *1863:*(Ex: "Casa <> *quod videas ante*) 261| P:To ponder, now Freedom's *1855:*ponder Freedom *1863:*Shall ponder, once Freedom 263| P:With the hated <> the Loraine's! *1855:*Go, hated *1863:*Loraine's, 264| P:hither. *1863:*hither! 265| P:prologuise *1863:*prologuize *1888:*prologize 266| P:Say proper things <> history— *1855:*Say fit things *1863:*Utter fit *1865:*history, 267| P:Set the true at <> and the false at a zero *1855:*Set truth at *1863:*Feel truth *1865:*and falsehood at zero 268| P:And make <> mystery! *1855:*Make *1863:*And make *1865:*Make <> mystery; 269| *1863:*Contrasting *1865:*Contrast 270| P:Show, monarchy its *1863:*monarchy ever its *1865:*Show—monarchy 271| P:shape to the chimera's— *1855:*chimæra's— *1863:*shape into Chimæra's— *1865:*into Chimæra's, 272| P:pure <> birth was still the republic's! *1855:*Pure <> birth being still *1863:*While Pure <> birth is still *1868:*republic's. 273| P:speech, curt *1855:*propose (in *1863:*propose in a speech (curt 274| P:Sober, expurgate, spare of an *"issimo,"* *1855:*"issimo,") *1863:*Expurgate and sober, with scarcely an

To end now our half-told tale of Cambuscan,
And turn the bell-tower's *alt* to *altissimo:*
And fine as the beak of a young beccaccia
The Campanile, the Duomo's fit ally,
Shall soar up in gold full fifty braccia,
Completing Florence, as Florence Italy.

XXXVI

Shall I be alive that morning the scaffold
Is broken away, and the long-pent fire,
Like the golden hope of the world, unbaffled
Springs from its sleep, and up goes the spire
While "God and the People" plain for its motto,
Thence the new tricolour flaps at the sky?
At least to foresee that glory of Giotto
And Florence together, the first am I!

275| P:To finish our *1855:* Ending our *1863:* To end now our 276| P:Turn the Bell-tower's alto to altissimo. *1855:* Turning the Bell-tower's altaltissimo. *1863:* And turn the Bell-tower's *alt* to *altissimo:* *1870:* bell-tower's 278| P:Shall the Campanile *1855:* The Campanile 279| P:Soars up in gold its full *1863:* Shall soar <> gold full 280| P:as Florence, Italy. *1888:* as Florence Italy. 281| P:So said, so done. That *1855:* Shall I be alive that 282| P:fire *1863:* fire, 283| P:world unbaffled *1863:* world, unbaffled 284| P:spire— *1863:* spire 285| P:When with "God *1855:* As, "God *1863:* While, "God *1870:* While "God 286| P:tricolor <> sky, *1855:* sky? *1863:* tricolour 287| P:Why, to hail him, the vindicated Giotto, *1855:* Forseeing, the day that vindicates Giotto *1863:* At least to forsee that glory of Giotto 288| P:Thanking God for it all, the *1855:* And Florence together, the

IN A BALCONY

PERSONS

Norbert
Constance
The Queen

IN A BALCONY

CONSTANCE and NORBERT

NORBERT Now!
CONSTANCE Not now!
NORBERT Give me them again, those hands:
Put them upon my forehead, how it throbs!
Press them before my eyes, the fire comes through!
You cruellest, you dearest in the world,
Let me! The Queen must grant whate'er I ask—
How can I gain you and not ask the Queen?
There she stays waiting for me, here stand you;
Some time or other this was to be asked;
Now is the one time—what I ask, I gain:
Let me ask now, Love!
CONSTANCE Do, and ruin us.
NORBERT Let it be now, Love! All my soul breaks forth.
How I do love you! Give my love its way!
A man can have but one life and one death,
One heaven, one hell. Let me fulfil my fate—
Grant me my heaven now! Let me know you mine,
Prove you mine, write my name upon your brow,
Hold you and have you, and then die away,
If God please, with completion in my soul!
CONSTANCE I am not yours then? How content this man!
I am not his—who change into himself,

IN A BALCONY §Subsequent placement: *1863:* Tragedies and Other Plays *1868:* uncategorized§
Title, etc.| P:*BALCONY / FIRST PART* / §rule§ / CONSTANCE *1863:BALCONY / A SCENE / 1855* / §rule§ / *In a Balcony* / CONSTANCE *1868:BALCONY* / §rule§ / CONSTANCE *1888:BALCONY / 1853* / §double rule§ / CONSTANCE 1| P: Now. CONSTANCE Not now. NORBERT <> hands— *1868:* Now! CONSTANCE Not now! NORBERT *1888:* hands: 3| P:through. *1868:* through! 5| P:the *1868:* me! The 7| P:you. *1868:* you; 8| P:asked, *1863:* asked; 9| P:gain— *1865:* gain: 10| *1868:* us! *1888:* us. 12| P:give *1868:* you! Give 15| P:now. Let. *1868:* now! Let 17| P:away *1870:* away, 18| P:please with <> soul. *1855:* please, with *1868:* soul! 19| P:how <> man? *1868:* then? How <> man! 20| P:his, who *1868:* his—who

Have passed into his heart and beat its beats,
Who give my hands to him, my eyes, my hair,
Give all that was of me away to him—
So well, that now, my spirit turned his own,
Takes part with him against the woman here,
Bids him not stumble at so mere a straw
As caring that the world be cognizant
How he loves her and how she worships him.
You have this woman, not as yet that world.
Go on, I bid, nor stop to care for me
By saving what I cease to care about,
The courtly name and pride of circumstance—
The name you'll pick up and be cumbered with
Just for the poor parade's sake, nothing more;
Just that the world may slip from under you—
Just that the world may cry "So much for him—
The man predestined to the heap of crowns:
There goes his chance of winning one, at least!"
NORBERT The world!
CONSTANCE You love it. Love me quite as well,
And see if I shall pray for this in vain!
Why must you ponder what it knows or thinks?
NORBERT You pray for—what, in vain?
CONSTANCE Oh my heart's heart,
How I do love you, Norbert! That is right:
But listen, or I take my hands away!
You say, "let it be now": you would go now
And tell the Queen, perhaps six steps from us,
You love me—so you do, thank God!
NORBERT Thank God!
CONSTANCE Yes, Norbert,—but you fain would tell your love,
And, what succeeds the telling, ask of her
My hand. Now take this rose and look at it,
Listening to me. You are the minister,

23| P:him *1868:* him— 27| P:cognisant *1888:* cognizant
34| P:more. *1855:* more; 37| P:crowns. *1855:* crowns! *1863:* crowns:
38| P:least." *1863:* least!" 39| *1868:* it! Love *1888:* it. Love 43| P:you, Norbert!—that is right! *1868:* you, Norbert! That is right: 44| P:away. *1868:* away! 45| P:now"—you *1868:* now:" you *1888:* now": you

The Queen's first favourite, nor without a cause.
To-night completes your wonderful year's-work
(This palace-feast is held to celebrate)
Made memorable by her life's success,
The junction of two crowns, on her sole head,
Her house had only dreamed of anciently:
That this mere dream is grown a stable truth,
To-night's feast makes authentic. Whose the praise?
Whose genius, patience, energy, achieved
What turned the many heads and broke the hearts?
You are the fate, your minute's in the heaven.
Next comes the Queen's turn. "Name your own reward!"
With leave to clench the past, chain the to-come,
Put out an arm and touch and take the sun
And fix it ever full-faced on your earth,
Possess yourself supremely of her life,—
You choose the single thing she will not grant;
Nay, very declaration of which choice
Will turn the scale and neutralize your work:
At best she will forgive you, if she can.
You think I'll let you choose—her cousin's hand?
NORBERT Wait. First, do you retain your old belief
The Queen is generous,—nay, is just?
CONSTANCE   There, there!
So men make women love them, while they know
No more of women's hearts than . . . look you here,
You that are just and generous beside,
Make it your own case! For example now,
I'll say—I let you kiss me, hold my hands—
Why? do you know why? I'll instruct you, then—
The kiss, because you have a name at court;
This hand and this, that you may shut in each
A jewel, if you please to pick up such.

56| P:That junction <> crowns on <> head *1863:* crowns, on <> head, *1865:* The junction 57| P:anciently. *1868:* anciently: 58| P:truth *1863:* truth, 62| P:fate—your *1868:* fate, your 63| P:turn. Name <> reward! *1863:* turn. "Name <> reward!" 64| *1863:* the Past <> To-come, *1868:* past <> to-come, 65| P:sun, *1855:* sun 67| P:life, *1863:* life,— 68| P:grant— *1863:* grant; 69| P:The very *1863:* Nay, very 70| P:neutralise <> work. *1863:* neutralize *1868:* work: 78| P:case. For *1868:* case! For 79| P:me and hold *1868:* me, hold 81| P:court, *1888:* court;

That's horrible? Apply it to the Queen—
Suppose I am the Queen to whom you speak:
"I was a nameless man; you needed me:
Why did I proffer you my aid? there stood
A certain pretty cousin at your side.
Why did I make such common cause with you?
Access to her had not been easy else.
You give my labour here abundant praise?
'Faith, labour, which she overlooked, grew play.
How shall your gratitude discharge itself?
Give me her hand!"
NORBERT And still I urge the same.
Is the Queen just? just—generous or no!
CONSTANCE Yes, just. You love a rose; no harm in that:
But was it for the rose's sake or mine
You put it in your bosom? mine, you said—
Then, mine you still must say or else be false.
You told the Queen you served her for herself;
If so, to serve her was to serve yourself,
She thinks, for all your unbelieving face!
I know her. In the hall, six steps from us,
One sees the twenty pictures; there's a life
Better than life, and yet no life at all.
Conceive her born in such a magic dome,
Pictures all round her! why, she sees the world,
Can recognize its given things and facts,
The fight of giants or the feast of gods,
Sages in senate, beauties at the bath,
Chases and battles, the whole earth's display,
Landscape and sea-piece, down to flowers and fruit—
And who shall question that she knows them all,

84| P:horrible! Apply *1868:* horrible? Apply 85| P:Suppose, I <> speak. *1868:* Suppose I *1888:* speak: 86| P:man: you *1863:* man; you 87| P:there crouched *1855:* there stood 88| P:pretty Cousin *1863:* cousin 91| P:labours <> praise: *1863:* praise? *1888:* labour 92| P:Which, labour, while she *1855:* 'Faith, labour *1863:* labour, which she 96| P:rose—no <> that— *1863:* rose; no <> that: 99| P:Then mine *1863:* Then, mine 100| P:herself: *1865:* herself; 101| P:yourself *1863:* yourself, 104| P:pictures—there's *1863:* pictures; there's 105| P:life—and <> all; *1863:* life, and <> all. 108| P:recognise *1863:* recognize 111| P:Chaces *C1870:* Chases 113| P:all *1863:* all,

In better semblance than the things outside?
Yet bring into the silent gallery
Some live thing to contrast in breath and blood,
Some lion, with the painted lion there—
You think she'll understand composedly?
—Say, "that's his fellow in the hunting-piece
Yonder, I've turned to praise a hundred times?"
Not so. Her knowledge of our actual earth,
Its hopes and fears, concerns and sympathies,
Must be too far, too mediate, too unreal.
The real exists for us outside, not her:
How should it, with that life in these four walls—
That father and that mother, first to last
No father and no mother—friends, a heap,
Lovers, no lack—a husband in due time,
And every one of them alike a lie!
Things painted by a Rubens out of nought
Into what kindness, friendship, love should be;
All better, all more grandiose than the life,
Only no life; mere cloth and surface-paint,
You feel, while you admire. How should she feel?
Yet now that she has stood thus fifty years
The sole spectator in that gallery,
You think to bring this warm real struggling love
In to her of a sudden, and suppose
She'll keep her state untroubled? Here's the truth—
She'll apprehend truth's value at a glance,
Prefer it to the pictured loyalty?
You only have to say, "so men are made,
For this they act; the thing has many names,
But this the right one: and now, Queen, be just!"

115| P:But bring *1855:* Yet bring 124| P:her— *1863:* her: 125| P:walls, *1888:* walls DC,BrU:walls— *1889:* walls— 129| P:everyone *1863:* every one 132| P:than life, *1888:* than the life, 133| P:surface-paint *1863:* surface-paint, 134| P:feel while *1863:* feel, while 135| P:And now *1863:* Yet now 140| P:apprehend its value *1868:* apprehend truth's value 141| P:loyalty! *1863:* loyalty? 142| P:say "so *1888:* say, "so 143| P:act, the <> names *1863:* act; the <> names, 144| P:one—and *1863:* one: and

Your life slips back; you lose her at the word:
You do not even for amends gain me.
He will not understand; oh, Norbert, Norbert,
Do you not understand?

NORBERT
The Queen's the Queen:
I am myself—no picture, but alive
In every nerve and every muscle, here
At the palace-window o'er the people's street,
As she in the gallery where the pictures glow:
The good of life is precious to us both.
She cannot love; what do I want with rule?
When first I saw your face a year ago
I knew my life's good, my soul heard one voice—
"The woman yonder, there's no use of life
But just to obtain her! heap earth's woes in one
And bear them—make a pile of all earth's joys
And spurn them, as they help or help not this;
Only, obtain her!" How was it to be?
I found you were the cousin of the Queen;
I must then serve the Queen to get to you.
No other way. Suppose there had been one,
And I, by saying prayers to some white star
With promise of my body and my soul,
Might gain you,—should I pray the star or no?
Instead, there was the Queen to serve! I served,
Helped, did what other servants failed to do.
Neither she sought nor I declared my end.
Her good is hers, my recompense be mine,—
I therefore name you as that recompense.
She dreamed that such a thing could never be?

145| P:And life <> back—you <> word— *1863:*back; you <> word: *1868:*Your life 147| P:understand! oh *1888:*understand: oh 148| P:the Queen, *1888:*the Queen DC,BrU:the Queen: *1889:*the Queen: 151| P:palace-window or in the *1863:*palace-window o'er the 152| P:glow. *1863:*glow: 154| P:love—what *1863:*love; what 156| P:good—my <> voice *1863:*good, my <> voice— 160| P:not here; *1863:*not this; 161| P:her!"—How *1868:*how *1888:*her!" How 162| P:found she was *1863:*found you were 163| P:get to her— *1863:*get to you. 165| P:And I by *1863:*And I, by 166| P:soul *1863:*soul, 169| P:And did *1863:*Helped, did 171| P:mine, *1888:*mine,— 172| P:And let me name *1863:*I therefore name

Let her wake now. She thinks there was more cause
In love of power, high fame, pure loyalty?
Perhaps she fancies men wear out their lives
Chasing such shades. Then, I've a fancy too;
I worked because I want you with my soul:
I therefore ask your hand. Let it be now!
CONSTANCE Had I not loved you from the very first,
Were I not yours, could we not steal out thus
So wickedly, so wildly, and so well,
You might become impatient. What's conceived
Of us without here, by the folk within?
Where are you now? immersed in cares of state—
Where am I now? intent on festal robes—
We two, embracing under death's spread hand!
What was this thought for, what that scruple of yours
Which broke the council up?—to bring about
One minute's meeting in the corridor!
And then the sudden sleights, strange secrecies,
Complots inscrutable, deep telegraphs,
Long-planned chance-meetings, hazards of a look,
"Does she know? does she not know? saved or lost?"
A year of this compression's ecstasy
All goes for nothing! you would give this up
For the old way, the open way, the world's,
His way who beats, and his who sells his wife!
What tempts you?—their notorious happiness
Makes you ashamed of ours? The best you'll gain
Will be—the Queen grants all that you require,

174| P:was some cause— *1863:* was more cause 175| P:The love of power, of fame *1863:* In love of power, high fame 176| P:—Perhaps *1863:* Perhaps 177| P:shades. Then I've <> too. *1863:* shades. Then, I've <> too; 178| P:soul— *1863:* soul: 179| P:now. *1863:* now! 183| P:might be thus impatient *1863:* might become impatient 184| P:folks DC,BrU:folk *1889:* folk 186| P:now?—intent *1888:* now? intent 188| P:for, what this scruple *1863:* for, what that scruple 189| P:up, to *1863:* up?—to 190| P:corridor? *1863:* corridor! 191| P:sleights, long secresies, *1863:* sleights, strange secrecies, 192| P:The plots inscrutable *1863:* Complots inscrutable 196| P:nothing? you *1863:* nothing! you 198| P:wife? *1863:* wife! 199| P:you? their <> happiness, *1863:* you?—their *1888:* happiness 200| P:That you're ashamed <> you'll get *1863:* you'll gain *1865:* That you are ashamed *1888:* Makes you ashamed 201| P:be, the *1868:* be—the

Concedes the cousin, rids herself of you
And me at once, and gives us ample leave
To live like our five hundred happy friends.
The world will show us with officious hand
Our chamber-entry, and stand sentinel
Where we so oft have stolen across its traps!
Get the world's warrant, ring the falcons' feet,
And make it duty to be bold and swift,
Which long ago was nature. Have it so!
We never hawked by rights till flung from fist?
Oh, the man's thought! no woman's such a fool.
NORBERT Yes, the man's thought and my thought, which is more—
One made to love you, let the world take note!
Have I done worthy work? be love's the praise,
Though hampered by restrictions, barred against
By set forms, blinded by forced secrecies!
Set free my love, and see what love can do
Shown in my life—what work will spring from that!
The world is used to have its business done
On other grounds, find great effects produced
For power's sake, fame's sake, motives in men's mouth.
So, good: but let my low ground shame their high!
Truth is the strong thing. Let man's life be true!
And love's the truth of mine. Time prove the rest!
I choose to wear you stamped all over me,
Your name upon my forehead and my breast,
You, from the sword's blade to the ribbon's edge,
That men may see, all over, you in me—
That pale loves may die out of their pretence

202| P:cousin, and gets rid of *1863:* cousin, rids herself of 203| P:And her at *1863:* And me at 204| P:live as our *1863:* live like our 206| P:chamber-entry and <> sentinel, *1888:* chamber-entry, and <> sentinel 207| P:When we <> across her traps! *1863:* Where we <> across its traps!' *1865:* traps! 208| P:falcon's foot, *1863:* falcons' feet, 210| P:When long ago 'twas nature *1863:* Which long ago was nature 211| P:He never *1863:* We never 212| P:thought!—no *1868:* thought! no 214| P:note. *1863:* note! 217| P:secresies. *1863:* secrecies! 218| P:my life, and <> love will do *1855:* my love, and *1863:* what love can do 222| P:motives you have named. *1863:* motives in men's mouth. 223| P:So good. But <> high. *1863:* So, good: but <> high! 226| P:to have you *1863:* to wear you

In face of mine, shames thrown on love fall off.
Permit this, Constance! Love has been so long
Subdued in me, eating me through and through,
That now 'tis all of me and must have way.
Think of my work, that chaos of intrigues,
Those hopes and fears, surprises and delays,
That long endeavour, earnest, patient, slow,
Trembling at last to its assured result:
Then think of this revulsion! I resume
Life after death, (it is no less than life,
After such long unlovely labouring days)
And liberate to beauty life's great need
O' the beautiful, which, while it prompted work,
Suppressed itself erewhile. This eve's the time,
This eve intense with yon first trembling star
We seem to pant and reach; scarce aught between
The earth that rises and the heaven that bends;
All nature self-abandoned, every tree
Flung as it will, pursuing its own thoughts
And fixed so, every flower and every weed,
No pride, no shame, no victory, no defeat;
All under God, each measured by itself.
These statues round us stand abrupt, distinct,
The strong in strength, the weak in weakness fixed,
The Muse for ever wedded to her lyre,
Nymph to her fawn, and Silence to her rose:
See God's approval on his universe!
Let us do so—aspire to live as these
In harmony with truth, ourselves being true!

231| P:off— *1863:* off. 234| P:it's *1868:* 'tis 238| P:result— *1888:* result: 239| P:revulsion. I *1863:* revulsion! I 240| P:Life, after <> life *1863:* Life after <> life, 243| P:Of *1870:* O' 244| P:Suppress <> time— *1868:* Suppressed <> time, 247| P:bends— *1863:* bends; 248| P:self-abandoned—even each tree *1855:* self-abandoned—every tree *1863:* self-abandoned, every 250| P:so, each small flower and weed the same, *1855:* so, every flower and every weed, 251| P:defeat— *1855:* defeat: *1863:* defeat; 252| P:itself! *1863:* itself. 253| P:us, each abrupt *1863:* us stand abrupt 256| The Nymph <> fawn, the Silence <> rose, *1863:* rose: *1888:* Nymph <> fawn, and Silence 257| P:And God's *1863:* See God's <> His *1868:* his 259| P:true. *1863:* true!

Take the first way, and let the second come!
My first is to possess myself of you;
The music sets the march-step—forward, then!
And there's the Queen, I go to claim you of,
The world to witness, wonder and applaud.
Our flower of life breaks open. No delay!
CONSTANCE And so shall we be ruined, both of us.
Norbert, I know her to the skin and bone:
You do not know her, were not born to it,
To feel what she can see or cannot see.
Love, she is generous,—ay, despite your smile,
Generous as you are: for, in that thin frame
Pain-twisted, punctured through and through with cares,
There lived a lavish soul until it starved,
Debarred of healthy food. Look to the soul—
Pity that, stoop to that, ere you begin
(The true man's-way) on justice and your rights,
Exactions and acquittance of the past!
Begin so—see what justice she will deal!
We women hate a debt as men a gift.
Suppose her some poor keeper of a school
Whose business is to sit thro' summer months
And dole out children leave to go and play,
Herself superior to such lightness—she
In the arm-chair's state and pædagogic pomp—
To the life, the laughter, sun and youth outside:
We wonder such a face looks black on us?
I do not bid you wake her tenderness,
(That were vain truly—none is left to wake)
But let her think her justice is engaged

260| P:come. *1863:* come! 262| P:forward then! *1863:* forward, then! 267| P:bone— *1865:* bone: *1888:* bone DC,BrU:bone: *1889:* bone: 270| P:generous, despite *1855:* generous,—ay, despite 271| P:are. Yes, in *1855:* are. For, in *1863:* are: for 273| P:a generous soul <> starved *1855:* a lavish soul *1888:* starved, 274| P:Debarred all healthy *1888:* Debarred of healthy 276| P:man's way *1863:* man's-way 277| P:past. *1863:* the Past! *1868:* past! 279| P:Men hate a gift as women hate a debt. *1855:* We women hate a debt as men a gift. 281| *1855:* summer-months *1865:* summer months 282| P:children's *1863:* children 284| P:pomp, *1888:* pomp— 285| P:outside— *1868:* outside: 286| P:such an one looks *1863:* such a face looks 288| P:—That <> wake— *1863:* (That <> wake) 289| P:But, let DC,BrU:But let *1889:* But let

To take the shape of tenderness, and mark
If she'll not coldly pay its warmest debt!
Does she love me, I ask you? not a whit:
Yet, thinking that her justice was engaged
To help a kinswoman, she took me up—
Did more on that bare ground than other loves
Would do on greater argument. For me,
I have no equivalent of such cold kind
To pay her with, but love alone to give
If I give anything. I give her love:
I feel I ought to help her, and I will.
So, for her sake, as yours, I tell you twice
That women hate a debt as men a gift.
If I were you, I could obtain this grace—
Could lay the whole I did to love's account,
Nor yet be very false as courtiers go—
Declaring my success was recompense;
It would be so, in fact: what were it else?
And then, once loose her generosity,—
Oh, how I see it!—then, were I but you,
To turn it, let it seem to move itself,
And make it offer what I really take,
Accepting just, in the poor cousin's hand,
Her value as the next thing to the Queen's—
Since none love Queens directly, none dare that,
And a thing's shadow or a name's mere echo
Suffices those who miss the name and thing!

291| P:coldly do its warmest deed! *1863:* coldly pay its warmest need! *C1870:* warmest debt! 292| P:whit. *1863:* whit: 297| P:of that cold *1863:* of such cold 298| P:with; my love *1863:* with, but love 299| P:love. *1863:* love: 301| P:So for *1863:* So, for 303| P:I could obtain this favour—I would lay *1855:* If I were you, I could obtain this grace— 304| P:The whole of what I *1855:* Would lay the whole I *1863:* Could lay 305| P:go; *1855:* go— 306| P:Declare that my <> recompense— *1855:* recompense *1863:* Declaring my 308| P:then, when flows her generosity *1855:* then, once loosed her *1863:* loose her generosity,— 309| P:As you will mark it—then,—were <> you *1863:* Oh, how I see it! then, were *1888:* it!—then <> you, 311| P:it give the thing I *1863:* it offer what I 312| P:Accepting so, in *1863:* Accepting just, in 313| P:All value <> queen— *1863:* Her value <> Queen's— 314| P:none loses her directly <> dares that! *1863:* loves Queens directly <> that, *1888:* love <> dare 315| P:A shadow of a thing, a *1863:* And a thing's shadow or 316| P:thing; *1863:* thing!

You pick up just a ribbon she has worn,
To keep in proof how near her breath you came.
Say, I'm so near I seem a piece of her—
Ask for me that way—(oh, you understand)
You'd find the same gift yielded with a grace,
Which, if you make the least show to extort . . .
—You'll see! and when you have ruined both of us,
Dissertate on the Queen's ingratitude!
NORBERT Then, if I turn it that way, you consent?
'Tis not my way; I have more hope in truth:
Still, if you won't have truth—why, this indeed,
Were scarcely false, as I'd express the sense.
Will you remain here?
CONSTANCE O best heart of mine,
How I have loved you! then, you take my way?
Are mine as you have been her minister,
Work out my thought, give it effect for me,
Paint plain my poor conceit and make it serve?
I owe that withered woman everything—
Life, fortune, you, remember! Take my part—
Help me to pay her! Stand upon your rights?
You, with my rose, my hands, my heart on you?
Your rights are mine—you have no rights but mine.
NORBERT Remain here. How you know me!
CONSTANCE Ah, but still—
[*He breaks from her: she remains. Dance-music from within.*

Enter the QUEEN

QUEEN Constance? She is here as he said. Speak quick!
Is it so? Is it true or false? One word!

317| P:worn *1863:* worn, 319| P:Say I'm *1863:* Say, I'm 321| P:And find *1863:* You'd find 322| P:Which if <> shew to extort *1863:* Which, if <> show to extort . . . 325| P:So, if *1855:* Then, if 326| P:truth. *1863:* truth: 327| P:Still if *1863:* Still, if 328| P:Is scarcely false, I'll turn it such a way. *1855:* false, I'll so express the sense. *1863:* Were scarcely false, as I'd express 339–40| P:*within.* / *SECOND PART.* / §rule§ / *Enter* *1863:within.* / §rule§ / *Enter* *1888:within.* / *Enter*
340| P:Constance!—She <> Speak! quick! *1868:* Constance? She <> Speak quick!
341| P:so? is it true—or *1868:* so? Is it true or <> word? *1888:* word!

CONSTANCE True.
QUEEN Mercifullest Mother, thanks to thee!
CONSTANCE Madam?
QUEEN I love you, Constance, from my soul.
Now say once more, with any words you will,
'Tis true, all true, as true as that I speak.
CONSTANCE Why should you doubt it?
QUEEN Ah, why doubt? why doubt?
Dear, make me see it! Do you see it so?
None see themselves; another sees them best.
You say "why doubt it?"—you see him and me.
It is because the Mother has such grace
That if we had but faith—wherein we fail—
Whate'er we yearn for would be granted us;
Yet still we let our whims prescribe despair,
Our fancies thwart and cramp our will and power,
And while, accepting life, abjure its use.
Constance, I had abjured the hope of love
And being loved, as truly as yon palm
The hope of seeing Egypt from that plot.
CONSTANCE Heaven!
QUEEN But it was so, Constance, it was so!
Men say—or do men say it? fancies say—
"Stop here, your life is set, you are grown old.
Too late—no love for you, too late for love—
Leave love to girls. Be queen: let Constance love."
One takes the hint—half meets it like a child,
Ashamed at any feelings that oppose.
"Oh love, true, never think of love again!
I am a queen: I rule, not love forsooth."

343| P:Madam! QUEEN *1868:* Madam? QUEEN 345| P:true—all true—as true *1863:* true, all true, as true 347| P:it. Do *1863:* it! Do 348| P:themselves—another *1863:* themselves; another 353| P:Howbeit we let such whims *1855:* let our whims *1888:* Yet still we 354| P:Such very fancies <> will, *1855:* Our very *1888:* Our fancies <> will and power, 355| P:And so accepting <> abjure ourselves! *1863:* so, accepting <> ourselves. *1888:* And while, accepting <> abjure its use. 357| P:And of being *1868:* And being 358| P:that turf. *1863:* that plot. 359| P:so, Constance, it was so. *1863:* so, Constance, it was so! 363| P:queen—let <> love!" *1863:* queen: let *1870:* love!' *1888:* let Constance love." 366| P:Oh, love <> of it again! *1855:* of love again! *1865:* Oh love, true 367| P:queen—I <> love, indeed. *1855:* indeed." *1863:* queen: I *1888:* love forsooth."

So it goes on; so a face grows like this,
Hair like this hair, poor arms as lean as these,
Till,—nay, it does not end so, I thank God!
CONSTANCE I cannot understand—
QUEEN The happier you!
Constance, I know not how it is with men:
For women (I am a woman now like you)
There is no good of life but love—but love!
What else looks good, is some shade flung from love;
Love gilds it, gives it worth. Be warned by me,
Never you cheat yourself one instant! Love,
Give love, ask only love, and leave the rest!
O Constance, how I love you!
CONSTANCE I love you.
QUEEN I do believe that all is come through you.
I took you to my heart to keep it warm
When the last chance of love seemed dead in me;
I thought your fresh youth warmed my withered heart.
Oh, I am very old now, am I not?
Not so! it is true and it shall be true!
CONSTANCE Tell it me: let me judge if true or false.
QUEEN Ah, but I fear you! you will look at me
And say, "she's old, she's grown unlovely quite
Who ne'er was beauteous: men want beauty still."
Well, so I feared—the curse! so I felt sure!
CONSTANCE Be calm. And now you feel not sure, you say?
QUEEN Constance, he came,—the coming was not strange—
Do not I stand and see men come and go?
I turned a half-look from my pedestal
Where I grow marble—"one young man the more!
He will love some one; that is nought to me:
What would he with my marble stateliness?"
Yet this seemed somewhat worse than heretofore;

372| P:men. *1863:* men: 373| P:women, (I *1868:* women (I 375| P:love— *1865:* love; 377| P:instant! Love, *1863:* instant! Love, 386| P:me! let *1863:* me: let 387 P:you—you *1863:* you! you 388| P:say "she's old *1868:* say, "she's old 389| P:beauteous! men *1863:* beauteous: men 390| P:sure. *1868:* sure! 392| P:came, the *1863:* came,—the 396| P:one,—that <> me— *1863:* me: *1865:* one; that

The man more gracious, youthful, like a god,
And I still older, with less flesh to change—
We two those dear extremes that long to touch.
It seemed still harder when he first began
To labour at those state-affairs, absorbed
The old way for the old end—interest.
Oh, to live with a thousand beating hearts
Around you, swift eyes, serviceable hands,
Professing they've no care but for your cause,
Thought but to help you, love but for yourself,—
And you the marble statue all the time
They praise and point at as preferred to life,
Yet leave for the first breathing woman's smile,
First dancer's, gipsy's or street baladine's!
Why, how I have ground my teeth to hear men's speech
Stifled for fear it should alarm my ear,
Their gait subdued lest step should startle me,
Their eyes declined, such queendom to respect,
Their hands alert, such treasure to preserve,
While not a man of them broke rank and spoke,
Wrote me a vulgar letter all of love,
Or caught my hand and pressed it like a hand!
There have been moments, if the sentinel
Lowering his halbert to salute the queen,
Had flung it brutally and clasped my knees,
I would have stooped and kissed him with my soul.
CONSTANCE Who could have comprehended?
QUEEN Ay, who—who?
Why, no one, Constance, but this one who did.
Not they, not you, not I. Even now perhaps
It comes too late—would you but tell the truth.
CONSTANCE I wait to tell it.
QUEEN Well, you see, he came,

403| P:Absorbed to labour at the state-affairs *1888:* To labour at those state-affairs, absorbed 404| P:end, interest. *1863:* end—interest. 408| P:yourself, *1888:* yourself,— 411| P:woman's cheek, *1888:* woman's smile, 412| P:gypsy's, or *1868:* gypsy's or 418| P:of these broke *1863:* of them broke 419| P:Or wrote *1888:* Wrote 420| P:a hand. *1868:* a hand! 423| P:knees *1855:* knees, 425| P:comprehend! QUEEN *1863:* comprehend? QUEEN

Outfaced the others, did a work this year
Exceeds in value all was ever done,
You know—it is not I who say it—all
Say it. And so (a second pang and worse)
I grew aware not only of what he did,
But why so wondrously. Oh, never work
Like his was done for work's ignoble sake—
Souls need a finer aim to light and lure!
I felt, I saw, he loved—loved somebody.
And Constance, my dear Constance, do you know,
I did believe this while 'twas you he loved.
CONSTANCE Me, madam?
QUEEN It did seem to me, your face
Met him where'er he looked: and whom but you
Was such a man to love? It seemed to me,
You saw he loved you, and approved his love,
And both of you were in intelligence.
You could not loiter in that garden, step
Into this balcony, but I straight was stung
And forced to understand. It seemed so true,
So right, so beautiful, so like you both,
That all this work should have been done by him
Not for the vulgar hope of recompense,
But that at last—suppose, some night like this—
Borne on to claim his due reward of me,
He might say "Give her hand and pay me so."
And I (O Constance, you shall love me now!)
I thought, surmounting all the bitterness,
—"And he shall have it. I will make her blest,
My flower of youth, my woman's self that was,
My happiest woman's self that might have been!

431| P:done *1863:* done, 437| P:It must have finer aims to spur it on! *1863:* to lure it *1888:* Souls need a finer aim to light and lure! 438| P:saw he *1863:* saw, he 441| P:to me your *1863:* to me, your 443| P:love? it <> me *1863:* me, *1868:* love? It 444| P:approved the love, *1888:* approved his love, 445| P:And that you both were *1863:* And so you *1888:* And both of you were <> intelligence DC,BrU:intelligence. *1889:* intelligence. 446| P:in the garden *1888:* in that garden 449| P:both *1863:* both, 452| P:suppose some *1863:* suppose, some 453| P:me *1863:* me, 454| P:say, "Give *1888:* say "Give 455| P:now) *1863:* now!) 457| P:blessed, *1855:* blest,

These two shall have their joy and leave me here."
Yes—yes!
CONSTANCE Thanks!
QUEEN And the word was on my lips
When he burst in upon me. I looked to hear
A mere calm statement of his just desire
For payment of his labour. When—O heaven,
How can I tell you? lightning on my eyes
And thunder in my ears proved that first word
Which told 'twas love of me, of me, did all—
He loved me—from the first step to the last,
Loved me!
CONSTANCE You hardly saw, scarce heard him speak
Of love: what if you should mistake?
QUEEN No, no—
No mistake! Ha, there shall be no mistake!
He had not dared to hint the love he felt—
You were my reflex—(how I understood!)
He said you were the ribbon I had worn,
He kissed my hand, he looked into my eyes,
And love, love came at end of every phrase.
Love is begun; this much is come to pass:
The rest is easy. Constance, I am yours!
I will learn, I will place my life on you,
Teach me but how to keep what I have won!
Am I so old? This hair was early grey;
But joy ere now has brought hair brown again,
And joy will bring the cheek's red back, I feel.
I could sing once too; that was in my youth.

461| P:Yes—yes—CONSTANCE *1868:* Yes—yes! CONSTANCE 463| P:Such a calm *1855:* A mere calm 464| P:In payment <> When, O Heaven, *1863:* For payment <> When—O *1868:* heaven, 465| P:you? cloud was on *1888:* you? lightning on 466| P:ears at that *1888:* ears proved that 469| P:CONSTANCE You did not hear . . . you thought he spoke *1888:* CONSTANCE You hardly saw, scarce heard him speak 470| P:love? what *1888:* love: what 473| P:reflex—how I understood! *1863:* reflex—(how I understood!) 474| P:riband *1855:* ribbon 476| P:love, love was the end *1888:* love, love came at end 477| P:begun—this <> pass, *1865:* begun; this <> pass: 478| P:yours— *1868:* yours! 480| P:But teach me how <> won. *1868:* won! *1888:* Teach me but how 481| P:old? this *1868:* old? This

Still, when men paint me, they declare me . . . yes,
Beautiful—for the last French painter did!
I know they flatter somewhat; you are frank—
I trust you. How I loved you from the first!
Some queens would hardly seek a cousin out
And set her by their side to take the eye:
I must have felt that good would come from you.
I am not generous—like him—like you!
But he is not your lover after all:
It was not you he looked at. Saw you him?
You have not been mistaking words or looks?
He said you were the reflex of myself.
And yet he is not such a paragon
To you, to younger women who may choose
Among a thousand Norberts. Speak the truth!
You know you never named his name to me:
You know, I cannot give him up—ah God,
Not up now, even to you!
CONSTANCE Then calm yourself.
QUEEN See, I am old—look here, you happy girl!
I will not play the fool, deceive—ah, whom?
'Tis all gone: put your cheek beside my cheek
And what a contrast does the moon behold!
But then I set my life upon one chance,
The last chance and the best—am *I* not left,
My soul, myself? All women love great men
If young or old; it is in all the tales:
Young beauties love old poets who can love—
Why should not he, the poems in my soul,
The passionate faith, the pride of sacrifice,
Life-long, death-long? I throw them at his feet.

493| P:all— *1865:* all: 495| P:looks! *1865:* looks? 496| P:myself— *1865:* myself. 500| P:me— *1888:* me: 503| P:girl, *1870:* girl *C1870:* girl! 504| P:deceive myself; *1888:* deceive—ah, whom? 505| P:gone— put <> my cheek— *1868:* gone: put *1888:* my cheek 506| P:Ah, what *1888:* And what 508| P:am I *1855:* am *I* 510| P:old—it <> tales— *1865:* old; it <> tales: 512| P:he the *1863:* he, the 513| P:The love, the passionate faith, the sacrifice, *1888:* The passionate faith, the pride of sacrifice, 514| P:The constancy? I *1888:* Life-long, death-long? I

Who cares to see the fountain's very shape,
Whether it be a Triton's or a Nymph's
That pours the foam, makes rainbows all around?
You could not praise indeed the empty conch;
But I'll pour floods of love and hide myself.
How I will love him! Cannot men love love?
Who was a queen and loved a poet once
Humpbacked, a dwarf? ah, women can do that!
Well, but men too; at least, they tell you so.
They love so many women in their youth,
And even in age they all love whom they please;
And yet the best of them confide to friends
That 'tis not beauty makes the lasting love—
They spend a day with such and tire the next:
They like soul,—well then, they like phantasy,
Novelty even. Let us confess the truth,
Horrible though it be, that prejudice,
Prescription . . . curses! they will love a queen.
They will, they do: and will not, does not—he?
CONSTANCE How can he? You are wedded: 'tis a name
We know, but still a bond. Your rank remains,
His rank remains. How can he, nobly souled
As you believe and I incline to think,
Aspire to be your favourite, shame and all?
QUEEN Hear her! There, there now—could she love like me?
What did I say of smooth-cheeked youth and grace?
See all it does or could do! so youth loves!
Oh, tell him, Constance, you could never do
What I will—you, it was not born in! I
Will drive these difficulties far and fast
As yonder mists curdling before the moon.
I'll use my light too, gloriously retrieve
My youth from its enforced calamity,

515| P:shape *1863:* shape, 516| P:And whether *1888:* Whether 520| P:him! cannot *1868:* him! Cannot 523| P:too! at *1863:* too; at 528| P:next; *1865:* next: 530| P:truth *1863:* truth, 531| P:be—that *1868:* be, that 532| P:Prescription . . . Curses *1863:* curses 533| P:will—they do. And *1868:* will, they do: and 534| P:wedded—'tis *1868:* wedded: 'tis 539| P:her! there, there *1868:* her! There, there 541| P:so, youth *1888:* so youth

Dissolve that hateful marriage, and be his,
His own in the eyes alike of God and man.
CONSTANCE You will do—dare do . . . pause on what you say!
QUEEN Hear her! I thank you, sweet, for that surprise.
You have the fair face: for the soul, see mine!
I have the strong soul: let me teach you, here.
I think I have borne enough and long enough,
And patiently enough, the world remarks,
To have my own way now, unblamed by all.
It does so happen (I rejoice for it)
This most unhoped-for issue cuts the knot.
There's not a better way of settling claims
Than this; God sends the accident express:
And were it for my subjects' good, no more,
'Twere best thus ordered. I am thankful now,
Mute, passive, acquiescent. I receive,
And bless God simply, or should almost fear
To walk so smoothly to my ends at last.
Why, how I baffle obstacles, spurn fate!
How strong I am! Could Norbert see me now!
CONSTANCE Let me consider. It is all too strange.
QUEEN You, Constance, learn of me; do you, like me!
You are young, beautiful: my own, best girl,
You will have many lovers, and love one—
Light hair, not hair like Norbert's, to suit yours:
Taller than he is, since yourself are tall.
Love him, like me! Give all away to him;
Think never of yourself; throw by your pride,
Hope, fear,—your own good as you saw it once,
And love him simply for his very self.
Remember, I (and what am I to you?)

550| P:dare do—Pause *1863:*dare do . . . pause 551| P:you, Sweet *1868:*sweet 555| P:enough the *1855:*enough, the 557| P:happen, I <> it, *1863:*happen (I <> it) 560| P:express; *1863:*express: 563| P:receive *1855:*receive, 567| P:am! could *1868:*am! Could 569| P:like me. *1863:*like me! 572| P:yours, *1888:*yours: 573| P:And taller <> is, for you are *1863:*for yourself are *1888:*Taller <> is, since yourself 574| P:him like me! give *1863:*him, like *1868:*me! Give

Would give up all for one, leave throne, lose life,
Do all but just unlove him! He loves me.
CONSTANCE He shall.
QUEEN You, step inside my inmost heart!
Give me your own heart: let us have one heart!
I'll come to you for counsel; "this he says,
This he does; what should this amount to, pray?
Beseech you, change it into current coin!
Is that worth kisses? Shall I please him there?"
And then we'll speak in turn of you—what else?
Your love, according to your beauty's worth,
For you shall have some noble love, all gold:
Whom choose you? we will get him at your choice.
—Constance, I leave you. Just a minute since,
I felt as I must die or be alone
Breathing my soul into an ear like yours:
Now, I would face the world with my new life,
Wear my new crown. I'll walk around the rooms,
And then come back and tell you how it feels.
How soon a smile of God can change the world!
How we are made for happiness—how work
Grows play, adversity a winning fight!
True, I have lost so many years: what then?
Many remain: God has been very good.
You, stay here! 'Tis as different from dreams,
From the mind's cold calm estimate of bliss,
As these stone statues from the flesh and blood.

580| P:him! he *1863:* him! He 581| P:heart. *1868:* heart! 582| P:heart—let <> heart— *1863:* heart: let <> heart. *1868:* one heart! 583| P:counsel; "This *1863:* this 584| P:does, what *1863:* does; what 585| P:coin. *1868:* coin! 586| P:shall *1868:* kisses? Shall 588| P:love (according <> worth) *1863:* love, according <> worth, 589| P:gold— *1863:* gold: 591| P:since *1863:* since, 593| P:yours. *1863:* yours: 595| P:With my *1888:* Wear my 598| P:are all made *1863:* are made 600| P:years. What *1868:* years: what 601| P:remain—God *1863:* remain: God 602| P:here. 'Tis <> dreams,— *1863:* dreams, *1868:* here! 'Tis

The comfort thou has caused mankind, God's moon!
[*She goes out, leaving* CONSTANCE. *Dance-music from within.*

NORBERT *enters.*

NORBERT Well? we have but one minute and one word!
CONSTANCE I am yours, Norbert!
NORBERT Yes, mine.
CONSTANCE Not till now!
You were mine. Now I give myself to you.
NORBERT Constance?
CONSTANCE Your own! I know the thriftier way
Of giving—haply, 'tis the wiser way.
Meaning to give a treasure, I might dole
Coin after coin out (each, as that were all,
With a new largess still at each despair)
And force you keep in sight the deed, preserve
Exhaustless till the end my part and yours,
My giving and your taking; both our joys
Dying together. Is it the wiser way?
I choose the simpler; I give all at once.
Know what you have to trust to, trade upon!
Use it, abuse it,—anything but think
Hereafter, "Had I known she loved me so,
And what my means, I might have thriven with it."
This is your means. I give you all myself.
NORBERT I take you and thank God.
CONSTANCE Look on through years!
We cannot kiss, a second day like this;
Else were this earth no earth.
NORBERT With this day's heat

605–606| P:*out. Dance-music* <> *within.* / *PART THIRD.* / §rule§ / NORBERT enters. *1863: out, leaving* CONSTANCE. Dance-music <> *within.* / NORBERT enters.
606| P:Well! we <> word— *1863:* word. *1868:* Well? we <> word!
609| P:Constance! CONSTANCE *1868:* Constance? CONSTANCE 614| P:deed, reserve *1863:* deed, preserve 616| P:taking, both *1863:* taking; both
619| P:upon. *1863:* upon! 620| P:but say *1863:* but think 625| P:kiss a <> this, *1863:* kiss, a <> this; 626| P:earth, no *1888:* earth no

We shall go on through years of cold.
CONSTANCE So, best!
—I try to see those years—I think I see.
You walk quick and new warmth comes; you look back
And lay all to the first glow—not sit down
For ever brooding on a day like this
While seeing embers whiten and love die.
Yes, love lives best in its effect; and mine,
Full in its own life, yearns to live in yours.
NORBERT Just so. I take and know you all at once.
Your soul is disengaged so easily,
Your face is there, I know you; give me time,
Let me be proud and think you shall know me.
My soul is slower: in a life I roll
The minute out whereto you condense yours—
The whole slow circle round you I must move,
To be just you. I look to a long life
To decompose this minute, prove its worth.
'Tis the sparks' long succession one by one
Shall show you, in the end, what fire was crammed
In that mere stone you struck: how could you know,
If it lay ever unproved in your sight,
As now my heart lies? your own warmth would hide
Its coldness, were it cold.
CONSTANCE But how prove, how?
NORBERT Prove in my life, you ask?
CONSTANCE Quick, Norbert—how?
NORBERT That's easy told. I count life just a stuff
To try the soul's strength on, educe the man.
Who keeps one end in view makes all things serve.
As with the body—he who hurls a lance
Or heaps up stone on stone, shows strength alike:
So must I seize and task all means to prove

627| P:CONSTANCE So best. *1863:*CONSTANCE So, best! 628| P:I try *1868:*—I try 632| P:seeing the embers *1888:*seeing embers 640| P:out in which you *1863:*out whereto you 645| P:you in the end what *1863:*you, in the end, what 646| P:struck: you could not know, *1863:*struck: how could you know, 655| P:shews <> alike, *1863:*shows *1888:*alike: 656| P:So I will seize and use all *1865:*prove, *C1870:*prove *1888:*So must I seize and task all

And show this soul of mine, you crown as yours,
And justify us both.
CONSTANCE Could you write books,
Paint pictures! One sits down in poverty
And writes or paints, with pity for the rich.
NORBERT And loves one's painting and one's writing, then,
And not one's mistress! All is best, believe,
And we best as no other than we are.
We live, and they experiment on life—
Those poets, painters, all who stand aloof
To overlook the farther. Let us be
The thing they look at! I might take your face
And write of it and paint it—to what end?
For whom? what pale dictatress in the air
Feeds, smiling sadly, her fine ghost-like form
With earth's real blood and breath, the beauteous life
She makes despised for ever? You are mine,
Made for me, not for others in the world,
Nor yet for that which I should call my art,
The cold calm power to see how fair you look.
I come to you; I leave you not, to write
Or paint. You are, I am: let Rubens there
Paint us!
CONSTANCE So, best!
NORBERT I understand your soul.
You live, and rightly sympathize with life,
With action, power, success. This way is straight;
And time were short beside, to let me change
The craft my childhood learnt: my craft shall serve.
Men set me here to subjugate, enclose,
Manure their barren lives, and force thence fruit

657| P:shew <> mine you *1863:*show *1868:*mine, you 659| P:pictures! one *1868:*pictures! One 661| P:writing too, *1863:*writing, then, 664| P:life *1863:*life— 667| P:take that face *1863:*take your face 675| P:That cold *1863:*The cold 676| P:you—I <> not to *1855:*not, to *1868:*you; I 677| P:am. Let *1868:*am: let 678| P:us. CONSTANCE So best *1863:*CONSTANCE So, best *1868:*us! CONSTANCE 679| P:sympathise *1863:*sympathize 680| P:success: this <> straight. *1863:*success. This <> straight; 681| P:And days were *1868:*And time were 682| P:learnt; my *1863:*learnt: my 684| P:lives and force the fruit *1863:*lives, and *1888:*force thence fruit

First for themselves, and afterward for me
In the due tithe; the task of some one soul,
Through ways of work appointed by the world.
I am not bid create—men see no star
Transfiguring my brow to warrant that—
But find and bind and bring to bear their wills.
So I began: to-night sees how I end.
What if it see, too, power's first outbreak here
Amid the warmth, surprise and sympathy,
And instincts of the heart that teach the head?
What if the people have discerned at length
The dawn of the next nature, novel brain
Whose will they venture in the place of theirs,
Whose work, they trust, shall find them as novel ways
To untried heights which yet he only sees?
I felt it when you kissed me. See this Queen,
This people—in our phrase, this mass of men—
See how the mass lies passive to my hand
Now that my hand is plastic, with you by
To make the muscles iron! Oh, an end
Shall crown this issue as this crowns the first!
My will be on this people! then, the strain,
The grappling of the potter with his clay,
The long uncertain struggle,—the success
And consummation of the spirit-work,
Some vase shaped to the curl of the god's lip,
While rounded fair for human sense to see

685| P:themselves and *1855:* themselves, and 686| P:one man, *1888:* one soul, 687| P:By ways <> by themselves. *1865:* Through ways *1888:* by the world. 688| P:create, they see *1863:* create—they *1888:* create—men see 690| P:But bind in one and carry out their *1888:* But find and bind and bring to bear their 692| P:too, my first *1888:* too, power's first 694| P:The instincts *1863:* And instincts 695| P:discerned in me *1863:* discerned at length 696| P:nature, the new man *1888:* nature, novel brain 698| P:And whom they trust to find them out new ways *1863:* And who, they trust, shall find *1888:* Whose work, they <> them as novel ways 699| P:To the new heights *1863:* To heights as new which *1888:* To untried heights which 701| *1863:* This People *1865:* people 703| P:And how my <> plastic, and you *1888:* Now that my <> plastic, with you 705| P:first. *1863:* first! 706| *1863:* this People *1865:* people 709| P:In that uprising of *1863:* And consummation of 710| P:The vase *1863:* Some vase 711| P:for lower men to *1888:* for human sense to

The Graces in a dance men recognize
With turbulent applause and laughs of heart!
So triumph ever shall renew itself;
Ever shall end in efforts higher yet,
Ever begin . . .
CONSTANCE I ever helping?
NORBERT Thus!
[*As he embraces her, the* QUEEN *enters.*
CONSTANCE Hist, madam! So have I performed my part.
You see your gratitude's true decency,
Norbert? A little slow in seeing it!
Begin, to end the sooner! What's a kiss?
NORBERT Constance?
CONSTANCE Why, must I teach it you again?
You want a witness to your dulness, sir?
What was I saying these ten minutes long?
Then I repeat—when some young handsome man
Like you has acted out a part like yours,
Is pleased to fall in love with one beyond,
So very far beyond him, as he says—
So hopelessly in love that but to speak
Would prove him mad,—he thinks judiciously,
And makes some insignificant good soul,
Like me, his friend, adviser, confidant,
And very stalking-horse to cover him
In following after what he dares not face.
When his end's gained—(sir, do you understand?)
When she, he dares not face, has loved him first,
—May I not say so, madam?—tops his hope,
And overpasses so his wildest dream,
With glad consent of all, and most of her

712| P:dance they recognise *1863:* dance all recognise *1888:* dance men recognize
715| P:Ever to end *1863:* Ever shall end 716| P:begun—CONSTANCE *1863:* begin . . . CONSTANCE 717| P:madam—so *1868:* madam! So
719| P:Norbert? a *1868:* Norbert? A 720| P:Begun to <> sooner. What's *1863:* Begin, to *1868:* sooner! What's 721| P:Constance! CONSTANCE *1868:* Constance? CONSTANCE 722| P:dullness *1868:* dulness 728| P:love, that *1870:* love that 729| P:mad, he *1863:* mad,—he 730| P:soul *1865:* soul,
731| P:confidant *1865:* confidant. *1868:* confidant, 733| P:face— *1888:* face.

The confidant who brought the same about—
Why, in the moment when such joy explodes,
I do hold that the merest gentleman
Will not start rudely from the stalking-horse,
Dismiss it with a "There, enough of you!"
Forget it, show his back unmannerly:
But like a liberal heart will rather turn
And say, "A tingling time of hope was ours;
Betwixt the fears and falterings, we two lived
A chanceful time in waiting for the prize:
The confidant, the Constance, served not ill.
And though I shall forget her in due time,
Her use being answered now, as reason bids,
Nay as herself bids from her heart of hearts,—
Still, she has rights, the first thanks go to her,
The first good praise goes to the prosperous tool,
And the first—which is the last—rewarding kiss."
NORBERT Constance, it is a dream—ah, see, you smile!
CONSTANCE So, now his part being properly performed,
Madam, I turn to you and finish mine
As duly; I do justice in my turn.
Yes, madam, he has loved you—long and well;
He could not hope to tell you so—'twas I
Who served to prove your soul accessible,
I led his thoughts on, drew them to their place
When they had wandered else into despair,
And kept love constant toward its natural aim.
Enough, my part is played; you stoop half-way

741| P:do say that *1863:* do hold that 744| P:unmannerly; *1888:* unmannerly: 746| P:ours— *1868:* ours; 747| P:faulterings—we *1863:* falterings *1868:* falterings, we 748| P:prize. *1863:* prize: 749| P:confidant, I grant too, served not ill; *1855:* confidant, the Constance, served *1863:* ill! *1865:* ill; *1868:* ill. 752| P:of hearts, *1868:* of hearts,— 755| P:last—thankful kiss." *1863:* last—rewarding kiss." 756| P:—Constance? it <> ah see you *1863:* Constance <> see, you *1868:* Constance, it <> ah, see 759| P:duly—I *1863:* duly; I 760| P:well— *1863:* well; 762| P:accessible. *1865:* accessible, 763| P:place, *1863:* place 764| P:When oft they had wandered out into *1863:* When else they *1888:* When they had wandered else into 766| P:Enough—my *1863:* Enough, my

And meet us royally and spare our fears:
'Tis like yourself. He thanks you, so do I.
Take him—with my full heart! my work is praised
By what comes of it. Be you happy, both!
Yourself—the only one on earth who can—
Do all for him, much more than a mere heart
Which though warm is not useful in its warmth
As the silk vesture of a queen! fold that
Around him gently, tenderly. For him—
For him,—he knows his own part!

NORBERT Have you done?
I take the jest at last. Should I speak now?
Was yours the wager, Constance, foolish child,
Or did you but accept it? Well—at least
You lose by it.

CONSTANCE Nay, madam, 'tis your turn!
Restrain him still from speech a little more,
And make him happier as more confident!
Pity him, madam, he is timid yet!
Mark, Norbert! Do not shrink now! Here I yield
My whole right in you to the Queen, observe!
With her go put in practice the great schemes
You teem with, follow the career else closed—
Be all you cannot be except by her!
Behold her!—Madam, say for pity's sake
Anything—frankly say you love him! Else
He'll not believe it: there's more earnest in
His fear than you conceive: I know the man!

NORBERT I know the woman somewhat, and confess
I thought she had jested better: she begins
To overcharge her part. I gravely wait
Your pleasure, madam: where is my reward?

767| P:fears— *1863:* fears: 768| P:yourself—he *1863:* yourself. He 776| P:part. NORBERT *1868:* part! NORBERT 779| P:least, *1863:* least 780| P:CONSTANCE Now madam <> turn. *1863:* CONSTANCE Nay, madam <> turn! 781| P:more *1863:* more, 782| P:happier and more *1888:* happier as more 783| P:yet. *1863:* yet! 784| P:do *1868:* Mark, Norbert! Do 789| P:her.—Madam *1863:* her!—Madam 790| P:him. Else *1863:* him! Else 792| P:conceive—I *1855:* man. *1863:* conceive: I *1868:* man! 794| P:better—she *1863:* better: she

QUEEN Norbert, this wild girl (whom I recognize
Scarce more than you do, in her fancy-fit,
Eccentric speech and variable mirth,
Not very wise perhaps and somewhat bold,
Yet suitable, the whole night's work being strange)
—May still be right: I may do well to speak
And make authentic what appears a dream
To even myself. For, what she says, is true:
Yes, Norbert—what you spoke just now of love,
Devotion, stirred no novel sense in me,
But justified a warmth felt long before.
Yes, from the first—I loved you, I shall say:
Strange! but I do grow stronger, now 'tis said.
Your courage helps mine: you did well to speak
To-night, the night that crowns your twelvemonths' toil:
But still I had not waited to discern
Your heart so long, believe me! From the first
The source of so much zeal was almost plain,
In absence even of your own words just now
Which hazarded the truth. 'Tis very strange,
But takes a happy ending—in your love
Which mine meets: be it so! as you chose me,
So I choose you.
NORBERT And worthily you choose.
I will not be unworthy your esteem,
No, madam. I do love you; I will meet
Your nature, now I know it. This was well.
I see,—you dare and you are justified:
But none had ventured such experiment,
Less versed than you in nobleness of heart,
Less confident of finding such in me.
I joy that thus you test me ere you grant

797| P:recognise *1888:* recognize 800| P:bold *1863:* bold, 804| P:true— *1865:* true: 805| P:spoke but now *1868:* spoke just now 808| P:say,— *1863:* say: 809| P:said, *1863:* said. 811| P:toil— *1865:* toil: 813| *1863:* me. From *1868:* me! From 816| P:Which opened out the <> Tis *1863:* 'Tis *1888:* Which hazarded the 818| P:so—as you choose *1863:* so: as *1868:* so! as *1888:* chose 819| P:worthily you choose! *1868:* worthily you choose. 821| P:you, I *1855:* you; I 822| P:it; this was well, *1863:* it. This was well. 826| P:finding it in *1863:* finding such in 827| P:I like that *1863:* I joy that

The dearest richest beauteousest and best
Of women to my arms: 'tis like yourself.
So—back again into my part's set words—
Devotion to the uttermost is yours,
But no, you cannot, madam, even you,
Create in me the love our Constance does.
Or—something truer to the tragic phrase—
Not yon magnolia-bell superb with scent
Invites a certain insect—that's myself—
But the small eye-flower nearer to the ground.
I take this lady.
CONSTANCE Stay—not hers, the trap—
Stay, Norbert—that mistake were worst of all!
He is too cunning, madam! It was I,
I Norbert, who . . .
NORBERT You, was it, Constance? Then,
But for the grace of this divinest hour
Which gives me you, I might not pardon here!
I am the Queen's; she only knows my brain:
She may experiment upon my heart
And I instruct her too by the result.
But you, sweet, you who know me, who so long
Have told my heart-beats over, held my life
In those white hands of yours,—it is not well!
CONSTANCE Tush! I have said it, did I not say it all?
The life, for her—the heart-beats, for her sake!
NORBERT Enough! my cheek grows red, I think. Your test?
There's not the meanest woman in the world,
Not she I least could love in all the world,
Whom, did she love me, had love proved itself,
I dare insult as you insult me now.

828| P:dearest, richest, beauteousest *1868:*dearest richest beauteousest 829| P:arms! 'tis <> yourself! *1863:*arms: 'tis <> yourself. 837| P:ground: *1863:*ground. 838| P:lady! CONSTANCE <> her's *1863:*lady. CONSTANCE <> hers 839| P:all. *1868:*all! 840| P:(He <> madam!) it *1863:*He <> madam! It 843| P:you, I should not <> here. *1863:*you, I might not *1868:*here! 844| P:the Queen's: she <> brain— *1865:*the Queen's; she <> brain: 845| P:experiment therefore on my *1888:*experiment upon my 846| P:result; *1863:*result. 847| *1863:*you, Sweet *1888:*sweet 852| P:test! *1863:*test? 855| P:me, did love prove *1888:*me, had love proved 856| P:dared *1888:*dare

Constance, I could say, if it must be said,
"Take back the soul you offer, I keep mine!"
But—"Take the soul still quivering on your hand,
The soul so offered, which I cannot use,
And, please you, give it to some playful friend,
For—what's the trifle he requites me with?"
I, tempt a woman, to amuse a man,
That two may mock her heart if it succumb?
No: fearing God and standing 'neath his heaven,
I would not dare insult a woman so,
Were she the meanest woman in the world,
And he, I cared to please, ten emperors!
CONSTANCE Norbert!
NORBERT I love once as I live but once.
What case is this to think or talk about?
I love you. Would it mend the case at all
If such a step as this killed love in me?
Your part were done: account to God for it!
But mine—could murdered love get up again,
And kneel to whom you please to designate,
And make you mirth? It is too horrible.
You did not know this, Constance? now you know
That body and soul have each one life, but one:
And here's my love, here, living, at your feet.
CONSTANCE See the Queen! Norbert—this one more last word—
If thus you have taken jest for earnest—thus
Loved me in earnest . . .
NORBERT Ah, no jest holds here!
Where is the laughter in which jests break up,
And what this horror that grows palpable?
Madam—why grasp you thus the balcony?
Have I done ill? Have I not spoken truth?
How could I other? Was it not your test,

858| P:offer—I <> mine" *1868:* offer, I <> mine!" 861| P:some friend of mine, *1863:* some playful friend, 863| P:woman to <> man *1855:* woman, to <> man, 865| P:No! fearing *1863:* 'neath His *1868:* No: fearing <> his 872| P:Should such <> kill *1888:* If such <> killed 873| P:it. *1868:* it! 875| P:pleased to designate *1863:* designate, *1865:* please 883| P:up? *1863:* up, 886| P:spoken the truth? *1888:* spoken truth?

To try me, what my love for Constance meant?
Madam, your royal soul itself approves,
The first, that I should choose thus! so one takes
A beggar,—asks him, what would buy his child?
And then approves the expected laugh of scorn
Returned as something noble from the rags.
Speak, Constance, I'm the beggar! Ha, what's this?
You two glare each at each like panthers now.
Constance, the world fades; only you stand there!
You did not, in to-night's wild whirl of things,
Sell me—your soul of souls, for any price?
No—no—'tis easy to believe in you!
Was it your love's mad trial to o'ertop
Mine by this vain self-sacrifice? well, still—
Though I might curse, I love you. I am love
And cannot change: love's self is at your feet!
[*The* QUEEN *goes out.*
CONSTANCE Feel my heart; let it die against your own!
NORBERT Against my own. Explain not; let this be!
This is life's height.
CONSTANCE Your, yours, yours!
NORBERT You and I—
Why care by what meanders we are here
I' the centre of the labyrinth? Men have died
Trying to find this place, which we have found.
CONSTANCE Found, found!
NORBERT Sweet, never fear what she can do!
We are past harm now.
CONSTANCE On the breast of God.
I thought of men—as if you were a man.

888| P:me, and what *1888:*me, what 891| P:beggar—asks him what <> child, *1868:*beggar,—asks him, what <> child? 896| P:Constance—the *1863:*Constance, the 897| P:not in <> things *1863:*not, in <> things, 899| P:you. *1868:*you! 902| P:Though I should curse *1888:*Though I might curse 903| P:change! love's <> feet. *1863:*change: love's *1868:*feet! 904| P:own. *1863:*own! 905| P:own! explain <> be. *1863:*own. Explain <> be! 906| P:CONSTANCE Yours! Yours! Yours *1868:*CONSTANCE Yours, yours, yours 908| P:In <> men *1868:*labyrinth? Men *1870:*I' 909| P:place out, which *1863:*place, which we have §line ends; word *found* and period omitted§ *1865:*have found. 910| P:do— *1863:*do!

Tempting him with a crown!
NORBERT This must end here:
It is too perfect.
CONSTANCE There's the music stopped.
What measured heavy tread? It is one blaze
About me and within me.
NORBERT Oh, some death
Will run its sudden finger round this spark
And sever us from the rest!
CONSTANCE And so do well.
Now the doors open.
NORBERT 'Tis the guard comes.
CONSTANCE Kiss!

913| P:here— *1868:* here: 914| P:perfect! CONSTANCE *1868:* perfect. CONSTANCE 915| P:it *1868:* tread? It 917| P:spark, *1863:* spark 918| P:rest— CONSTANCE *1868:* rest! CONSTANCE 919| P:open— NORBERT *1868:* open. NORBERT *1888:* CONSTANCE Kiss DC,BrU:CONSTANCE Kiss! *1889:* CONSTANCE Kiss!

SAUL

I

Said Abner, "At last thou art come! Ere I tell, ere thou speak,
Kiss my cheek, wish me well!" Then I wished it, and did kiss his cheek.
And he, "Since the King, O my friend, for thy countenance sent,
Neither drunken nor eaten have we; nor until from his tent
Thou return with the joyful assurance the King liveth yet,
Shall our lip with the honey be bright, with the water be wet.
For out of the black mid-tent's silence, a space of three days,
Not a sound hath escaped to thy servants, of prayer nor of praise,
To betoken that Saul and the Spirit have ended their strife,
And that, faint in his triumph, the monarch sinks back upon life.

II

"Yet now my heart leaps, O beloved! God's child with his dew
On thy gracious gold hair, and those lilies still living and blue
Just broken to twine round thy harp-strings, as if no wild heat
Were now raging to torture the desert!"

III

                                        Then I, as was meet,
Knelt down to the God of my fathers, and rose on my feet,
And ran o'er the sand burnt to powder. The tent was unlooped;
I pulled up the spear that obstructed, and under I stooped;

SAUL §Additional eds. 1845, 1849; see Editorial Notes for description of 1845 line divisions. Subsequent placement: *1863:* DL§ 1| *1845:* speak,— P:speak, 2| *1845:* cheek: P:cheek. 3| *1845:* the King, oh P:the King, O 4| *1845:* Nor drunken <> Nor, until P:Neither drunken <> nor until 5| *1845:* king P:assurance the King 6| *1845:* be brightened, / —The water, be P:be bright, with the water be 8| *1845:* No sound P:Not a sound <> or *1865:* nor 9-11| *1845:* the Spirit / Have gone their dread ways. / "Yet <> child, with *1849:* the Spirit / Have ended their strife, / And that faint in his triumph the monarch / Sinks back upon life. / "Yet P:strife, / And that, faint <> triumph, the *1863:* with His *1868:* child with his 13| *1845:* As thou brak'st them to P:Just broken to 14| *1845:* Were raging P:Were now raging

Hands and knees on the slippery grass-patch, all withered and gone,
That extends to the second enclosure, I groped my way on
Till I felt where the foldskirts fly open. Then once more I prayed,
And opened the foldskirts and entered, and was not afraid
But spoke, "Here is David, thy servant!" And no voice replied.
At the first I saw nought but the blackness; but soon I descried
A something more black than the blackness—the vast, the upright
Main prop which sustains the pavilion: and slow into sight
Grew a figure against it, gigantic and blackest of all.
Then a sunbeam, that burst thro' the tent-roof, showed Saul.

IV

He stood as erect as that tent-prop, both arms stretched out wide
On the great cross-support in the centre, that goes to each side;
He relaxed not a muscle, but hung there as, caught in his pangs
And waiting his change, the king-serpent all heavily hangs,
Far away from his kind, in the pine, till deliverance come
With the spring-time,—so agonized Saul, drear and stark, blind and dumb.

18| *1845:* knees o'er the <> grass-patch— / All <> gone— P:knees on the <> grass-patch, all <> gone, 19| *1845:* That leads to <> on, P:That extends to <> on 20| *1845:* open; / Then P:open. Then 21| *1845:* afraid: P:afraid, *1865:* afraid 22| *1845:* And spoke <> replied; P:But spoke <> replied. 23| *1845:* And first P:At the first 24| *1855:* vast the *1868:* vast, the 25| *1845:* Main-prop <> pavilion,— / And P:Main prop <> pavilion: and 26| *1845:* figure, gigantic, against it, / And <> all;— P:figure against it, gigantic and *1863:* all: *1865:* all. 27| P:tent-roof,— showed *1863:* tent-roof, showed 28| *1845:* tent-prop; / Both *1868:* tent-prop, both 29| *1845:* centre / That <> side: P:centre, that *1863:* side; 30| *1845:* So he bent not a muscle but *1849:* muscle, but P:He relaxed not <> there,—as *1863:* there, as *1865:* there as 31| *1845:* change the *1849:* change, the P:change the *1863:* change, the 32| *1845:* the Pine *1849:* pine 33| *1845:* the Spring-time <> and black, blind *1849:* and stark, blind P:spring-time

V

Then I tuned my harp,—took off the lilies we twine round its
chords
Lest they snap 'neath the stress of the noontide—those sunbeams
like swords!
And I first played the tune all our sheep know, as, one after one,
So docile they come to the pen-door till folding be done.
They are white and untorn by the bushes, for lo, they have fed
Where the long grasses stifle the water within the stream's bed;
And now one after one seeks its lodging, as star follows star
Into eve and the blue far above us,—so blue and so far!

VI

—Then the tune, for which quails on the cornland will each
leave his mate
To fly after the player; then, what makes the crickets elate
Till for boldness they fight one another: and then, what has
weight
To set the quick jerboa a-musing outside his sand house—
There are none such as he for a wonder, half bird and half
mouse!
God made all the creatures and gave them our love and our fear,
To give sign, we and they are his children, one family here.

VII

Then I played the help-tune of our reapers, their wine-song,
when hand
Grasps at hand, eye lights eye in good friendship, and great
hearts expand

37| *1845:* done *1849:* done; P:Very docile <> pen-door, till <> done. *1855:* So docile *1865:* pen-door till 38| *1845:* —They P:They 39| *1849:* bed: P:bed; 40| *1845:* How one after P:And now one after 42| *1845:* Then the tune for <> Will leave each his P:—Then the tune, for <> will each leave his 43| *1845:* To follow the P:To fly after the <> elate, *1868:* elate 45| *1845:* house P:house— 46| *1845:* —There <> wonder— / Half bird P:There <> wonder, half bird <> mouse!— *1863:* mouse! 47| *1845:* —God P:God 48| *1845:* To show, we P:To give sign, we *1863:* are His *1868:* his 49| *1845:* our Reapers *1849:* reapers 50| *1845:* Grasps hand <> expand, P:Grasps at hand <> expand

And grow one in the sense of this world's life.—And then, the last song
When the dead man is praised on his journey—"Bear, bear him along
With his few faults shut up like dead flowerets! Are balm-seeds not here
To console us? The land has none left such as he on the bier.
Oh, would we might keep thee, my brother!"—And then, the glad chaunt
Of the marriage,—first go the young maidens, next, she whom we vaunt
As the beauty, the pride of our dwelling.—And then, the great march
Wherein man runs to man to assist him and buttress an arch
Nought can break; who shall harm them, our friends?—Then, the chorus intoned
As the Levites go up to the altar in glory enthroned.
But I stopped here: for here in the darkness Saul groaned.

VIII

And I paused, held my breath in such silence, and listened apart;
And the tent shook, for mighty Saul shuddered: and sparkles 'gan dart
From the jewels that woke in his turban, at once with a start,
All its lordly male-sapphires, and rubies courageous at heart.

51| *1845:* life; / And <> the low song P:life.—And <> the last song 52| *1870:* journey—"Bear bear *1888:* journey—"Bear, bear 53| *1845:* flowerets; / Are P:flowerets! are *1868:* flowerets! Are 54| *1845:* has got none such <> bier— *1849:* land is left none P:land has none left, such <> bier. *1863:* left such 55| *1845:* brother!" / And P:brother!"—And 56| *1845:* maidens— / Next *1849:* maidens, / Next 57| *1845:* dwelling: / And P:dwelling.—And 58| *1845:* When man runs *1849:* him, / And P:Wherein man runs <> him and 59| *1845:* break . . . who <> our brothers? / Then *1849:* our friends? / Then P:break; who <> friends?—Then 60| *1845:* enthroned— P:enthroned . . . *1863:* enthroned. 61| *1845:* here—for here, in the darkness, / Saul groaned: *1849:* groaned. P:for here in the darkness Saul *1855:* darkness, Saul *1865:* here: for *1868:* darkness Saul 62| *1845:* silence! / And <> apart— *1849:* apart; P:silence, and <> apart, *1855:* apart; 63| *1845:* shuddered,— / And *1863:* shuddered—and *1865:* shuddered: and 64| *1845:* turban / —At <> start P:turban at <> start— *1865:* start, *1870:* start *1888:* turban, at <> start, 65| *1845:* All the lordly <> heart; *1849:* All its lordly P:heart.

So the head: but the body still moved not, still hung there erect.
And I bent once again to my playing, pursued it unchecked,
As I sang,—

IX

"Oh, our manhood's prime vigour! No spirit feels waste,
Not a muscle is stopped in its playing nor sinew unbraced.
Oh, the wild joys of living! the leaping from rock up to rock,
The strong rending of boughs from the fir-tree, the cool silver
shock
Of the plunge in a pool's living water, the hunt of the bear,
And the sultriness showing the lion is couched in his lair.
And the meal, the rich dates yellowed over with gold dust divine,
And the locust-flesh steeped in the pitcher, the full draught of
wine,
And the sleep in the dried river-channel where bulrushes tell
That the water was wont to go warbling so softly and well.
How good is man's life, the mere living! how fit to employ
All the heart and the soul and the senses for ever in joy!
Hast thou loved the white locks of thy father, whose sword thou
didst guard
When he trusted thee forth with the armies, for glorious reward?
Didst thou see the thin hands of thy mother, held up as men
sung

66| *1845:* head, but <> not,— / Still *1849:* head—but <> not, / Still *1865:* head: but 68| *1845:* sang, "Oh <> vigour! / —No P:sang,— §section IX begins§ "Oh <> vigour! no *1868:* vigour! No 69| *1845:* No muscle <> No <> unbraced,— *1849:* playing, / No <> unbraced;— P:Not a muscle <> nor <> unbraced. *1865:* playing nor 70| *1845:* And the wild <> to rock— P:Oh, the wild *1865:* to rock, 71| *1845:* The rending their boughs <> palm-trees,— / The P:The strong rending of boughs <> fir-tree,—the *1865:* fir-tree, the 72| *1845:* Of a plunge in the pool's <> water— / The hunt *1849:* haunt P:Of the plunge in a pool's <> water,—the hunt *1865:* water, the hunt 73| *1845:* lair: P:shewing <> lair. *1863:* showing 74| *1845:* meal—the <> dates—yellowed *1863:* dates yellowed *1865:* meal, the 75| *1845:* locust's-flesh <> pitcher— / The *1849:* pitcher, / The P:pitcher; the *1863:* pitcher! the *1865:* pitcher, the *1868:* locust-flesh 76| *1845:* river channel / Where tall rushes tell P:river-channel where bull-rushes tell *1863:* bulrushes 77| *1845:* The water <> well,— P:That the water <> well. 78| *1845:* life here, mere P:life, the mere 79| *1845:* The heart P:All the heart <> senses, for *1865:* senses for 80| *1845:* father / Whose P:father, whose 81| *1845:* forth to the wolf hunt / For P:forth with the armies, for 82| *1845:* mother / Held up, as P:mother, held up as

The low song of the nearly-departed, and hear her faint tongue
Joining in while it could to the witness, 'Let one more attest,
I have lived, seen God's hand thro' a lifetime, and all was for best'?
Then they sung thro' their tears in strong triumph, not much, but the rest.
And thy brothers, the help and the contest, the working whence grew
Such result as, from seething grape-bundles, the spirit strained true:
And the friends of thy boyhood—that boyhood of wonder and hope,
Present promise and wealth of the future beyond the eye's scope,—
Till lo, thou art grown to a monarch; a people is thine;
And all gifts, which the world offers singly, on one head combine!
On one head, all the beauty and strength, love and rage (like the throe
That, a-work in the rock, helps its labour and lets the gold go)
High ambition and deeds which surpass it, fame crowning them,—all
Brought to blaze on the head of one creature—King Saul!"

83| *1845:*The song <> heard P:The low song *1865:*hear 84| *1845:*witness / "Let P:witness, "Let *1855:*witness, 'Let 85| *1845:*thro' that life-time <> best . . ." P:thro' a lifetime *1855:*best . . .' *1863:*best!' *1888:*best'?
86| *1845:*tears, in <> much,—but the rest! P:tears in <> rest. *1863:*much—but *1865:*much, but 87| *1845:*brothers—the help P:brothers, the help
88| *1845:*result, as from <> grape-bundles / The spirit so true— *1849:*true: P:result as from <> grape-bundles, the spirit strained true! *1863:*as, from *1868:*true:
89| *1845:*that boyhood / With wonder P:that boyhood of wonder 90| *1845:*And the promise <> future,— / The eye's eagle scope,— *1849:*Present promise P:promise, and <> future beyond the eye's scope,— *1868:*promise and 91| *1845:*monarch, / A <> thine! P:monarch; a <> thine; *1888:*is hine; *1889:*is thine; §see Editorial Notes§
92| *1845:*Oh all, all the <> combine, *1849:*Oh all gifts the P:And all gifts which the <> combine! *1863:*gifts, which 93| *1845:*head the joy and the pride, / Even rage like P:head, all the beauty and strength, love and rage, like *1863:*rage (like 94| *1845:*That opes the rock <> its glad labour, / And <> go— P:That, a-work in the rock <> its labour <> go: *1863:*labour and <> go) 95| *1845:*And ambition that sees a sun lead it / Oh, all of these—all *1849:*it— / Oh P:High ambition and deeds which surpass it, fame crowning it,—all *1865:*crowning them,—all 96| *1845:*Combine to unite in one creature/—Saul P:Brought to blaze on the head of one creature—King Saul!" End note| *1845:(End of Part the First.)* *1849:*END OF PART THE FIRST P:§note dropped§

X

And lo, with that leap of my spirit,—heart, hand, harp and voice,
Each lifting Saul's name out of sorrow, each bidding rejoice
Saul's fame in the light it was made for—as when, dare I say,
The Lord's army, in rapture of service, strains through its array,
And upsoareth the cherubim-chariot—"Saul!" cried I, and stopped,
And waited the thing that should follow. Then Saul, who hung propped
By the tent's cross-support in the centre, was struck by his name.
Have ye seen when Spring's arrowy summons goes right to the aim,
And some mountain, the last to withstand her, that held (he alone,
While the vale laughed in freedom and flowers) on a broad bust of stone
A year's snow bound about for a breastplate,—leaves grasp of the sheet?
Fold on fold all at once it crowds thunderously down to his feet,
And there fronts you, stark, black, but alive yet, your mountain of old,
With his rents, the successive bequeathings of ages untold—
Yea, each harm got in fighting your battles, each furrow and scar
Of his head thrust 'twixt you and the tempest—all hail, there they are!
—Now again to be softened with verdure, again hold the nest
Of the dove, tempt the goat and its young to the green on his crest
For their food in the ardours of summer. One long shudder thrilled
All the tent till the very air tingled, then sank and was stilled
At the King's self left standing before me, released and aware.

97| P:spirit, heart *1863:*spirit,—heart 100| P:army in *1863:*army, in 102| P:propt *1863:*propped 105| P:held, (he *1863:*held (he 109| P:black but *1863:*black, but 113| P:Now *1868:*—Now 114| P:on its crest *1865:*on his crest 115| P:summer! One *1868:*summer. One 116| P:stilled, *1863:*stilled

What was gone, what remained? All to traverse, 'twixt hope and despair;
Death was past, life not come: so he waited. Awhile his right hand
Held the brow, helped the eyes left too vacant forthwith to remand
To their place what new objects should enter: 'twas Saul as before.
I looked up and dared gaze at those eyes, nor was hurt any more
Than by slow pallid sunsets in autumn, ye watch from the shore,
At their sad level gaze o'er the ocean—a sun's slow decline
Over hills which, resolved in stern silence, o'erlap and entwine
Base with base to knit strength more intensely: so, arm folded arm
O'er the chest whose slow heavings subsided.

XI

What spell or what charm,
(For, awhile there was trouble within me) what next should I urge
To sustain him where song had restored him?—Song filled to the verge
His cup with the wine of this life, pressing all that it yields
Of mere fruitage, the strength and the beauty: beyond, on what fields,
Glean a vintage more potent and perfect to brighten the eye
And bring blood to the lip, and commend them the cup they put by?
He saith, "It is good;" still he drinks not: he lets me praise life,
Gives assent, yet would die for his own part.

118| P:all to traverse 'twixt <> despair— *1863:* despair; *1868:* remained? All <> despair. *1870:* despair, *1888:* traverse, 'twixt <> despair; 119| P:come—so *1863:* come: so 123| P:shore *1863:* shore, 126| P:intense <> folded in arm *1868:* intensely <> folded arm 131| P:beauty! Beyond *1868:* beauty: beyond 134| P:not—he *1863:* not: he

XII

Then fancies grew rife
Which had come long ago on the pasture, when round me the sheep
Fed in silence—above, the one eagle wheeled slow as in sleep;
And I lay in my hollow and mused on the world that might lie
'Neath his ken, though I saw but the strip 'twixt the hill and the sky:
And I laughed—"Since my days are ordained to be passed with my flocks,
Let me people at least, with my fancies, the plains and the rocks,
Dream the life I am never to mix with, and image the show
Of mankind as they live in those fashions I hardly shall know!
Schemes of life, its best rules and right uses, the courage that gains,
And the prudence that keeps what men strive for." And now these old trains
Of vague thought came again; I grew surer; so, once more the string
Of my harp made response to my spirit, as thus—

XIII

"Yea, my King,"
I began—"thou dost well in rejecting mere comforts that spring
From the mere mortal life held in common by man and by brute:
In our flesh grows the branch of this life, in our soul it bears fruit.
Thou hast marked the slow rise of the tree,—how its stem trembled first
Till it passed the kid's lip, the stag's antler; then safely outburst
The fan-branches all round; and thou mindest when these too, in turn

---

136| P:I had sought long <> pastures *1855:* Which had come long *1865:* pasture 137| P:silence, above the <> sleep, *1855:* silence—above, the *1863:* sleep; 138| P:hollow, and *1868:* hollow and 141| P: least with *1863:* least, with 146| P:so once *1863:* so, once 147| P:king," *1863:* my King," 153| P:mindedst *1870:* mindest

Broke a-bloom and the palm-tree seemed perfect: yet more was to learn,
E'en the good that comes in with the palm-fruit. Our dates shall we slight,
When their juice brings a cure for all sorrow? or care for the plight
Of the palm's self whose slow growth produced them? Not so! stem and branch
Shall decay, nor be known in their place, while the palm-wine shall staunch
Every wound of man's spirit in winter. I pour thee such wine.
Leave the flesh to the fate it was fit for! the spirit be thine!
By the spirit, when age shall o'ercome thee, thou still shalt enjoy
More indeed, than at first when inconscious, the life of a boy.
Crush that life, and behold its wine running! Each deed thou hast done
Dies, revives, goes to work in the world; until e'en as the sun
Looking down on the earth, though clouds spoil him, though tempests efface,
Can find nothing his own deed produced not, must everywhere trace
The results of his past summer-prime,—so, each ray of thy will,
Every flash of thy passion and prowess, long over, shall thrill
Thy whole people, the countless, with ardour, till they too give forth
A like cheer to their sons, who in turn, fill the South and the North
With the radiance thy deed was the germ of. Carouse in the past!
But the license of age has its limit; thou diest at last:
As the lion when age dims his eyeball, the rose at her height,
So with man—so his power and his beauty for ever take flight.

154| P:palm-tree stood perfect; yet *1855:* palm-tree seemed perfect *1863:* perfect: yet 155| P:Even *1855:* Ev'n *1868:* E'en 159| P:wine! *1855:* wine. 163| P:each *1868:* running! Each 166| P: every where *1863:* everywhere 167| P:summer-prime: so *1855:* summer-prime,—so 169| P:people the *1888:* people, the 170| P:south <> north *1863:* the South <> North 171| P:past. *1863:* in the Past! *1868:* past! 172| P:last. *1863:* last: 173| P:eye-ball <> height, *1863:* eyeball *1888:* heigh DC,BrU:height, *1889:* height §emended to§ height, §see Editorial Notes§

No! Again a long draught of my soul-wine! Look forth o'er the years!
Thou hast done now with eyes for the actual; begin with the seer's!
Is Saul dead? In the depth of the vale make his tomb—bid arise
A grey mountain of marble heaped four-square, till, built to the skies,
Let it mark where the great First King slumbers: whose fame would ye know?
Up above see the rock's naked face, where the record shall go
In great characters cut by the scribe,—Such was Saul, so he did;
With the sages directing the work, by the populace chid,—
For not half, they'll affirm, is comprised there! Which fault to amend,
In the grove with his kind grows the cedar, whereon they shall spend
(See, in tablets 'tis level before them) their praise, and record
With the gold of the graver, Saul's story,—the statesman's great word
Side by side with the poet's sweet comment. The river's a-wave
With smooth paper-reeds grazing each other when prophet-winds rave:
So the pen gives unborn generations their due and their part
In thy being! Then, first of the mighty, thank God that thou art!"

XIV

And behold while I sang . . . but O Thou who didst grant me that day,
And before it not seldom hast granted thy help to essay,
Carry on and complete an adventure,—my shield and my sword

175| P:again <> of the spirit! look <> years— *1855:* of my soul-wine! look *1868:* No! Again <> Look <> years! 177| P:in *1868:* dead? In 178| P:till built <> skies. *1863:* till, built <> skies, 179| P:slumbers—whose *1863:* slumbers: whose 188| P:prophet winds *1863:* prophet-winds 190| P:art." *1863:* art!" 191| P:sang . . But *1868:* but *1888:* sang . . . but 192| P:granted, thy <> essay *1863:* granted Thy *1865:* essay, *1868:* thy 193| P:my Shield <> Sword, *1855:* my Shield and my Sword *1868:* shield <> sword

In that act where my soul was thy servant, thy word was my word,—
Still be with me, who then at the summit of human endeavour
And scaling the highest, man's thought could, gazed hopeless as ever
On the new stretch of heaven above me—till, mighty to save,
Just one lift of thy hand cleared that distance—God's throne from man's grave!
Let me tell out my tale to its ending—my voice to my heart
Which can scarce dare believe in what marvels last night I took part,
As this morning I gather the fragments, alone with my sheep,
And still fear lest the terrible glory evanish like sleep!
For I wake in the grey dewy covert, while Hebron upheaves
The dawn struggling with night on his shoulder, and Kidron retrieves
Slow the damage of yesterday's sunshine.

XV

I say then,—my song
While I sang thus, assuring the monarch, and ever more strong
Made a proffer of good to console him—he slowly resumed
His old motions and habitudes kingly. The right-hand replumed
His black locks to their wonted composure, adjusted the swathes
Of his turban, and see—the huge sweat that his countenance bathes,
He wipes off with the robe; and he girds now his loins as of yore,
And feels slow for the armlets of price, with the clasp set before.
He is Saul, ye remember in glory,—ere error had bent
The broad brow from the daily communion; and still, though much spent

---

194| *1863:* was Thy <> Thy *1868:* thy <> thy 195| P:who reaching the *1855:* who then at the 196| P:highest man's <> can *1855:* could *1863:* highest, man's 197| P:of Heaven <> Mighty *1863:* mighty *1868:* heaven 198| *1863:* of Thy *1868:* thy 199| P:heart, *1863:* heart 200| P:marvels that night *1863:* marvels last night 208| P:right hand *1888:* right-hand

Be the life and the bearing that front you, the same, God did choose,
To receive what a man may waste, desecrate, never quite lose.
So sank he along by the tent-prop till, stayed by the pile
Of his armour and war-cloak and garments, he leaned there awhile,
And sat out my singing,—one arm round the tent-prop, to raise
His bent head, and the other hung slack—till I touched on the praise
I foresaw from all men in all time, to the man patient there;
And thus ended, the harp falling forward. Then first I was 'ware
That he sat, as I say, with my head just above his vast knees
Which were thrust out on each side around me, like oak-roots which please
To encircle a lamb when it slumbers. I looked up to know
If the best I could do had brought solace: he spoke not, but slow
Lifted up the hand slack at his side, till he laid it with care
Soft and grave, but in mild settled will, on my brow: thro' my hair
The large fingers were pushed, and he bent back my head, with kind power—
All my face back, intent to peruse it, as men do a flower.
Thus held he me there with his great eyes that scrutinized mine—
And oh, all my heart how it loved him! but where was the sign?
I yearned—"Could I help thee, my father, inventing a bliss,
I would add, to that life of the past, both the future and this;
I would give thee new life altogether, as good, ages hence,
As this moment,—had love but the warrant, love's heart to dispense!"

XVI

Then the truth came upon me. No harp more—no song more! outbroke—

217| P:tent-prop, till *1863:* tent-prop till 219| P:And so sat *1865:* And sat 221| P:times <> there, *1863:* there; *1865:* time 222| P:was, ware *1855:* was 'ware 224| *1863:* oak roots *1888:* oak-roots 231| P:scrutinised *1863:* scrutinized 234| P:add to <> this. *1863:* the Past <> Future and this; *1868:* add, to <> past <> future 237| P:out-broke— *1888:* outbroke—

XVII

"I have gone the whole round of creation: I saw and I spoke:
I, a work of God's hand for that purpose, received in my brain
And pronounced on the rest of his handwork—returned him
again
His creation's approval or censure: I spoke as I saw:
I report, as a man may of God's work—all's love, yet all's law.
Now I lay down the judgeship he lent me. Each faculty tasked
To perceive him, has gained an abyss, where a dew-drop was
asked.
Have I knowledge? confounded it shrivels at Wisdom laid bare.
Have I forethought? how purblind, how blank, to the Infinite
Care!
Do I task any faculty highest, to image success?
I but open my eyes,—and perfection, no more and no less,
In the kind I imagined, full-fronts me, and God is seen God
In the star, in the stone, in the flesh, in the soul and the clod.
And thus looking within and around me, I ever renew
(With that stoop of the soul which in bending upraises it too)
The submission of man's nothing-perfect to God's all-complete,
As by each new obeisance in spirit, I climb to his feet.
Yet with all this abounding experience, this deity known,
I shall dare to discover some province, some gift of my own.
There's a faculty pleasant to exercise, hard to hoodwink,
I am fain to keep still in abeyance, (I laugh as I think)
Lest, insisting to claim and parade in it, wot ye, I worst
E'en the Giver in one gift.—Behold, I could love if I durst!
But I sink the pretension as fearing a man may o'ertake
God's own speed in the one way of love: I abstain for love's sake.
—What, my soul? see thus far and no farther? when doors great
and small,

238| P:of Creation <> spoke! *1868:* creation <> spoke: 240| *1863:* of His <> Him *1868:* his <> him 241| P:saw. *1888:* saw: 242| P:law! *1868:* law. 243| *1863:* judgeship He *1868:* he 244| *1863:* perceive Him *1868:* him 245| P:wisdom *1863:* at Wisdom 246| P:care! *1863:* the Infinite Care! 253| P:of Man's <> All-Complete, *1868:* man's <> all-complete, 254| P:feet! *1863:* to His *1868:* his feet. 255| P:experience, this Deity *1868:* deity 257| P:There's one faculty *1863:* There's a faculty 260| P:gift.—Behold! I could *1868:* gift.—Behold, I could 262| P:abstain, for <> sake! *1863:* abstain for <> sake.

Nine-and-ninety flew ope at our touch, should the hundredth appal?
In the least things have faith, yet distrust in the greatest of all?
Do I find love so full in my nature, God's ultimate gift,
That I doubt his own love can compete with it? Here, the parts shift?
Here, the creature surpass the Creator,—the end, what Began?
Would I fain in my impotent yearning do all for this man,
And dare doubt he alone shall not help him, who yet alone can?
Would it ever have entered my mind, the bare will, much less power,
To bestow on this Saul what I sang of, the marvellous dower
Of the life he was gifted and filled with? to make such a soul,
Such a body, and then such an earth for insphering the whole?
And doth it not enter my mind (as my warm tears attest)
These good things being given, to go on, and give one more, the best?
Ay, to save and redeem and restore him, maintain at the height
This perfection,—succeed with life's dayspring, death's minute of night?
Interpose at the difficult minute, snatch Saul the mistake,
Saul the failure, the ruin he seems now,—and bid him awake
From the dream, the probation, the prelude, to find himself set
Clear and safe in new light and new life,—a new harmony yet
To be run, and continued, and ended—who knows?—or endure!
The man taught enough, by life's dream, of the rest to make sure;
By the pain-throb, triumphantly winning intensified bliss,
And the next world's reward and repose, by the struggles in this.

265| P:things, have *1865:* things have 267| P:here *1863:* doubt His *1868:* his <> Here 268| P:surpass the Creator, the <> Began?— *1868:* surpass the Creator,—the <> Began? 270| P:doubt He *1868:* he 279| P:snatch Saul, the *1888:* snatch Saul the 280| P:Saul, the failure *1888:* Saul the failure 284| P:enough by <> sure. *1863:* sure; DC,BrU:enough, by *1889:* enough, by 286| P:struggle *1863:* struggles

XVIII

"I believe it! 'Tis thou, God, that givest, 'tis I who receive:
In the first is the last, in thy will is my power to believe.
All's one gift: thou canst grant it moreover, as prompt to my
prayer
As I breathe out this breath, as I open these arms to the air.
From thy will, stream the worlds, life and nature, thy dread
Sabaoth:
I will?—the mere atoms despise me! Why am I not loth
To look that, even that in the face too? Why is it I dare
Think but lightly of such impuissance? What stops my despair?
This;—'tis not what man Does which exalts him, but what man
Would do!
See the King—I would help him but cannot, the wishes fall
through.
Could I wrestle to raise him from sorrow, grow poor to enrich,
To fill up his life, starve my own out, I would—knowing which,
I know that my service is perfect. Oh, speak through me now!
Would I suffer for him that I love? So wouldst thou—so wilt
thou!
So shall crown thee the topmost, ineffablest, uttermost crown—
And thy love fill infinitude wholly, nor leave up nor down
One spot for the creature to stand in! It is by no breath,
Turn of eye, wave of hand, that salvation joins issue with death!
As thy Love is discovered almighty, almighty be proved
Thy power, that exists with and for it, of being Beloved!
He who did most, shall bear most; the strongest shall stand the
most weak.
'Tis the weakness in strength, that I cry for! my flesh, that I seek

---

287| P:it! 'tis Thou *1868:*it! 'Tis thou 288| *1863:*last, in Thy *1868:*thy 289| *1863:*gift: Thou *1868:*thou 291| *1863:*From Thy *1868:*thy 292| P:I will,—the <> me! and why am I loth *1855:I* will?—the *1863:*me! why am I not loth *1868:*me! Why 293| P:why *1868:*too? Why 294| P:what *1868:*impuissance? What 295| P:does <> would *1855:*man Does <> Would 296| P:king *1863:*the King 299| P:perfect.—Oh *1863:*perfect. Oh 300| P:love? So wilt Thou <> Thou! *1863:*love? So wouldst *1868:*thou <> thou! 301| P:uttermost Crown— *1863:*crown Thee <> crown— *1868:*thee 302| *1863:*And Thy *1868:*thy 304| P:that Salvation *1863:*salvation 305| *1863:*As Thy *1868:*thy 306| P:of Being beloved! *1863:*being Beloved! 308| P:strength that I cry *1863:*strength, that I cry

In the Godhead! I seek and I find it. O Saul, it shall be
A Face like my face that receives thee; a Man like to me,
Thou shalt love and be loved by, for ever: a Hand like this hand
Shall throw open the gates of new life to thee! See the Christ
stand!"

XIX

I know not too well how I found my way home in the night.
There were witnesses, cohorts about me, to left and to right,
Angels, powers, the unuttered, unseen, the alive, the aware:
I repressed, I got through them as hardly, as strugglingly there,
As a runner beset by the populace famished for news—
Life or death. The whole earth was awakened, hell loosed with
her crews;
And the stars of night beat with emotion, and tingled and shot
Out in fire the strong pain of pent knowledge: but I fainted not,
For the Hand still impelled me at once and supported,
suppressed
All the tumult, and quenched it with quiet, and holy behest,
Till the rapture was shut in itself, and the earth sank to rest.
Anon at the dawn, all that trouble had withered from earth—
Not so much, but I saw it die out in the day's tender birth;
In the gathered intensity brought to the grey of the hills;
In the shuddering forests' held breath; in the sudden
wind-thrills;
In the startled wild beasts that bore off, each with eye sidling
still
Though averted with wonder and dread; in the birds stiff and
chill
That rose heavily, as I approached them, made stupid with awe:
E'en the serpent that slid away silent,—he felt the new law.

310| P:thee: a *1863:* thee; a 311| P:ever! a *1863:* ever: a 315| P:alive—the aware— *1863:* alive, the *1865:* aware: 320| P:not. *1863:* not, 321| P:supported—suppressed *1863:* supported, suppressed 327| P:forests' new awe; in *1868:* forests' held breath; in 328| P:bore off, each *1870:* bore oft, each §emended to§ off §see Editorial Notes§ 329| P:Tho' averted, in wonder and dread; and the *1863:* Though averted with wonder and dread; in the 330| P:heavily as <> awe! *1855:* heavily, as *1868:* awe: 331| P:Even <> Law. *1855:* E'en *1868:* law.

The same stared in the white humid faces upturned by the
flowers;
The same worked in the heart of the cedar and moved the
vine-bowers:
And the little brooks witnessing murmured, persistent and low,
With their obstinate, all but hushed voices—"E'en so, it is so!"

333| P:cedar, and <> vine-bowers. *1863:* vine-bowers: *1868:* cedar and
335| P:voices—E'en so! it is so. *1863:* voices—"E'en so, it is so!"

"DE GUSTIBUS—"

I

Your ghost will walk, you lover of trees,
(If our loves remain)
In an English lane,
By a cornfield-side a-flutter with poppies.
Hark, those two in the hazel coppice—
A boy and a girl, if the good fates please,
Making love, say,—
The happier they!
Draw yourself up from the light of the moon,
And let them pass, as they will too soon,
With the bean-flowers' boon,
And the blackbird's tune,
And May, and June!

II

What I love best in all the world
Is a castle, precipice-encurled,
In a gash of the wind-grieved Apennine.
Or look for me, old fellow of mine,
(If I get my head from out the mouth
O' the grave, and loose my spirit's bands,
And come again to the land of lands)—
In a sea-side house to the farther South,
Where the baked cicala dies of drouth,
And one sharp tree—'tis a cypress—stands,
By the many hundred years red-rusted,
Rough iron-spiked, ripe fruit-o'ercrusted,
My sentinel to guard the sands
To the water's edge. For, what expands
Before the house, but the great opaque

"DE GUSTIBUS—" §Subsequent placement: *1863:* DL§ 2| P:(If loves *1863:* (If our loves 6| P:please! *1855:* please, 11| P:beanflowers' *1888:* bean-flowers' 14| P:world, *1865:* world 15| P:Is, a *1865:* Is a 21| P:south, *1863:* farther South, 22| P:cicalas die *1870:* cicala dies 23| P:tree ('tis a cypress) stands, *1863:* tree—'tis a cypress—stands, 28| P:Without the house *1863:* Before the house

Blue breadth of sea without a break?
While, in the house, for ever crumbles
Some fragment of the frescoed walls,
From blisters where a scorpion sprawls.
A girl bare-footed brings, and tumbles
Down on the pavement, green-flesh melons,
And says there's news to-day—the king
Was shot at, touched in the liver-wing,
Goes with his Bourbon arm in a sling:
—She hopes they have not caught the felons.
Italy, my Italy!
Queen Mary's saying serves for me—
(When fortune's malice
Lost her—Calais)—
Open my heart and you will see
Graved inside of it, "Italy."
Such lovers old are I and she:
So it always was, so shall ever be!

29| P:sea, and not a *1863:* sea without a 33| P:brings and *1863:* brings, and 37| P:sling. *1863:* sling: 38| P:felons! *1855:* felons. 42| P:her, Calais.) *1863:* her, Calais) *1888:* her—Calais)— 44| P:it—"Italy"— *1855:* it, "Italy." 45| P:she— *1855:* she; *1870:* she: 46| P:was, so it still shall be! *1863:* was, so shall ever be!

WOMEN AND ROSES

I

I dream of a red-rose tree.
And which of its roses three
Is the dearest rose to me?

II

Round and round, like a dance of snow
In a dazzling drift, as its guardians, go
Floating the women faded for ages,
Sculptured in stone, on the poet's pages.
Then follow women fresh and gay,
Living and loving and loved to-day.
Last, in the rear, flee the multitude of maidens,
Beauties yet unborn. And all, to one cadence,
They circle their rose on my rose tree.

III

Dear rose, thy term is reached,
Thy leaf hangs loose and bleached:
Bees pass it unimpeached.

IV

Stay then, stoop, since I cannot climb,
You, great shapes of the antique time!
How shall I fix you, fire you, freeze you,
Break my heart at your feet to please you?
Oh, to possess and be possessed!
Hearts that beat 'neath each pallid breast!
Once but of love, the poesy, the passion,
Drink but once and die!—In vain, the same fashion,
They circle their rose on my rose tree.

WOMEN AND ROSES §Subsequent placement: *1863:* DL§ [11]| P:Beauties unborn *1868:* Beauties yet unborn [17]| *1865:* time *1868:* time! [20]| P:Oh! to possess, and *1863:* Oh, to *1868:* possess and [22]| P:But once of *1868:* Once but of [23]| P:Drink once *1868:* Drink but once

V

Dear rose, thy joy's undimmed,
Thy cup is ruby-rimmed,
Thy cup's heart nectar-brimmed.

VI

Deep, as drops from a statue's plinth
The bee sucked in by the hyacinth,
So will I bury me while burning,
Quench like him at a plunge my yearning,
Eyes in your eyes, lips on your lips!
Fold me fast where the cincture slips,
Prison all my soul in eternities of pleasure,
Girdle me for once! But no—the old measure,
They circle their rose on my rose tree.

VII

Dear rose without a thorn,
Thy bud's the babe unborn:
First streak of a new morn.

VIII

Wings, lend wings for the cold, the clear!
What is far conquers what is near.
Roses will bloom nor want beholders,
Sprung from the dust where our flesh moulders.
What shall arrive with the cycle's change?
A novel grace and a beauty strange.
I will make an Eve, be the artist that began her,
Shaped her to his mind!—Alas! in like manner
They circle their rose on my rose tree.

25| P:undimmed; *1870:* undimmed *1888:* undimmed, 28| P:Deep as *1865:* Deep, as 34| P:pleasure! *1865:* pleasure *1868:* pleasure, 35| P:me once <> no—in their old measure *1865:* no—the old measure, *1868:* me for once 40| *1865:* clear *1868:* clear! 41| P:What's far *1865:* What is far 43| P:our own flesh *1865:* our flesh

PROTUS

Among these latter busts we count by scores,
Half-emperors and quarter-emperors,
Each with his bay-leaf fillet, loose-thonged vest,
Loric and low-browed Gorgon on the breast,—
One loves a baby face, with violets there,
Violets instead of laurel in the hair,
As those were all the little locks could bear.

Now read here. "Protus ends a period
Of empery beginning with a god;
Born in the porphyry chamber at Byzant,
Queens by his cradle, proud and ministrant:
And if he quickened breath there, 'twould like fire
Pantingly through the dim vast realm transpire.
A fame that he was missing spread afar:
The world from its four corners, rose in war,
Till he was borne out on a balcony
To pacify the world when it should see.
The captains ranged before him, one, his hand
Made baby points at, gained the chief command.
And day by day more beautiful he grew
In shape, all said, in feature and in hue,
While young Greek sculptors, gazing on the child,
Became with old Greek sculpture reconciled.
Already sages laboured to condense
In easy tomes a life's experience:
And artists took grave counsel to impart
In one breath and one hand-sweep, all their art—
To make his graces prompt as blossoming
Of plentifully-watered palms in spring:

PROTUS §Subsequent placement: *1863:* DR§ [4]| P:low-browed Fury on the breast, *1855:* low-browed Gorgon on the breast *1863:* breast,— [9]| P:god: *1863:* god; [10]| P:at Byzant; *1863:* at Byzant, [11]| P:ministrant. *1863:* ministrant: [14]| P:missing, spread afar— *1865:* afar: *1888:* missing spread [15]| P:world, from *1888:* world from [22]| P:sculptors gazing <> child *1888:* sculptors, gazing <> child, [23]| P:Were, so, with <> sculpture, reconciled. *1863:* Became, with *1888:* Became with <> sculpture reconciled.

Since well beseems it, whoso mounts the throne,
For beauty, knowledge, strength, should stand alone,
And mortals love the letters of his name."

—Stop! Have you turned two pages? Still the same.
New reign, same date. The scribe goes on to say
How that same year, on such a month and day,
"John the Pannonian, groundedly believed
A blacksmith's bastard, whose hard hand reprieved
The Empire from its fate the year before,—
Came, had a mind to take the crown, and wore
The same for six years (during which the Huns
Kept off their fingers from us), till his sons
Put something in his liquor"—and so forth.
Then a new reign. Stay—"Take at its just worth"
(Subjoins an annotator) "what I give
As hearsay. Some think, John let Protus live
And slip away. 'Tis said, he reached man's age
At some blind northern court; made, first a page,
Then tutor to the children; last, of use
About the hunting-stables. I deduce
He wrote the little tract 'On worming dogs,'
Whereof the name in sundry catalogues
Is extant yet. A Protus of the race
Is rumoured to have died a monk in Thrace,—
And if the same, he reached senility."

Here's John the Smith's rough-hammered head. Great eye,
Gross jaw and griped lips do what granite can
To give you the crown-grasper. What a man!

40| P:years, (during *1888:* years (during 41| P:us) till *1888:* us), till
45| P:think John *1863:* think, John 47| P:made first *1863:* made, first
48| P:Then, tutor < > children—last *1863:* children; last *1865:* Then tutor
52| P:the Race *1863:* race 55| P:eye *1868:* eye,

HOLY-CROSS DAY

ON WHICH THE JEWS WERE FORCED TO ATTEND AN ANNUAL CHRISTIAN SERMON IN ROME.

["Now was come about Holy-Cross Day, and now must my lord preach his first sermon to the Jews: as it was of old cared for in the merciful bowels of the Church, that, so to speak, a crumb at least from her conspicuous table here in Rome should be, though but once yearly, cast to the famishing dogs, under-trampled and bespitten-upon beneath the feet of the guests. And a moving sight in truth, this, of so many of the besotted blind restif and ready-to-perish Hebrews! now maternally brought—nay (for He saith, 'Compel them to come in') haled, as it were, by the head and hair, and against their obstinate hearts, to partake of the heavenly grace. What awakening, what striving with tears, what working of a yeasty conscience! Nor was my lord wanting to himself on so apt an occasion; witness the abundance of conversions which did incontinently reward him: though not to my lord be altogether the glory."—*Diary by the Bishop's Secretary,* 1600.]

What the Jews really said, on thus being driven to church, was rather to this effect:—

I

Fee, faw, fum! bubble and squeak!
Blessedest Thursday's the fat of the week.
Rumble and tumble, sleek and rough,
Stinking and savoury, smug and gruff,
Take the church-road, for the bell's due chime
Gives us the summons—'tis sermon-time!

HOLY-CROSS DAY §Subsequent placement: *1863:* DR§ *Subtitle*| P:(ON, <> ROME) *1855:* ON <> ROME *Prefatory note:* 4| P:Rome, should *1888:* Rome should 7| P:besotted, blind, restive *1868:* besotted blind restif 8| P:now paternally *1863:* now maternally 8| P:nay, (for *1888:* nay (for 13| P:occasion—witness *1855:* occasion; witness 14| P:him—though *1855:* him: though 16| *1855:* Though what *1865:* What

5| P:church road *1855:* church-road 6| P:sermon-time. *1865:* sermon-time *1868:* sermon-time!

II

Boh, here's Barnabas! Job, that's you?
Up stumps Solomon—bustling too?
Shame, man! greedy beyond your years
To handsel the bishop's shaving-shears?
Fair play's a jewel! Leave friends in the lurch?
Stand on a line ere you start for the church!

III

Higgledy piggledy, packed we lie,
Rats in a hamper, swine in a stye,
Wasps in a bottle, frogs in a sieve,
Worms in a carcase, fleas in a sleeve.
Hist! square shoulders, settle your thumbs
And buzz for the bishop—here he comes.

IV

Bow, wow, wow—a bone for the dog!
I liken his Grace to an acorned hog.
What, a boy at his side, with the bloom of a lass,
To help and handle my lord's hour-glass!
Didst ever behold so lithe a chine?
His cheek hath laps like a fresh-singed swine.

V

Aaron's asleep—shove hip to haunch,
Or somebody deal him a dig in the paunch!
Look at the purse with the tassel and knob,
And the gown with the angel and thingumbob!
What's he at, quotha? reading his text!
Now you've his curtsey—and what comes next.

11| P:leave *1868:* jewel! Leave 12| P:church. *1868:* church! 28| P:thingumbob. *1868:* thingumbob! 30| P:next? *1888:* next DC,BrU:next. *1889:* next.

VI

See to our converts—you doomed black dozen—
No stealing away—nor cog nor cozen!
You five, that were thieves, deserve it fairly;
You seven, that were beggars, will live less sparely;
You took your turn and dipped in the hat,
Got fortune—and fortune gets you; mind that!

VII

Give your first groan—compunction's at work;
And soft! from a Jew you mount to a Turk.
Lo, Micah,—the selfsame beard on chin
He was four times already converted in!
Here's a knife, clip quick—it's a sign of grace—
Or he ruins us all with his hanging-face.

VIII

Whom now is the bishop a-leering at?
I know a point where his text falls pat.
I'll tell him to-morrow, a word just now
Went to my heart and made me vow
I meddle no more with the worst of trades—
Let somebody else pay his serenades.

IX

Groan all together now, whee—hee—hee!
It's a-work, it's a-work, ah, woe is me!
It began, when a herd of us, picked and placed,
Were spurred through the Corso, stripped to the waist;
Jew brutes, with sweat and blood well spent
To usher in worthily Christian Lent.

33| P:five that *1868:* five, that 34| P:seven that <> sparely. *1855:* sparely *1863:* sparely; *1868:* seven, that 45| P:to-morrow a *1855:* to-morrow, a 53| P:Jew-brutes *1868:* Jew brutes

X

It grew, when the hangman entered our bounds,
Yelled, pricked us out to his church like hounds:
It got to a pitch, when the hand indeed
Which gutted my purse would throttle my creed:
And it overflows when, to even the odd,
Men I helped to their sins help me to their God.

XI

But now, while the scapegoats leave our flock,
And the rest sit silent and count the clock,
Since forced to muse the appointed time
On these precious facts and truths sublime,—
Let us fitly employ it, under our breath,
In saying Ben Ezra's Song of Death.

XII

For Rabbi Ben Ezra, the night he died,
Called sons and sons' sons to his side,
And spoke, "This world has been harsh and strange;
Something is wrong: there needeth a change.
But what, or where? at the last or first?
In one point only we sinned, at worst.

XIII

"The Lord will have mercy on Jacob yet,
And again in his border see Israel set.
When Judah beholds Jerusalem,
The stranger-seed shall be joined to them:
To Jacob's House shall the Gentiles cleave.
So the Prophet saith and his sons believe.

56| P:to this church <> hounds. *1863:* to his church *1865:* hounds: 58| P:purse, would <> creed. *1865:* creed: *1888:* purse would 59| P:overflows, when *1888:* overflows when 60| P:sins, help *1888:* sins help 69| P:strange, *1863:* strange; 70| P:wrong, there *1863:* wrong: there 71| P:last, or *1865:* last or

XIV

"Ay, the children of the chosen race
Shall carry and bring them to their place:
In the land of the Lord shall lead the same,
Bondsmen and handmaids. Who shall blame,
When the slaves enslave, the oppressed ones o'er
The oppressor triumph for evermore?

XV

"God spoke, and gave us the word to keep,
Bade never fold the hands nor sleep
'Mid a faithless world,—at watch and ward,
Till Christ at the end relieve our guard.
By His servant Moses the watch was set:
Though near upon cock-crow, we keep it yet.

XVI

"Thou! if thou wast He, who at mid-watch came,
By the starlight, naming a dubious name!
And if, too heavy with sleep—too rash
With fear—O Thou, if that martyr-gash
Fell on Thee coming to take thine own,
And we gave the Cross, when we owed the Throne—

XVII

"Thou art the Judge. We are bruised thus.
But, the Judgment over, join sides with us!
Thine too is the cause! and not more thine
Than ours, is the work of these dogs and swine,
Whose life laughs through and spits at their creed!
Who maintain Thee in word, and defy Thee in deed!

84| P:oppressor, triumph *1855:* oppressor triumph 85| P:keep: *1888:* keep DC,BrU:keep, *1889:* keep, 90| P:cock-crow—we *1863:* cock-crow, we 92| P:starlight naming <> Name! *1863:* starlight, naming *1868:* name! 93| P:if we were too *1863:* if, too 94| *1868:* thou *1888:* fear—O Thou 95| P:thee *1863:* on Thee <> Thine *1868:* thee <> thine *1888:* on Thee 98| P:judgment *1868:* the Judgment 99| *1863:* more Thine *1868:* thine 101| P:creed, *1888:* creed! 102| P:thee <> thee *1863:* maintain Thee <> Thee

XVIII

"We withstood Christ then? Be mindful how
At least we withstand Barabbas now!
Was our outrage sore? But the worst we spared,
To have called these—Christians, had we dared!
Let defiance to them pay mistrust of Thee,
And Rome make amends for Calvary!

XIX

"By the torture, prolonged from age to age,
By the infamy, Israel's heritage,
By the Ghetto's plague, by the garb's disgrace,
By the badge of shame, by the felon's place,
By the branding-tool, the bloody whip,
And the summons to Christian fellowship,—

XX

"We boast our proof that at least the Jew
Would wrest Christ's name from the Devil's crew.
Thy face took never so deep a shade
But we fought them in it, God our aid!
A trophy to bear, as we march, thy band,
South, East, and on to the Pleasant Land!"

[*Pope Gregory XVI abolished this bad business of the Sermon.*—R. B.]

103| P:be *1868:* then? Be 105| P:but *1868:* sore? But 106| P:these—Christians,—had *1863:* these—Christians, had 107| P:them, pay <> thee, *1863:* them pay <> Thee, *1868:* thee, *1888:* of Thee, 112| P:place— *1855:* place, 113| P:Each heavier to us as these braggarts waxed, *1855:* By the branding-tool, the bloody whip, 114| P:Each lighter whenever their power relaxed— *1855:* And the summons to Christian fellowship, *1863:* fellowship,— 115| P:proofs, that *1863:* proofs that 119| P:march, a band *1863:* march, Thy band *1868:* thy *1888:* band, 120| P:east *1863:* South, East *End note*| P:[*The Present Pope abolished* <> *business.*—R. B.] *1855: business of the sermon.*—R. B.] *1868: the Sermon* *1888:* [*Pope Gregory XVI. abolished*

THE GUARDIAN-ANGEL

A PICTURE AT FANO

I

Dear and great Angel, wouldst thou only leave
    That child, when thou hast done with him, for me!
Let me sit all the day here, that when eve
    Shall find performed thy special ministry,
And time come for departure, thou, suspending
Thy flight, mayst see another child for tending,
    Another still, to quiet and retrieve.

II

Then I shall feel thee step one step, no more,
    From where thou standest now, to where I gaze,
—And suddenly my head is covered o'er
    With those wings, white above the child who prays
Now on that tomb—and I shall feel thee guarding
Me, out of all the world; for me, discarding
    Yon heaven thy home, that waits and opes its door.

III

I would not look up thither past thy head
    Because the door opes, like that child, I know,
For I should have thy gracious face instead,
    Thou bird of God! And wilt thou bend me low
Like him, and lay, like his, my hands together,
And lift them up to pray, and gently tether
    Me, as thy lamb there, with thy garment's spread?

THE GUARDIAN-ANGEL §Subsequent placement: *1863:* DL§ *Title*| P:*GUARDIAN-ANGEL:* *1863:GUARDIAN-ANGEL.* 4| P:ministry *1865:* ministry, 6| *1863:* may'st *1888:* mayst 7| P:One more, to stay with, quiet, and *1855:* Another still, to quiet and 10| P:And <> head be covered *1863:* —And <> head is covered 14| P:door! *1863:* Yon Heaven *1865:* door. *1868:* heaven

IV

If this was ever granted, I would rest
My head beneath thine, while thy healing hands
Close-covered both my eyes beside thy breast,
Pressing the brain, which too much thought expands,
Back to its proper size again, and smoothing
Distortion down till every nerve had soothing,
And all lay quiet, happy and suppressed.

V

How soon all worldly wrong would be repaired!
I think how I should view the earth and skies
And sea, when once again my brow was bared
After thy healing, with such different eyes.
O world, as God has made it! All is beauty:
And knowing this, is love, and love is duty.
What further may be sought for or declared?

VI

Guercino drew this angel I saw teach
(Alfred, dear friend!)—that little child to pray,
Holding the little hands up, each to each
Pressed gently,—with his own head turned away
Over the earth where so much lay before him
Of work to do, though heaven was opening o'er him,
And he was left at Fano by the beach.

VII

We were at Fano, and three times we went
To sit and see him in his chapel there,
And drink his beauty to our soul's content
—My angel with me too: and since I care

25| *1868:* brain which *1888:* brain, which 28| P:suppress. *1868:* suppressed. 33| P:O, world <> all *1865:* O world *1868:* it! All 37| P:friend)—that *1863:* friend!)—that 41| *1863:* though Heaven *1868:* heaven

For dear Guercino's fame (to which in power
And glory comes this picture for a dower,
Fraught with a pathos so magnificent)—

VIII

And since he did not work thus earnestly
At all times, and has else endured some wrong—
I took one thought his picture struck from me,
And spread it out, translating it to song.
My love is here. Where are you, dear old friend?
How rolls the Wairoa at your world's far end?
This is Ancona, yonder is the sea.

47| P:fame, (to *1863:* fame (to 49| P:magnificent) *1888:* magnificent)—
50| P:work so earnestly *1865:* work thus earnestly 51| P:wrong,—
1863: wrong— 54| P:My Love *1868:* love

CLEON

"As certain also of your own poets have said"—

Cleon the poet (from the sprinkled isles,
Lily on lily, that o'erlace the sea,
And laugh their pride when the light wave lisps "Greece")—
To Protus in his Tyranny: much health!

They give thy letter to me, even now:
I read and seem as if I heard thee speak.
The master of thy galley still unlades
Gift after gift; they block my court at last
And pile themselves along its portico
Royal with sunset, like a thought of thee:
And one white she-slave from the group dispersed
Of black and white slaves (like the chequer-work
Pavement, at once my nation's work and gift,
Now covered with this settle-down of doves),
One lyric woman, in her crocus vest
Woven of sea-wools, with her two white hands
Commends to me the strainer and the cup
Thy lip hath bettered ere it blesses mine.

Well-counselled, king, in thy munificence!
For so shall men remark, in such an act
Of love for him whose song gives life its joy,
Thy recognition of the use of life;
Nor call thy spirit barely adequate
To help on life in straight ways, broad enough
For vulgar souls, by ruling and the rest.
Thou, in the daily building of thy tower,—
Whether in fierce and sudden spasms of toil,
Or through dim lulls of unapparent growth,

CLEON §Subsequent placement: *1863:* MW§ [1]| P:poet, (from *1888:* poet (from [4]| P:To Protos *1865:* To Protus [12]| P:slaves, (like *1888:* slaves (like [14]| P:doves) *1888:* doves), [19]| *1888:* munificence DC,BrU:munificence! *1889:* munificence! [26]| P:tower, *1888:* tower,—

Or when the general work 'mid good acclaim
Climbed with the eye to cheer the architect,—
Didst ne'er engage in work for mere work's sake—
Hadst ever in thy heart the luring hope
Of some eventual rest a-top of it,
Whence, all the tumult of the building hushed,
Thou first of men mightst look out to the East:
The vulgar saw thy tower, thou sawest the sun.
For this, I promise on thy festival
To pour libation, looking o'er the sea,
Making this slave narrate thy fortunes, speak
Thy great words, and describe thy royal face—
Wishing thee wholly where Zeus lives the most,
Within the eventual element of calm.

Thy letter's first requirement meets me here.
It is as thou hast heard: in one short life
I, Cleon, have effected all those things
Thou wonderingly dost enumerate.
That epos on thy hundred plates of gold
Is mine,—and also mine the little chant,
So sure to rise from every fishing-bark
When, lights at prow, the seamen haul their net.
The image of the sun-god on the phare,
Men turn from the sun's self to see, is mine;
The Pœcile, o'er-storied its whole length,
As thou didst hear, with painting, is mine too.
I know the true proportions of a man
And woman also, not observed before;
And I have written three books on the soul,
Proving absurd all written hitherto,
And putting us to ignorance again.
For music,—why, I have combined the moods,
Inventing one. In brief, all arts are mine;
Thus much the people know and recognize,

30| P:architect, *1888:* architect,— 35| P:the East *1855:* east. *1863:* the East: 36| P:tower; thou *1863:* tower, thou 41| P:most *1868:* most, 48| P:chaunt, *1863:* chant, 50| P:nets. *1865:* net. 51| P:phare *1865:* phare, 60| *1888:* moods DC,BrU:moods, *1889:* moods, 62| P:recognise, *1888:* recognize,

Throughout our seventeen islands. Marvel not.
We of these latter days, with greater mind
Than our forerunners, since more composite,
Look not so great, beside their simple way,
To a judge who only sees one way at once,
One mind-point and no other at a time,—
Compares the small part of a man of us
With some whole man of the heroic age,
Great in his way—not ours, nor meant for ours.
And ours is greater, had we skill to know:
For, what we call this life of men on earth,
This sequence of the soul's achievements here
Being, as I find much reason to conceive,
Intended to be viewed eventually
As a great whole, not analyzed to parts,
But each part having reference to all,—
How shall a certain part, pronounced complete,
Endure effacement by another part?
Was the thing done?—then, what's to do again?
See, in the chequered pavement opposite,
Suppose the artist made a perfect rhomb,
And next a lozenge, then a trapezoid—
He did not overlay them, superimpose
The new upon the old and blot it out,
But laid them on a level in his work,
Making at last a picture; there it lies.
So, first the perfect separate forms were made,
The portions of mankind; and after, so,
Occurred the combination of the same.
For where had been a progress, otherwise?
Mankind, made up of all the single men,—
In such a synthesis the labour ends.

66| P:great (beside <> way) *1863:* great, beside <> way, 68| P:mind-point, and *1865:* mind-point and 71| P:way,—not <> for ours, *1863:* way—not <> for ours; *1868:* for ours. 72| P:know. *1868:* know: 73| P:Yet, what *1863:* For, what 74| P:here, *1888:* here 77| P:analysed *1888:* analyzed 81| P:done?—Then what's *1863:* done?—Then, what's *1868:* then 89| *1865:* So first *1888:* So, first 90| P:mankind—and *1865:* mankind; and 91| *1865:* same: *1868:* same. 92| P:Or where *1868:* For where

Now mark me! those divine men of old time
Have reached, thou sayest well, each at one point
The outside verge that rounds our faculty;
And where they reached, who can do more than reach?
It takes but little water just to touch
At some one point the inside of a sphere,
And, as we turn the sphere, touch all the rest
In due succession: but the finer air
Which not so palpably nor obviously,
Though no less universally, can touch
The whole circumference of that emptied sphere,
Fills it more fully than the water did;
Holds thrice the weight of water in itself
Resolved into a subtler element.
And yet the vulgar call the sphere first full
Up to the visible height—and after, void;
Not knowing air's more hidden properties.
And thus our soul, misknown, cries out to Zeus
To vindicate his purpose in our life:
Why stay we on the earth unless to grow?
Long since, I imaged, wrote the fiction out,
That he or other god descended here
And, once for all, showed simultaneously
What, in its nature, never can be shown,
Piecemeal or in succession;—showed, I say,
The worth both absolute and relative
Of all his children from the birth of time,
His instruments for all appointed work.
I now go on to image,—might we hear
The judgment which should give the due to each,
Show where the labour lay and where the ease,
And prove Zeus' self, the latent everywhere!
This is a dream:—but no dream, let us hope,
That years and days, the summers and the springs,

95| P:Now, mark me—those *1865:* Now mark *1868:* me! those 113| P:in its life— *1863:* in our life— *1865:* life: 116| P:other God, descended *1865:* other God descended *1868:* god 118| P:shown *1888:* shown, 121| P:all His *1863:* his 125| P:Shew *1863:* Show 126| P:latent, everywhere! *1865:* latent everywhere! 127| P:dream. But *1865:* dream:—but 128| P:springs *1865:* springs,

Follow each other with unwaning powers.
The grapes which dye thy wine are richer far,
Through culture, than the wild wealth of the rock;
The suave plum than the savage-tasted drupe;
The pastured honey-bee drops choicer sweet;
The flowers turn double, and the leaves turn flowers;
That young and tender crescent-moon, thy slave,
Sleeping above her robe as buoyed by clouds,
Refines upon the women of my youth.
What, and the soul alone deteriorates?
I have not chanted verse like Homer, no—
Nor swept string like Terpander, no—nor carved
And painted men like Phidias and his friend:
I am not great as they are, point by point.
But I have entered into sympathy
With these four, running these into one soul,
Who, separate, ignored eachother's art.
Say, is it nothing that I know them all?
The wild flower was the larger; I have dashed
Rose-blood upon its petals, pricked its cup's
Honey with wine, and driven its seed to fruit,
And show a better flower if not so large:
I stand myself. Refer this to the gods
Whose gift alone it is! which, shall I dare
(All pride apart) upon the absurd pretext
That such a gift by chance lay in my hand,
Discourse of lightly or depreciate?
It might have fallen to another's hand: what then?
I pass too surely: let at least truth stay!

And next, of what thou followest on to ask.
This being with me as I declare, O king,

129| P:powers— *1863:* powers; *1865:* powers. 130| P:wine, are <> far *1888:* wine are <> far, 135| *1865:* crescent moon *1888:* crescent-moon 136–37| P:Refines <> youth— / Sleeping upon her robe as if on clouds. *1855:* Sleeping <> clouds, / Refines <> youth. *1888:* Sleeping above her robe as buoyed by clouds, 139| P:like Homer's *1868:* like Homer 142| P:by point: *1868:* by point. 145| P:each others' arts. *1888:* eachother's art. 147| P:larger—I *1865:* larger; I 150| P:large. *1865:* large: 151| P:stand, myself *1865:* stand myself 156| P:hand—what *1865:* hand: what 157| P:surely—let *1863:* surely: let

My works, in all these varicoloured kinds,
So done by me, accepted so by men—
Thou askest, if (my soul thus in men's hearts)
I must not be accounted to attain
The very crown and proper end of life?
Inquiring thence how, now life closeth up,
I face death with success in my right hand:
Whether I fear death less than dost thyself
The fortunate of men? "For" (writest thou)
"Thou leavest much behind, while I leave nought.
Thy life stays in the poems men shall sing,
The pictures men shall study; while my life,
Complete and whole now in its power and joy,
Dies altogether with my brain and arm,
Is lost indeed; since, what survives myself?
The brazen statue to o'erlook my grave,
Set on the promontory which I named.
And that—some supple courtier of my heir
Shall use its robed and sceptred arm, perhaps,
To fix the rope to, which best drags it down.
I go then: triumph thou, who dost not go!"

Nay, thou art worthy of hearing my whole mind.
Is this apparent, when thou turn'st to muse
Upon the scheme of earth and man in chief,
That admiration grows as knowledge grows?
That imperfection means perfection hid,
Reserved in part, to grace the after-time?
If, in the morning of philosophy,
Ere aught had been recorded, nay perceived,
Thou, with the light now in thee, couldst have looked
On all earth's tenantry, from worm to bird,
Ere man, her last, appeared upon the stage—

162| P:askest if *1865:* askest, if 164| P:life. *1865:* life? 167| P:less even than thyself *1855:* less than dost thyself 168| P:men. "For *1865:* men? "For 169| P:nought: *1865:* nought. 174| P:since,—what *1863:* since, what 175| P:statue that o'erlooks *1865:* statue to o'erlook 176| P:named, *1855:* named. 177| P:that, some *1855:* that—some 178| P:use—its *1855:* use its 180| P:go, then *1865:* go then 188| P:recorded, aught perceived, *1865:* recorded, nay perceived, 191| P:man had yet appeared *1865:* man, her last appeared

Thou wouldst have seen them perfect, and deduced
The perfectness of others yet unseen.
Conceding which,—had Zeus then questioned thee
"Shall I go on a step, improve on this,
Do more for visible creatures than is done?"
Thou wouldst have answered, "Ay, by making each
Grow conscious in himself—by that alone.
All's perfect else: the shell sucks fast the rock,
The fish strikes through the sea, the snake both swims
And slides, forth range the beasts, the birds take flight,
Till life's mechanics can no further go—
And all this joy in natural life is put
Like fire from off thy finger into each,
So exquisitely perfect is the same.
But 'tis pure fire, and they mere matter are;
It has them, not they it: and so I choose
For man, thy last premeditated work
(If I might add a glory to the scheme)
That a third thing should stand apart from both,
A quality arise within his soul,
Which, intro-active, made to supervise
And feel the force it has, may view itself,
And so be happy." Man might live at first
The animal life: but is there nothing more?
In due time, let him critically learn
How he lives; and, the more he gets to know
Of his own life's adaptabilities,
The more joy-giving will his life become.
Thus man, who hath this quality, is best.

But thou, king, hadst more reasonably said:
"Let progress end at once,—man make no step

195| P:"Wilt thou go *1863:*"Shall I go 201| P:slides; the birds take flight, forth range the beasts, *1863:*slides, the *1870:*slides, forth <> beasts, the <> flight, 203| P:life, is put, *1888:*life is put 204| P:off Thy *1865:*thy 206| P:fire—and *1865:*fire, and 207| P:choose, *1863:*choose 208| P:man, Thy *1865:*thy 209| P:to this scheme) *1863:*to the scheme) 211| P:within the soul, *1865:*within his soul, 220| P:The man who *1865:*Thus man, who

Beyond the natural man, the better beast,
Using his senses, not the sense of sense."
In man there's failure, only since he left
The lower and inconscious forms of life.
We called it an advance, the rendering plain
Man's spirit might grow conscious of man's life,
And, by new lore so added to the old,
Take each step higher over the brute's head.
This grew the only life, the pleasure-house,
Watch-tower and treasure-fortress of the soul,
Which whole surrounding flats of natural life
Seemed only fit to yield subsistence to;
A tower that crowns a country. But alas,
The soul now climbs it just to perish there!
For thence we have discovered ('tis no dream—
We know this, which we had not else perceived)
That there's a world of capability
For joy, spread round about us, meant for us,
Inviting us; and still the soul craves all,
And still the flesh replies, "Take no jot more
Than ere thou clombst the tower to look abroad!
Nay, so much less as that fatigue has brought
Deduction to it." We struggle, fain to enlarge
Our bounded physical recipiency,
Increase our power, supply fresh oil to life,
Repair the waste of age and sickness: no,
It skills not! life's inadequate to joy,
As the soul sees joy, tempting life to take.
They praise a fountain in my garden here
Wherein a Naiad sends the water-bow
Thin from her tube; she smiles to see it rise.
What if I told her, it is just a thread
From that great river which the hills shut up,

225| P:There's failure in man, only *1855:* In man there's failure, only 228| A spirit <> of that life, *1865:* Man's spirit <> of man's life, 229| P:And by *1855:* And, by 235| P:alas! *1865:* alas, 236| P:there, *1865:* there! 243| P:ere you climbed *1863:* ere thou climbedst *1870:* clombst 244| P:less, as *1865:* less as 245| P:struggle—fain *1865:* struggle, fain 248| P:sickness. No, *1868:* sickness: no, 249| P:not: life's *1868:* not! life's 252| P:the water-spurt *1863:* the water-bow

And mock her with my leave to take the same?
The artificer has given her one small tube
Past power to widen or exchange—what boots
To know she might spout oceans if she could?
She cannot lift beyond her first thin thread:
And so a man can use but a man's joy
While he sees God's. Is it for Zeus to boast,
"See, man, how happy I live, and despair—
That I may be still happier—for thy use!"
If this were so, we could not thank our lord,
As hearts beat on to doing; 'tis not so—
Malice it is not. Is it carelessness?
Still, no. If care—where is the sign? I ask,
And get no answer, and agree in sum,
O king, with thy profound discouragement,
Who seest the wider but to sigh the more.
Most progress is most failure: thou sayest well.

The last point now:—thou dost except a case—
Holding joy not impossible to one
With artist-gifts—to such a man as I
Who leave behind me living works indeed;
For, such a poem, such a painting lives.
What? dost thou verily trip upon a word,
Confound the accurate view of what joy is
(Caught somewhat clearer by my eyes than thine)
With feeling joy? confound the knowing how
And showing how to live (my faculty)
With actually living?—Otherwise
Where is the artist's vantage o'er the king?
Because in my great epos I display
How divers men young, strong, fair, wise, can act—
Is this as though I acted? if I paint,
Carve the young Phœbus, am I therefore young?

260| P:first straight thread. *1863:* first thin thread, *1865:* thread: 262| P:it, for <> boast *1888:* it for <> boast, 265| *1855:* our Lord, *1868:* lord, 266| P:doing: 'tis *1888:* doing; 'tis 268| P:sign, I ask— *1865:* sign? I ask, 269| P:answer: and *1865:* answer, and 272| P:failure! thou *1865:* failure: thou *1888:* savest DC,BrU:sayest *1889:* sayest 275| P:as I— *1865:* as I 280| P:clearer with my *1855:* clearer by my

Methinks I'm older that I bowed myself
The many years of pain that taught me art!
Indeed, to know is something, and to prove
How all this beauty might be enjoyed, is more:
But, knowing nought, to enjoy is something too.
Yon rower, with the moulded muscles there,
Lowering the sail, is nearer it than I.
I can write love-odes: thy fair slave's an ode.
I get to sing of love, when grown too grey
For being beloved: she turns to that young man,
The muscles all a-ripple on his back.
I know the joy of kingship: well, thou art king!

"But," sayest thou—(and I marvel, I repeat,
To find thee trip on such a mere word) "what
Thou writest, paintest, stays; that does not die:
Sappho survives, because we sing her songs,
And Æschylus, because we read his plays!"
Why, if they live still, let them come and take
Thy slave in my despite, drink from thy cup,
Speak in my place. Thou diest while I survive?
Say rather that my fate is deadlier still,
In this, that every day my sense of joy
Grows more acute, my soul (intensified
By power and insight) more enlarged, more keen;
While every day my hairs fall more and more,
My hand shakes, and the heavy years increase—
The horror quickening still from year to year,
The consummation coming past escape
When I shall know most, and yet least enjoy—
When all my works wherein I prove my worth,
Being present still to mock me in men's mouths,

294| P:rower with <> there *1865:* rower, with <> there, 296| P:love-odes—thy *1865:* love-odes: thy 298| P:man *1863:* man, 300| P:well—thou *1865:* well, thou 301| P:repeat, *1888:* §punctuation at end of line decayed§ *1889:* §punctuation at end of line missing; emended to§ repeat, §see Editorial Notes§ 302| P:tripping on a *1888:* trip on such a 303| P:stays: that *1865:* stays; that 307| P:despite—drink <> cup— *1863:* despite, drink <> cup, 309| P:Say wiselier that <> still,— *1855:* Say rather that *1863:* still, 312| P:In power *1863:* By power 316| *1863:* escape, *1888:* escape

Alive still, in the praise of such as thou,
I, I the feeling, thinking, acting man,
The man who loved his life so over-much,
Sleep in my urn. It is so horrible,
I dare at times imagine to my need
Some future state revealed to us by Zeus,
Unlimited in capability
For joy, as this is in desire for joy,
—To seek which, the joy-hunger forces us:
That, stung by straitness of our life, made strait
On purpose to make prized the life at large—
Freed by the throbbing impulse we call death,
We burst there as the worm into the fly,
Who, while a worm still, wants his wings. But no!
Zeus has not yet revealed it; and alas,
He must have done so, were it possible!

Live long and happy, and in that thought die:
Glad for what was! Farewell. And for the rest,
I cannot tell thy messenger aright
Where to deliver what he bears of thine
To one called Paulus; we have heard his fame
Indeed, if Christus be not one with him—
I know not, nor am troubled much to know.
Thou canst not think a mere barbarian Jew
As Paulus proves to be, one circumcized,
Hath access to a secret shut from us?
Thou wrongest our philosophy, O king,
In stooping to inquire of such an one,

320| P:the phrase of *1888:* the praise of 321| P:I, I, the *1865:* I, I the 322| P:over much, *1863:* over-much, 323| *1855:* Shall sleep *1888:* Sleep 328| P:To <> us. *1863:* —To <> us: 330| P:make sweet the *1865:* make prized the 331| P:death *1870:* death, 333| P:wings. But, no! *1865:* wings. But no! 334| P:and, alas! *1863:* alas, *1865:* and alas, 335| P:so—were *1863:* so, were 336| P:die, *1888:* die: 337| P:was. Farewell *1868:* was! Farewell 340| P:called Paulus—we *1865:* called Paulus; we 343| P:think that a barbarian Jew, *1855:* think a mere barbarian *1888:* barbarian Jew 344| P:be—one circumcised— *1855:* be, one circumcised, *1888:* circumcized, 347| P:such a one, *1855:* such an one,

As if his answer could impose at all!
He writeth, doth he? well, and he may write.
Oh, the Jew findeth scholars! certain slaves
Who touched on this same isle, preached him and Christ;
And (as I gathered from a bystander)
Their doctrine could be held by no sane man.

348| P:all. *1865:* all! 351| P:isle,—preached <> Christ— *1855:* isle, preached <> Christ; 353| P:doctrines *1865:* doctrine

THE TWINS

"Give" and "It-shall-be-given-unto-you"

I

Grand rough old Martin Luther
    Bloomed fables—flowers on furze,
The better the uncouther:
    Do roses stick like burrs?

II

A beggar asked an alms
    One day at an abbey-door,
Said Luther; but, seized with qualms,
    The abbot replied, "We're poor!

III

"Poor, who had plenty once,
    When gifts fell thick as rain:
But they give us nought, for the nonce,
    And how should we give again?"

IV

Then the beggar, "See your sins!
    Of old, unless I err,
Ye had brothers for inmates, twins,
    Date and Dabitur.

THE TWINS §MS and 1854 text: see Editorial Notes; subsequent placement: *1863:* DR§ *Title and subtitle*| §MS:written as one line§ *1854:* §printed as two lines§ [6]| MS:abbey door, P:abbey-door, [8]| MS:replied "We're poor!" *1854:* replied, "We're *1863:* poor! [12]| *1863:* again? *1865:* again?" [16]| MS:§throughout the MS, *Date* and *Dabitur* are double-underlined, calling for upper-case letters. 1854 follows this, but P-1889 only the initial letter of each name is capitalized§ *1854:* and Dabitur." *1863:* and Dabitur.

V

"While Date was in good case
Dabitur flourished too:
For Dabitur's lenten face
No wonder if Date rue.

VI

"Would ye retrieve the one?
Try and make plump the other!
When Date's penance is done,
Dabitur helps his brother.

VII

"Only, beware relapse!"
The Abbot hung his head.
This beggar might be perhaps
An angel, Luther said.

[20]| *1854:*rue." *1863:*rue. [23]| MS:done *1854:*done, [24]| MS:Dabitur joins his *1854:*brother." P:Dabitur help his *1855:*helps *1863:*brother. [26]| MS:—The *1854:*The [27]| MS:This Beggar <> be, perhaps, *1855:*beggar *1865:*be perhaps §MS signed§ *Robert Browning* §and dated§ *Rome, March 30, '54* *1854:*§year printed as§ 1854 P:§name and date dropped§

POPULARITY

I

Stand still, true poet that you are!
    I know you; let me try and draw you.
Some night you'll fail us: when afar
    You rise, remember one man saw you,
Knew you, and named a star!

II

My star, God's glow-worm! Why extend
    That loving hand of his which leads you,
Yet locks you safe from end to end
    Of this dark world, unless he needs you,
Just saves your light to spend?

III

His clenched hand shall unclose at last,
    I know, and let out all the beauty:
My poet holds the future fast,
    Accepts the coming ages' duty,
Their present for this past.

IV

That day, the earth's feast-master's brow
    Shall clear, to God the chalice raising;
"Others give best at first, but thou
    Forever set'st our table praising,
Keep'st the good wine till now!"

POPULARITY §Subsequent placement: *1863:* DL§ 1| P:are, *1863:* are! 2| P:you—let *1855:* you; let 3| P:us. When *1863:* us: when 5| P:star. *1863:* star! 7| P:of His *1868:* his 9| P:unless He <> you— *1865:* you, *1868:* he 11| P:That clenched Hand <> last *1855:* His clenched *1863:* last, *1868:* hand 12| P:beauty. *1863:* beauty: 13| *1863:* the Future *1868:* future 15| *1863:* Their Present <> Past. *1868:* present <> past. 16| P:brow, *1855:* brow 18| P:but Thou *1868:* thou 19| P:praising,— *1863:* praising, 20| P:now."

V

Meantime, I'll draw you as you stand,
With few or none to watch and wonder:
I'll say—a fisher, on the sand
By Tyre the old, with ocean-plunder,
A netful, brought to land.

VI

Who has not heard how Tyrian shells
Enclosed the blue, that dye of dyes
Whereof one drop worked miracles,
And coloured like Astarte's eyes
Raw silk the merchant sells?

VII

And each bystander of them all
Could criticize, and quote tradition
How depths of blue sublimed some pall
—To get which, pricked a king's ambition;
Worth sceptre, crown and ball.

VIII

Yet there's the dye, in that rough mesh,
The sea has only just o'erwhispered!
Live whelks, each lip's beard dripping fresh,
As if they still the water's lisp heard
Through foam the rock-weeds thresh.

IX

Enough to furnish Solomon
Such hangings for his cedar-house,

1863: now!" [22]| P:wonder. *1863:* wonder: [23]| P:fisher (on *1863:* fisher, on [24]| P:the Old) his ocean-plunder, *1863:* the Old, with ocean-plunder, *1868:* old [32]| P:criticise *1863:* criticize [33]| P:pall, *1863:* pall [34]| P:To <> ambition: *1855:* ambition; *1863:* —To [36]| P:dye,—in *1863:* dye, in [37]| P:o'er-whispered! *1888:* o'erwhispered! [38]| P:whelks, the lip's-beard *1863:* whelks, each lip's beard

That, when gold-robed he took the throne
In that abyss of blue, the Spouse
Might swear his presence shone

X

Most like the centre-spike of gold
Which burns deep in the blue-bell's womb,
What time, with ardours manifold,
The bee goes singing to her groom,
Drunken and overbold.

XI

Mere conchs! not fit for warp or woof!
Till cunning come to pound and squeeze
And clarify,—refine to proof
The liquor filtered by degrees,
While the world stands aloof.

XII

And there's the extract, flasked and fine,
And priced and saleable at last!
And Hobbs, Nobbs, Stokes and Nokes combine
To paint the future from the past,
Put blue into their line.

XIII

Hobbs hints blue,—straight he turtle eats:
Nobbs prints blue,—claret crowns his cup:
Nokes outdares Stokes in azure feats,—
Both gorge. Who fished the murex up?
What porridge had John Keats?

43| P:That when *1863:* That, when 47| *1868:* womb *1888:* womb, 52| P:Till art comes,—comes to *1863:* Till cunning comes to *1865:* come 53| P:refines *1863:* refine 56| P:And, there's *1855:* And there's 57| P:priced, and *1863:* priced and 59| *1863:* the Future <> Past, *1868:* future <> past, 61| P:eats. *1863:* eats: 62| P:cup. *1863:* cup:

THE HERETIC'S TRAGEDY

A MIDDLE-AGE INTERLUDE

ROSA MUNDI; SEU, FULCITE ME FLORIBUS. A CONCEIT OF MASTER GYSBRECHT, CANON-REGULAR OF SAINT JODOCUS-BY-THE-BAR, YPRES CITY. CANTUQUE, *Virgilius.* AND HATH OFTEN BEEN SUNG AT HOCK-TIDE AND FESTIVALS. GAVISUS ERAM, *Jessides.*

(It would seem to be a glimpse from the burning of Jacques du Bourg-Molay, at Paris, A.D. 1314; as distorted by the refraction from Flemish brain to brain, during the course of a couple of centuries.)

I

PREADMONISHETH THE ABBOT DEODAET

The Lord, we look to once for all,
    Is the Lord we should look at, all at once:
He knows not to vary, saith Saint Paul,
    Nor the shadow of turning, for the nonce.
See him no other than as he is!
    Give both the infinitudes their due—
Infinite mercy, but, I wis,
    As infinite a justice too.

[*Organ: plagal-cadence.*

    As infinite a justice too.

II

ONE SINGETH

John, Master of the Temple of God,
    Falling to sin the Unknown Sin,
What he bought of Emperor Aldabrod,
    He sold it to Sultan Saladin:

THE HERETIC'S TRAGEDY §Subsequent placement: *1863:* DR§ *Prefatory note:* [1]| P:(*In the original*) *ROSA* *1863:ROSA* [8]| P:centuries.—R. B.) *1863:* centuries.)

[3]| P:saith St. *1863:* saith Saint [5]| P:See Him <> is; *1863:* as He is! *1868:* him <> he [6]| P:the Infinites their *1863:* the Infinitudes their *1868:* infinitudes [13]| P:to Sultan Saladin— *1863:* to Sultan Saladin:

Till, caught by Pope Clement, a-buzzing there,
Hornet-prince of the mad wasps' hive,
And clipt of his wings in Paris square,
They bring him now to be burned alive.
[*And wanteth there grace of lute or clavicithern,*
ye shall say to confirm him who singeth—
We bring John now to be burned alive.

III

In the midst is a goodly gallows built;
'Twixt fork and fork, a stake is stuck;
But first they set divers tumbrils a-tilt,
Make a trench all round with the city muck;
Inside they pile log upon log, good store;
Faggots no few, blocks great and small,
Reach a man's mid-thigh, no less, no more,—
For they mean he should roast in the sight of all.

CHORUS

We mean he should roast in the sight of all.

IV

Good sappy bavins that kindle forthwith;
Billets that blaze substantial and slow;
Pine-stump split deftly, dry as pith;
Larch-heart that chars to a chalk-white glow:
Then up they hoist me John in a chafe,
Sling him fast like a hog to scorch,
Spit in his face, then leap back safe,
Sing "Laudes" and bid clap-to the torch.

CHORUS

Laus Deo—who bids clap-to the torch.

17| P:They have brought him *1855:* They bring him 18| P:We have brought John *1855:* We bring John 24| P:Faggots not few *1888:* Faggots no few 32| P:they all hoist *1855:* they hoist

V

John of the Temple, whose fame so bragged,
Is burning alive in Paris square!
How can he curse, if his mouth is gagged?
Or wriggle his neck, with a collar there?
Or heave his chest, which a band goes round?
Or threat with his fist, since his arms are spliced?
Or kick with his feet, now his legs are bound?
—Thinks John, I will call upon Jesus Christ.
[*Here one crosseth himself.*

VI

Jesus Christ—John had bought and sold,
Jesus Christ—John had eaten and drunk;
To him, the Flesh meant silver and gold.
(*Salvâ reverentiâ.*)
Now it was, "Saviour, bountiful lamb,
I have roasted thee Turks, though men roast me!
See thy servant, the plight wherein I am!
Art thou a saviour? Save thou me!"

CHORUS

'Tis John the mocker cries, "Save thou me!"

VII

Who maketh God's menace an idle word?
—Saith, it no more means what it proclaims,
Than a damsel's threat to her wanton bird?—
For she too prattles of ugly names.
—Saith, he knoweth but one thing,—what he knows?
That God is good and the rest is breath;

41| P:chest, while a *1888:* chest, which a 44| P:—Thinks John—I *1863:* —Thinks John, I 50| P:me. *1863:* roasted Thee *1865:* me! *1868:* thee 51| *1863:* See Thy *1868:* thy 52| P:a Saviour *1863:* Art Thou <> Thou *1868:* thou a saviour <> thou 53| P:It is <> Save <> me! *1855:* 'Tis *1863:* cries, Save Thou *1865:* cries, "Save <> me!" *1868:* thou 56| P:bird,— *1855:* bird?—

Why else is the same styled Sharon's rose?
  Once a rose, ever a rose, he saith.

CHORUS

O, John shall yet find a rose, he saith!

VIII

Alack, there be roses and roses, John!
  Some, honied of taste like your leman's tongue:
Some, bitter; for why? (roast gaily on!)
  Their tree struck root in devil's-dung.
When Paul once reasoned of righteousness
  And of temperance and of judgment to come,
Good Felix trembled, he could no less:
  John, snickering, crook'd his wicked thumb.

CHORUS

What cometh to John of the wicked thumb?

IX

Ha ha, John plucketh now at his rose
  To rid himself of a sorrow at heart!
Lo,—petal on petal, fierce rays unclose;
  Anther on anther, sharp spikes outstart;
And with blood for dew, the bosom boils;
  And a gust of sulphur is all its smell;
And lo, he is horribly in the toils
  Of a coal-black giant flower of hell!

CHORUS

What maketh heaven, That maketh hell.

60| P:styled, Sharon's *1868:* styled Sharon's 64| P:tongue. *1863:* tongue: 65| P:bitter—for *1865:* bitter; for 66| P:devil's dung! *1865:* devil's dung. *1888:* devil's-dung. 69| P:less— *1865:* less: 72| P:plucks *1863:* plucketh 79| of Hell! *1868:* hell! 80| P:maketh Heaven, that <> Hell. *1863:* maketh Heaven, That *1868:* heaven <> hell.

X

So, as John called now, through the fire amain,
    On the Name, he had cursed with, all his life—
To the Person, he bought and sold again—
    For the Face, with his daily buffets rife—
Feature by feature It took its place:
    And his voice, like a mad dog's choking bark,
At the steady whole of the Judge's face—
    Died. Forth John's soul flared into the dark.

SUBJOINETH THE ABBOT DEODAET

God help all poor souls lost in the dark!

85| P:place! *1865:* place: 86| P:voice like <> bark *1863:* voice, like <> bark, 87| P:steady Whole <> Face— *1868:* whole <> face—

TWO IN THE CAMPAGNA

I

I wonder do you feel to-day
As I have felt since, hand in hand,
We sat down on the grass, to stray
In spirit better through the land,
This morn of Rome and May?

II

For me, I touched a thought, I know,
Has tantalized me many times,
(Like turns of thread the spiders throw
Mocking across our path) for rhymes
To catch at and let go.

III

Help me to hold it! First it left
The yellowing fennel, run to seed
There, branching from the brickwork's cleft,
Some old tomb's ruin: yonder weed
Took up the floating weft,

IV

Where one small orange cup amassed
Five beetles,—blind and green they grope
Among the honey-meal: and last,
Everywhere on the grassy slope
I traced it. Hold it fast!

V

The champaign with its endless fleece
Of feathery grasses everywhere!

TWO IN THE CAMPAGNA §Subsequent placement: *1863:* DL§ 2| P:felt, since *1865:* felt since 7| P:tantalised *1863:* tantalized 10| *1888:* go DC,BrU:go. *1889:* go. 11| P:it: first *1863:* it! First 14| *1863:* ruin; yonder *1868:* ruin: yonder 18| P:honey-meal,—and last *1863:* honey-meal: and last,

Silence and passion, joy and peace,
An everlasting wash of air—
Rome's ghost since her decease.

VI

Such life here, through such lengths of hours,
Such miracles performed in play,
Such primal naked forms of flowers,
Such letting nature have her way
While heaven looks from its towers!

VII

How say you? Let us, O my dove,
Let us be unashamed of soul,
As earth lies bare to heaven above!
How is it under our control
To love or not to love?

VIII

I would that you were all to me,
You that are just so much, no more.
Nor yours nor mine, nor slave nor free!
Where does the fault lie? What the core
O' the wound, since wound must be?

IX

I would I could adopt your will,
See with your eyes, and set my heart
Beating by yours, and drink my fill
At your soul's springs,—your part my part
In life, for good and ill.

26| P:life there, through *1868:* life here, through 29| P:letting Nature *1868:* nature 30| P:While Heaven <> towers. *1863:* towers! *1868:* heaven 33| P:above. *1863:* above! 37| P:more— *1863:* more. 38| P:yours, nor mine,—nor slave *1865:* yours nor mine, nor slave 39| P:what *1868:* lie? What 40| P:Of *1870:* O' 44| P:part, my *1888:* part my

X

No. I yearn upward, touch you close,
    Then stand away. I kiss your cheek,
Catch your soul's warmth,—I pluck the rose
    And love it more than tongue can speak—
Then the good minute goes.

XI

Already how am I so far
    Out of that minute? Must I go
Still like the thistle-ball, no bar,
    Onward, whenever light winds blow,
Fixed by no friendly star?

XII

Just when I seemed about to learn!
    Where is the thread now? Off again!
The old trick! Only I discern—
    Infinite passion, and the pain
Of finite hearts that yearn.

46| P:upward—touch *1863:*upward, touch 54| *1875:*§comma after *blow* decayed to period§ *1888:*blow DC,BrU:blow, *1889:*blow,
59| P:passion and *1863:*passion, and

A GRAMMARIAN'S FUNERAL

SHORTLY AFTER THE REVIVAL OF LEARNING IN EUROPE.

Let us begin and carry up this corpse,
    Singing together.
Leave we the common crofts, the vulgar thorpes
    Each in its tether
Sleeping safe on the bosom of the plain,
    Cared-for till cock-crow:
Look out if yonder be not day again
    Rimming the rock-row!
That's the appropriate country; there, man's thought,
    Rarer, intenser,
Self-gathered for an outbreak, as it ought,
    Chafes in the censer.
Leave we the unlettered plain its herd and crop;
    Seek we sepulture
On a tall mountain, citied to the top,
    Crowded with culture!
All the peaks soar, but one the rest excels;
    Clouds overcome it;
No! yonder sparkle is the citadel's
    Circling its summit.
Thither our path lies; wind we up the heights:
    Wait ye the warning?
Our low life was the level's and the night's;
    He's for the morning.
Step to a tune, square chests, erect each head,
    'Ware the beholders!

A GRAMMARIAN'S FUNERAL §Subsequent placement: *1863:* DR§ *Title*| P:*FUNERAL.* *1865:FUNERAL,* *Subtitle*| P:[*Time*—Shortly <> Europe.] *1865:* SHORTLY <> EUROPE. 3| P:thorpes, *1888:* thorpes 6| P:cock-crow. *1863:* cock-crow: 7| P:yonder's not the day *1863:* yonder be not day 9| P:country—there *1863:* country; there 12| P:censer! *1865:* censer. 18| P:it— *1855:* it; 19| P:No, yonder *1888:* No! yonder 20| P:summit! *1865:* summit. 21| P:lies—wind <> heights— *1863:* lies; wind <> heights: 23| P:night's— *1855:* night's; 24| P:morning! *1865:* morning. 25| P:erect the head, *1865:* erect each head,

This is our master, famous calm and dead,
Borne on our shoulders.

Sleep, crop and herd! sleep, darkling thorpe and croft,
Safe from the weather!
He, whom we convoy to his grave aloft,
Singing together,
He was a man born with thy face and throat,
Lyric Apollo!
Long he lived nameless: how should spring take note
Winter would follow?
Till lo, the little touch, and youth was gone!
Cramped and diminished,
Moaned he, "New measures, other feet anon!
My dance is finished?"
No, that's the world's way: (keep the mountain-side,
Make for the city!)
He knew the signal, and stepped on with pride
Over men's pity;
Left play for work, and grappled with the world
Bent on escaping:
"What's in the scroll," quoth he, "thou keepest furled?
Show me their shaping,
Theirs who most studied man, the bard and sage,—
Give!"—So, he gowned him,
Straight got by heart that book to its last page:
Learned, we found him.
Yea, but we found him bald too, eyes like lead,
Accents uncertain:
"Time to taste life," another would have said,
"Up with the curtain!"
This man said rather, "Actual life comes next?
Patience a moment!

27| P:famous, calm, and *1868:* famous calm and 28| *1888:* shoulders DC,BrU:shoulders. *1889:* shoulders. 29| *1865:* croft *1888:* croft, 41| P:way! (keep *1865:* way: (keep 42| P:city.) *1863:* city,) *1865:* city!) 44| P:pity: *1855:* pity; 48| P:Shew *1863:* Show 49| P:Theirs, who *1865:* Theirs who 50| P:Give!"—So he *1865:* Give!"—So, he 52| P:him! *1865:* him. 53| P:too—eyes *1865:* too, eyes 56| *1863:* curtain!"— *1865:* curtain!"

Grant I have mastered learning's crabbed text,
Still there's the comment.
Let me know all! Prate not of most or least,
Painful or easy!
Even to the crumbs I'd fain eat up the feast,
Ay, nor feel queasy."
Oh, such a life as he resolved to live,
When he had learned it,
When he had gathered all books had to give!
Sooner, he spurned it.
Image the whole, then execute the parts—
Fancy the fabric
Quite, ere you build, ere steel strike fire from quartz,
Ere mortar dab brick!

(Here's the town-gate reached: there's the market-place
Gaping before us.)
Yea, this in him was the peculiar grace
(Hearten our chorus!)
That before living he'd learn how to live—
No end to learning:
Earn the means first—God surely will contrive
Use for our earning.
Others mistrust and say, "But time escapes:
Live now or never!"
He said, "What's time? Leave Now for dogs and apes!
Man has Forever."
Back to his book then: deeper drooped his head:
Calculus racked him:
Leaden before, his eyes grew dross of lead:
Tussis attacked him.
"Now, master, take a little rest!"—not he!

60| P:Still, there's the comment! *1855:*comment. *1865:*Still there's 61| P:all. Prate *1863:*all! Prate 62| P:easy: *1865:*easy! 64| P:queasy!" *1865:*queasy." 67| P:give— *1855:*give; *1863:*give! 68| P:it! *1863:*it. 76| P:chorus) *1865:*chorus!) 77| P:Still before *1863:*That before 78| P:learning. *1863:*learning: 81| P:say—"But <> escapes,— *1863:*escapes! *1865:*say, "But *1868:*escapes: 83| P:said, "What's Time? leave <> apes, *1855:*apes! *1863:*time *1868:*time? Leave 84| P:has For ever!" *1855:*ever." *1863:*has Forever." 85| P:head; *1863:*head: 87| P:lead; *1863:*lead: 89| P:"Now, Master *1868:*master

(Caution redoubled,
Step two abreast, the way winds narrowly!)
Not a whit troubled
Back to his studies, fresher than at first,
Fierce as a dragon
He (soul-hydroptic with a sacred thirst)
Sucked at the flagon.
Oh, if we draw a circle premature,
Heedless of far gain,
Greedy for quick returns of profit, sure
Bad is our bargain!
Was it not great? did not he throw on God,
(He loves the burthen)—
God's task to make the heavenly period
Perfect the earthen?
Did not he magnify the mind, show clear
Just what it all meant?
He would not discount life, as fools do here,
Paid by instalment.
He ventured neck or nothing—heaven's success
Found, or earth's failure:
"Wilt thou trust death or not?" He answered "Yes:
Hence with life's pale lure!"
That low man seeks a little thing to do,
Sees it and does it:
This high man, with a great thing to pursue,
Dies ere he knows it.
That low man goes on adding one to one,
His hundred's soon hit:
This high man, aiming at a million,
Misses an unit.

90| P:redoubled! *1865:* redoubled, 91| P:a-breast <> narrowly.) *1863:* narrowly) *1865:* narrowly!) *1888:* abreast 92| *1855:* troubled, *1888:* troubled 94| P:dragon, *1855:* dragon 95| P:He, (soul-hydroptic *1863:* He (soul-hydroptic 99| *1855:* sure, *1865:* sure 104| P:Complete the *1855:* Perfect the 105| P:he make the most of mind, shew *1855:* he magnify the mind *1863:* show 107| P:He did not *1855:* He would not 108| P:instalment! *1865:* instalment. 109| *1863:* nothing—Heaven's *1868:* heaven's 111| P:"Will you trust <> he <> "Yes. *1855:* "Wilt thou trust *1863:* not?" He <> "Yes! *1888:* answered "Yes DC,BrU:answered "Yes: *1889:* answered "Yes:

That, has the world here—should he need the next,
Let the world mind him!
This, throws himself on God, and unperplexed
Seeking shall find him.
So, with the throttling hands of death at strife,
Ground he at grammar;
Still, thro' the rattle, parts of speech were rife:
While he could stammer
He settled *Hoti's* business—let it be!—
Properly based *Oun*—
Gave us the doctrine of the enclitic *De*,
Dead from the waist down.
Well, here's the platform, here's the proper place:
Hail to your purlieus,
All ye highfliers of the feathered race,
Swallows and curlews!
Here's the top-peak; the multitude below
Live, for they can, there:
This man decided not to Live but Know—
Bury this man there?
Here—here's his place, where meteors shoot, clouds form,
Lightnings are loosened,
Stars come and go! Let joy break with the storm,
Peace let the dew send!
Lofty designs must close in like effects:
Loftily lying,
Leave him—still loftier than the world suspects,
Living and dying.

123| P:unperplext *1868:*unperplexed 124| *1855:*find Him. *1865:*him.
125| P:of Death *1868:*death 127| P:rife. *1863:*rife: 129| P:settled *Oti's* *1855:*settled *Hoti's* 133| P:place. *1868:*place: 134| P:purlieus *1863:*purlieus, 137| P:top-peak! the *1865:*top-peak; the 138| P:can there. *1863:*can, there: 143| P:go! let <> storm— *1863:*storm, *1865:*go! Let

ONE WAY OF LOVE

I

All June I bound the rose in sheaves.
Now, rose by rose, I strip the leaves
And strew them where Pauline may pass.
She will not turn aside? Alas!
Let them lie. Suppose they die?
The chance was they might take her eye.

II

How many a month I strove to suit
These stubborn fingers to the lute!
To-day I venture all I know.
She will not hear my music? So!
Break the string; fold music's wing:
Suppose Pauline had bade me sing!

III

My whole life long I learned to love.
This hour my utmost art I prove
And speak my passion—heaven or hell?
She will not give me heaven? 'Tis well!
Lose who may—I still can say,
Those who win heaven, blest are they!

ONE WAY OF LOVE §Subsequent placement: *1863:* DL§ 2| P:leaves, *1863:* leaves
11| string—fold <> wing. *1863:* string; fold <> wing: 12| P:sing? *1855:* sing!
15| P:passion.—Heaven or hell? *1863:* or Hell? *1868:* passion—heaven or hell?
16| *1863:* me Heaven *1868:* heaven 18| *1863:* win Heaven *1868:* heaven

ANOTHER WAY OF LOVE

I

June was not over
  Though past the full,
And the best of her roses
  Had yet to blow,
  When a man I know
(But shall not discover,
  Since ears are dull,
And time discloses)
Turned him and said with a man's true air,
Half sighing a smile in a yawn, as 'twere,—
"If I tire of your June, will she greatly care?"

II

Well, dear, in-doors with you!
  True! serene deadness
Tries a man's temper.
  What's in the blossom
  June wears on her bosom?
Can it clear scores with you?
  Sweetness and redness.
  Eadem semper!
Go, let me care for it greatly or slightly!
If June mend her bower now, your hand left unsightly
By plucking the roses,—my June will do rightly.

III

And after, for pastime,
  If June be refulgent
With flowers in completeness,
  All petals, no prickles,
  Delicious as trickles

ANOTHER WAY OF LOVE §Subsequent placement: *1863:* DL§ 1| P:over, *1865:* over 12| P:Well, Dear *1868:* dear 13| P:True, serene *1865:* True! serene 18| P:redness, *1888:* redness. 21| P:mends her bowers *1868:* mend her bower 22| P:plucking their roses *1863:* rightly, *1865:* rightly. *1868:* plucking the roses

Of wine poured at mass-time,—
And choose One indulgent
To redness and sweetness:
Or if, with experience of man and of spider,
June use my June-lightning, the strong insect-ridder,
And stop the fresh film-work,—why, June will consider.

32| P:She use *1863:* June use 33| P:To stop the fresh spinning,—why *1863:* And stop *1865:* fresh film-work,—why

"TRANSCENDENTALISM: A POEM IN TWELVE BOOKS"

Stop playing, poet! May a brother speak?
'Tis you speak, that's your error. Song's our art:
Whereas you please to speak these naked thoughts
Instead of draping them in sights and sounds.
—True thoughts, good thoughts, thoughts fit to treasure up!
But why such long prolusion and display,
Such turning and adjustment of the harp,
And taking it upon your breast, at length,
Only to speak dry words across its strings?
Stark-naked thought is in request enough:
Speak prose and hollo it till Europe hears!
The six-foot Swiss tube, braced about with bark,
Which helps the hunter's voice from Alp to Alp—
Exchange our harp for that,—who hinders you?
But here's your fault; grown men want thought, you think;
Thought's what they mean by verse, and seek in verse.
Boys seek for images and melody,
Men must have reason—so, you aim at men.
Quite otherwise! Objects throng our youth, 'tis true;
We see and hear and do not wonder much:
If you could tell us what they mean, indeed!
As German Boehme never cared for plants
Until it happed, a-walking in the fields,
He noticed all at once that plants could speak,
Nay, turned with loosened tongue to talk with him.
That day the daisy had an eye indeed—
Colloquized with the cowslip on such themes!
We find them extant yet in Jacob's prose.
But by the time youth slips a stage or two
While reading prose in that tough book he wrote

"TRANSCENDENTALISM: A POEM IN TWELVE BOOKS" §Subsequent placement: *1863:* MW§ 1| P:may *1868:* poet! May 8| P:breast at *1863:* breast, at 10| P:enough— *1863:* enough: 11| P:holloa *1863:* hollo 16| P:in verse: *1888:* in verse DC,BrU:in verse. *1889:* in verse. 18| P:so you *1863:* so, you 19| P:true— *1855:* true, *1863:* true; 20| *1855:* much. *1863:* much: 22| P:As Swedish Boehme *1868:* As German Boehme 25| P:him: *1855:* him. 27| P:Colloquised *1888:* Colloquized 28-29| *1863:* §space between lines§ *1868:* §space closed up§ 30| P:wrote, *1888:* wrote

(Collating and emendating the same
And settling on the sense most to our mind),
We shut the clasps and find life's summer past.
Then, who helps more, pray, to repair our loss—
Another Boehme with a tougher book
And subtler meanings of what roses say,—
Or some stout Mage like him of Halberstadt,
John, who made things Boehme wrote thoughts about?
He with a "look you!" vents a brace of rhymes,
And in there breaks the sudden rose herself,
Over us, under, round us every side,
Nay, in and out the tables and the chairs
And musty volumes, Boehme's book and all,—
Buries us with a glory, young once more,
Pouring heaven into this shut house of life.

So come, the harp back to your heart again!
You are a poem, though your poem's naught.
The best of all you showed before, believe,
Was your own boy-face o'er the finer chords
Bent, following the cherub at the top
That points to God with his paired half-moon wings.

31| P:(Collating, and *1863:* (Collating and 32| P:mind) *1888:* mind), 45| *1863:* Pouring Heaven *1868:* heaven 48| P:you did before *1868:* you showed before 49| P:boy's-face *1868:* boy-face

MISCONCEPTIONS

I

This is a spray the Bird clung to,
Making it blossom with pleasure,
Ere the high tree-top she sprung to,
Fit for her nest and her treasure.
Oh, what a hope beyond measure
Was the poor spray's, which the flying feet hung to,—
So to be singled out, built in, and sung to!

II

This is a heart the Queen leant on,
Thrilled in a minute erratic,
Ere the true bosom she bent on,
Meet for love's regal dalmatic.
Oh, what a fancy ecstatic
Was the poor heart's, ere the wanderer went on—
Love to be saved for it, proffered to, spent on!

MISCONCEPTIONS §Subsequent placement: *1863:* DL§ 8| *1868:* on. DC,BrU:on, *1889:* on, 14| P:it, matched with, and spent *1855:* it, proffered to, spent

*ONE WORD MORE**

TO E. B. B.

1855

I

There they are, my fifty men and women
Naming me the fifty poems finished!
Take them, Love, the book and me together:
Where the heart lies, let the brain lie also.

II

Rafael made a century of sonnets,
Made and wrote them in a certain volume
Dinted with the silver-pointed pencil
Else he only used to draw Madonnas:
These, the world might view—but one, the volume.
Who that one, you ask? Your heart instructs you.
Did she live and love it all her life-time?
Did she drop, his lady of the sonnets,
Die, and let it drop beside her pillow
Where it lay in place of Rafael's glory,
Rafael's cheek so duteous and so loving—

* Originally appended to the collection of Poems called "Men and Women," the greater portion of which has now been, more correctly, distributed under the other titles of this edition.

ONE WORD MORE §MS:see Editorial Notes; subsequent placement: *1863:* MW§ *Title*| MS:*A LAST WORD* P:*ONE WORD MORE* *Date*| MS:§date at end of poem; see below§ P:§no date§ *1863: London, September,* 1855. *1888:* 1855 *Section arrangement*| §see Editorial Notes§ *Footnote*| MS:§no note§ *1863:* this volume. *1868:* this edition. [2]| P:finished: *1855:* finished! [3]| MS:together— P:together. *1863:* together: [4]| MS:heart is, let *1855:* heart lies, let [9]| MS:but §inserted above§ one eye §crossed out§ , the volume: P:volume. [10]| MS:Whose §last two letters crossed out§ that eye §crossed out and replaced above by§ one [11]| MS:life-time— P:life-time? [13]| MS:Die and P:Die, and

Cheek, the world was wont to hail a painter's,
Rafael's cheek, her love had turned a poet's?

III

You and I would rather read that volume,
(Taken to his beating bosom by it)
Lean and list the bosom-beats of Rafael,
Would we not? than wonder at Madonnas—
Her, San Sisto names, and Her, Foligno,
Her, that visits Florence in a vision,
Her, that's left with lilies in the Louvre—
Seen by us and all the world in circle.

IV

You and I will never read that volume.
Guido Reni, like his own eye's apple
Guarded long the treasure-book and loved it.
Guido Reni dying, all Bologna
Cried, and the world cried too, "Ours, the treasure!"
Suddenly, as rare things will, it vanished.

V

Dante once prepared to paint an angel:
Whom to please? You whisper "Beatrice."
While he mused and traced it and retraced it,
(Peradventure with a pen corroded
Still by drops of that hot ink he dipped for,

16| MS:Cheek, a world <> hail, the painter's, P:Cheek, the world <> hail a painter's, 17–18| MS:§marginal note calling for new ¶ numbered 3§ P:§section 3§ 18| MS:read the §last letter crossed out and replaced above by *at* forming *that*§ 21| MS:at Madonnas P:at Madonnas— 22| MS:—Her, San P:Her, San 25| MS:and the whole world P:and all the world 26| MS:read the §last letter crossed out and replaced above by *at* forming *that*§ 27| MS:his eyesights' §crossed out and replaced above by two words§ own eye's 28| MS:Laid away the <> it; P:Guarded long the <> it. 30| MS:world with it, Ours—the treasure! P:it, "Ours <> treasure!" *1863:* world cried too, "Ours *1865:* too, "Ours, the 33| MS:please? Your §last letter crossed out§ own heart §last two words crossed out and replaced by§ whisper, §comma crossed out§ "Bice." §crossed out and replaced by§ Beatrice. P:whisper "Beatrice." 35| MS:Peradventure *1855:* (Peradventure 36| MS:for P:for,

When, his left-hand i' the hair o' the wicked,
Back he held the brow and pricked its stigma,
Bit into the live man's flesh for parchment,
Loosed him, laughed to see the writing rankle,
Let the wretch go festering through Florence)—
Dante, who loved well because he hated,
Hated wickedness that hinders loving,
Dante standing, studying his angel,—
In there broke the folk of his Inferno.
Says he—"Certain people of importance"
(Such he gave his daily dreadful line to)
"Entered and would seize, forsooth, the poet."
Says the poet—"Then I stopped my painting."

VI

You and I would rather see that angel,
Painted by the tenderness of Dante,
Would we not?—than read a fresh Inferno.

VII

You and I will never see that picture.
While he mused on love and Beatrice,
While he softened o'er his outlined angel,
In they broke, those "people of importance:"
We and Bice bear the loss for ever.

41| MS:thro' Florence. P:thro' Florence,— *1855:* thro' Florence)— *1863:* through 42| MS:Dante then, who loved because *1855:* Dante, who loved well because 44| MS:Dante stood and studied thus §last four words crossed out and replaced above by two words§ standing, studying his angel, P:angel, 47| MS:daily, dreadful *1868:* daily dreadful 48| MS:Entered and would see §crossed out and replaced above by one word§ sieze, <> poet: P:poet. *1863:* "Entered <> poet." 49| MS:poet—Then <> painting. P:poet—"Then <> painting." 49–50| MS:§marginal note calling for new ¶ numbered 6§ P:§section 6§ 50| MS:angel P:angel, 53| MS:see the §last letter crossed out and replaced above by *at* forming *that*§ 54| MS:on heaven §crossed out and replaced above by one word§ love and on Bice, §last two words crossed out and replaced above by§ Beatrice 57| MS:forever *1863:* for ever.

VIII

What of Rafael's sonnets, Dante's picture?
This: no artist lives and loves, that longs not
Once, and only once, and for one only,
(Ah, the prize!) to find his love a language
Fit and fair and simple and sufficient—
Using nature that's an art to others,
Not, this one time, art that's turned his nature.
Ay, of all the artists living, loving,
None but would forego his proper dowry,—
Does he paint? he fain would write a poem,—
Does he write? he fain would paint a picture,
Put to proof art alien to the artist's,
Once, and only once, and for one only,
So to be the man and leave the artist,
Gain the man's joy, miss the artist's sorrow.

IX

Wherefore? Heaven's gift takes earth's abatement!
He who smites the rock and spreads the water,
Bidding drink and live a crowd beneath him,
Even he, the minute makes immortal,
Proves, perchance, but mortal in the minute,
Desecrates, belike, the deed in doing.
While he smites, how can he but remember,
So he smote before, in such a peril,
When they stood and mocked—"Shall smiting help us?"

58| MS:§line stands alone as section 8§ *1863:*§line joined with ll. 59-72 to form section 8§
59| MS:§section 9 begins§ loves that *1863:*§becomes part of section 8§ loves, that
60| MS:only once, and but once only, P:only once, and for One only, *1868:*one
64| MS:this time, an art P:this one time, art 65| MS:Out of P:Ay, of
66| MS:dowry, P:dowry,— 67| MS:—Does <> poem, P:Does <> poem,—
68| MS:—Does P:Does 69| P:artists', *1855:*artist's, 70| P:for One *1868:*one
72| MS:Save the man's *1863:*Gain the man's 73| MS:§section 10 begins§ Ah,—for heaven's <> abatement. P:Wherefore? Heaven's <> abatement! *1863:*§section renumbered 9§ 75| MS:him P:him, 76| MS:—Even P:Even
77| MS:Brings, perchance, his mortal P:Proves, perchance *1865:*perchance, but mortal 78| MS:doing: P:doing. 79| MS:remember P:remember,

When they drank and sneered—"A stroke is easy!"
When they wiped their mouths and went their journey,
Throwing him for thanks—"But drought was pleasant."
Thus old memories mar the actual triumph;
Thus the doing savours of disrelish;
Thus achievement lacks a gracious somewhat;
O'er-importuned brows becloud the mandate,
Carelessness or consciousness—the gesture.
For he bears an ancient wrong about him,
Sees and knows again those phalanxed faces,
Hears, yet one time more, the 'customed prelude—
"How shouldst thou, of all men, smite, and save us?"
Guesses what is like to prove the sequel—
"Egypt's flesh-pots—nay, the drought was better."

X

Oh, the crowd must have emphatic warrant!
Theirs, the Sinai-forehead's cloven brilliance,
Right-arm's rod-sweep, tongue's imperial fiat.
Never dares the man put off the prophet.

XI

Did he love one face from out the thousands,
(Were she Jethro's daughter, white and wifely,

82| MS:Then §first letter crossed out and replaced above by *W* forming *When*§ <> and smiled—"A *1855:* and sneered—"A 83| MS:Last §crossed out and replaced above by§ When <> journey P:journey, 84| MS:Throwing me §crossed out and replaced above by§ him 85| MS:So past §two words crossed out and replaced above by§ Thus old 86| MS:So §crossed out and replaced above by§ Thus <> disrelish, P:disrelish; 87| MS:So §crossed out and replaced above by§ Thus
89–90| MS:consciousness, the gesture— / Makes precipitate or more retarding,— §entire line crossed out; last two words questionable§ / For <> ancient grudge about P:gesture. / For <> ancient wrong about *1865:* consciousness—the 91| MS:those faces phalanxed, §last two words each circled and numbered to indicate transposition§ P:those phalanxed faces, 92| MS:Hears yet <> more the customed P:Hears, yet <> more, the 'customed 93| MS:smite and P:smite, and 95–96| MS:§marginal note calling for new ¶ numbered 11§ P:§section 11§ *1863:* §section renumbered 10§
97| MS:prophet-forehead's §first word crossed out and replaced above by§ Sinai
98| MS:rod-sweep and tongue's royal fiat— P:rod-sweep, tongue's imperial fiat.
100| MS:§section 12 begins§ *1863:* §section renumbered 11§ 101| MS:Were P:(Were

Were she but the Æthiopian bondslave,)
He would envy yon dumb patient camel,
Keeping a reserve of scanty water
Meant to save his own life in the desert;
Ready in the desert to deliver
(Kneeling down to let his breast be opened)
Hoard and life together for his mistress.

XII

I shall never, in the years remaining,
Paint you pictures, no, nor carve you statues,
Make you music that should all-express me;
So it seems: I stand on my attainment.
This of verse alone, one life allows me;
Verse and nothing else have I to give you.
Other heights in other lives, God willing:
All the gifts from all the heights, your own, Love!

XIII

Yet a semblance of resource avails us—
Shade so finely touched, love's sense must seize it.
Take these lines, look lovingly and nearly,
Lines I write the first time and the last time.
He who works in fresco, steals a hair-brush,
Curbs the liberal hand, subservient proudly,

102| MS:bondslave, P:bondslave,) 103| MS:Why—he'd envy <> camel P:*He would* envy <> camel, *1855:* He would 104| MS:Dowered with his reserve §first word crossed out and replaced above by§ Gifted §crossed out; first three words crossed out and replaced in L margin by two words§ Keeping a <> scanty drinking, §crossed out and replaced above by§ water §retaining comma§ P:water 105| MS:desert, P:desert; 106| MS:desert—might he yield it;— §dashes and last four words crossed out and replaced above by three words§ to be yielded §last two words crossed out and replaced in R margin by§ deliver 108| MS:together to §crossed out and replaced above by§ for 109| MS:§section 13 begins§ *1863:* §section renumbered 12§ 111| MS:me. P:me; 112| Ms:attainment: P:attainment. 113| MS:alone one <> me, *1855:* alone, one <> me; 114| MS:you, P:you; *1855:* you. *1868:* you *C1870:* you. 115| MS:willing— *1865:* willing: 116| *1868:* love! *1888:* own, Love! 117| MS:§section 14 begins§ *1863:* §section renumbered 13§ 119| MS:Take this verse, look P:Take these lines, look 120| MS:Verse I P:Lines I 121| MS:a paint-brush, §first two words crossed out and replaced above by two words§ an oil- P:a hair-brush, 122| MS:the callous §crossed out and replaced above by§ liberal

Cramps his spirit, crowds its all in little,
Makes a strange art of an art familiar,
Fills his lady's missal-marge with flowerets.
He who blows thro' bronze, may breathe thro' silver,
Fitly serenade a slumbrous princess.
He who writes, may write for once as I do.

XIV

Love, you saw me gather men and women,
Live or dead or fashioned by my fancy,
Enter each and all, and use their service,
Speak from every mouth,—the speech, a poem.
Hardly shall I tell my joys and sorrows,
Hopes and fears, belief and disbelieving:
I am mine and yours—the rest be all men's,
Karshish, Cleon, Norbert and the fifty.
Let me speak this once in my true person,
Not as Lippo, Roland or Andrea,
Though the fruit of speech be just this sentence:
Pray you, look on these my men and women,
Take and keep my fifty poems finished;
Where my heart lies, let my brain lie also!
Poor the speech; be how I speak, for all things.

XV

Not but that you know me! Lo, the moon's self!
Here in London, yonder late in Florence,
Still we find her face, the thrice-transfigured.
Curving on a sky imbrued with colour,
Drifted over Fiesole by twilight,

125| *1870:* flowerets *C1870:* flowerets. 128| MS:once, as *1865:* once as
129| MS:§section 15 begins§ *1863:* §section renumbered 14§ 131| MS:all, and claim §crossed out and replaced above by§ use 135| MS:mens', P:men's,
136| MS:Karshook, Cleon *1870:* Karshish, Cleon 139| MS:sentence P:sentence— *1888:* sentence DC,BrU:sentence: *1889:* sentence: 140| MS:—Pray P:Pray
141| MS:finished, P:finished; 142| MS:heart is, let *1855:* heart lies, let
144| MS:§section 16 begins§ *1863:* §section renumbered 15§ 145| MS:in Florence— *1855:* in Florence, 147| MS:colours, *1855:* colour,
148| MS:Drifted as o'er §last two words crossed out and replaced above by§ over

Came she, our new crescent of a hair's-breadth.
Full she flared it, lamping Samminiato,
Rounder 'twixt the cypresses and rounder,
Perfect till the nightingales applauded.
Now, a piece of her old self, impoverished,
Hard to greet, she traverses the houseroofs,
Hurries with unhandsome thrift of silver,
Goes dispiritedly, glad to finish.

XVI

What, there's nothing in the moon noteworthy?
Nay: for if that moon could love a mortal,
Use, to charm him (so to fit a fancy)
All her magic ('tis the old sweet mythos)
She would turn a new side to her mortal,
Side unseen of herdsman, huntsman, steersman—
Blank to Zoroaster on his terrace,
Blind to Galileo on his turret,
Dumb to Homer, dumb to Keats—him, even!
Think, the wonder of the moonstruck mortal—
When she turns round, comes again in heaven,
Opens out anew for worse or better!
Proves she like some portent of an iceberg
Swimming full upon the ship it founders,
Hungry with huge teeth of splintered crystals?

---

[151]| MS:Rounded 'twixt §above word illegibly crossed out, perhaps *a-top*§ the cypresses §last two letters inserted above, followed by word illegibly crossed out, perhaps *walls*§ P:Rounder [154]| MS:house-roofs, P:houseroofs, [156]| MS:All §crossed out and replaced above by§ Goes dispiritedly, and §crossed out§ glad P:dispiritedly,—glad *1863:* dispiritedly, glad [156–57]| MS:§marginal note calling for new ¶ numbered 17§ P:§section 17§ *1863:* §section renumbered 16§ [157]| MS:note-worthy? *1888:* noteworthy? [158]| MS:Nay—for *1865:* Nay: for *1888:* mortal DC,BrU:mortal, *1889:* mortal, [159]| MS:Gave to grace him §first and third words crossed out and replaced above by, respectively§ Use §and§ charm <> fancy) *1855:* Use, to *1888:* fancy BrU:fancy, *1889:* fancy, §emended to§ fancy) §see Editorial Notes§ [160]| MS:her pleasure §crossed out and replaced above by§ magic [162]| MS:of shepherd, huntsman P:of herdsman, huntsman [166]| MS:Think the wonder P:Think, the wonder [167]| MS:What §last two letters crossed out and replaced above by *en* forming *When*§ she §inserted above§ <> round, and §crossed out§ [168]| MS:better? *1865:* better! [169]| MS:Proves it §crossed out and replaced above by two words§ she like some white §crossed out§ <> ice-berg *1863:* iceberg [171]| MS:chrystals? *1863:* crystals?

Proves she as the paved work of a sapphire
Seen by Moses when he climbed the mountain?
Moses, Aaron, Nadab and Abihu
Climbed and saw the very God, the Highest,
Stand upon the paved work of a sapphire.
Like the bodied heaven in his clearness
Shone the stone, the sapphire of that paved work,
When they ate and drank and saw God also!

XVII

What were seen? None knows, none ever shall know.
Only this is sure—the sight were other,
Not the moon's same side, born late in Florence,
Dying now impoverished here in London.
God be thanked, the meanest of his creatures
Boasts two soul-sides, one to face the world with,
One to show a woman when he loves her!

XVIII

This I say of me, but think of you, Love!
This to you—yourself my moon of poets!
Ah, but that's the world's side, there's the wonder,
Thus they see you, praise you, think they know you!
There, in turn I stand with them and praise you—
Out of my own self, I dare to phrase it.
But the best is when I glide from out them,

172–73| MS:Proves it §crossed out and replaced above by one word§ she as when Moses climbed the mountain, / Saw the paved-work of a stone, a sapphire, P:Proves she as the paved-work of a sapphire / Seen by Moses when he climbed the mountain— *1855:*mountain? *1868:*paved work 174| MS:—Moses <> Abihu, P:Moses <> Abihu 176| MS:paved-work <> sapphire? P:sapphire. *1865:*paved work 178| P:paved-work, *1868:*paved work, *1888:*work DC,BrU:work, *1889:*work, 180| MS:§section numbered 16§ Which §last three letters crossed out and replaced above by ***at*** forming ***What***§ P:§section numbered 18§ *1863:*§section renumbered 17§ 186| MS:woman if he <> her. P:woman when he *1865:*her! 187| MS:§section numbered 17§ P:§section numbered 19§ *1863:*§section renumbered 18§ 189| MS:side—there's the wonder— *1863:*side, there's the wonder, 190| MS:know you. *1865:*know you! 191| MS:you, *1865:*you. *C1870:*you— 192–93| MS:sell—(I <> it) / Seeing—mine with all the eyes—our wonder. / But P:it:) / But *1855:*self, I <> it. / But

Cross a step or two of dubious twilight,
Come out on the other side, the novel
Silent silver lights and darks undreamed of,
Where I hush and bless myself with silence.

XIX

Oh, their Rafael of the dear Madonnas,
Oh, their Dante of the dread Inferno,
Wrote one song—and in my brain I sing it,
Drew one angel—borne, see, on my bosom!

R. B.

197| MS:with beauty. P:with silence. 197–98| MS:§no section division§ 198| MS:§section 20 begins§ *1863:*§section renumbered 19§ 201| MS:§first word, perhaps *Did,* illegibly crossed out and altered to§ Drew <> angel,—borne P:angel—borne *Date*| MS:London, Sept 22. 1855. §at L margin and underlined§ P:§no date§ *Signature*| MS: *R. B.* §at R margin and underlined§ P:§no signature§ *1863:R. B.* §at R margin§ *MS Note*| MS:End of Vol II. §at L margin§ P:The End

BEN KARSHOOK'S WISDOM

Edited by Allan C. Dooley and Susan E. Dooley

BEN KARSHOOK'S WISDOM

I

"Would a man 'scape the rod?"
Rabbi Ben Karshook saith,
"See that he turn to God
The day before his death."

"Ay, could a man inquire
When it shall come!" I say.
The Rabbi's eye shoots fire—
"Then let him turn to-day!"

II

Quoth a young Sadducee:
"Reader of many rolls,
Is it so certain we
Have, as they tell us, souls?"

"Son, there is no reply!"
The Rabbi bit his beard:
"Certain, a soul have *I*—
We may have none," he sneered.

Thus Karshook, the Hiram's-Hammer,
The Right-hand Temple-column,
Taught babes in grace their grammar,
And struck the simple, solemn.

Rome, April 27, 1854

§This and the following page reproduce the "Dedication" and "Advertisement" that B provided for *Last Poems by Elizabeth Barrett Browning,* published by Chapman and Hall in 1862.§

TO "GRATEFUL FLORENCE,"
TO THE MUNICIPALITY, HER REPRESENTATIVE
AND TO TOMMASEO, ITS SPOKESMAN,
MOST GRATEFULLY.

ADVERTISEMENT

These poems are given as they occur on a list drawn up last June. A few had already been printed in periodicals.

There is hardly such direct warrant for publishing the Translations; which were only intended, many years ago, to accompany and explain certain Engravings after ancient Gems, in the projected work of a friend, by whose kindness they are now recovered: but as two of the original series (the 'Adonis' of Bion, and 'Song to the Rose' from Achilles Tatius) have subsequently appeared, it is presumed that the remainder may not improperly follow.

A single recent version is added.

London, *February,* 1862

§This page reproduces the "Advertisement" that B provided for *The Greek Christian Poets and the English Poets by Elizabeth Barrett Browning,* published by Chapman and Hall in 1863.§

ADVERTISEMENT

The following pieces, first printed in 1842 by the 'Athenæum,' are now reprinted with the liberal permission of that Journal.

It was intended by its Writer, that the account of the Greek Christian Poets should receive corrections, or certainly additions: a project which new objects of interest came to delay. The glancing series of notes upon the English Poets seems suggested by, as well as consequent upon, the account; unless it arose from the publication of Wordsworth's 'Poems of early and late years, including The Borderers, '—in the form of a review of which, the latter part of the paper originally appeared: the former was occasioned by 'The Book of the Poets,' a compilation of the day.

Both performances, laid away long ago, and only lately unfolded for the first time, were perhaps almost forgotten by their Author; but on the whole, in all likelihood, some way or other reproduction was desired: and this is effected accordingly.

A name, which occurs unworthily enough toward the close, should be withdrawn were it found possible: its presence may be pardoned as serving at least to mark more dates than one.

London, February, 1863

§This and the following pages reproduce the title page, B's dedication and notes, and the table of contents of his 1863 and 1865 collected editions. The 1865 edition, while textually distinct, differs in its preliminary pages from 1863 only in the date and the description "Fourth Edition" on the title page.§

THE POETICAL WORKS
OF
ROBERT BROWNING

VOL. I
LYRICS, ROMANCES, MEN, AND WOMEN

THIRD EDITION

LONDON:
CHAPMAN AND HALL, 193, PICCADILLY
1863

§Vol. II / Tragedies, and other Plays.§ §Vol. III / Paracelsus, Christmas-Eve and Easter-Day, and Sordello.§

I DEDICATE THESE VOLUMES
TO
MY OLD FRIEND JOHN FORSTER,
GLAD AND GRATEFUL THAT HE WHO, FROM THE FIRST
PUBLICATION OF THE VARIOUS POEMS THEY INCLUDE,
HAS BEEN THEIR PROMPTEST AND STAUNCHEST HELPER,
SHOULD SEEM EVEN NEARER TO ME NOW THAN
THIRTY YEARS AGO.

R. B.

London, April 21, 1863.

CONTENTS

VOLUME I

LYRICS

CAVALIER TUNES
I. MARCHING ALONG
II. GIVE A ROUSE
III. BOOT AND SADDLE
THE LOST LEADER
"HOW THEY BROUGHT THE GOOD NEWS FROM GHENT TO AIX"
THROUGH THE METIDJA TO ABD-EL-KADR
NATIONALITY IN DRINKS
GARDEN FANCIES
I. THE FLOWER'S NAME
II. SIBRANDUS SCHAFNABURGENSIS
SOLILOQUY OF THE SPANISH CLOISTER
THE LABORATORY
THE CONFESSIONAL
CRISTINA
THE LOST MISTRESS
EARTH'S IMMORTALITIES
MEETING AT NIGHT
PARTING AT MORNING
SONG
A WOMAN'S LAST WORD
EVELYN HOPE
LOVE AMONG THE RUINS
A LOVERS' QUARREL
UP AT A VILLA—DOWN IN THE CITY
A TOCCATA OF GALUPPI'S
OLD PICTURES IN FLORENCE
"DE GUSTIBUS—"
HOME-THOUGHTS, FROM ABROAD
HOME-THOUGHTS, FROM THE SEA
SAUL
MY STAR
BY THE FIRESIDE
ANY WIFE TO ANY HUSBAND
TWO IN THE CAMPAGNA
MISCONCEPTIONS
A SERENADE AT THE VILLA
ONE WAY OF LOVE
ANOTHER WAY OF LOVE
A PRETTY WOMAN

RESPECTABILITY
LOVE IN A LIFE
LIFE IN A LOVE
IN THREE DAYS
IN A YEAR
WOMEN AND ROSES
BEFORE
AFTER
THE GUARDIAN-ANGEL—A PICTURE AT FANO
MEMORABILIA
POPULARITY
MASTER HUGUES OF SAXE-GOTHA

ROMANCES

INCIDENT OF THE FRENCH CAMP
THE PATRIOT—AN OLD STORY
MY LAST DUCHESS—FERRARA
COUNT GISMOND—AIX IN PROVENCE
THE BOY AND THE ANGEL
INSTANS TYRANNUS
MESMERISM
THE GLOVE
TIME'S REVENGES
THE ITALIAN IN ENGLAND
THE ENGLISHMAN IN ITALY—PIANO DI SORRENTO
IN A GONDOLA
WARING
THE TWINS
A LIGHT WOMAN
THE LAST RIDE TOGETHER
THE PIED PIPER OF HAMELIN; A CHILD'S STORY
THE FLIGHT OF THE DUCHESS
A GRAMMARIAN'S FUNERAL
JOHANNES AGRICOLA IN MEDITATION
THE HERETIC'S TRAGEDY—A MIDDLE AGE INTERLUDE
HOLY-CROSS DAY
PROTUS
THE STATUE AND THE BUST
PORPHYRIA'S LOVER
"CHILDE ROLAND TO THE DARK TOWER CAME"

MEN, AND WOMEN

'TRANSCENDENTALISM:' A POEM IN TWELVE BOOKS
HOW IT STRIKES A CONTEMPORARY
ARTEMIS PROLOGIZES

AN EPISTLE CONTAINING THE STRANGE MEDICAL EXPERIENCE OF KARSHISH, THE ARAB PHYSICIAN
PICTOR IGNOTUS
FRA LIPPO LIPPI
ANDREA DEL SARTO
THE BISHOP ORDERS HIS TOMB AT SAINT PRAXED'S CHURCH
BISHOP BLOUGRAM'S APOLOGY
CLEON
RUDEL TO THE LADY OF TRIPOLI
ONE WORD MORE

VOLUME II

PIPPA PASSES—A DRAMA
KING VICTOR AND KING CHARLES—A TRAGEDY
THE RETURN OF THE DRUSES—A TRAGEDY
A BLOT IN THE 'SCUTCHEON—A TRAGEDY
COLOMBE'S BIRTHDAY—A PLAY
LURIA—A TRAGEDY
A SOUL'S TRAGEDY
IN A BALCONY—A SCENE
STRAFFORD—A TRAGEDY

VOLUME III

PARACELSUS
CHRISTMAS-EVE AND EASTER-DAY
SORDELLO

§The following notes appear in Volume I.§

In this Volume are collected and redistributed the pieces first published in 1842, 1845, and 1855, respectively, under the titles of "Dramatic Lyrics," "Dramatic Romances," and "Men and Women."

Part of these were inscribed to my dear friend John Kenyon: I hope the whole may obtain the honor of an association with his memory.

R. B.

* Such Poems as the majority in this volume might also come properly enough, I suppose, under the head of "Dramatic Pieces;" being, though often Lyric in expression, always Dramatic in principle, and so many utterances of so many imaginary persons, not mine.—

R. B.

EURYDICE TO ORPHEUS

Text edited by John C. Berkey
Annotations by Allan C. Dooley and Susan E. Dooley

EURYDICE TO ORPHEUS

A PICTURE BY LEIGHTON

But give them me, the mouth, the eyes, the brow!
Let them once more absorb me! One look now
Will lap me round for ever, not to pass
Out of its light, though darkness lie beyond:
Hold me but safe again within the bond
Of one immortal look! All woe that was,
Forgotten, and all terror that may be,
Defied,—no past is mine, no future: look at me!

---

§Ed. 1864, 1868, 1870, 1888, 1889. For MSS, see Editorial Notes.§ *EURYDICE TO ORPHEUS* *1864:*§printed as prose§ *1868:*§printed as verse; subsequent placement: *1868:*DP§ [1]| *1864:*"But <> me—the <> brow. *1868:*But <> me, the <> brow! [4]| *1864:*beyond! *1868:*beyond: [6]| *1864:*was *1868:*was, [7]| *1864:*be *1868:*be, [8]| *1864:*defied; no <> future! look at me!" *1868:*Defied,—no <> future: look at me! §Signature, *1864* only§ *Robert Browning. A Fragment.*

DRAMATIS PERSONÆ

Text edited by John C. Berkey
Annotations by Allan C. Dooley and Susan E. Dooley

DRAMATIS PERSONÆ

DRAMATIS PERSONÆ

1864

JAMES LEE'S WIFE

I —JAMES LEE'S WIFE SPEAKS AT THE WINDOW

I

Ah, Love, but a day
    And the world has changed!
The sun's away,
    And the bird estranged;
The wind has dropped,
    And the sky's deranged:
Summer has stopped.

II

Look in my eyes!
    Wilt thou change too?
Should I fear surprise?
    Shall I find aught new
In the old and dear,
    In the good and true,
With the changing year?

III

Thou art a man,
    But I am thy love.

---

§MS in Pierpont Morgan Library, New York. Ed. P1864a, CP1864a, 1864a, 1864a(r), 1864b, 1868, 1870, C1870, 1875, 1888, 1889. See Editorial Notes and Table of Editions§
JAMES LEE'S WIFE §*1836:* lines 152-81 titled "LINES" in *The Monthly Repository* *1857:* MS lines 244-69. See Editorial Notes.§ *Title*| MS:James Lee. *1868:* JAMES LEE'S WIFE. MS:§no section titles§ *P1864a:* AT THE WINDOW. *1864a(r):* §in R margin, *James Lee's Wife Speaks* marked for insertion before AT§ 1| MS:day, *P1864a:* love *1870:* Ah, Love *1888:* day
4| MS:bird's estranged: *P1864a:* estranged; *1868:* bird estranged;
6| MS:deranged— *P1864a:* deranged: 16| MS:love! *1868:* love.

For the lake, its swan;
    For the dell, its dove;
And for thee—(oh, haste!)
    Me, to bend above,
Me, to hold embraced.

II —BY THE FIREFSIDE

I

Is all our fire of shipwreck wood,
        Oak and pine?
Oh, for the ills half-understood,
        The dim dead woe
        Long ago
Befallen this bitter coast of France!
Well, poor sailors took their chance;
        I take mine.

II

A ruddy shaft our fire must shoot
        O'er the sea:
Do sailors eye the casement—mute,
        Drenched and stark,
        From their bark—
And envy, gnash their teeth for hate
O' the warm safe house and happy freight
        —Thee and me?

III

God help you, sailors, at your need!
        Spare the curse!

17| MS:swan— *P1864a:*swan; 18| MS:dove— *P1864a:*dove; 21| MS:embraced! *1868:*embraced. 25| MS:dim, dead *1868:* dim dead 28| MS:chance, *P1864a:*chance; 32| *1868:* mute DC,BrU:mute, *1889:*mute, 36| MS:Of *P1864a:*O'

For some ships, safe in port indeed,
Rot and rust,
Run to dust,
All through worms i' the wood, which crept,
Gnawed our hearts out while we slept:
That is worse.

IV

Who lived here before us two?
Old-world pairs.
Did a woman ever—would I knew!—
Watch the man
With whom began
Love's voyage full-sail,—(now, gnash your teeth!)
When planks start, open hell beneath
Unawares?

III —IN THE DOORWAY

I

The swallow has set her six young on the rail,
And looks sea-ward:
The water's in stripes like a snake, olive-pale
To the leeward,—
On the weather-side, black, spotted white with the wind.
"Good fortune departs, and disaster's behind,"—
Hark, the wind with its wants and its infinite wail!

II

Our fig-tree, that leaned for the saltness, has furled
Her five fingers,
Each leaf like a hand opened wide to the world
Where there lingers

45| MS:worse! *1868:* worse. 46| MS:two? §over possibly *too?*§ 47| MS:pairs! *1868:* pairs. 54| MS:her six §over illegible word§ 55| MS:sea-ward; *P1864a:* sea-ward: 58| MS:black—spotted <> wind: *P1864a:* black, spotted *1870:* wind. 59| MS:departs and <> behind"— *P1864a:* departs, and <> behind,"—

No glint of the gold, Summer sent for her sake:
How the vines writhe in rows, each impaled on its stake!
My heart shrivels up and my spirit shrinks curled.

III

Yet here are we two; we have love, house enough,
With the field there,
This house of four rooms, that field red and rough,
Though it yield there,
For the rabbit that robs, scarce a blade or a bent;
If a magpie alight now, it seems an event;
And they both will be gone at November's rebuff.

IV

But why must cold spread? but wherefore bring change
To the spirit,
God meant should mate his with an infinite range,
And inherit
His power to put life in the darkness and cold?
Oh, live and love worthily, bear and be bold!
Whom Summer made friends of, let Winter estrange!

IV —ALONG THE BEACH

I

I will be quiet and talk with you,
And reason why you are wrong.
You wanted my love—is that much true?
And so I did love, so I do:
What has come of it all along?

65| MS:gold, summer *P1864a:*gold, Summer 66| *1870:*stake *1875:*stake! 67| MS:up, and *1868:*up and 72| MS:For rabbits that rob §altered to§ For the §inserted above§ rabbit that robs <> bent— *P1864a:*bent; 73| MS:event— *P1864a:*event; 75| MS:But §over illegible erasure§ spread? And wherefore *P1864a:*spread? but wherefore 77| MS:mate His *1868:*mate his 79| MS:life into darkness *P1864a:*life in the darkness 83| MS:Will reason <> wrong: *P1864a:*And reason *1868:*wrong.

II

I took you—how could I otherwise?
For a world to me, and more;
For all, love greatens and glorifies
Till God's a-glow, to the loving eyes,
In what was mere earth before.

III

Yes, earth—yes, mere ignoble earth!
Now do I mis-state, mistake?
Do I wrong your weakness and call it worth?
Expect all harvest, dread no dearth,
Seal my sense up for your sake?

IV

Oh, Love, Love, no, Love! not so, indeed!
You were just weak earth, I knew:
With much in you waste, with many a weed,
And plenty of passions run to seed,
But a little good grain too.

V

And such as you were, I took you for mine:
Did not you find me yours,
To watch the olive and wait the vine,
And wonder when rivers of oil and wine
Would flow, as the Book assures?

VI

Well, and if none of these good things came,
What did the failure prove?

87| MS:otherwise?— *P1864a:* otherwise? 88| MS:more— *P1864a:* more; 89| MS:all, love §over illegible erasure§ 92| MS:earth—just mere *P1864a:* earth—yes, mere 93| MS:misstate *P1864a:* misstate 95| MS:—Expect all beauty, dread *P1864a:* Expect all harvest, dread 97| MS:no, Love! Not so *P1864a:* Oh, love, love, no, love! not so *1870:* Oh, Love, Love, no, Love! not 101| MS:too! *P1864a:* too. 103| MS:yours *P1864a:* yours,

The man was my whole world, all the same,
With his flowers to praise or his weeds to blame,
    And, either or both, to love.

VII

Yet this turns now to a fault—there! there!
    That I do love, watch too long,
And wait too well, and weary and wear;
And 'tis all an old story, and my despair
    Fit subject for some new song:

VIII

"How the light, light love, he has wings to fly
    At suspicion of a bond:
My wisdom has bidden your pleasure good-bye,
Which will turn up next in a laughing eye,
    And why should you look beyond?"

V —ON THE CLIFF

I

I leaned on the turf,
I looked at a rock
Left dry by the surf;
For the turf, to call it grass were to mock:
Dead to the roots, so deep was done
The work of the summer sun.

110| MS:praise, or *1868:*praise or 111| MS:—But, either *P1864a:*And, either 112| MS:And this *P1864a:*Yet this 113| MS:love—watch *P1864a:*love, watch 114| MS:wear,— *P1864a:*wear; 116| MS:song— *P1864a:*song: 117| MS:How *1868:*"How 119| MS:And the wisdom <> bidden the pleasure *P1864a:*How my wisdom <> bidden your pleasure *1868:*My wisdom 120| MS:Which turns up *P1864a:*Which will turn up 121| MS:should love look beyond? *P1864a:*should you look *1868:*beyond?" 123| MS:And looked *P1864a:*I looked 124| MS:surf: *P1864:*surf; 125| MS:turf,—to <> mock! *P1864a:*turf, to <> mock: 126| MS:Red to *P1864a:*Dead to

II

And the rock lay flat
As an anvil's face:
No iron like that!
Baked dry; of a weed, of a shell, no trace:
Sunshine outside, but ice at the core,
Death's altar by the lone shore.

III

On the turf, sprang gay
With his films of blue,
No cricket, I'll say,
But a warhorse, barded and chanfroned too,
The gift of a quixote-mage to his knight,
Real fairy, with wings all right.

IV

On the rock, they scorch
Like a drop of fire
From a brandished torch,
Fall two red fans of a butterfly:
No turf, no rock: in their ugly stead,
See, wonderful blue and red!

V

Is it not so
With the minds of men?
The level and low,
The burnt and bare, in themselves; but then

131| MS:weed, of §over *or*§ 133| MS:—Death's *P1864a:* Death's 134| MS:turf sprang *P1864a:* turf, sprang 136| MS:—No *P1864a:* No 139| MS:right! *P1864a:* right. 140| MS:rock,—they *P1864a:* rock, they 142| MS:torch,— *P1864a:* torch, 143| MS:The two *P1864a:* Fell two *1868:* Fall two 144| MS:rock—in <> stead *P1864a:* rock, in <> stead, *1888:* rock: in 145–46| MS:§stanza incorrectly numbered 7§ 147| MS:men?— *P1864a:* men? 148| MS:low *P1864a:* low, 149| MS:themselves—but *P1864a:* themselves; but

With such a blue and red grace, not theirs,—
Love settling unawares!

VI —READING A BOOK, UNDER THE CLIFF

I

"Still ailing, Wind? Wilt be appeased or no?
Which needs the other's office, thou or I?
Dost want to be disburthened of a woe,
And can, in truth, my voice untie
Its links, and let it go?

II

"Art thou a dumb wronged thing that would be righted,
Entrusting thus thy cause to me? Forbear!
No tongue can mend such pleadings; faith, requited
With falsehood,—love, at last aware
Of scorn,—hopes, early blighted,—

III

"We have them; but I know not any tone
So fit as thine to falter forth a sorrow:
Dost think men would go mad without a moan,
If they knew any way to borrow
A pathos like thy own?

150| MS:theirs, *1888:* theirs,— 151–52| *P1864a:* UNDER THE CLIFF. *1864a(r):* §in L margin, *Reading a Book,* marked for insertion before UNDER§ 152| *1836:* Still <> wind? wilt be MS:"Still ailing, Wind? Wilt be 154| *1836:* disburdened MS:disburthened 155| *1836:* can in truth my MS:can, in truth, my 157| *1836:* dumb wrong'd thing MS:dumb, wronged thing 158| *1836:* forbear: MS:me? Forbear *P1864a:* me? Forbear. *1868:* me? Forbear! 159| *1836:* faith required MS:faith, requited 160| *1836:* love at MS:love, at 161| *1836:* hopes early MS:hopes, early 162| *1836:* them—but MS:them,—but *P1864a:* them; but 164| *1836:* moan MS:moan, 166| *1836:* like thine own MS:like thy own

IV

"Which sigh wouldst mock, of all the sighs? The one
So long escaping from lips starved and blue,
That lasts while on her pallet-bed the nun
Stretches her length; her foot comes through
The straw she shivers on;

V

"You had not thought she was so tall: and spent,
Her shrunk lids open, her lean fingers shut
Close, close, their sharp and livid nails indent
The clammy palm; then all is mute:
That way, the spirit went.

VI

"Or wouldst thou rather that I understand
Thy will to help me?—like the dog I found
Once, pacing sad this solitary strand,
Who would not take my food, poor hound,
But whined and licked my hand."

VII

All this, and more, comes from some young man's pride
Of power to see,—in failure and mistake,
Relinquishment, disgrace, on every side,—

167| *1836:* would'st mock of <> sighs? that one MS:mock, of <> sighs? That one *P1864a:* wouldst <> sighs? The one 168| *1836:* starv'd MS:starved <> blue *P1864a:* blue, 169| *1836:* Which lasts MS:That lasts 170| *1836:* length—her *P1864:* length; her 171| *1836:* on, MS:on,— *P1864a:* on; 172| *1836:* tall,—and MS:tall! and *P1864a:* tall: and 173| *1836:* ope MS:open 174| *1836:* So close *P1864a:* Close, close 175| *1836:* palm: then <> mute— MS:palm; then <> mute: 176| *1836:* way the MS:way, the 177| *1836:* would'st MS:woulds't *P1864a:* wouldst 178| *1836:* me—like *P1864a:* me?—like 179| *1836:* Once pacing sad the solitary MS:sad this solitary *P1864a:* Once, pacing 180| *1836:* That would MS:Who would 181| *1836:* whined, and <> hand? §signed Z.§ MS:whined and <> hand?" *P1864a:* hand." 181–82| MS:§no rule§ *P1864a:* §rule added§ 183| MS:see, in *P1864a:* see,—in 184| MS:side, *P1864a:* side,—

Merely examples for his sake,
Helps to his path untried:

VIII

Instances he must—simply recognize?
Oh, more than so!—must, with a learner's zeal,
Make doubly prominent, twice emphasize,
By added touches that reveal
The god in babe's disguise.

IX

Oh, he knows what defeat means, and the rest!
Himself the undefeated that shall be:
Failure, disgrace, he flings them you to test,—
His triumph, in eternity
Too plainly manifest!

X

Whence, judge if he learn forthwith what the wind
Means in its moaning—by the happy prompt
Instinctive way of youth, I mean; for kind
Calm years, exacting their accompt
Of pain, mature the mind:

XI

And some midsummer morning, at the lull
Just about daybreak, as he looks across
A sparkling foreign country, wonderful
To the sea's edge for gloom and gloss,
Next minute must annul,—

185| MS:— Merely *P1864a:* Merely 187| MS:Instances, he must . . simply *P1864a:* Instances he must—simply 188| MS:zeal *P1864a:* zeal, 191| MS:The §over illegible word§ <> disguise: *P1864a:* disguise. 193| MS:—Himself, the *P1864a:* Himself the 195| MS:in serenity §over perhaps *eternity*§ *P1864a:* in eternity 196| MS:So plainly *P1864a:* Too plainly 198| MS:happy, prompt, *1868:* happy prompt 199| MS:mean,—for *P1864a:* mean; for 200| MS:Long years *P1864a:* Calm years 203| MS:Just before day-break *P1864a:* Just about daybreak 205| MS:gloss *P1864a:* gloss,

XII

Then, when the wind begins among the vines,
    So low, so low, what shall it say but this?
"Here is the change beginning, here the lines
    Circumscribe beauty, set to bliss
The limit time assigns."

XIII

Nothing can be as it has been before;
    Better, so call it, only not the same.
To draw one beauty into our hearts' core,
    And keep it changeless! such our claim;
So answered,—Never more!

XIV

Simple? Why this is the old woe o' the world;
    Tune, to whose rise and fall we live and die.
Rise with it, then! Rejoice that man is hurled
    From change to change unceasingly,
His soul's wings never furled!

XV

That's a new question; still replies the fact,
    Nothing endures: the wind moans, saying so;
We moan in acquiescence: there's life's pact,
    Perhaps probation—do *I* know?
God does: endure his act!

208| MS:low, so low,—what shall it mean but *P1864a:* low, so low, what *1868:* it say but 209| MS:Here <> beginning—here *P1864a:* "Here <> beginning, here 211| MS:assigns: *P1864a:* assigns." 212| MS:before! *P1864a:* before; 213| MS:Better,—so <> same: *P1864a:* Better, so <> same. 214| MS:core *P1864a:* core, 215| MS:changelessly,— §last two letters crossed out§ such <> claim, *P1864a:* changeless! such <> claim; 217| MS:world, *P1864a:* world; *1889:* o §emended to§ o' the §see Editorial Notes§ 218| MS:—Tune, to <> die: *P1864a:* Tune, to <> die. 219| MS:Rise through it *P1864a:* Rise with it 220| *P1864a:* unceasingly. *1864a:* unceasingly, *1864b:* unceasingly. *1875:* unceasingly, 222| MS:still remains the *P1864a:* still replies the 223| MS:endures—the <> so, *P1864a:* endures: the <> so; 224| MS:acquiescence—there's *P1864a:* acquiescence: there's 225| MS:—Perhaps, probation *P1864a:* Perhaps probation 226| MS:endure His *1868:* endure his

XVI

Only, for man, how bitter not to grave
    On his soul's hands' palms one fair good wise thing
Just as he grasped it! For himself, death's wave;
    While time first washes—ah, the sting!—
O'er all he'd sink to save.

VII —AMONG THE ROCKS

I

Oh, good gigantic smile o' the brown old earth,
    This autumn morning! How he sets his bones
To bask i' the sun, and thrusts out knees and feet
For the ripple to run over in its mirth;
    Listening the while, where on the heap of stones
The white breast of the sea-lark twitters sweet.

II

That is the doctrine, simple, ancient, true;
    Such is life's trial, as old earth smiles and knows.
If you loved only what were worth your love,
Love were clear gain, and wholly well for you:
    Make the low nature better by your throes!
Give earth yourself, go up for gain above!

227| MS:man—how *P1864a:* man, how 228| MS:On our soul's <> fair, good, wise *P1864a:* On his soul's *1868:* fair good wise 229| MS:as we grasped <> For ourselves, death's wave— *P1864a:* as he grasped <> For himself, death's wave; 230| MS:time o'er §crossed out and replaced above by§ first ripples—ah, the sting— *P1864a:* first washes—ah, the sting!— 231| MS:First, §crossed out and replaced above by§ O'er all we'd sink to save! *P1864a:* all he'd sink to save. 231–32| MS:§no rule§ *1868:* §rule added§ 232| MS:earth *P1864a:* earth, 234| MS:out arms and *P1864a:* out knees and 235| MS:mirth *P1864a:* mirth; 236| MS:stones, *P1864a:* stones 237| MS:sweet! *P1864a:* sweet. 238| MS:simple, old and true: *P1864a:* simple, ancient, true; 239| MS:trial, the old <> knows: *P1864a:* trial, as old <> knows. 240| MS:what worth *P1864a:* what were worth 242| MS:Give the low nature comfort by *P1864a:* Make the low nature better by 243| MS:Leave to yourself *P1864a:* Give earth yourself

VIII —BESIDE THE DRAWING BOARD

I

"As like as a Hand to another Hand!"
Whoever said that foolish thing,
Could not have studied to understand
The counsels of God in fashioning,
Out of the infinite love of his heart,
This Hand, whose beauty I praise, apart
From the world of wonder left to praise,
If I tried to learn the other ways
Of love in its skill, or love in its power.
"As like as a Hand to another Hand":
Who said that, never took his stand,
Found and followed, like me, an hour,
The beauty in this,—how free, how fine
To fear, almost,—of the limit-line!
As I looked at this, and learned and drew,
Drew and learned, and looked again,
While fast the happy minutes flew,
Its beauty mounted into my brain,
And a fancy seized me; I was fain
To efface my work, begin anew,

243–44| *P1864a:* DRAWING-BOARD. *1888:* DRAWING BOARD. 244| *1857:* a hand is to a hand!" MS:a Hand to another Hand"! *P1864a:* another Hand:" *1868:* another Hand!" 245| *1857:* says *P1864a:* said 246| *1857:* Cannot have *P1864a:* Could not have 247| *1857:* fashioning *P1864a:* fashioning, 248| *1857:* of his heart MS:of His heart, *1868:* his 249| *1857:* whose Beauty praise apart MS:Hand—whose beauty I praise, apart *P1864:* Hand, whose 250| *1857:* From a world <> praise MS:From the world <> praise, 251| *1857:* Should one try and learn MS:If I tried to learn 252| *1857:* Of that love in the Skill, that love in the Power. MS:Of Love, in its Skill, or Love, in its power: *P1864a:* Of love, in its skill, or love, <> power.
252–55| *1857:* the Power. / Oh, never he followed, a single hour, MS:its power: / "As like a Hand to another Hand!" / Who says that, never §over illegible erasure§ took his stand, / Found and followed like me, an hour *P1864a:* another Hand:" / Who said <> / <> followed, like <> hour, *1888:* another Hand": 256| *1857:* The Beauty alone, so free, so fine MS:The beauty in this,—how free, how fine 257| *1857:* fear almost,—of MS:fear, almost,—of 258| *1857:* at it, and learned, and MS:at this, and learned and 259| *1857:* And drew, and MS:Drew and learned and *P1864a:* learned, and 261| *1857:* The beauty <> brain MS:Its beauty <> brain, 262| MS:me,—I *P1864a:* me; I 263| *1857:* work and begin MS:work, begin

Kiss what before I only drew;
Ay, laying the red chalk 'twixt my lips,
        With soul to help if the mere lips failed,
        I kissed all right where the drawing ailed,
Kissed fast the grace that somehow slips
Still from one's soulless finger-tips.

II

'Tis a clay cast, the perfect thing,
        From Hand live once, dead long ago:
Princess-like it wears the ring
        To fancy's eye, by which we know
That here at length a master found
        His match, a proud lone soul its mate,
As soaring genius sank to ground,
        And pencil could not emulate
The beauty in this,—how free, how fine
To fear almost!—of the limit-line.
Long ago the god, like me
The worm, learned, each in our degree:
Looked and loved, learned and drew,
        Drew and learned and loved again,
While fast the happy minutes flew,
        Till beauty mounted into his brain
And on the finger which outvied
        His art he placed the ring that's there,
Still by fancy's eye descried,
        In token of a marriage rare:
        For him on earth, his art's despair,
For him in heaven, his soul's fit bride.

264| *1857:*what, before, I simply drew— MS:what before I *P1864a:*before I only drew; 266| *1857:*With my soul close by, if the weak lips ailed, MS:With soul to help if the mere lips failed, 267| *1857:*I would kiss all safe where the drawing failed MS:I kissed all right where the drawing ailed— *P1864a:*ailed, 268| *1857:*—Kiss down the MS:Kissed fast the 269| MS:finger-tips! *1864a:*finger-tips. 269–70| *1857:*§signed§ *Robert Browning* 276| *1868:*ground *1888:*ground,

III

Little girl with the poor coarse hand
I turned from to a cold clay cast—
I have my lesson, understand
The worth of flesh and blood at last.
Nothing but beauty in a Hand?
Because he could not change the hue,
Mend the lines and make them true
To this which met his soul's demand,—
Would Da Vinci turn from you?
I hear him laugh my woes to scorn—
"The fool forsooth is all forlorn
Because the beauty, she thinks best,
Lived long ago or was never born,—
Because no beauty bears the test
In this rough peasant Hand! Confessed!
'Art is null and study void!'
So sayest thou? So said not I,
Who threw the faulty pencil by,
And years instead of hours employed,
Learning the veritable use
Of flesh and bone and nerve beneath
Lines and hue of the outer sheath,
If haply I might reproduce
One motive of the powers profuse,
Flesh and bone and nerve that make
The poorest coarsest human hand
An object worthy to be scanned
A whole life long for their sole sake.
Shall earth and the cramped moment-space
Yield the heavenly crowning grace?
Now the parts and then the whole!
Who art thou, with stinted soul
And stunted body, thus to cry
'I love,—shall that be life's strait dole?
I must live beloved or die!'

295| *1868:* last! *1888:* last. 306| *1868:* peasant Hand! Confessed *1888:* Confessed! 315| *1868:* the mechanism, *1888:* the powers profuse,

This peasant hand that spins the wool
  And bakes the bread, why lives it on,
  Poor and coarse with beauty gone,—
What use survives the beauty?" Fool!

Go, little girl with the poor coarse hand!
I have my lesson, shall understand.

IX —ON DECK

I

There is nothing to remember in me,
  Nothing I ever said with a grace,
Nothing I did that you care to see,
  Nothing I was that deserves a place
In your mind, now I leave you, set you free.

II

Conceded! In turn, concede to me,
  Such things have been as a mutual flame.
Your soul's locked fast; but, love for a key,
  You might let it loose, till I grew the same
In your eyes, as in mine you stand: strange plea!

III

For then, then, what would it matter to me
  That I was the harsh ill-favoured one?
We both should be like as pea and pea;
  It was ever so since the world begun:
So, let me proceed with my reverie.

330| *1868:* beauty? Fool!" *1888:* beauty?" Fool! 331| MS:girl, with *1868:* girl with 335| MS:cared *1868:* care 336| MS:Nothing I was, §last two words over illegible erasure§ that *P1864a:* was that 338| MS:Conceded! In §over illegible erasure§ 339| MS:flame: *P1864a:* flame. 340| MS:My soul's <> fast, but <> for your key, *P1864a:* Your soul's <> fast; but <> for a key, 341| MS:let §inserted above§ loose mine till *P1864a:* let it loose, till 344| MS:harsh, ill-favoured *1888:* harsh ill-favoured 345| MS:should turn like as—pea and pea! *P1864a:* should be like as pea and pea; 346| MS:begun, *P1864a:* begun: 347| MS:So,—let *P1864a:* So, let

IV

How strange it were if you had all me,
  As I have all you in my heart and brain,
You, whose least word brought gloom or glee,
  Who never lifted the hand in vain—
Will hold mine yet, from over the sea!

V

Strange, if a face, when you thought of me,
  Rose like your own face present now,
With eyes as dear in their due degree,
  Much such a mouth, and as bright a brow,
Till you saw yourself, while you cried " 'Tis She!"

VI

Well, you may, you must, set down to me
  Love that was life, life that was love;
A tenure of breath at your lips' decree,
  A passion to stand as your thoughts approve,
A rapture to fall where your foot might be.

VII

But did one touch of such love for me
  Come in a word or a look of yours,
Whose words and looks will, circling, flee
  Round me and round while life endures,—
Could I fancy "As I feel, thus feels he";

348| MS:me *P1864a:* me, 349| MS:brain,— *P1864a:* brain, 351| MS:vain *1888:* vain— 352| MS:Which §crossed out§ will still holds mine from <> sea. *P1864a:* Will hold mine yet, from <> sea! 356| MS:mouth and *P1864a:* mouth, and 357| MS:yourself while *P1864a:* yourself, while 358| MS:may, or §crossed out§ you *P1864a:* may, or you *1868:* may, you 359| MS:love, *P1864a:* love; 365| MS:and whose §inserted above and crossed out§ <> circling, free *P1864a:* circling, flee 367| MS:feels He,"— *P1864a:* feels He;" *1888:* feels he";

VIII

Why, fade you might to a thing like me,
    And your hair grow these coarse hanks of hair,
Your skin, this bark of a gnarled tree,—
    You might turn myself!—should I know or care
When I should be dead of joy, James Lee?

370| MS:And your skin *1868:* Your skin   371| MS:myself, I should know nor care, *P1864a:* myself; should I know or care, *1868:* myself!—should   372| MS:For I should <> Lee! *P1864a:* When I should <> Lee?

GOLD HAIR: A STORY OF PORNIC

I

Oh, the beautiful girl, too white,
    Who lived at Pornic, down by the sea,
Just where the sea and the Loire unite!
    And a boasted name in Brittany
She bore, which I will not write.

II

Too white, for the flower of life is red;
    Her flesh was the soft seraphic screen
Of a soul that is meant (her parents said)
    To just see earth, and hardly be seen,
And blossom in heaven instead.

III

Yet earth saw one thing, one how fair!
    One grace that grew to its full on earth:
Smiles might be sparse on her cheek so spare,
    And her waist want half a girdle's girth,
But she had her great gold hair.

IV

Hair, such a wonder of flix and floss,
    Freshness and fragrance—floods of it, too!
Gold, did I say? Nay, gold's mere dross:
    Here, Life smiled, "Think what I meant to do!"
And Love sighed, "Fancy my loss!"

GOLD HAIR *Title*| MS:Gold hair: / a Legend of Pornic. *1864a:*LEGEND §crossed out§ STORY §in R margin§ [2]| MS:at Pornic down *P1864a:*Pornic, down [6]| MS:white—for *P1864a:*white, for [7]| MS:soft, seraphic *1868:*soft seraphic [9]| MS:just §over illegible word§ [10]| MS:in Heaven *1868:*heaven [11]| MS:thing, and how *P1864a:*thing, one how [12]| MS:to the full *P1864a:*to its full [14]| MS:a §over illegible erasure§ [16]| MS:of gloom and gloss, *P1864a:*of flix and floss, [17]| MS:fragrance—heaps of *P1864a:*fragrance—floods of [18]| MS:dross— *P1864a:*dross: [19]| MS:smiled "Think *P1864a:*smiled, "Think [20]| MS:sighed "Fancy *P1864a:*sighed,"Fancy *1868:*sighed, "Fancy, my *C1870:*sighed, "Fancy my

V

So, when she died, it was scarce more strange
Than that, when delicate evening dies,
And you follow its spent sun's pallid range,
There's a shoot of colour startles the skies
With sudden, violent change,—

VI

That, while the breath was nearly to seek,
As they put the little cross to her lips,
She changed; a spot came out on her cheek,
A spark from her eye in mid-eclipse,
And she broke forth, "I must speak!"

VII

"Not my hair!" made the girl her moan—
"All the rest is gone or to go;
But the last, last grace, my all, my own,
Let it stay in the grave, that the ghosts may know!
Leave my poor gold hair alone!"

VIII

The passion thus vented, dead lay she;
Her parents sobbed their worst on that;
All friends joined in, nor observed degree:
For indeed the hair was to wonder at,
As it spread—not flowing free,

IX

But curled around her brow, like a crown,
And coiled beside her cheeks, like a cap,

21| MS:So when *P1864a:* So, when 22| MS:when some delicate <> dies *P1864a:* dies, *1888:* when delicate 26| MS:seek *P1864a:* seek, 28| MS:changed, a *P1864a:* changed; a 30| MS:forth "I *P1864a:* forth, "I 32| MS:go, *P1864a:* go; 35| MS:alone! *P1864a:* alone!" 36| MS:she: *P1864a:* she; 37| MS:worst at that, *P1864a:* worst on that, *1888:* that; 38| MS:in nor <> degree— *P1864a:* in, nor <> degree: 39| MS:at *P1864a:* at, 41| MS:brow like *P1864a:* brow, like 42| MS:cheeks like *P1864a:* cheeks, like

And calmed about her neck—ay, down
        To her breast, pressed flat, without a gap
I' the gold, it reached her gown.

X

All kissed that face, like a silver wedge
        Mid the yellow wealth, nor disturbed its hair:
E'en the priest allowed death's privilege,
        As he planted the crucifix with care
On her breast, 'twixt edge and edge.

XI

And thus was she buried, inviolate
        Of body and soul, in the very space
By the altar; keeping saintly state
        In Pornic church, for her pride of race,
Pure life and piteous fate.

XII

And in after-time would your fresh tear fall,
        Though your mouth might twitch with a dubious smile,
As they told you of gold, both robe and pall,
        How she prayed them leave it alone awhile,
So it never was touched at all.

XIII

Years flew; this legend grew at last
        The life of the lady; all she had done,
All been, in the memories fading fast

45| MS:In *P1864a:*I' 46| MS:kissed her face, like a fine white wedge *P1864a:*kissed that face, like a silver wedge 47| MS:In the <> disturbed that hair; *P1864a:*Mid the <> disturbed its hair; *1868:*hair: 48| MS:privilege *P1864a:*privilege, 50| MS:twixt *P1864a:*'twixt 51| MS:And so was she buried inviolate *P1864a:*And thus was she buried, inviolate 52| MS:soul in *P1864a:*soul, in 53| MS:altar, keeping *P1864a:*altar; keeping 55| MS:life, and *1868:*life and 56| MS:after time *P1864a:*after-time 58| MS:gold both <> pall— *P1864a:*pall, *1888:*gold, both 61| MS:Years came; this *P1864a:*Years flew; this 62| MS:lady—all *P1864a:*lady; all

Of lover and friend, was summed in one
Sentence survivors passed:

XIV

To wit, she was meant for heaven, not earth;
Had turned an angel before the time:
Yet, since she was mortal, in such dearth
Of frailty, all you could count a crime
Was—she knew her gold hair's worth.

XV

At little pleasant Pornic church,
It chanced, the pavement wanted repair,
Was taken to pieces: left in the lurch,
A certain sacred space lay bare,
And the boys began research.

XVI

'Twas the space where our sires would lay a saint,
A benefactor,—a bishop, suppose,
A baron with armour-adornments quaint,
Dame with chased ring and jewelled rose,
Things sanctity saves from taint;

64| MS:in §over illegible erasure§ 65| MS:passed— *P1864a:* passed: 66| MS:for Heaven not earth, *P1864a:* for Heaven, not earth; *1868:* for heaven, not 67| MS:And turned <> time, *P1864a:* Had turned <> time: 71| MS:In little *P1864a:* At little 73| MS:So §erased§ was §altered to§ Was 74| MS:A sacred space in the midst lay bare *P1864a:* A certain sacred space lay bare, 75| MS:Where the boys began their search. *P1864a:* And the boys began research. 77| *P1864a:* suppose; *1864a(r):* suppose; §altered to§ suppose, 78| *P1864a:* quaint; *1864a(r):* quaint; §altered to§ quaint, 79| MS:A dame with <> rose— *P1864a:* rose, *1868:* Dame with 80| MS:Things, sanctity <> taint— *P1864a:* Things sanctity <> taint: *1864a(r):* taint: §altered to§ taint;

XVII

So we come to find them in after-days
    When the corpse is presumed to have done with gauds
Of use to the living, in many ways:
    For the boys get pelf, and the town applauds,
And the church deserves the praise.

XVIII

They grubbed with a will: and at length—*O cor*
    Humanum, pectora cæca, and the rest!—
They found—no gaud they were prying for,
    No ring, no rose, but—who would have guessed?—
A double Louis-d'or!

XIX

Here was a case for the priest: he heard,
    Marked, inwardly digested, laid
Finger on nose, smiled, "There's a bird
    Chirps in my ear": then, "Bring a spade,
Dig deeper!"—he gave the word.

XX

And lo, when they came to the coffin-lid,
    Or rotten planks which composed it once,
Why, there lay the girl's skull wedged amid
    A mint of money, it served for the nonce
To hold in its hair-heaps hid!

83| MS:ways, *P1864a:* ways; *1864a(r):* ways; §altered to§ ways: 85| MS:church receives the *P1864a:* church deserves the 88| MS:found to §erased§ —no gauds *1868:* no gaud 89| MS:Nor §erased to read§ No 93| MS:nose, said "A little bird *P1864a:* nose, smiled, "A *1888:* smiled, "There's a bird 94| MS:ear:" and "Bring *P1864a:* ear:" then, "Bring *1888:* ear": then 96| *P1864a:* lo! when *1864a(r):* lo! §altered to§ lo, when 97| MS:Or the rotten planks which *1868:* Or rotten 100| MS:hid. *1864a(r):* hid. §altered to§ hid! 100–16| *1864a(r):* §three

XXI

Hid there? Why? Could the girl be wont
(She the stainless soul) to treasure up
Money, earth's trash and heaven's affront?
Had a spider found out the communion-cup,
Was a toad in the christening-font?

XXII

Truth is truth: too true it was.
Gold! She hoarded and hugged it first,
Longed for it, leaned o'er it, loved it—alas—
Till the humour grew to a head and burst,
And she cried, at the final pass,—

XXIII

"Talk not of God, my heart is stone!
Nor lover nor friend—be gold for both!
Gold I lack; and, my all, my own,
It shall hide in my hair. I scarce die loth
If they let my hair alone!"

XXIV

Louis-d'or, some six times five,
And duly double, every piece.
Now do you see? With the priest to shrive,
With parents preventing her soul's release
By kisses that kept alive,—

XXV

With heaven's gold gates about to ope,
With friends' praise, gold-like, lingering still,

---

stanzas added; see Editorial Notes§ 102| *1864a(r):*(She, the *1868:*(She the 103| *1864a(r):*and Heaven's *1868:*heaven's 110| *1864a(r):*final §above illegible erasure§ 116| MS:Louis-d'ors some *1864a:*Louis-d'ors, some <> five; *1864a(r):*five; §altered to§ five, *1888:*Louis-d'or 118| MS:Now, do *1888:*Now do 120| MS:keep *1864a(r):*keep §altered to§ kept 121| MS:With Heaven's *1868:*heaven's 122| MS:With Earth's praise *P1864a:*With friends' praise

An instinct had bidden the girl's hand grope
    For gold, the true sort—"Gold in heaven, if you will;
But I keep earth's too, I hope."

XXVI

Enough! The priest took the grave's grim yield:
    The parents, they eyed that price of sin
As if *thirty pieces* lay revealed
    On the place *to bury strangers in,*
The hideous Potter's Field.

XXVII

But the priest bethought him: " 'Milk that's spilt'
    —You know the adage! Watch and pray!
Saints tumble to earth with so slight a tilt!
    It would build a new altar; that, we may!"
And the altar therewith was built.

XXVIII

Why I deliver this horrible verse?
    As the text of a sermon, which now I preach:
Evil or good may be better or worse
    In the human heart, but the mixture of each
Is a marvel and a curse.

XXIX

The candid incline to surmise of late
    That the Christian faith proves false, I find;

123| MS:What *1864a(r):* An §*What* crossed out, *An* in L margin§ 124| MS:sort—"gold in Heaven, I hope, *P1864a:* sort—"Gold <> hope; *1864a(r):* in Heaven, if you will; *1868:* heaven 125| MS:keep this, if God will!" *P1864a:* keep earth's, if *1864a(r):* earth's too, I hope!" *1864b:* hope." 126| MS:Enough! §over illegible erasure§ 127| MS:parents—they *P1864a:* parents, they 131| MS:him—"Milk that's spilt *P1864a:* him: " 'Milk that's spilt' 134| MS:altar—that we *P1864a:* altar; that, we 135| MS:altar there with was §last three words over illegible erasure§ *P1864a:* therewith 135–36| MS:§space and rule called for in margin§ *1868:* §no rule§ 137| MS:which thus I *P1864a:* which now I 139| MS:human heart §over illegible erasure§ 141| MS:The public inclines to *P1864a:* The candid incline to 142| MS:faith may be false, I find, *P1864a:* find; *1888:* faith proves false

For our Essays-and-Reviews' debate
Begins to tell on the public mind,
And Colenso's words have weight:

XXX

I still, to suppose it true, for my part,
See reasons and reasons; this, to begin:
'Tis the faith that launched point-blank her dart
At the head of a lie—taught Original Sin,
The Corruption of Man's Heart.

144| MS:the candid mind, *P1864a:* the public mind, 146| MS:still must suppose *P1864a:* still, to suppose 147| MS:For reasons and reasons—this, to begin— *P1864a:* See reasons and reasons; this, to begin: 149| MS:the heart §crossed out and replaced above by§ head <> Taught *P1864a:* taught 150| MS:And §crossed out and replaced above by§ The <> man's heart. *P1864a:* of Man's Heart.

THE WORST OF IT

I

Would it were I had been false, not you!
    I that am nothing, not you that are all:
I, never the worse for a touch or two
    On my speckled hide; not you, the pride
Of the day, my swan, that a first fleck's fall
    On her wonder of white must unswan, undo!

II

I had dipped in life's struggle and, out again,
    Bore specks of it here, there, easy to see,
When I found my swan and the cure was plain;
    The dull turned bright as I caught your white
On my bosom: you saved me—saved in vain
    If you ruined yourself, and all through me!

III

Yes, all through the speckled beast that I am,
    Who taught you to stoop; you gave me yourself,
And bound your soul by the vows that damn:
    Since on better thought you break, as you ought,
Vows—words, no angel set down, some elf
    Mistook,—for an oath, an epigram!

IV

Yes, might I judge you, here were my heart,
    And a hundred its like, to treat as you pleased!
I choose to be yours, for my proper part,
    Yours, leave or take, or mar me or make;

THE WORST OF IT 2| MS:all,— *P1864a:* all: 3| MS:never §over illegible erasure§ 4| MS:hide, not you the *P1864a:* hide; not you, the 7| MS:struggle, was out *P1864a:* struggle, and out *1870:* struggle and, out 9| MS:plain, *P1864a:* plain; 14| MS:yourself: *P1864a:* yourself, 15| MS:damn— *P1864a:* damn: 17| MS:down—some *P1864a:* down, some 19| MS:heart *P1864a:* heart, 22| MS:make,— *P1864a:* make;

If I acquiesce, why should you be teased
With the conscience-prick and the memory-smart?

V

But what will God say? Oh, my sweet,
Think, and be sorry you did this thing!
Though earth were unworthy to feel your feet,
There's a heaven above may deserve your love:
Should you forfeit heaven for a snapt gold ring
And a promise broke, were it just or meet?

VI

And I to have tempted you! I, who tried
Your soul, no doubt, till it sank! Unwise,
I loved and was lowly, loved and aspired,
Loved, grieving or glad, till I made you mad,
And you meant to have hated and despised—
Whereas, you deceived me nor inquired!

VII

She, ruined? How? No heaven for her?
Crowns to give, and none for the brow
That looked like marble and smelt like myrrh?
Shall the robe be worn, and the palm-branch borne,
And she go graceless, she graced now
Beyond all saints, as themselves aver?

VIII

Hardly! That must be understood!
The earth is your place of penance, then;

26| MS:thing! *1888:* thing §emended to§ thing! §see Editorial Notes§
28| *P1864a:* a Heaven *1868:* heaven 29| *P1864a:* forfeit Heaven *1868:* heaven
31| MS:you—I *P1864a:* you! I 33| *P1864a:* loved, and was *C1870:* loved and was 34| MS:Was grieving or glad till *P1864a:* Loved, grieving or glad, till
37| MS:ruined? How—no *P1864a:* ruined? How? No Heaven *1868:* heaven
42| MS:saints as *P1864a:* saints, as 43| MS:must §over illegible erasure§

And what will it prove? I desire your good,
But, plot as I may, I can find no way
How a blow should fall, such as falls on men,
Nor prove too much for your womanhood.

IX

It will come, I suspect, at the end of life,
When you walk alone, and review the past;
And I, who so long shall have done with strife,
And journeyed my stage and earned my wage
And retired as was right,—I am called at last
When the devil stabs you, to lend the knife.

X

He stabs for the minute of trivial wrong,
Nor the other hours are able to save,
The happy, that lasted my whole life long:
For a promise broke, not for first words spoke,
The true, the only, that turn my grave
To a blaze of joy and a crash of song.

XI

Witness beforehand! Off I trip
On a safe path gay through the flowers you flung:
My very name made great by your lip,
And my heart a-glow with the good I know
Of a perfect year when we both were young,
And I tasted the angels' fellowship.

XII

And witness, moreover . . . Ah, but wait!
I spy the loop whence an arrow shoots!
It may be for yourself, when you meditate,

50| MS:alone and *P1864a:* alone, and 52| MS:wage, *P1864a:* stage, and *1868:* stage and <> wage 57| MS:happy that <> long! *P1864a:* happy, that <> long: 60| MS:song! *P1864a:* song. 62| MS:safe §over illegible erasure§ 67| MS:witness moreover . . ah *P1864a:* witness, moreover . . . Ah

That you grieve—for slain ruth, murdered truth.
"Though falsehood escape in the end, what boots?
        How truth would have triumphed!"—you sigh too late.

XIII

Ay, who would have triumphed like you, I say!
        Well, it is lost now; well, you must bear,
Abide and grow fit for a better day:
        You should hardly grudge, could I be your judge!
But hush! For you, can be no despair:
        There's amends: 'tis a secret: hope and pray!

XIV

For I was true at least—oh, true enough!
        And, Dear, truth is not as good as it seems!
Commend me to conscience! Idle stuff!
        Much help is in mine, as I mope and pine,
And skulk through day, and scowl in my dreams
        At my swan's obtaining the crow's rebuff.

XV

Men tell me of truth now—"False!" I cry:
        Of beauty—"A mask, friend! Look beneath!"
We take our own method, the devil and I,
        With pleasant and fair and wise and rare:
And the best we wish to what lives, is—death;
        Which even in wishing, perhaps we lie!

XVI

Far better commit a fault and have done—
        As you, Dear!—for ever; and choose the pure,
And look where the healing waters run,
        And strive and strain to be good again,

70| MS:truth— *P1864a:* truth: *1888:* truth DC,BrU:truth. *1889:* truth. 75| MS:Or bide and *P1864a:* Abide and 80| MS:dear *1870:* And, Dear 86| MS:—Of <> friend—look *P1864a:* Of <> friend! Look 88| MS:rare— *P1864a:* rare: 89| MS:death— *P1864a:* death; 92| MS:dear!—for ever—and

And a place in the other world ensure,
All glass and gold, with God for its sun.

XVII

Misery! What shall I say or do?
I cannot advise, or, at least, persuade:
Most like, you are glad you deceived me—rue
No whit of the wrong: you endured too long,
Have done no evil and want no aid,
Will live the old life out and chance the new.

XVIII

And your sentence is written all the same,
And I can do nothing,—pray, perhaps:
But somehow the world pursues its game,—
If I pray, if I curse,—for better or worse:
And my faith is torn to a thousand scraps,
And my heart feels ice while my words breathe flame.

XIX

Dear, I look from my hiding-place.
Are you still so fair? Have you still the eyes?
Be happy! Add but the other grace,
Be good! Why want what the angels vaunt?
I knew you once: but in Paradise,
If we meet, I will pass nor turn my face.

P1864a: ever; and *1870:* you, Dear 95| *P1864a:* insure, *1868:* ensure,
100| MS:long— *P1864a:* long, 105| MS:game, *1870:* game,—
106| MS:worse,— *P1864a:* worse: 113| MS:in Paradise *P1864a:* in Paradise,

DÎS ALITER VISUM; OR, LE BYRON DE NOS JOURS

I

Stop, let me have the truth of that!
Is that all true? I say, the day
Ten years ago when both of us
Met on a morning, friends—as thus
We meet this evening, friends or what?—

II

Did you—because I took your arm
And sillily smiled, "A mass of brass
That sea looks, blazing underneath!"
While up the cliff-road edged with heath,
We took the turns nor came to harm—

III

Did you consider "Now makes twice
That I have seen her, walked and talked
With this poor pretty thoughtful thing,
Whose worth I weigh: she tries to sing;
Draws, hopes in time the eye grows nice;

IV

"Reads verse and thinks she understands;
Loves all, at any rate, that's great,
Good, beautiful; but much as we
Down at the bath-house love the sea,
Who breathe its salt and bruise its sands:

DÎS ALITER VISUM; OR, LE BYRON DE NOS JOURS *Title*| MS:visum: or *P1864a: VISUM; OR* [8]| MS:underneath"! *P1864a:* underneath!" [9]| MS:heath *P1864a:* heath, [13]| MS:thing *P1864a:* thing, [14]| MS:sing, *P1864a:* sing; [15]| MS:nice,— *P1864a:* nice; [16]| MS:understands, *P1864a:* understands; [18]| MS:beautiful—but *P1864a:* beautiful; but [19]| the Bath-house *1868:* bath-house [20]| MS:sands— *P1864a:* sands:

V

"While . . . do but follow the fishing-gull
That flaps and floats from wave to cave!
There's the sea-lover, fair my friend!
What then? Be patient, mark and mend!
Had you the making of your scull?"

VI

And did you, when we faced the church
With spire and sad slate roof, aloof
From human fellowship so far,
Where a few graveyard crosses are,
And garlands for the swallows' perch,—

VII

Did you determine, as we stepped
O'er the lone stone fence, "Let me get
Her for myself, and what's the earth
With all its art, verse, music, worth—
Compared with love, found, gained, and kept?

VIII

"Schumann's our music-maker now;
Has his march-movement youth and mouth?
Ingres's the modern man that paints;
Which will lean on me, of his saints?
Heine for songs; for kisses, how?"

IX

And did you, when we entered, reached
The votive frigate, soft aloft
Riding on air this hundred years,

21| MS:While . . do *1888:* While . . . do 25| MS:scull? *P1864a:* scull?"
26| MS:—And *P1864a:* And 31| MS:determine . . §altered to§ determine, as
35| MS:gained and *P1864a:* gained, and 40| MS:songs! For *P1864a:* songs; for

Safe-smiling at old hopes and fears,—
Did you draw profit while she preached?

X

Resolving, "Fools we wise men grow!
Yes, I could easily blurt out curt
Some question that might find reply
As prompt in her stopped lips, dropped eye,
And rush of red to cheek and brow:

XI

"Thus were a match made, sure and fast,
'Mid the blue weed-flowers round the mound
Where, issuing, we shall stand and stay
For one more look at baths and bay,
Sands, sea-gulls, and the old church last—

XII

"A match 'twixt me, bent, wigged and lamed,
Famous, however, for verse and worse,
Sure of the Fortieth spare Arm-chair
When gout and glory seat me there,
So, one whose love-freaks pass unblamed,—

XIII

"And this young beauty, round and sound
As a mountain-apple, youth and truth
With loves and doves, at all events
With money in the Three per Cents;
Whose choice of me would seem profound:—

44| MS:fears, *P1864a:* fears,— 45| MS:—Did *P1864a:* Did 46| MS:Resolving "Fools *P1864a:* Resolving, "Fools 51| MS:So were *P1864a:* Thus were 54| MS:at Baths *1868:* baths 56| *P1864a:* wigged, and *1868:* wigged and 57| MS:however, through verse *P1864a:* however, for verse 58| MS:arm-chair *P1864a:* spare Arm-chair 59| MS:there,— *P1864a:* there, 60| MS:unblamed— *P1864a:* unblamed,— 63| MS:doves,—at *P1864a:* doves, at 64| MS:per cents,— *P1864a:* per Cents; 65| MS:profound;— *P1864a:* profound:—

XIV

"She might take me as I take her.
Perfect the hour would pass, alas!
Climb high, love high, what matter? Still,
Feet, feelings, must descend the hill:
An hour's perfection can't recur.

XV

"Then follows Paris and full time
For both to reason: 'Thus with us!'
She'll sigh, 'Thus girls give body and soul
At first word, think they gain the goal,
When 'tis the starting-place they climb!

XVI

" 'My friend makes verse and gets renown;
Have they all fifty years, his peers?
He knows the world, firm, quiet and gay;
Boys will become as much one day:
They're fools; he cheats, with beard less brown.

XVII

" 'For boys say, *Love me or I die!*
He did not say, *The truth is, youth*
I want, who am old and know too much;
I'd catch youth: lend me sight and touch!
Drop heart's blood where life's wheels grate dry!'

66| MS:her, *P1864a:* her. 69| MS:hill— *P1864a:* hill: 72| MS:reason: "Thus with us!" *P1864a:* reason: 'Thus with us!' 73| MS:sigh, "So girls *P1864a:* sigh, 'Thus girls 74| MS:word—think *P1864a:* word, think 78| *P1864a:* quiet, and *1868:* quiet and 81| MS:"For boys say 'Love me or I die!' *P1864a:* " 'For boys say, *Love me or I die!* 82| MS:say 'The truth is, youth *P1864a:* say, *The truth is, youth* 83-85| MS:§no italics called for§ *P1864a:* §italic type§ 83| MS:much,— *P1864a: much;* 85| MS:dry!' *P1864a: dry! 1889: dry!* §emended to§ *dry!'* §see Editorial Notes§

XVIII

"While I should make rejoinder"—(then
It was, no doubt, you ceased that least
Light pressure of my arm in yours)
" 'I can conceive of cheaper cures
For a yawning-fit o'er books and men.

XIX

" 'What? All I am, was, and might be,
All, books taught, art brought, life's whole strife,
Painful results since precious, just
Were fitly exchanged, in wise disgust,
For two cheeks freshened by youth and sea?

XX

" 'All for a nosegay!—what came first;
With fields on flower, untried each side;
I rally, need my books and men,
And find a nosegay': drop it, then,
No match yet made for best or worst!"

XXI

That ended me. You judged the porch
We left by, Norman; took our look
At sea and sky; wondered so few
Find out the place for air and view;
Remarked the sun began to scorch;

89| MS:"I *P1864a:*" 'I 90| MS:men! *P1864a:*men. 93| MS:precious—just *P1864a:*precious, just 94| MS:Were a fit exchange in wise digust *P1864a:*Were fitly exchanged in *1868:*exchanged, in <> digust, 96| MS:first! *P1864a:*first; 97| MS:side! *P1864a:*side; 99| MS:nosegay: drop <> then! *P1864a:*then, *1868:*nosegay:' drop *1888:*nosegay': drop 100| *P1864a:*worst!' " *1868:*worst!" 101| MS:me! You *P1864a:*me. You 104| MS:Found out *P1864a:*Find out

XXII

Descended, soon regained the baths,
    And then, good-bye! Years ten since then:
Ten years! We meet: you tell me, now,
    By a window-seat for that cliff-brow,
On carpet-stripes for those sand-paths.

XXIII

Now I may speak: you fool, for all
    Your lore! WHO made things plain in vain?
What was the sea for? What, the grey
    Sad church, that solitary day,
Crosses and graves and swallows' call?

XXIV

Was there nought better than to enjoy?
    No feat which, done, would make time break,
And let us pent-up creatures through
    Into eternity, our due?
No forcing earth teach heaven's employ?

XXV

No wise beginning, here and now,
    What cannot grow complete (earth's feat)
And heaven must finish, there and then?
    No tasting earth's true food for men,
Its sweet in sad, its sad in sweet?

106| MS:the Baths, *1868:*baths, 107| MS:And so, good bye <> then— *P1864a:*And then, good <> then: *1870:*good-bye 108| MS:now,— *P1864a:*now,
117| MS:break *P1864a:*break, 120| MS:teach Heavens *P1864a:*teach Heaven's *1868:*heaven's 122| MS:complete—earth's feat— *P1864a:*complete (earth's feat)
123| MS:So Heaven must finish there *P1864a:*And Heaven must finish, there *1868:*heaven
125| MS:Her sweet in sad, her sad *P1864a:*Its sweet in sad, its sad

XXVI

No grasping at love, gaining a share
    O' the sole spark from God's life at strife
With death, so, sure of range above
    The limits here? For us and love,
Failure; but, when God fails, despair.

XXVII

This you call wisdom? Thus you add
    Good unto good again, in vain?
You loved, with body worn and weak;
    I loved, with faculties to seek:
Were both loves worthless since ill-clad?

XXVIII

Let the mere star-fish in his vault
    Crawl in a wash of weed, indeed,
Rose-jacynth to the finger-tips:
    He, whole in body and soul, outstrips
Man, found with either in default.

XXIX

But what's whole, can increase no more,
    Is dwarfed and dies, since here's its sphere.
The devil laughed at you in his sleeve!
    You knew not? That I well believe;
Or you had saved two souls: nay, four.

126| MS:love—gaining *P1864a:* love, gaining   127| MS:Of *P1864a:* O'   128| MS:death,—so, sure *P1864a:* death, so, sure   129| MS:limits now: for <> love *P1864a:* limits here? For <> love,   130| MS:Failure!—but *P1864a:* Failure; but   131| MS:call progress? Thus *P1864a:* call wisdom? Thus   133| MS:weak— *P1864a:* weak;   134| MS:seek— *P1864a:* seek: 135| MS:Both loves worth nothing since ill-clad! *P1864a:* Were both loves worthless since ill-clad?   141| MS:What's whole now, can *P1864a:* But what's whole, can   142| MS:Dies or is dwarfed, since <> sphere: *P1864a:* Is dwarfed and dies, since <> sphere.   144| MS:not? That, I well believe— *P1864a:* believe; *1868:* not? That I   145| MS:souls—nay, four— *P1864a:* souls: nay, four.

XXX

For Stephanie sprained last night her wrist,
    Ankle or something. "Pooh," cry you?
At any rate she danced, all say,
    Vilely; her vogue has had its day.
Here comes my husband from his whist.

147| MS:Ancle or something: "Pooh," cry *P1864a:* Ancle, or something. "Pooh," cry *1868:* Ankle 149| MS:Vilely: her <> day! *P1864a:* day. *1868:* Vilely; her 150| MS:my Husband *P1864a:* husband

TOO LATE

I

Here was I with my arm and heart
    And brain, all yours for a word, a want
Put into a look—just a look, your part,—
    While mine, to repay it . . . vainest vaunt,
Were the woman, that's dead, alive to hear,
    Had her lover, that's lost, love's proof to show!
But I cannot show it; you cannot speak
    From the churchyard neither, miles removed,
Though I feel by a pulse within my cheek,
    Which stabs and stops, that the woman I loved
Needs help in her grave and finds none near,
    Wants warmth from the heart which sends it—so!

II

Did I speak once angrily, all the drear days
    You lived, you woman I loved so well,
Who married the other? Blame or praise,
    Where was the use then? Time would tell,
And the end declare what man for you,
    What woman for me, was the choice of God.
But, Edith dead! no doubting more!
    I used to sit and look at my life
As it rippled and ran till, right before,
    A great stone stopped it: oh, the strife
Of waves at the stone some devil threw
    In my life's midcurrent, thwarting God!

III

But either I thought, "They may churn and chide
    Awhile, my waves which came for their joy

TOO LATE 2| MS:brain—all *P1864a:*brain, all 7| MS:it—you *P1864a:*it; you 18| MS:me was *1888:*me, was 19| MS:dead! No *P1864a:*no 23| MS:at that stone *1868:*at the stone 25| MS:thought "They *P1864a:*thought, "They 26| MS:Awhile, my §over illegible erasure§

And found this horrible stone full-tide:
    Yet I see just a thread escape, deploy
Through the evening-country, silent and safe,
    And it suffers no more till it finds the sea."
Or else I would think, "Perhaps some night
    When new things happen, a meteor-ball
May slip through the sky in a line of light,
    And earth breathe hard, and landmarks fall,
And my waves no longer champ nor chafe,
    Since a stone will have rolled from its place: let be!"

IV

But, dead! All's done with: wait who may,
    Watch and wear and wonder who will.
Oh, my whole life that ends to-day!
    Oh, my soul's sentence, sounding still,
"The woman is dead that was none of his;
    And the man that was none of hers may go!"
There's only the past left: worry that!
    Wreak, like a bull, on the empty coat,
Rage, its late wearer is laughing at!
    Tear the collar to rags, having missed his throat;
Strike stupidly on—"This, this and this,
    Where I would that a bosom received the blow!"

V

I ought to have done more: once my speech,
    And once your answer, and there, the end,
And Edith was henceforth out of reach!
    Why, men do more to deserve a friend,
Be rid of a foe, get rich, grow wise,
    Nor, folding their arms, stare fate in the face.
Why, better even have burst like a thief

31| MS:think "Perhaps *P1864a:* think, "Perhaps 36| *1870:* be!' *1875:* be!" 38| MS:will! *P1864a:* will. 41| MS:his— *P1864a:* his; 42| MS:hers, may *1888:* hers may 43| MS:the Past *P1864a:* past 46| MS:throat— *P1864a:* throat; 47| MS:on "This, this and this— *P1864a:* on—"This, this and this, 50| MS:once her answer, and so, the *P1864a:* once your answer, and there, the 52| MS:friend *P1864a:* friend, 55| MS:And better *P1864a:* Why, better

And borne you away to a rock for us two,
In a moment's horror, bright, bloody and brief:
Then changed to myself again—"I slew
Myself in that moment; a ruffian lies
Somewhere: your slave, see, born in his place!"

VI

What did the other do? You be judge!
Look at us, Edith! Here are we both!
Give him his six whole years: I grudge
None of the life with you, nay, loathe
Myself that I grudged his start in advance
Of me who could overtake and pass.
But, as if he loved you! No, not he,
Nor anyone else in the world, 'tis plain:
Who ever heard that another, free
As I, young, prosperous, sound and sane,
Poured life out, proffered it—"Half a glance
Of those eyes of yours and I drop the glass!"

VII

Handsome, were you? 'Tis more than they held,
More than they said; I was 'ware and watched:
I was the 'scapegrace, this rat belled
The cat, this fool got his whiskers scratched:
The others? No head that was turned, no heart
Broken, my lady, assure yourself!
Each soon made his mind up; so and so
Married a dancer, such and such
Stole his friend's wife, stagnated slow,

56| MS:borne her away <> two *P1864a:* borne you away *1868:* two, 57| MS:brief, *1888:* brief: 59| MS:moment—a *P1864a:* moment; a 60| MS:Somewhere—your *P1864a:* Somewhere: your 61| MS:do? Let her judge! *P1864a:* do? You be judge! 64| MS:you—nay, I loathe *P1864a:* you, nay *1888:* nay, loathe 66| MS:pass! *P1864a:* pass. 71| MS:Poured his life out, proffered §last two words over illegible erasures§ *P1864a:* Poured life 73| MS:held— *P1864a:* held, 74| MS:said,—I *P1864a:* said; I 75| MS:'scapegrace—this *P1864a:* 'scapegrace, this 76| MS:scratched! *P1864a:* scratched: 79| MS:up—so *P1864a:* up; so 81| MS:slow— *P1864a:* slow,

Or maundered, unable to do as much,
And muttered of peace where he had no part:
While, hid in the closet, laid on the shelf,—

VIII

On the whole, you were let alone, I think!
So, you looked to the other, who acquiesced;
My rival, the proud man,—prize your pink
Of poets! A poet he was! I've guessed:
He rhymed you his rubbish nobody read,
Loved you and doved you—did not I laugh!
There was a prize! But we both were tried.
Oh, heart of mine, marked broad with her mark,
Tekel, found wanting, set aside,
Scorned! See, I bleed these tears in the dark
Till comfort come and the last be bled:
He? He is tagging your epitaph.

IX

If it would only come over again!
—Time to be patient with me, and probe
This heart till you punctured the proper vein,
Just to learn what blood is: twitch the robe
From that blank lay-figure your fancy draped,
Prick the leathern heart till the—verses spirt!
And late it was easy; late, you walked
Where a friend might meet you; Edith's name
Arose to one's lip if one laughed or talked;
If I heard good news, you heard the same;
When I woke, I knew that your breath escaped;
I could bide my time, keep alive, alert.

X

And alive I shall keep and long, you will see!
I knew a man, was kicked like a dog

84| MS:Thus, hid *P1864a:* While, hid 86| MS:And you <> acquiesced— *P1864a:* So, you <> acquiesced; 91| *1868:* tried *1870:* tried.

From gutter to cesspool; what cared he
    So long as he picked from the filth his prog?
He saw youth, beauty and genius die,
    And jollily lived to his hundredth year.
But I will live otherwise: none of such life!
    At once I begin as I mean to end.
Go on with the world, get gold in its strife,
    Give your spouse the slip and betray your friend!
There are two who decline, a woman and I,
    And enjoy our death in the darkness here.

XI

I liked that way you had with your curls
    Wound to a ball in a net behind:
Your cheek was chaste as a quaker-girl's,
    And your mouth—there was never, to my mind,
Such a funny mouth, for it would not shut;
    And the dented chin too—what a chin!
There were certain ways when you spoke, some words
    That you know you never could pronounce:
You were thin, however; like a bird's
    Your hand seemed—some would say, the pounce
Of a scaly-footed hawk—all but!
    The world was right when it called you thin.

XII

But I turn my back on the world: I take
    Your hand, and kneel, and lay to my lips.
Bid me live, Edith! Let me slake
    Thirst at your presence! Fear no slips:

111| MS:cess-pool—what *P1864a:* cesspool; what 113| *P1864a:* beauty, and *1868:* beauty and 116| MS:For here I *P1864a:* At once I 118| MS:your wife the slip, and *CP1864a:* your wife §crossed out and replaced above by§ spouse *1868:* slip and 125| MS:shut— *P1864a:* shut; 126| MS:chin, too *1868:* chin too 127| MS:spoke—some *P1864a:* spoke, some 129| MS:however—like *P1864a:* however; like 130| *1870:* pounce, *C1870:* pounce 134| MS:lips: *P1864a:* lips. 136| MS:My thirst at <> slips— *P1864a:* Thirst at <> slips! *1888:* slips:

'Tis your slave shall pay, while his soul endures,
    Full due, love's whole debt, *summum jus.*
My queen shall have high observance, planned
    Courtship made perfect, no least line
Crossed without warrant. There you stand,
    Warm too, and white too: would this wine
Had washed all over that body of yours,
    Ere I drank it, and you down with it, thus!

138| MS:dues *CP1864a:* dues §altered to§ due 142| MS:Warm, too, and white, too *P1864a:* Warm too, and white too

ABT VOGLER

(AFTER HE HAS BEEN EXTEMPORIZING UPON THE MUSICAL INSTRUMENT OF HIS INVENTION.)

I

Would that the structure brave, the manifold music I build,
    Bidding my organ obey, calling its keys to their work,
Claiming each slave of the sound, at a touch, as when Solomon willed
    Armies of angels that soar, legions of demons that lurk,
Man, brute, reptile, fly,—alien of end and of aim,
    Adverse, each from the other heaven-high, hell-deep removed,—
Should rush into sight at once as he named the ineffable Name,
    And pile him a palace straight, to pleasure the princess he loved!

II

Would it might tarry like his, the beautiful building of mine,
    This which my keys in a crowd pressed and importuned to raise!
Ah, one and all, how they helped, would dispart now and now combine,
    Zealous to hasten the work, heighten their master his praise!
And one would bury his brow with a blind plunge down to hell,
    Burrow awhile and build, broad on the roots of things,
Then up again swim into sight, having based me my palace well,
    Founded it, fearless of flame, flat on the nether springs.

III

And another would mount and march, like the excellent minion he was,

---

ABT VOGLER *Subtitle*| MS:(after extemporising upon the musical instrument of his invention.) *P1864a:*(AFTER HE HAS BEEN EXTEMPORIZING
3| MS:touch—as *P1864a:*touch, as 10| MS:which the keys *P1864a:*which my keys 11| MS:helped—would *P1864a:*helped, would

Ay, another and yet another, one crowd but with many a crest,
Raising my rampired walls of gold as transparent as glass,
Eager to do and die, yield each his place to the rest:
For higher still and higher (as a runner tips with fire,
When a great illumination surprises a festal night—
Outlining round and round Rome's dome from space to spire)
Up, the pinnacled glory reached, and the pride of my soul was in sight.

IV

In sight? Not half! for it seemed, it was certain, to match man's birth,
Nature in turn conceived, obeying an impulse as I;
And the emulous heaven yearned down, made effort to reach the earth,
As the earth had done her best, in my passion, to scale the sky:
Novel splendours burst forth, grew familiar and dwelt with mine,
Not a point nor peak but found and fixed its wandering star;
Meteor-moons, balls of blaze: and they did not pale nor pine,
For earth had attained to heaven, there was no more near nor far.

V

Nay more; for there wanted not who walked in the glare and glow,
Presences plain in the place; or, fresh from the Protoplast,

19| MS:glass *P1864a:*glass, 21| MS:higher, as <> fire *P1864a:*higher (as <> fire, 22| MS:—When *P1864a:*When 23| MS:spire, *P1864a:*spire) 25| MS:half!—for <> Man's *P1864a:*half! for <> man's 26| MS:as I, *P1864a:*as I; 27| MS:emulous Heaven *P1864a:*heaven 28| MS:passion to *P1864a:*passion, to 29| MS:splendors burst §over illegible erasure§ *1864a:*splendours 30| MS:star— *P1864a:*star; 31| blaze, and *P1864a:*blaze: and 32| MS:to Heaven *P1864a:*heaven 33| MS:more—for *P1864a:*more; for 34| MS:place—or *P1864a:*place; or

Furnished for ages to come, when a kindlier wind should blow,
Lured now to begin and live, in a house to their liking at last;
Or else the wonderful Dead who have passed through the body and gone,
But were back once more to breathe in an old world worth their new:
What never had been, was now; what was, as it shall be anon;
And what is,—shall I say, matched both? for I was made perfect too.

VI

All through my keys that gave their sounds to a wish of my soul,
All through my soul that praised as its wish flowed visibly forth,
All through music and me! For think, had I painted the whole,
Why, there it had stood, to see, nor the process so wonder-worth:
Had I written the same, made verse—still, effect proceeds from cause,
Ye know why the forms are fair, ye hear how the tale is told;
It is all triumphant art, but art in obedience to laws,
Painter and poet are proud in the artist-list enrolled:—

VII

But here is the finger of God, a flash of the will that can,
Existent behind all laws, that made them and, lo, they are!

38| MS:new; *P1864a:* new: 39| MS:now,—what <> anon, *P1864a:* now; what <> anon; 40| MS:is,—shall I say, §last four words over illegible erasure§ §two words illegibly erased and placed above by§ matched both? 41| MS:through these keys *P1864a:* through my keys 42| MS:And through §inserted above§ my <> praised the while §last two words crossed out and replaced above by§ as *P1864a:* All through 43| MS:me!—for *P1864a:* me! For 46| MS:told, *P1864a:* told; 47| MS:triumphant art §over illegible erasure§ but art §over illegible erasure§ *P1864a:* triumphant art, but 49| MS:of God—a flash §over illegible word§ *P1864a:* of God, a 50| MS:and, there §crossed out and replaced above by§ lo,

And I know not if, save in this, such gift be allowed to man,
    That out of three sounds he frame, not a fourth sound, but a
      star.
Consider it well: each tone of our scale in itself is nought;
    It is everywhere in the world—loud, soft, and all is said:
Give it to me to use! I mix it with two in my thought:
    And, there! Ye have heard and seen: consider and bow the
      head!

VIII

Well, it is gone at last, the palace of music I reared;
    Gone! and the good tears start, the praises that come too
      slow;
For one is assured at first, one scarce can say that he feared,
    That he even gave it a thought, the gone thing was to go.
Never to be again! But many more of the kind
    As good, nay, better perchance: is this your comfort to me?
To me, who must be saved because I cling with my mind
    To the same, same self, same love, same God: ay, what was,
      shall be.

IX

Therefore to whom turn I but to thee, the ineffable Name?
    Builder and maker, thou, of houses not made with hands!
What, have fear of change from thee who art ever the same?
    Doubt that thy power can fill the heart that thy power
      expands?

51| MS:man *P1864a:* man, 52| MS:frames §over illegible erasure§ —not <> star: *P1864a:* frame, not <> star. 53| MS:well—each tone of our §last three words over illegible erasure§ <> nought— *P1864a:* well: each <> nought; 55| MS:thought— *P1864a:* thought; *1868:* thought *1870:* thoughts *C1870:* thought *1888:* thought: 57| MS:reared— *P1864a:* reared; 59| MS:first—one *P1864a:* first, one 60| MS:it thought that the gone <> go: *P1864a:* it a thought, the gone <> go. 61| MS:kind, *P1864a:* kind 63| MS:who hope to §last two words crossed out and replaced above by one word§ shall be *P1864a:* who must be 64| MS:same God: for, §inserted above§ what was once §erased and replaced by comma§ shall *P1864a:* same God: ay, what 65| MS:to Thee *1868:* thee 66| MS:maker, Thou, of houses §over illegible erasure§ *P1864a:* thou 67| MS:from Thee *1868:* thee 68| MS:that Thy <> Thy *1888:* thy <> thy

There shall never be one lost good! What was, shall live as before;
The evil is null, is nought, is silence implying sound;
What was good shall be good, with, for evil, so much good more;
On the earth the broken arcs; in the heaven, a perfect round.

X

All we have willed or hoped or dreamed of good shall exist;
Not its semblance, but itself; no beauty, nor good, nor power
Whose voice has gone forth, but each survives for the melodist
When eternity affirms the conception of an hour.
The high that proved too high, the heroic for earth too hard,
The passion that left the ground to lose itself in the sky,
Are music sent up to God by the lover and the bard;
Enough that he heard it once: we shall hear it by-and-by.

XI

And what is our failure here but a triumph's evidence
For the fulness of the days? Have we withered or agonized?
Why else was the pause prolonged but that singing might issue thence?
Why rushed the discords in but that harmony should be prized?

69| MS:shall be as before, *P1864a:*shall live as before; 70| MS:evil is null, is §last two words inserted above§ nought—defeated the §last two words crossed out and replaced above by§ is silence *P1864a:*nought, is 71| MS:was good, shall be good,—with, for <> more, *P1864a:*be good, with, for <> more; *1888:*was good shall 72| MS:On §over perhaps *O'er*§ the earth <> arcs, in the Heaven *P1864a:*arcs; in the heaven
73| MS:have hoped or willed or <> good, shall exist— *P1864a:*have willed or hoped or <> exist; *1888:*good shall 74| MS:its likeness, but itself: no *1864a:*its semblance, but <> good, power *1864a(r):*good, power §*nor* in R margin, marked for insertion before *power*§ 75| MS:but still shall §crossed out§ survives *P1864a:*but each survives
76| MS:When Eternity *P1864a:*eternity 77| MS:The High <> Heroic *P1864a:*The high <> heroic 79| MS:Are the §crossed out§ music 80| MS:that He heard them §crossed out and replaced above by§ it once; we <> hear them §crossed out and replaced above by§ it by and by. *P1864a:*once: we <> it by-and-by. *1868:*he
81| MS:For what *P1864a:*And what 82| MS:In the *P1864a:*For the
83| MS:Will, §crossed out§ Why else §inserted above§ 84| MS:in, but *1888:*in but

Sorrow is hard to bear, and doubt is slow to clear,
    Each sufferer says his say, his scheme of the weal and woe:
But God has a few of us whom he whispers in the ear;
    The rest may reason and welcome: 'tis we musicians know.

XII

Well, it is earth with me; silence resumes her reign:
    I will be patient and proud, and soberly acquiesce.
Give me the keys. I feel for the common chord again,
    Sliding by semitones, till I sink to the minor,—yes
And I blunt it into a ninth, and I stand on alien ground,
    Surveying awhile the heights I rolled from into the deep;
Which, hark, I have dared and done, for my resting-place is
        found,
    The C Major of this life: so, now I will try to sleep.

86| MS:sufferer says §over illegible erasure§ his <> woe,— *P1864a:* woe:
87| MS:whom He *1868:* he 89| MS:reign; *P1864a:* reign: 90| MS:acquiesce: *P1864a:* acquiesce. 91| MS:keys—I *P1864a:* keys. I 92| MS:Sliding §over illegible erasure§ by <> I sink §over illegible erasure§ 94| MS:deep *P1864a:* deep;
95| MS:—Which, see, I <> done—for *P1864a:* Which, hark, I <> done, for

RABBI BEN EZRA

I

Grow old along with me!
The best is yet to be,
The last of life, for which the first was made:
Our times are in His hand
Who saith "A whole I planned,
Youth shows but half; trust God: see all nor be afraid!"

II

Not that, amassing flowers,
Youth sighed "Which rose make ours,
Which lily leave and then as best recall?"
Not that, admiring stars,
It yearned "Nor Jove, nor Mars;
Mine be some figured flame which blends, transcends them all!"

III

Not for such hopes and fears
Annulling youth's brief years,
Do I remonstrate: folly wide the mark!
Rather I prize the doubt
Low kinds exist without,
Finished and finite clods, untroubled by a spark.

IV

Poor vaunt of life indeed,
Were man but formed to feed
On joy, to solely seek and find and feast:

RABBI BEN EZRA [5]| MS:planned— *P1864a:* planned, [6]| MS:half: trust <> all, nor *P1864a:* half; trust *1888:* all nor [7]| MS:flowers *P1864a:* flowers, [8]| *1870:* ours *C1870:* ours, [10]| MS:stars *P1864a:* stars, [11]| MS:nor Mars— *1864a:* nor Mars; [14]| MS:years *P1864a:* years, [15]| MS:remonstrate—folly *P1864a:* remonstrate: folly [19]| MS:indeed *P1864a:* indeed,

Such feasting ended, then
As sure an end to men;
Irks care the crop-full bird? Frets doubt the maw-crammed beast?

V

Rejoice we are allied
To That which doth provide
And not partake, effect and not receive!
A spark disturbs our clod;
Nearer we hold of God
Who gives, than of His tribes that take, I must believe.

VI

Then, welcome each rebuff
That turns earth's smoothness rough,
Each sting that bids nor sit nor stand but go!
Be our joys three-parts pain!
Strive, and hold cheap the strain;
Learn, nor account the pang; dare, never grudge the throe!

VII

For thence,—a paradox
Which comforts while it mocks,—
Shall life succeed in that it seems to fail:
What I aspired to be,
And was not, comforts me:
A brute I might have been, but would not sink i' the scale.

VIII

What is he but a brute
Whose flesh has soul to suit,
Whose spirit works lest arms and legs want play?

23| MS:men: *P1864a:* men; 24| MS:crop full *P1864a:* crop-full 34| MS:three parts *P1864a:* three-parts 43| MS:brute, *P1864a:* brute 44| MS:hath *1888:* has

To man, propose this test—
Thy body at its best,
How far can that project thy soul on its lone way?

IX

Yet gifts should prove their use:
I own the Past profuse
Of power each side, perfection every turn:
Eyes, ears took in their dole,
Brain treasured up the whole;
Should not the heart beat once "How good to live and learn?"

X

Not once beat "Praise be Thine!
I see the whole design,
I, who saw power, see now love perfect too:
Perfect I call Thy plan:
Thanks that I was a man!
Maker, remake, complete,—I trust what Thou shalt do!"

XI

For pleasant is this flesh;
Our soul, in its rose-mesh
Pulled ever to the earth, still yearns for rest;
Would we some prize might hold
To match those manifold
Possessions of the brute,—gain most, as we did best!

XII

Let us not always say
"Spite of this flesh to-day
I strove, made head, gained ground upon the whole!"

51| MS:side, perfection §over *of*§ 52| MS:in the §altered to§ their 53| MS:whole, *P1864a:* whole; 57| MS:saw Power, shall see Love perfect *CP1864:* saw Power; now §over *shall*§ see *1864a:* saw Power, see now Love perfect *1868:* power *1888:* love
60| MS:do! *P1864a:* do!" 62| MS:soul in *P1864a:* soul, in
63| MS:rest: *1888:* rest; 68| MS:of the flesh *P1864a:* of this flesh

As the bird wings and sings,
Let us cry "All good things
Are ours, nor soul helps flesh more, now, than flesh helps soul!"

XIII

Therefore I summon age
To grant youth's heritage,
Life's struggle having so far reached its term:
Thence shall I pass, approved
A man, for aye removed
From the developed brute; a god though in the germ.

XIV

And I shall thereupon
Take rest, ere I be gone
Once more on my adventure brave and new:
Fearless and unperplexed,
When I wage battle next,
What weapons to select, what armour to indue.

XV

Youth ended, I shall try
My gain or loss thereby;
Leave the fire ashes, what survives is gold:
And I shall weigh the same,
Give life its praise or blame:
Young, all lay in dispute; I shall know, being old.

XVI

For note, when evening shuts,
A certain moment cuts
The deed off, calls the glory from the grey:

72| MS:more than flesh helps the soul!" *P1864a:* more, now, than flesh helps soul!" 78| MS:brute, a God *P1864a:* brute; a *1888:* god 82| MS:—Fearless *P1864a:* Fearless 83| MS:next *P1864a:* next, 86| MS:thereby— *P1864a:* thereby; 87| MS:Be the fire <> gold; *P1864a:* gold: *1868:* Leave the fire 89| MS:blame; *P1864a:* blame: 90| MS:Young,—all <> dispute: I *P1864a:* Young, all <> dispute; I

A whisper from the west
Shoots—"Add this to the rest,
Take it and try its worth: here dies another day."

XVII

So, still within this life,
Though lifted o'er its strife,
Let me discern, compare, pronounce at last,
"This rage was right i' the main,
That acquiescence vain:
The Future I may face now I have proved the Past."

XVIII

For more is not reserved
To man, with soul just nerved
To act to-morrow what he learns to-day:
Here, work enough to watch
The Master work, and catch
Hints of the proper craft, tricks of the tool's true play.

XIX

As it was better, youth
Should strive, through acts uncouth,
Toward making, than repose on aught found made:
So, better, age, exempt
From strife, should know, than tempt
Further. Thou waitedest age: wait death nor be afraid!

94| MS:the West *P1864a:* west 95| MS:Shoots—"add *P1864a:* Shoots—"Add 99| MS:last— *P1864a:* last, 101| MS:vain; *P1864a:* vain: 104| MS:man, whose soul is nerved *P1864a:* man, with soul just nerved 105| MS:what it learns *P1864a:* what he learns 111| MS:on what was made,— *P1864a:* on aught found made; *1870:* made! *1888:* made: 113| MS:than §over illegible erasure§ 114| MS:Further: thou waitedst age, wait *P1864a:* Further. Thou <> age; wait *1870:* age: wait *1888:* waitedest

XX

Enough now, if the Right
And Good and Infinite
Be named here, as thou callest thy hand thine own,
With knowledge absolute,
Subject to no dispute
From fools that crowded youth, nor let thee feel alone.

XXI

Be there, for once and all,
Severed great minds from small,
Announced to each his station in the Past!
Was I, the world arraigned,
Were they, my soul disdained,
Right? Let age speak the truth and give us peace at last!

XXII

Now, who shall arbitrate?
Ten men love what I hate,
Shun what I follow, slight what I receive;
Ten, who in ears and eyes
Match me: we all surmise,
They this thing, and I that: whom shall my soul believe?

XXIII

Not on the vulgar mass
Called "work," must sentence pass,
Things done, that took the eye and had the price;

115| MS:now, that the *P1864a:* now, if the 117| MS:Are named <> own; *P1864a:* Be named <> own, 120| MS:From that crowd round youth, nor *P1864a:* From fools that crowded youth, nor 123| MS:the Past: *P1864a:* the Past! 131| MS:surmise,— *P1864a:* surmise, 132| MS:They, this thing, and I, that: whom shall a man believe? *P1864a:* shall my soul believe? *1888:* They this thing, and I that 134| MS:"work," will sentence pass *P1864a:* "work," must sentence pass, 135| MS:—Things *P1864a:* Things

O'er which, from level stand,
The low world laid its hand,
Found straightway to its mind, could value in a trice:

XXIV

But all, the world's coarse thumb
And finger failed to plumb,
So passed in making up the main account;
All instincts immature,
All purposes unsure,
That weighed not as his work, yet swelled the man's amount:

XXV

Thoughts hardly to be packed
Into a narrow act,
Fancies that broke through language and escaped;
All I could never be,
All, men ignored in me,
This, I was worth to God, whose wheel the pitcher shaped.

XXVI

Ay, note that Potter's wheel,
That metaphor! and feel
Why time spins fast, why passive lies our clay,—
Thou, to whom fools propound,
When the wine makes its round,
"Since life fleets, all is change; the Past gone, seize to-day!"

136| MS:Whereon, from *P1864a:* O'er which, from 138| MS:mind, and valued in *P1864a:* mind, could value in 141| MS:passed by, making <> account,— *P1864a:* passed in making <> account; 142| MS:The instincts *P1864a:* All instincts 143| MS:The purposes unsure *P1864a:* All purposes unsure, 144| MS:weigh <> swell §over illegible erasure§ *P1864a:* weighed <> swelled 145| MS:Thoughts, hardly §over illegible word§ *P1864a:* Thoughts hardly 146| MS:act— *P1864a:* act, 148| MS:—All *P1864a:* All 150| MS:All, I *P1864a:* This, I *1870:* shaped *C1870:* shaped. 153| MS:time turns round, why *P1864a:* time spins fast, why 154| MS:propound *P1864a:* propound, 156| MS:fleets, earth in change, the past gone *P1864a:* fleets, all is change; the Past gone

XXVII

Fool! All that is, at all,
Lasts ever, past recall;
Earth changes, but thy soul and God stand sure:
What entered into thee,
That was, is, and shall be:
Time's wheel runs back or stops: Potter and clay endure.

XXVIII

He fixed thee mid this dance
Of plastic circumstance,
This Present, thou, forsooth, wouldst fain arrest:
Machinery just meant
To give thy soul its bent,
Try thee and turn thee forth, sufficiently impressed.

XXIX

What though the earlier grooves
Which ran the laughing loves
Around thy base, no longer pause and press?
What though, about thy rim,
Scull-things in order grim
Grow out, in graver mood, obey the sterner stress?

XXX

Look not thou down but up!
To uses of a cup,
The festal board, lamp's flash and trumpet's peal,
The new wine's foaming flow,
The Master's lips a-glow!

158| MS:recall,— *P1864a:* recall; 159| MS:Earth passes, but the soul *P1864a:* Earth changes, but thy soul 160| MS:thee *P1864a:* thee, 162| MS:Time's §over illegible erasure§ <> stops; Potter *1868:* stops: Potter 163| MS:mid that dance *P1864a:* mid this dance 165| MS:That Present *P1864a:* This Present
166| MS:—Machinery *P1864a:* Machinery 167| MS:soul the bent, *P1864a:* soul its bent, 170| MS:That ran *P1864a:* Which ran 171| MS:press,— *P1864a:* press?
174| MS:stress,— *P1864a:* stress? 177| MS:peal— *P1864a:* peal,

Thou, heaven's consummate cup, what need'st thou with earth's wheel?

XXXI

But I need, now as then,
Thee, God, who mouldest men;
And since, not even while the whirl was worst,
Did I,—to the wheel of life
With shapes and colours rife,
Bound dizzily,—mistake my end, to slake Thy thirst:

XXXII

So, take and use Thy work:
Amend what flaws may lurk,
What strain o' the stuff, what warpings past the aim!
My times be in Thy hand!
Perfect the cup as planned!
Let age approve of youth, and death complete the same!

180| MS:Thou, Heaven's <> needst *P1864a:* heaven's *1888:* need'st 182| MS:men! *P1864a:* men; 183| MS:since not *P1864a:* since, not 184| MS:of live *P1864a:* of life 185| MS:colors *P1864a:* colours 186| MS:thirst— *P1864a:* thirst: 187| MS:work! *1870:* work: 189| MS:The strain <> stuff, the warpings <> aim; *P1864a:* What strain <> stuff, what warpings <> aim! 190| MS:hand; *P1864a:* hand! 191| MS:Perfect Thy work as planned; *P1864a:* Perfect the cup as planned! 192| MS:Let Age <> youth and *P1864a:* age <> youth, and

A DEATH IN THE DESERT

[Supposed of Pamphylax the Antiochene:
It is a parchment, of my rolls the fifth,
Hath three skins glued together, is all Greek
And goeth from *Epsilon* down to *Mu*:
Lies second in the surnamed Chosen Chest,
Stained and conserved with juice of terebinth,
Covered with cloth of hair, and lettered *Xi*,
From Xanthus, my wife's uncle, now at peace:
Mu and *Epsilon* stand for my own name.
I may not write it, but I make a cross
To show I wait His coming, with the rest,
And leave off here: beginneth Pamphylax.]

I said, "If one should wet his lips with wine,
And slip the broadest plantain-leaf we find,
Or else the lappet of a linen robe,
Into the water-vessel, lay it right,
And cool his forehead just above the eyes,
The while a brother, kneeling either side,
Should chafe each hand and try to make it warm,—
He is not so far gone but he might speak."

This did not happen in the outer cave,
Nor in the secret chamber of the rock
Where, sixty days since the decree was out,
We had him, bedded on a camel-skin,
And waited for his dying all the while;
But in the midmost grotto: since noon's light
Reached there a little, and we would not lose
The last of what might happen on his face.

I at the head, and Xanthus at the feet,
With Valens and the Boy, had lifted him,

A DEATH IN THE DESERT 3| MS:all Greek, *1888:* all Greek 7| MS:hair and *P1864a:* hair, and 9| MS:name, *1888:* name. 17| MS:eyes,— *P1864a:* eyes, 22| MS:rock, DC,BrU:rock *1889:* rock 25| MS:while: *P1864a:* while; 26| MS:grotto,—for noon's *P1864a:* grotto: since noon's 30| MS:him *P1864a:* him,

And brought him from the chamber in the depths,
And laid him in the light where we might see:
For certain smiles began about his mouth,
And his lids moved, presageful of the end.

Beyond, and half way up the mouth o' the cave,
The Bactrian convert, having his desire,
Kept watch, and made pretence to graze a goat
That gave us milk, on rags of various herb,
Plantain and quitch, the rocks' shade keeps alive:
So that if any thief or soldier passed,
(Because the persecution was aware)
Yielding the goat up promptly with his life,
Such man might pass on, joyful at a prize,
Nor care to pry into the cool o' the cave.
Outside was all noon and the burning blue.

"Here is wine," answered Xanthus,—dropped drop;
I stooped and placed the lap of cloth aright,
Then chafed his right hand, and the Boy his left:
But Valens had bethought him, and produced
And broke a ball of nard, and made perfume.
Only, he did—not so much wake, as—turn
And smile a little, as a sleeper does
If any dear one call him, touch his face—
And smiles and loves, but will not be disturbed.

Then Xanthus said a prayer, but still he slept:
It is the Xanthus that escaped to Rome,
Was burned, and could not write the chronicle.

Then the Boy sprang up from his knees, and ran,
Stung by the splendour of a sudden thought,
And fetched the seventh plate of graven lead
Out of the secret chamber, found a place,
Pressing with finger on the deeper dints,

---

[32]| MS:see: *1888:* see §emended to§ see: §see Editorial Notes§
[35]| MS:half-way *P1864a:* half way [48]| MS:right hand *P1864a:* right-hand [59]| MS:splendor *P1864a:* splendour

And spoke, as 'twere his mouth proclaiming first,
"I am the Resurrection and the Life."

Whereat he opened his eyes wide at once,
And sat up of himself, and looked at us;
And thenceforth nobody pronounced a word:
Only, outside, the Bactrian cried his cry
Like the lone desert-bird that wears the ruff,
As signal we were safe, from time to time.

First he said, "If a friend declared to me,
This my son Valens, this my other son,
Were James and Peter,—nay, declared as well
This lad was very John,—I could believe!
—Could, for a moment, doubtlessly believe:
So is myself withdrawn into my depths,
The soul retreated from the perished brain
Whence it was wont to feel and use the world
Through these dull members, done with long ago.
Yet I myself remain; I feel myself:
And there is nothing lost. Let be, awhile!"

[This is the doctrine he was wont to teach,
How divers persons witness in each man,
Three souls which make up one soul: first, to wit,
A soul of each and all the bodily parts,
Seated therein, which works, and is what Does,
And has the use of earth, and ends the man
Downward: but, tending upward for advice,
Grows into, and again is grown into
By the next soul, which, seated in the brain,
Useth the first with its collected use,
And feeleth, thinketh, willeth,—is what Knows:

63| MS:first— *P1864a:* first, 65| MS:Whereat he opened §last three words over illegible erasure§ 69| MS:wears §over illegible erasure§ 70| MS:From §altered to§ from time to time. §last four words circled and marked for transposition to end of line§ as §altered to§ As 75| MS:believe— *P1864a:* believe: 84| MS:to-wit, *P1864a:* to wit, 87| MS:earth and *P1864a:* earth, and 89| MS:into and *P1864a:* into, and

Which, duly tending upward in its turn,
Grows into, and again is grown into
By the last soul, that uses both the first,
Subsisting whether they assist or no,
And, constituting man's self, is what Is—
And leans upon the former, makes it play,
As that played off the first: and, tending up,
Holds, is upheld by, God, and ends the man
Upward in that dread point of intercourse,
Nor needs a place, for it returns to Him.
What Does, what Knows, what Is; three souls, one man.
I give the glossa of Theotypas.]

And then, "A stick, once fire from end to end;
Now, ashes save the tip that holds a spark!
Yet, blow the spark, it runs back, spreads itself
A little where the fire was: thus I urge
The soul that served me, till it task once more
What ashes of my brain have kept their shape,
And these make effort on the last o' the flesh,
Trying to taste again the truth of things—"
(He smiled)—"their very superficial truth;
As that ye are my sons, that it is long
Since James and Peter had release by death,
And I am only he, your brother John,
Who saw and heard, and could remember all.
Remember all! It is not much to say.
What if the truth broke on me from above
As once and oft-times? Such might hap again:
Doubtlessly He might stand in presence here,
With head wool-white, eyes flame, and feet like brass,
The sword and the seven stars, as I have seen—

94| MS:into and *P1864a:* into, and 96| MS:assist §over illegible erasure§ 97| MS:what Is,— *P1864a:* what Is— 99| MS:first,—and *P1864a:* first: and 100| MS:by, God,—and *P1864a:* by, God and 102| MS:to Him: *P1864a:* to Him. *1888:* to Him DC,BrU:to Him. *1889:* to Him. 113| MS:truth— *P1864a:* truth; 117| MS:heard and *P1864a:* heard, and 122| *1868:* eyes, flame *1888:* eyes flame

I who now shudder only and surmise
'How did your brother bear that sight and live?'

"If I live yet, it is for good, more love
Through me to men: be nought but ashes here
That keep awhile my semblance, who was John,—
Still, when they scatter, there is left on earth
No one alive who knew (consider this!)
—Saw with his eyes and handled with his hands
That which was from the first, the Word of Life.
How will it be when none more saith 'I saw'?

"Such ever was love's way: to rise, it stoops.
Since I, whom Christ's mouth taught, was bidden teach,
I went, for many years, about the world,
Saying 'It was so; so I heard and saw,'
Speaking as the case asked: and men believed.
Afterward came the message to myself
In Patmos isle; I was not bidden teach,
But simply listen, take a book and write,
Nor set down other than the given word,
With nothing left to my arbitrament
To choose or change: I wrote, and men believed.
Then, for my time grew brief, no message more,
No call to write again, I found a way,
And, reasoning from my knowledge, merely taught
Men should, for love's sake, in love's strength believe;
Or I would pen a letter to a friend
And urge the same as friend, nor less nor more:
Friends said I reasoned rightly, and believed.
But at the last, why, I seemed left alive
Like a sea-jelly weak on Patmos strand,
To tell dry sea-beach gazers how I fared
When there was mid-sea, and the mighty things;
Left to repeat, 'I saw, I heard, I knew,'

125| MS:that §over *the*§ sight 130| MS:knew—consider this! *P1864a:* knew (consider this!) 137| MS:was so, so *P1864a:* was so; so 148| MS:strength, believe; *1888:* strength believe; 150| MS:same, as *P1864a:* same as 152| MS:last,—why, I seemed §over illegible erasure§ *P1864a:* last, why 155| MS:mid-sea and <> things— *P1864a:* mid-sea, and <> things; 156| MS:repeat 'I *P1864a:* repeat, 'I

And go all over the old ground again,
With Antichrist already in the world,
And many Antichrists, who answered prompt
'Am I not Jasper as thyself art John?
Nay, young, whereas through age thou mayest forget:
Wherefore, explain, or how shall we believe?'
I never thought to call down fire on such,
Or, as in wonderful and early days,
Pick up the scorpion, tread the serpent dumb;
But patient stated much of the Lord's life
Forgotten or misdelivered, and let it work:
Since much that at the first, in deed and word,
Lay simply and sufficiently exposed,
Had grown (or else my soul was grown to match,
Fed through such years, familiar with such light,
Guarded and guided still to see and speak)
Of new significance and fresh result;
What first were guessed as points, I now knew stars,
And named them in the Gospel I have writ.
For men said, 'It is getting long ago:
Where is the promise of His coming?'—asked
These young ones in their strength, as loth to wait,
Of me who, when their sires were born, was old.
I, for I loved them, answered, joyfully,
Since I was there, and helpful in my age;
And, in the main, I think such men believed.
Finally, thus endeavouring, I fell sick,
Ye brought me here, and I supposed the end,
And went to sleep with one thought that, at least,
Though the whole earth should lie in wickedness,

162| MS:Therefore, explain *P1864a:* Wherefore, explain 165| MS:dumb,— *P1864a:* dumb; 168| MS:Since §over illegible erasure§ 169| MS:Lay §over illegible erasure§ 170| MS:grown—or <> was §over illegible erasure§ *P1864a:* grown (or 172| MS:speak— *P1864:* speak) 175| MS:named them §over illegible word§ 176| MS:For §over illegible erasure§ <> said 'It <> ago:' *P1864a:* said, 'It *1888:* ago: 177| MS:'Where *1870:* Where 179| MS:—Of <> old: *P1864a:* Of <> old. 180| MS:joyfully *P1864a:* joyfully, 181| MS:That I was there and <> age, *P1864a:* Since I was there, and <> age; 183| MS:Finally, so §over illegible erasure§ endeavouring *P1864a:* Finally, thus endeavouring

We had the truth, might leave the rest to God.
Yet now I wake in such decrepitude
As I had slidden down and fallen afar,
Past even the presence of my former self,
Grasping the while for stay at facts which snap,
Till I am found away from my own world,
Feeling for foot-hold through a blank profound,
Along with unborn people in strange lands,
Who say—I hear said or conceive they say—
'Was John at all, and did he say he saw?
Assure us, ere we ask what he might see!'

"And how shall I assure them? Can they share
—They, who have flesh, a veil of youth and strength
About each spirit, that needs must bide its time,
Living and learning still as years assist
Which wear the thickness thin, and let man see—
With me who hardly am withheld at all,
But shudderingly, scarce a shred between,
Lie bare to the universal prick of light?
Is it for nothing we grow old and weak,
We whom God loves? When pain ends, gain ends too.
To me, that story—ay, that Life and Death
Of which I wrote 'it was'—to me, it is;
—Is, here and now: I apprehend nought else.
Is not God now i' the world His power first made?
Is not His love at issue still with sin
Visibly when a wrong is done on earth?

187| MS:truth and left the <> God: *P1864a:* truth, might leave the <> God. 190| MS:former §over illegible erasure§ 191| MS:snap, §over illegible erasure§ 193| MS:through the blank *P1864a:* through a blank 199| MS:—They, with the flesh, the veil *P1864a:* —They, who have flesh, a veil 200| MS:that §erasure§ must *P1864a:* that needs must 201| MS:still as §last two words over illegible erasure§ 202| MS:thin and *P1864a:* thin, and 203| MS:all *P1864a:* all, 209| MS:me it §over illegible erasure§ is *P1864a:* me, it is; 210| MS:else: *P1864a:* else. 211| MS:For §erased§ Is not God in the §over *this*§ world His power once made? *P1864a:* not God now i' the <> power first made? 212| MS:Is §over illegible erasure§ not <> at struggle here with sin, *P1864a:* at issue still with DC,BrU:sin *1889:* sin 212–13| MS:sin, / Closed with and cast and conquered, crucified / Visibly *1868:* §line deleted§ 213| MS:on it? §over *earth*§ *P1864a:* on earth? *C1870:* Visibly, when §change not made in subsequent texts§

Love, wrong, and pain, what see I else around?
Yea, and the Resurrection and Uprise
To the right hand of the throne—what is it beside,
When such truth, breaking bounds, o'erfloods my soul,
And, as I saw the sin and death, even so
See I the need yet transiency of both,
The good and glory consummated thence?
I saw the power; I see the Love, once weak,
Resume the Power: and in this word 'I see,'
Lo, there is recognized the Spirit of both
That moving o'er the spirit of man, unblinds
His eye and bids him look. These are, I see;
But ye, the children, His beloved ones too,
Ye need,—as I should use an optic glass
I wondered at erewhile, somewhere i' the world,
It had been given a crafty smith to make;
A tube, he turned on objects brought too close,
Lying confusedly insubordinate
For the unassisted eye to master once:
Look through his tube, at distance now they lay,
Become succinct, distinct, so small, so clear!
Just thus, ye needs must apprehend what truth
I see, reduced to plain historic fact,
Diminished into clearness, proved a point
And far away: ye would withdraw your sense
From out eternity, strain it upon time,
Then stand before that fact, that Life and Death,
Stay there at gaze, till it dispart, dispread,

216| MS:right-hand *P1864a:* right hand 217| MS:When such §over illegible erasure§ truth breaking §*ing* over erasure§ bounds o'erfloods *P1864a:* truth, breaking bounds, o'erfloods 221| MS:the Power <> once §over illegible erasure§ *1870:* power 222| MS:see'. *P1864a:* see,' 223| MS:—Lo, there §over illegible erasure§ is §inserted above§ *P1864a:* Lo 224| *P1864a:* That, moving *1868:* That moving 225| MS:look: These §over illegible erasure§ are §inserted above§ :I see. *P1864a:* look. These are, I see; 226| MS:beloved too, *P1864a:* beloved ones too, 227| MS:an §over illegible erasure§ 229| MS:make— *P1864a:* make; 232| MS:master thus: *P1864a:* master once: 233| MS:tube, they lay, §last two words circled and marked for transposition to end of line§ 235| MS:Just so, ye <> must §inserted above§ *P1864a:* Just thus, ye 237| MS:clearness, proved a §last two words over illegible erasure§ 239| MS:out Eternity <> Time, *P1864a:* eternity <> time,

As though a star should open out, all sides,
Grow the world on you, as it is my world.

"For life, with all it yields of joy and woe,
And hope and fear,—believe the aged friend,—
Is just our chance o' the prize of learning love,
How love might be, hath been indeed, and is;
And that we hold thenceforth to the uttermost
Such prize despite the envy of the world,
And, having gained truth, keep truth: that is all.
But see the double way wherein we are led,
How the soul learns diversely from the flesh!
With flesh, that hath so little time to stay,
And yields mere basement for the soul's emprise,
Expect prompt teaching. Helpful was the light,
And warmth was cherishing and food was choice
To every man's flesh, thousand years ago,
As now to yours and mine; the body sprang
At once to the height, and stayed: but the soul,—no!
Since sages who, this noontide, meditate
In Rome or Athens, may descry some point
Of the eternal power, hid yestereve;
And, as thereby the power's whole mass extends,
So much extends the æther floating o'er,
The love that tops the might, the Christ in God.
Then, as new lessons shall be learned in these
Till earth's work stop and useless time run out,
So duly, daily, needs provision be

243| MS:And grow <> you: it *P1864a:* you, as it *1870:* Grow 247| MS:How it might <> is— *P1864a:* How love might <> is; 250| MS:And truth once gained, §last four words crossed out and replaced above by three words§ Having gained truth, dare keep truth—that *P1864a:* And, having *P1864a:* gained truth, keep truth: that 253| MS:With §over illegible erasure§ 255| MS:teaching; helpful *P1864a:* teaching. Helpful
260| MS:this §followed by illegible erasure§ noontide, §over illegible erasure§
261| MS:In Rome, or Athens, may §over illegible erasure§ *P1864a:* In Rome or
262| MS:the Eternal <> yesterday §altered to§ yestereve; *P1864a:* eternal
263| MS:And as *C1870:* And, as 264| MS:much hath waxed the æther §over illegible erasure§ <> o'er, §over illegible word§ *P1864a:* much extends the <> o'er *CP1864a:* o'er, *1870:* o'er DC,BrU:o'er, *1889:* o'er, 265| MS:the might, §over illegible erasure§
266| MS:And as <> These *P1864a:* Then, as <> these 267| MS:stop §over illegible erasure§ and <> time run out, §last two words over illegible erasure§

For keeping the soul's prowess possible,
Building new barriers as the old decay,
Saving us from evasion of life's proof,
Putting the question ever, 'Does God love,
And will ye hold that truth against the world?'
Ye know there needs no second proof with good
Gained for our flesh from any earthly source:
We might go freezing, ages,—give us fire,
Thereafter we judge fire at its full worth,
And guard it safe through every chance, ye know!
That fable of Prometheus and his theft,
How mortals gained Jove's fiery flower, grows old
(I have been used to hear the pagans own)
And out of mind; but fire, howe'er its birth,
Here is it, precious to the sophist now
Who laughs the myth of Æschylus to scorn,
As precious to those satyrs of his play,
Who touched it in gay wonder at the thing.
While were it so with the soul,—this gift of truth
Once grasped, were this our soul's gain safe, and sure
To prosper as the body's gain is wont,—
Why, man's probation would conclude, his earth
Crumble; for he both reasons and decides,
Weighs first, then chooses: will he give up fire
For gold or purple once he knows its worth?
Could he give Christ up were His worth as plain?
Therefore, I say, to test man, the proofs shift,

272| MS:ever, 'Doth God §last two words over illegible erasure§ *P1864a:*ever, 'Does
273| MS:world? *P1864a:*world?' *1868:*'world!' *1870:*world?' 275| MS:for man's flesh <> earthly §over illegible erasure§ *P1864a:*for our flesh 276| MS:He might go freezing §over illegible erasure§ ages,—give him fire, *P1864a:* We might go freezing, ages,—give us fire, 277| MS:Thereafter he will judge <> its worth, *P1864a:*Thereafter we judge <> its full worth, 279| MS:and the theft— *P1864a:*and his theft, 280| MS:gained Jove's §over illegible erasure§ <> flower—grows *P1864a:*flower, grows 284| MS:the tale of *P1864a:*the myth of 285| MS:of your §above partially erased *the*§ bard, *P1864a:*of his play, 286| MS:thing: *P1864a:*thing.
287| MS:But were *P1864a:*While were 288| MS:safe and *P1864a:*safe, and
289| MS:wont, *P1864a:*wont,— 291| MS:Crumble,—for *P1864a:*Crumble; for
292| MS:Weighs first, then §last two words over illegible erasure§ 294| MS:Could §over *Would*§ 295| MS:man, shift the proofs, *1868:*man, the proofs shift,

Nor may he grasp that fact like other fact,
And straightway in his life acknowledge it,
As, say, the indubitable bliss of fire.
Sigh ye, 'It had been easier once than now'?
To give you answer I am left alive;
Look at me who was present from the first!
Ye know what things I saw; then came a test,
My first, befitting me who so had seen:
'Forsake the Christ thou sawest transfigured, Him
Who trod the sea and brought the dead to life?
What should wring this from thee!'—ye laugh and ask.
What wrung it? Even a torchlight and a noise,
The sudden Roman faces, violent hands,
And fear of what the Jews might do! Just that,
And it is written, 'I forsook and fled:'
There was my trial, and it ended thus.
Ay, but my soul had gained its truth, could grow:
Another year or two,—what little child,
What tender woman that had seen no least
Of all my sights, but barely heard them told,
Who did not clasp the cross with a light laugh,
Or wrap the burning robe round, thanking God?
Well, was truth safe for ever, then? Not so.
Already had begun the silent work
Whereby truth, deadened of its absolute blaze,
Might need love's eye to pierce the o'erstretched doubt.
Teachers were busy, whispering 'All is true

298| MS:As, say, §last word and comma inserted above§ 299| MS:now?' *1888:* now'?
300| MS:give that answer <> alive, *P1864a:* give you answer <> alive;
303| MS:The first, befitting him who *P1864a:* My first, befitting me who
304| MS:transfigured, Him, §comma erased§ 306| MS:should do this with thee?'—Ye laugh *P1864a:* should wring this from thee?'—ye *1868:* thee!'—ye *1870:* ask; *C1870:* ask.
307| MS:What did it *P1864a:* What wrung it 309| MS:might §over illegible erasure§ do— just *P1864a:* do! Just 310| MS:And, it <> fled'— *P1864a:* fled': *1868:* And it <> fled:' 311| MS:trial and it issued thus. §over *so*§ *P1864a:* trial, and it ended thus. 312| MS:but the soul <> could §over illegible erasure§ *P1864a:* but my soul 314| MS:woman who had *P1864a:* woman that had 315| MS:sights but <> heard of §erased§ them, §comma erased§ told, *P1864a:* sights, but
318| MS:forever <> so— *P1864a:* for ever <> so. 321| MS:Should need love's eye §inserted above§ to <> o'erstretched §over illegible erasure§ doubt: *P1864a:* Might need *1868:* doubt; *1870:* doubt. 322| MS:busy, saying 'All *P1864a:* busy, whispering 'All

As the aged ones report; but youth can reach
Where age gropes dimly, weak with stir and strain,
And the full doctrine slumbers till to-day.'
Thus, what the Roman's lowered spear was found,
A bar to me who touched and handled truth,
Now proved the glozing of some new shrewd tongue,
This Ebion, this Cerinthus or their mates,
Till imminent was the outcry 'Save our Christ!'
Whereon I stated much of the Lord's life
Forgotten or misdelivered, and let it work.
Such work done, as it will be, what comes next?
What do I hear say, or conceive men say,
'Was John at all, and did he say he saw?
Assure us, ere we ask what he might see!'

"Is this indeed a burthen for late days,
And may I help to bear it with you all,
Using my weakness which becomes your strength?
For if a babe were born inside this grot,
Grew to a boy here, heard us praise the sun,
Yet had but yon sole glimmer in light's place,—
One loving him and wishful he should learn,
Would much rejoice himself was blinded first
Month by month here, so made to understand
How eyes, born darkling, apprehend amiss:
I think I could explain to such a child
There was more glow outside than gleams he caught,
Ay, nor need urge 'I saw it, so believe!'

---

[323]| MS:aged ones §over illegible erasure§ <> can §over illegible erasure§
[324]| MS:gropes §over illegible erasure§ dimly, through its §over illegible erasure§ stir *P1864a:* dimly, weak with stir [325]| MS:And §over illegible erasure§ the <> slumbered §altered to§ slumbers—till today'— §last two words over illegible erasure§ *P1864a:* slumbers till to-day.' [326]| MS:Thus, §over illegible erasure§
[328]| MS:comment §crossed out and replaced above by§ glozing <> tongue, §over illegible erasure§ [329]| MS:mates— *P1864a:* mates, [330]| MS:And so the cry came to me §last seven words crossed out and replaced above by five words§ Till the outcry was imminent 'Save us Christ!' *P1864a:* Till imminent was the outcry 'Save us *1868:* outcry 'Save our Christ!' [333]| MS:Such work done, §last three words over illegible erasure§
[334]| MS:What did I <> men said, *P1864a:* What do I <> men say,
[337]| MS:days *P1864a:* days, [338]| MS:with you all, §last two words over illegible erasure§ [345]| MS:here, and §over illegible word§ made *P1864a:* here, so made

It is a heavy burthen you shall bear
In latter days, new lands, or old grown strange,
Left without me, which must be very soon.
What is the doubt, my brothers? Quick with it!
I see you stand conversing, each new face,
Either in fields, of yellow summer eves,
On islets yet unnamed amid the sea;
Or pace for shelter 'neath a portico
Out of the crowd in some enormous town
Where now the larks sing in a solitude;
Or muse upon blank heaps of stone and sand
Idly conjectured to be Ephesus:
And no one asks his fellow any more
'Where is the promise of His coming?' but
Was He revealed in any of His lives,
As Power, as Love, as Influencing Soul?'

"Quick, for time presses, tell the whole mind out,
And let us ask and answer and be saved!
My book speaks on, because it cannot pass;
One listens quietly, nor scoffs but pleads
'Here is a tale of things done ages since;
What truth was ever told the second day?
Wonders, that would prove doctrine, go for nought.
Remains the doctrine, love; well, we must love,
And what we love most, power and love in one,
Let us acknowledge on the record here,
Accepting these in Christ: must Christ then be?
Has He been? Did not we ourselves make Him?
Our mind receives but what it holds, no more.
First of the love, then; we acknowledge Christ—

351| MS:lands or *P1864a:* lands, or 356| MS:sea,— *P1864a:* sea; 359| MS:solitude,— *P1864a:* solitude; 361| MS:Barely conjectured <> Ephesus,— *P1864a:* Idly conjectured <> Ephesus: 363| MS:coming?'—But— *P1864a:* coming?' but 364| *P1864a:* 'Was He *1888:* he *1889:* he §emended to§ 'Was He §see Editorial Notes§ 368| MS:book speaks on §last two words over illegible erasure§ <> pass— *P1864a:* pass; 369| MS:listens §over illegible erasure§ <> pleads— *P1864a:* pleads 372| MS:Then wonders that prove *P1864a:* Wonders, that would prove 373| MS:doctrine, Love; well, we, §over illegible erasure§ *P1864a:* love 377| MS:he *P1864a:* Has He 378| MS:holds—no more: *P1864a:* holds, no more. 379| MS:the Love *P1864a:* love

A proof we comprehend His love, a proof
We had such love already in ourselves,
Knew first what else we should not recognize.
'Tis mere projection from man's inmost mind,
And, what he loves, thus falls reflected back,
Becomes accounted somewhat out of him;
He throws it up in air, it drops down earth's,
With shape, name, story added, man's old way.
How prove you Christ came otherwise at least?
Next try the power: He made and rules the world:
Certes there is a world once made, now ruled,
Unless things have been ever as we see.
Our sires declared a charioteer's yoked steeds
Brought the sun up the east and down the west,
Which only of itself now rises, sets,
As if a hand impelled it and a will,—
Thus they long thought, they who had will and hands:
But the new question's whisper is distinct,
Wherefore must all force needs be like ourselves?
We have the hands, the will; what made and drives
The sun is force, is law, is named, not known,
While will and love we do know; marks of these,
Eye-witnesses attest, so books declare—
As that, to punish or reward our race,
The sun at undue times arose or set
Or else stood still: what do not men affirm?
But earth requires as urgently reward
Or punishment to-day as years ago,
And none expects the sun will interpose:
Therefore it was mere passion and mistake,

382| MS:recognize; *P1864a:* recognize. *1870:* recognise. *1888:* recognize.
383| MS:from man's §over illegible erasure§ 384| MS:loves, so falls <> back *P1864a:* loves, thus falls <> back, 385| MS:him,— *P1864a:* him; 387| MS:way: *P1864a:* way. 389| MS:the Power *P1864a:* power 391| MS:been §over illegible word§ <> see: *P1864a:* see. 393| MS:the East <> West— *P1864a:* east <> west, 396| MS:Thus we long thought, we who have *P1864a:* Thus they long thought, they who had 397| MS:distinct *P1864a:* distinct,
399| MS:will,—what *P1864a:* will; what 400| MS:known— *P1864a:* known,
402| MS:Eye-witnesses, it is affirmed, attest— *P1864a:* Eye-witnesses attest, so books declare— 404| MS:The sun arose or set §last three words circled and marked for transposition to end of line§ at undue times 405| MS:still—what *P1864a:* still: what

Or erring zeal for right, which changed the truth.
Go back, far, farther, to the birth of things;
Ever the will, the intelligence, the love,
Man's!—which he gives, supposing he but finds,
As late he gave head, body, hands and feet,
To help these in what forms he called his gods.
First, Jove's brow, Juno's eyes were swept away,
But Jove's wrath, Juno's pride continued long;
As last, will, power, and love discarded these,
So law in turn discards power, love, and will.
What proveth God is otherwise at least?
All else, projection from the mind of man!'

"Nay, do not give me wine, for I am strong,
But place my gospel where I put my hands.

"I say that man was made to grow, not stop;
That help, he needed once, and needs no more,
Having grown but an inch by, is withdrawn:
For he hath new needs, and new helps to these.
This imports solely, man should mount on each
New height in view; the help whereby he mounts,
The ladder-rung his foot has left, may fall,
Since all things suffer change save God the Truth.
Man apprehends Him newly at each stage
Whereat earth's ladder drops, its service done;
And nothing shall prove twice what once was proved.
You stick a garden-plot with ordered twigs
To show inside lie germs of herbs unborn,

411| MS:things; §over illegible erasure§ 414| MS:feet *P1864a:* feet, 415| MS:what §over illegible erasure§ 416| MS:Now, Jove's <> are *P1864a:* First, Jove's <> were 417| MS:wrath §over illegible erasure§ <> continued §over illegible erasure§ 418| MS:last Will, Power, and Love *P1864a:* last, will, power, and love 419| MS:Power shall in turn discard Power, Love, and Will. *P1864a:* So law in turn discards power, love, and will. 421| MS:All else—§over illegible word§ projection *P1864a:* All else, projection 426| MS:grown up but <> withdrawn, *P1864a:* withdrawn: *1870:* grown but 427| MS:these: *P1864a:* these. 429| MS:view,—the *P1864a:* view; the 430| MS:What §over illegible erasure§ ladder-rung *P1864a:* The ladder-rung 431| MS:Since §over illegible erasure§ 433| MS:done, *P1864a:* done; 436| MS:lie germs of §last two words inserted above§ herbs as yet §last two words crossed out§ unborn,

And check the careless step would spoil their birth;
But when herbs wave, the guardian twigs may go,
Since should ye doubt of virtues, question kinds,
It is no longer for old twigs ye look,
Which proved once underneath lay store of seed,
But to the herb's self, by what light ye boast,
For what fruit's signs are. This book's fruit is plain,
Nor miracles need prove it any more.
Doth the fruit show? Then miracles bade 'ware
At first of root and stem, saved both till now
From trampling ox, rough boar and wanton goat.
What? Was man made a wheelwork to wind up,
And be discharged, and straight wound up anew?
No!—grown, his growth lasts; taught, he ne'er forgets:
May learn a thousand things, not twice the same.

"This might be pagan teaching: now hear mine.

"I say, that as the babe, you feed awhile,
Becomes a boy and fit to feed himself,
So, minds at first must be spoon-fed with truth:
When they can eat, babe's-nurture is withdrawn.
I fed the babe whether it would or no:
I bid the boy or feed himself or starve.
I cried once, 'That ye may believe in Christ,
Behold this blind man shall receive his sight!'
I cry now, 'Urgest thou, *for I am shrewd*

437| MS:spoil §over illegible erasure§ <> birth *P1864a:* birth; 439| MS:virtue, question kind, *P1864a:* virtues, question kinds, 441| MS:proved that there §crossed out and replaced above by§ underneath <> seed, to save, §last two words and comma crossed out§ *P1864a:* proved once underneath 443| MS:are. This Book's <> plain, §over illegible erasure§ *P1864a:* book's 444| MS:miracles shall prove *P1864a:* miracles need prove 445| MS:miracles bade 'ware §las two words over illegible erasure§ 447| MS:trampling ox, rough §last two words over illegible erasure§ 448| MS:What? Was Man *P1864a:* man 450| MS:lasts—taught, <> forgets, *P1864a:* lasts; taught, <> forgets: 451–52| MS:§no ¶§ *P1864a:* §¶§
452| MS:This is a pagan teaching—now *P1864a:* This might be pagan teaching: now
453| MS:say that *P1864a:* say, that 455| MS:spoon fed *P1864a:* spoon-fed
456| MS:When he can <> withdrawn; *P1864a:* When they can eat, babe's nurture is withdrawn. *1888:* babe's-nurture 459| MS:once—'That *P1864a:* once, 'That 461| MS:now 'Urgest *P1864a:* now, 'Urgest

And smile at stories how John's word could cure—
Repeat that miracle and take my faith?'
I say, that miracle was duly wrought
When, save for it, no faith was possible.
Whether a change were wrought i' the shows o' the world,
Whether the change came from our minds which see
Of shows o' the world so much as and no more
Than God wills for His purpose,—(what do I
See now, suppose you, there where you see rock
Round us?)—I know not; such was the effect,
So faith grew, making void more miracles
Because too much: they would compel, not help.
I say, the acknowledgment of God in Christ
Accepted by thy reason, solves for thee
All questions in the earth and out of it,
And has so far advanced thee to be wise.
Wouldst thou unprove this to re-prove the proved?
In life's mere minute, with power to use that proof,
Leave knowledge and revert to how it sprung?
Thou hast it; use it and forthwith, or die!

"For I say, this is death and the sole death,
When a man's loss comes to him from his gain,
Darkness from light, from knowledge ignorance,
And lack of love from love made manifest;
A lamp's death when, replete with oil, it chokes;
A stomach's when, surcharged with food, it starves.
With ignorance was surety of a cure.

463| MS:*faith?* *1868:faith?'* 464| MS:say that *P1864a:*say, that 465| MS:possible: *P1864a:*possible. 466| MS:was *P1864a:*were 468| MS:Of the shows <> world just so much and *P1864a:*world so much as and *1870:*Of shows 469| MS:As God *P1864a:*Than God 471| MS:effect; *P1864a:*effect, 472| MS:So §over illegible erasure§ 473| MS:much,—they *1864a:*much: they 474| MS:say the acknowledgement of *P1864a:*say, the acknowledgment of 477| MS:wise: *P1864a:*wise. 478| MS:unprove this §over illegible erasure§ to reprove *P1864a:*re-prove 479| MS:—In <> minute, thy power §last two words over illegible erasure§ *P1864a:*In <> minute, with power 480| MS:Leave knowledge §over illegible erasure§ 481| MS:die. *P1864a:*die! 485| MS:manifest— *P1864a:*manifest; 486| MS:it choaks— *P1864a:*it chokes; 488| MS:With Ignorance <> cure; *P1864a:*ignorance <> cure.

When man, appalled at nature, questioned first
'What if there lurk a might behind this might?'
He needed satisfaction God could give,
And did give, as ye have the written word:
But when he finds might still redouble might,
Yet asks, 'Since all is might, what use of will?'
—Will, the one source of might,—he being man
With a man's will and a man's might, to teach
In little how the two combine in large,—
That man has turned round on himself and stands,
Which in the course of nature is, to die.

"And when man questioned, 'What if there be love
Behind the will and might, as real as they?'—
He needed satisfaction God could give,
And did give, as ye have the written word:
But when, beholding that love everywhere,
He reasons, 'Since such love is everywhere,
And since ourselves can love and would be loved,
We ourselves make the love, and Christ was not,'—
How shall ye help this man who knows himself,
That he must love and would be loved again,
Yet, owning his own love that proveth Christ,
Rejecteth Christ through very need of Him?
The lamp o'erswims with oil, the stomach flags
Loaded with nurture, and that man's soul dies.

"If he rejoin, 'But this was all the while
A trick; the fault was, first of all, in thee,
Thy story of the places, names and dates,
Where, when and how the ultimate truth had rise,
—Thy prior truth, at last discovered none,
Whence now the second suffers detriment.

494| MS:Yet §over illegible erasure§ 500| MS:questioned 'What <> Love *P1864a:*questioned, 'What <> love 501| MS:the Will and Might <> they?' *P1864a:*will and might <> they?'— 504| MS:that Love *P1864a:*love 505| MS:reasons 'Since such Love *P1864a:*reasons, 'Since such love 509| MS:would §over illegible erasure§ 515| MS:trick, the *P1864a:*trick; the 516| MS:That story *P1864a:*Thy story 519| MS:detriment! *P1864a:*detriment.

What good of giving knowledge if, because
O' the manner of the gift, its profit fail?
And why refuse what modicum of help
Had stopped the after-doubt, impossible
I' the face of truth—truth absolute, uniform?
Why must I hit of this and miss of that,
Distinguish just as I be weak or strong,
And not ask of thee and have answer prompt,
Was this once, was it not once?—then and now
And evermore, plain truth from man to man.
Is John's procedure just the heathen bard's?
Put question of his famous play again
How for the ephemerals' sake Jove's fire was filched,
And carried in a cane and brought to earth:
The fact is in the fable, cry the wise,
Mortals obtained the boon, so much is fact,
Though fire be spirit and produced on earth.
As with the Titan's, so now with thy tale:
Why breed in us perplexity, mistake,
Nor tell the whole truth in the proper words?'

"I answer, Have ye yet to argue out
The very primal thesis, plainest law,
—Man is not God but hath God's end to serve,
A master to obey, a course to take,
Somewhat to cast off, somewhat to become?
Grant this, then man must pass from old to new,
From vain to real, from mistake to fact,
From what once seemed good, to what now proves best.
How could man have progression otherwise?

521| MS:Of <> profit pass,— *P1864a:*profit fail? *1870:*O' 524| MS:of truth, absolute *P1864a:*of truth—truth absolute 526| MS:Distinguish right as *P1864a:*Distinguish just as 527| MS:and have §inserted above§ answered §altered to§ answer 528| MS:once?—Then *P1864a:*once?—then
531| MS:famous tale again *P1864a:*famous play again 532| MS:for ephemerals' sake, Jove's *P1864a:*for the ephemerals' *1888:*sake Jove's
533| MS:earth— *P1864a:*earth: 534| MS:fable,' cry the wise, §last two words over illegible erasure§ *P1864a:fable,* cry 536| MS:earth'— *P1864a:earth.*
534–36| MS:§no italics§ *P1864a:*§italics§ 537| MS:the Titan, so <> tale, *P1864a:*the Titan's, so <> tale: 542| MS:serve— *P1864a:*serve, 545| MS:this, and man *P1864a:*this, then man 546| MS:fact, §over illegible erasure§

Before the point was mooted 'What is God?'
No savage man inquired 'What am myself?'
Much less replied, 'First, last, and best of things.'
Man takes that title now if he believes
Might can exist with neither will nor love,
In God's case—what he names now Nature's Law—
While in himself he recognizes love
No less than might and will: and rightly takes.
Since if man prove the sole existent thing
Where these combine, whatever their degree,
However weak the might or will or love,
So they be found there, put in evidence,—
He is as surely higher in the scale
Than any might with neither love nor will,
As life, apparent in the poorest midge,
(When the faint dust-speck flits, ye guess its wing)
Is marvellous beyond dead Atlas' self—
Given to the nobler midge for resting-place!
Thus, man proves best and highest—God, in fine,
And thus the victory leads but to defeat,
The gain to loss, best rise to the worst fall,
His life becomes impossible, which is death.

"But if, appealing thence, he cower, avouch
He is mere man, and in humility

550| MS:inquired "What is myself?' *P1864a:* inquired 'What am myself?' 551| MS:replied, "Man, §partially erased§ "first and last and best §last two words inserted above§ of things': *P1864a:* replied, 'First and last and best of things.' *CP1864a(Yale):* replied, 'First §comma inserted§ and §crossed out§ last §comma inserted§ and *CP1864a(Berg):* replied, 'First §comma inserted§ and §crossed out§ *1864a:* replied, 'First, last, and 552| MS:He takes *P1864a:* Man takes 553| MS:neither Will nor Love, *P1864a:* will nor love, 555| MS:recognizes Love *P1864a:* love 556| MS:than Might and Will—and <> takes: *P1864a:* might and will: and <> takes. 557| MS:if Man *P1864a:* man 559| MS:the Might <> Love— *P1864a:* might <> love, 562| MS:any Might with Love nor Will, §comma crossed out§ *P1864a:* might with love nor will, 563| MS:life apparent <> midge,— *P1864a:* life, apparent <> midge, 564| MS:When the poor dust-speck flits, §over illegible erasure§ <> wing,— *P1864a:* the faint dust-speck <> wing, *1868:* (When <> wing) 565| MS:marvelous *P1864a:* marvellous <> self: *1870:* self— 566| MS:I give such to the midge *1870:* Given to the nobler midge 567| MS:Man proves the best *P1864a:* Thus, man proves best 569| MS:loss, most rise *P1864a:* loss, best rise 571| MS:avouch §over illegible erasure§ 572| MS:He is §both words over illegible erasure§

Neither may know God nor mistake himself;
I point to the immediate consequence
And say, by such confession straight he falls
Into man's place, a thing nor God nor beast,
Made to know that he can know and not more:
Lower than God who knows all and can all,
Higher than beasts which know and can so far
As each beast's limit, perfect to an end,
Nor conscious that they know, nor craving more;
While man knows partly but conceives beside,
Creeps ever on from fancies to the fact,
And in this striving, this converting air
Into a solid he may grasp and use,
Finds progress, man's distinctive mark alone,
Not God's, and not the beasts': God is, they are,
Man partly is and wholly hopes to be.
Such progress could no more attend his soul
Were all it struggles after found at first
And guesses changed to knowledge absolute,
Than motion wait his body, were all else
Than it the solid earth on every side,
Where now through space he moves from rest to rest.
Man, therefore, thus conditioned, must expect
He could not, what he knows now, know at first;
What he considers that he knows to-day,
Come but to-morrow, he will find misknown;
Getting increase of knowledge, since he learns
Because he lives, which is to be a man,

573| MS:himself,— *P1864a:* himself; 576| MS:Into Man's *P1864a:* man's 577| MS:more, *P1864a:* more: 579| MS:beasts §over illegible erasure§ 581| MS:they §over illegible erasure§ <> more, *P1864a:* more; 583| MS:from fancy to the fact,— *P1864a:* from fancies to the fact, 586| MS:progress, only §partially erased§ Man's *P1864a:* progress, man's 587| MS:beasts—God *P1864a:* beasts': God 588| MS:be: *P1864a:* be. *1870:* be: *1875:* be. 589| MS:more be for his *P1864a:* more attend his 592| MS:motion for his *P1864a:* motion wait his 593| MS:it made solid *P1864a:* it the solid 594| MS:Whereas through *P1864a:* Where now through 596| MS:What he knows now, he could not know at first, *P1864a:* He could not, what he knows now, know at first; 597| MS:he considers §over illegible erasure§ 598| MS:misknown, *P1864a:* misknown; 599| MS:Bringing §crossed out and replaced above by§ Getting 600| MS:man,— *P1864a:* man,

Set to instruct himself by his past self:
First, like the brute, obliged by facts to learn,
Next, as man may, obliged by his own mind,
Bent, habit, nature, knowledge turned to law.
God's gift was that man should conceive of truth
And yearn to gain it, catching at mistake,
As midway help till he reach fact indeed.
The statuary ere he mould a shape
Boasts a like gift, the shape's idea, and next
The aspiration to produce the same;
So, taking clay, he calls his shape thereout,
Cries ever 'Now I have the thing I see':
Yet all the while goes changing what was wrought,
From falsehood like the truth, to truth itself.
How were it had he cried 'I see no face,
No breast, no feet i' the ineffectual clay'?
Rather commend him that he clapped his hands,
And laughed 'It is my shape and lives again!'
Enjoyed the falsehood, touched it on to truth,
Until yourselves applaud the flesh indeed
In what is still flesh-imitating clay.
Right in you, right in him, such way be man's!
God only makes the live shape at a jet.
Will ye renounce this pact of creatureship?
The pattern on the Mount subsists no more,
Seemed awhile, then returned to nothingness;
But copies, Moses strove to make thereby,
Serve still and are replaced as time requires:
By these, make newest vessels, reach the type!
If ye demur, this judgment on your head,
Never to reach the ultimate, angels' law,

601| MS:self *P1864a:*self: 603| MS:own soul, *P1864a:*own mind, 604| MS:knowledge turned to §last two words over illegible erasure§ 607| MS:As §over illegible erasure§ <> indeed: *P1864a:*indeed. 609| MS:Boasts §over illegible erasure§ 612| MS:Cries §over illegible erasure§ <> see'— *P1864a:*see': *1868:*see:' *1888:*see': 614| MS:itself: *P1864a:*itself. 616| MS:No breast, §over illegible erasure§ <> i' §over illegible erasure§ <> clay?' *1888:*clay'? 618| MS:is thy §altered to§ my 622| MS:way is man's— *P1864a:*way be man's! 623| MS:jet! *P1864a:*jet. 627| MS:copies Moses *P1864a:*copies, Moses 628| MS:requires— *P1864a:*requires: 630| MS:judgement <> head *P1864a:*judgment <> head, 631| MS:reach §over illegible erasure§ <> law *P1864a:*law,

Indulging every instinct of the soul
There where law, life, joy, impulse are one thing!

"Such is the burthen of the latest time.
I have survived to hear it with my ears,
Answer it with my lips: does this suffice?
For if there be a further woe than such,
Wherein my brothers struggling need a hand,
So long as any pulse is left in mine,
May I be absent even longer yet,
Plucking the blind ones back from the abyss,
Though I should tarry a new hundred years!"

But he was dead; 'twas about noon, the day
Somewhat declining: we five buried him
That eve, and then, dividing, went five ways,
And I, disguised, returned to Ephesus.

By this, the cave's mouth must be filled with sand.
Valens is lost, I know not of his trace;
The Bactrian was but a wild childish man,
And could not write nor speak, but only loved:
So, lest the memory of this go quite,
Seeing that I to-morrow fight the beasts,
I tell the same to Phœbas, whom believe!
For many look again to find that face,
Beloved John's to whom I ministered,
Somewhere in life about the world; they err:
Either mistaking what was darkly spoke
At ending of his book, as he relates,
Or misconceiving somewhat of this speech
Scattered from mouth to mouth, as I suppose.

632| MS:instinct §over illegible word§ 634| MS:time: *P1864a:* time. 636| MS:lips §over illegible erasure§ 637| MS:such, §over illegible erasure§ 638| MS:hand,— *P1864a:* hand, 639| MS:is §over illegible erasure§ 643| MS:dead: 'twas *1888:* dead; 'twas 645| MS:dividing went *P1864a:* dividing, went 646| BrU:to Ephesus. §period called for; see Editorial Notes§ 647| MS:this the *P1864a:* this, the 649| MS:wild, childish *1868:* wild childish 656| MS:world: they err— *P1864a:* world; they err: 657| MS:darkly said *P1864a:* darkly spoke

Believe ye will not see him any more
About the world with his divine regard!
For all was as I say, and now the man
Lies as he lay once, breast to breast with God.

[Cerinthus read and mused; one added this:

"If Christ, as thou affirmest, be of men
Mere man, the first and best but nothing more,—
Account Him, for reward of what He was,
Now and for ever, wretchedest of all.
For see; Himself conceived of life as love,
Conceived of love as what must enter in,
Fill up, make one with His each soul He loved:
Thus much for man's joy, all men's joy for Him.
Well, He is gone, thou sayest, to fit reward.
But by this time are many souls set free,
And very many still retained alive:
Nay, should His coming be delayed awhile,
Say, ten years longer (twelve years, some compute)
See if, for every finger of thy hands,
There be not found, that day the world shall end,
Hundreds of souls, each holding by Christ's word
That He will grow incorporate with all,
With me as Pamphylax, with him as John,
Groom for each bride! Can a mere man do this?
Yet Christ saith, this He lived and died to do.
Call Christ, then, the illimitable God,
Or lost!"

But 'twas Cerinthus that is lost.]

662| MS:regard, *P1864a:*regard! 664–65| MS:§no rule§ *P1864a:*§rule§ 670| MS:see,—Himself *P1864a:*see; Himself 672| MS:his <> loved— *P1864a:*with His <> loved: 673| MS:for His *P1864a:*for Him. 674| MS:reward: *P1864a:*reward. 675| MS:By this time there are *P1864a:*But by this time are 676| MS:alive, *P1864a:*alive: 677| MS:—Nay <> awhile *P1864a:*Nay <> awhile, 679| MS:hands *P1864a:*hands, 684| MS:bride: can *P1864a:*bride! Can

CALIBAN UPON SETEBOS; OR, NATURAL THEOLOGY IN THE ISLAND

"Thou thoughtest that I was altogether such a one as thyself."

['Will sprawl, now that the heat of day is best,
Flat on his belly in the pit's much mire,
With elbows wide, fists clenched to prop his chin.
And, while he kicks both feet in the cool slush,
And feels about his spine small eft-things course,
Run in and out each arm, and make him laugh:
And while above his head a pompion-plant,
Coating the cave-top as a brow its eye,
Creeps down to touch and tickle hair and beard,
And now a flower drops with a bee inside,
And now a fruit to snap at, catch and crunch,—
He looks out o'er yon sea which sunbeams cross
And recross till they weave a spider-web
(Meshes of fire, some great fish breaks at times)
And talks to his own self, howe'er he please,
Touching that other, whom his dam called God.
Because to talk about Him, vexes—ha,
Could He but know! and time to vex is now,
When talk is safer than in winter-time.
Moreover Prosper and Miranda sleep
In confidence he drudges at their task,

CALIBAN UPON SETEBOS *Title*| MS:upon Setebos, or *P1864a:*SETEBOS; OR *Epigraph*| MS:Thou <> such an one as thyself. Ps:50. *P1864a:*"THOU <> THYSELF." *1868:*§Epigraph omitted§ *1888:*§Epigraph restored§ such a one 1| MS:'Will *P1864a:*['Will 3| MS:chin; *1888:*chin. 4| MS:And while *P1864a:*And, while 5| MS:feels small eft-things course about his spine, *P1864a:*feels about his spine small eft-things course, 6| MS:arm and <> laugh— *P1864a:*arm, and <> laugh; *1888:*laugh: 10| MS:—And *P1864a:*And 11| *P1864a:*crunch: *1868:*crunch,— 13| MS:spider-web, *1888:*spider-web 14| MS:Meshes <> times,— *P1864a:*(Meshes <> times) 16| MS:that Other, whom his Dam called God— *P1864a:*other <> dam called God. 17| MS:ha! *P1864a:*ha, 18| MS:know—and <> now *P1864a:*know! and <> now,

And it is good to cheat the pair, and gibe,
Letting the rank tongue blossom into speech.]

Setebos, Setebos, and Setebos!
'Thinketh, He dwelleth i' the cold o' the moon.

'Thinketh He made it, with the sun to match,
But not the stars; the stars came otherwise;
Only made clouds, winds, meteors, such as that:
Also this isle, what lives and grows thereon,
And snaky sea which rounds and ends the same.

'Thinketh, it came of being ill at ease:
He hated that He cannot change His cold,
Nor cure its ache. 'Hath spied an icy fish
That longed to 'scape the rock-stream where she lived,
And thaw herself within the lukewarm brine
O' the lazy sea her stream thrusts far amid,
A crystal spike 'twixt two warm walls of wave;
Only, she ever sickened, found repulse
At the other kind of water, not her life,
(Green-dense and dim-delicious, bred o' the sun)
Flounced back from bliss she was not born to breathe,
And in her old bounds buried her despair,
Hating and loving warmth alike: so He.

'Thinketh, He made thereat the sun, this isle,
Trees and the fowls here, beast and creeping thing.
Yon otter, sleek-wet, black, lithe as a leech;
Yon auk, one fire-eye in a ball of foam,
That floats and feeds; a certain badger brown
He hath watched hunt with that slant white-wedge eye

23| MS:speech. *P1864a:* speech.] 25| MS:moon: *P1864a:* moon. 27| MS:otherwise: *P1864a:* otherwise; 28| MS:Only the clouds <> that— *P1864a:* Only made clouds <> that: 29| MS:this Isle *P1864a:* isle 33| MS:ache: 'hath *P1864a:* ache. 'Hath 36| MS:far into, *P1864a:* far amid, 37| MS:wave, §comma erased§ *P1864a:* wave; 38| MS:Only she *1888:* Only, she 40| MS:Green-dense <> sun,— *P1864a:* (Green-dense <> sun) 44| MS:this Isle, *P1864a:* isle, 45| MS:thing; *P1864a:* thing. 46| MS:leech— *P1864a:* leech; 47| MS:foam,— *P1864a:* foam, 48| MS:feeds—a *P1864a:* feeds; a

By moonlight; and the pie with the long tongue
That pricks deep into oakwarts for a worm,
And says a plain word when she finds her prize,
But will not eat the ants; the ants themselves
That build a wall of seeds and settled stalks
About their hole—He made all these and more,
Made all we see, and us, in spite: how else?
He could not, Himself, make a second self
To be His mate; as well have made Himself:
He would not make what He mislikes or slights,
An eyesore to Him, or not worth His pains:
But did, in envy, listlessness or sport,
Make what Himself would fain, in a manner, be—
Weaker in most points, stronger in a few,
Worthy, and yet mere playthings all the while,
Things He admires and mocks too,—that is it.
Because, so brave, so better though they be,
It nothing skills if He begin to plague.
Look now, I melt a gourd-fruit into mash,
Add honeycomb and pods, I have perceived,
Which bite like finches when they bill and kiss,—
Then, when froth rises bladdery, drink up all,
Quick, quick, till maggots scamper through my brain;
Last, throw me on my back i' the seeded thyme,
And wanton, wishing I were born a bird.
Put case, unable to be what I wish,
I yet could make a live bird out of clay:
Would not I take clay, pinch my Caliban
Able to fly?—for, there, see, he hath wings,

50| MS:moonlight—and *P1864a:* moonlight; and 51| MS:deep §over illegible erasure§ <> worm *P1864a:* worm, 52| MS:when he finds his prize *P1864a:* when she finds her prize, 53| MS:ants—the *P1864a:* ants; the 56| MS:us—in *P1864a:* us, in 59| MS:what He *1870:* he *1889:* he §emended to§ what He §see Editorial Notes§ 60| MS:pains, *P1864a:* pains: 61| MS:listlessness and sport, *P1864a:* listlessness or sport, 65| MS:He could admire and mock too,—that is it: *P1864a:* Things He admires and mocks too,—that is it. 67| MS:plague: *P1864a:* plague. 69| MS:honey comb *P1864a:* honeycomb 70| MS:That bite *P1864a:* Which bite 71| MS:And, §over illegible erasure§ when *P1864a:* Then, when 72| MS:quick, while maggots <> brain, *P1864a:* quick, till maggots <> brain; 73| MS:Then throw <> thyme *P1864a:* And throw <> thyme, *1888:* Last, throw 76| MS:clay— *P1864a:* clay:

And great comb like the hoopoe's to admire,
And there, a sting to do his foes offence,
There, and I will that he begin to live,
Fly to yon rock-top, nip me off the horns
Of grigs high up that make the merry din,
Saucy through their veined wings, and mind me not.
In which feat, if his leg snapped, brittle clay,
And he lay stupid-like,—why, I should laugh;
And if he, spying me, should fall to weep,
Beseech me to be good, repair his wrong,
Bid his poor leg smart less or grow again,—
Well, as the chance were, this might take or else
Not take my fancy: I might hear his cry,
And give the mankin three sound legs for one,
Or pluck the other off, leave him like an egg,
And lessoned he was mine and merely clay.
Were this no pleasure, lying in the thyme,
Drinking the mash, with brain become alive,
Making and marring clay at will? So He.

'Thinketh, such shows nor right nor wrong in Him,
Nor kind, nor cruel: He is strong and Lord.
'Am strong myself compared to yonder crabs
That march now from the mountain to the sea,
'Let twenty pass, and stone the twenty-first,
Loving not, hating not, just choosing so.
'Say, the first straggler that boasts purple spots
Shall join the file, one pincer twisted off;
'Say, this bruised fellow shall receive a worm,

79| MS:And a great *P1864a:* And great 81| MS:begin to walk, *P1864a:* begin to live, 83| MS:Of flies high *P1864a:* Of grigs high 84| MS:through great veined <> not— *P1864a:* through their veined <> not. 85| MS:if §over illegible erasure§ 87| MS:weep *P1864a:* weep, 88| MS:repair §over illegible word§ 91| MS:his prayer *P1864a:* his cry, 92| MS:mankin three legs for his one, *P1864a:* manikin *1868:* three legs for one, *1888:* mankin three sound legs 93| MS:pluck that one off *P1864a:* pluck the other off 98| MS:such §over illegible erasure§ is nor *P1864a:* such shows nor 100| MS:myself to yonder crawling crabs *P1864a:* myself compared to yonder crabs 102| MS:Let <> pass and *P1864a:* 'Let <> pass, and 103| MS:just willing so: *P1864a:* just choosing so. 105| MS:off— *P1864a:* off;

And two worms he whose nippers end in red;
As it likes me each time, I do: so He.

Well then, 'supposeth He is good i' the main,
Placable if His mind and ways were guessed,
But rougher than His handiwork, be sure!
Oh, He hath made things worthier than Himself,
And envieth that, so helped, such things do more
Than He who made them! What consoles but this?
That they, unless through Him, do nought at all,
And must submit: what other use in things?
'Hath cut a pipe of pithless elder joint
That, blown through, gives exact the scream o' the jay
When from her wing you twitch the feathers blue:
Sound this, and little birds that hate the jay
Flock within stone's throw, glad their foe is hurt:
Put case such pipe could prattle and boast forsooth
"I catch the birds, I am the crafty thing,
I make the cry my maker cannot make
With his great round mouth; he must blow through mine!"
Would not I smash it with my foot? So He.

But wherefore rough, why cold and ill at ease?
Aha, that is a question! Ask, for that,
What knows,—the something over Setebos
That made Him, or He, may be, found and fought,
Worsted, drove off and did to nothing, perchance.
There may be something quiet o'er His head,
Out of His reach, that feels nor joy nor grief,

107| MS:red— *P1864a:* red; 108| MS:me, each *P1864a:* me each 112| MS:Oh, yes! 'Hath *P1864a:* Oh, He hath 114| MS:them: what <> this— *P1864a:* them! What <> this? 116| MS:submit? What other §over illegible word§ in them? *P1864a:* submit: what <> in things? 117| MS:cut §over illegible erasure§ <> pithless elder-tree *P1864a:* pithless elder-joint 118| MS:Which, blown *P1864a:* That, blown 122| MS:boast and say *P1864a:* boast forsooth 125| MS:mouth, he <> through me!" *P1864a:* mouth; he <> through mine!" 126| MS:not he smash it with his foot *P1864a:* not I smash it with my foot 130| MS:made, or, may be, He found §last two words over illegible erasure§ out and fought, *P1864a:* made Him, or He, may be, found and fought, 131| MS:nothing, mayhap: *P1864a:* nothing, perchance.
132| MS:be some live quiet §altered to§ Quiet *P1864a:* be something quiet

Since both derive from weakness in some way.
I joy because the quails come; would not joy
Could I bring quails here when I have a mind:
This Quiet, all it hath a mind to, doth.
'Esteemeth stars the outposts of its couch,
But never spends much thought nor care that way.
It may look up, work up,—the worse for those
It works on! 'Careth but for Setebos
The many-handed as a cuttle-fish,
Who, making Himself feared through what He does,
Looks up, first, and perceives he cannot soar
To what is quiet and hath happy life;
Next looks down here, and out of very spite
Makes this a bauble-world to ape yon real,
These good things to match those as hips do grapes.
'Tis solace making baubles, ay, and sport.
Himself peeped late, eyed Prosper at his books
Careless and lofty, lord now of the isle:
Vexed, 'stitched a book of broad leaves, arrow-shaped,
Wrote thereon, he knows what, prodigious words;
Has peeled a wand and called it by a name;
Weareth at whiles for an enchanter's robe
The eyed skin of a supple oncelot;
And hath an ounce sleeker than youngling mole,
A four-legged serpent he makes cower and couch,
Now snarl, now hold its breath and mind his eye,
And saith she is Miranda and my wife:

134| MS:Since each derives from <> way: *P1864a:* Since both derive from <> way. 137| MS:This other, all it §over illegible erasure§ *P1864a:* This Quiet, all 139| MS:spends a §partially erased§ much §inserted above§ thought, nor cares that way, *P1864a:* much thought nor care that way. 141| MS:on! Careth all for *P1864a:* on! 'Careth but for 143| MS:That makes Himself be feared *P1864a:* Who, making Himself feared 144| MS:perceives He *1868:* he 145| MS:and a happy life, *P1864a:* and hath happy life; 146| MS:So looks <> here and *P1864a:* Next looks <> here, and 147| MS:Made this the bauble-world *P1864a:* Makes this a bauble-world 148| MS:Our good things matching those *P1864a:* These good things to match those 149| MS:sport: *P1864a:* sport. 151| MS:the Isle;— *P1864a:* isle: 152| MS:stitched *P1864a:* 'stitched 153| MS:Writes *P1864a:* Wrote 154| MS:name, *P1864a:* name; 156| MS:oncelot, *P1864a:* oncelot; 159| MS:snarl now *P1864a:* snarl, now

'Keeps for his Ariel a tall pouch-bill crane
He bids go wade for fish and straight disgorge;
Also a sea-beast, lumpish, which he snared,
Blinded the eyes of, and brought somewhat tame,
And split its toe-webs, and now pens the drudge
In a hole o' the rock and calls him Caliban;
A bitter heart that bides its time and bites.
'Plays thus at being Prosper in a way,
Taketh his mirth with make-believes: so He.

His dam held that the Quiet made all things
Which Setebos vexed only: 'holds not so.
Who made them weak, meant weakness He might vex.
Had He meant other, while His hand was in,
Why not make horny eyes no thorn could prick,
Or plate my scalp with bone against the snow,
Or overscale my flesh 'neath joint and joint,
Like an orc's armour? Ay,—so spoil His sport!
He is the One now: only He doth all.

'Saith, He may like, perchance, what profits Him.
Ay, himself loves what does him good; but why?
'Gets good no otherwise. This blinded beast
Loves who so places flesh-meat on his nose,
But, had he eyes, would want no help, but hate
Or love, just as it liked him: He hath eyes.
Also it pleaseth Setebos to work,

161| MS:Keeps *P1864a:*'Keeps 162| MS:He biddeth wade < > disgorge, *P1864a:* He bids go wade < > disgorge; 164| MS:and made somewhat *P1864a:* and brought somewhat 165| MS:toe-webs and *P1864a:* toe-webs, and 166| MS:him Caliban— *P1864a:* him Caliban; 167| MS:heart, that *1868:* heart that
168| MS:Plays *P1864a:*'Plays 169| MS:make-believes: §first word over illegible erasure§ 170| MS:quiet *P1864a:* the Quiet 171| MS:Which §over illegible erasure§ < > vexes only: "holds not so: *P1864a:* vexed only: 'holds not so.
172| MS:weakness should be vexed. *P1864a:* weakness He might vex. 173| MS:his *P1864a:* while His 174| MS:thorn pricks through, *P1864a:* thorn could prick,
175| MS:plate the scalp *P1864a:* plate my scalp 176| MS:overscale the §erased§ soft flesh < > and joint. *P1864a:* overscale my flesh < > and joint,
177| MS:his *P1864a:* spoil His 179| MS:profits Him: *P1864a:* profits Him.
181| MS:Gets < > otherwise: this *P1864a:*'Gets < > otherwise. This
182| MS:whoso §over illegible word§ places fleshmeat *P1864a:* flesh-meat

Use all His hands, and exercise much craft,
By no means for the love of what is worked.
'Tasteth, himself, no finer good i' the world
When all goes right, in this safe summer-time,
And he wants little, hungers, aches not much,
Than trying what to do with wit and strength.
'Falls to make something: 'piled yon pile of turfs,
And squared and stuck there squares of soft white chalk,
And, with a fish-tooth, scratched a moon on each,
And set up endwise certain spikes of tree,
And crowned the whole with a sloth's skull a-top,
Found dead i' the woods, too hard for one to kill.
No use at all i' the work, for work's sole sake;
'Shall some day knock it down again: so He.

'Saith He is terrible: watch His feats in proof!
One hurricane will spoil six good months' hope.
He hath a spite against me, that I know,
Just as He favours Prosper, who knows why?
So it is, all the same, as well I find.
'Wove wattles half the winter, fenced them firm
With stone and stake to stop she-tortoises
Crawling to lay their eggs here: well, one wave,
Feeling the foot of Him upon its neck,
Gaped as a snake does, lolled out its large tongue,
And licked the whole labour flat: so much for spite.
'Saw a ball flame down late (yonder it lies)

186| MS:hands and *P1864a:* hands, and 187| MS:worked: *P1864a:* worked. 189| MS:summer time, *1864b:* summer-time, 190| MS:Wanting for little, hungering, aching not, *P1864a:* And he wants little, hungers, aches not much, 192| MS:Falls <> something: piled *P1864a:* 'Falls <> something: 'piled 194| MS:And with a fish-tooth scratched *P1864a:* And, with a fish-tooth, scratched 195| MS:tree *P1864a:* tree, 197| MS:kill— *P1864a:* kill. 198| MS:sake, *P1864a:* sake; 199| MS:Shall *P1864a:* 'Shall 200| MS:terrible—watch *P1864a:* terrible: watch 201| MS:spoil the six months' *P1864a:* spoil six good months' 203| MS:favours Prosper,—who *P1864a:* favours Prosper, who 204| MS:well I know. *P1864a:* well I find. 205| MS:'Wove §over illegible erasure§ 209| MS:lolled §over perhaps *curled*§ out its long tongue, *P1864a:* its large tongue, 210| MS:flat,—so <> spite: *P1864a:* flat: so <> spite. *1868:* spite *1870:* spite.
211| MS:down once—yonder it lies— *P1864a:* down late (yonder it lies)

Where, half an hour before, I slept i' the shade:
Often they scatter sparkles: there is force!
'Dug up a newt He may have envied once
And turned to stone, shut up inside a stone.
Please Him and hinder this?—What Prosper does?
Aha, if He would tell me how! Not He!
There is the sport: discover how or die!
All need not die, for of the things o' the isle
Some flee afar, some dive, some run up trees;
Those at His mercy,—why, they please Him most
When . . when . . well, never try the same way twice!
Repeat what act has pleased, He may grow wroth.
You must not know His ways, and play Him off,
Sure of the issue. 'Doth the like himself:
'Spareth a squirrel that it nothing fears
But steals the nut from underneath my thumb,
And when I threat, bites stoutly in defence:
'Spareth an urchin that contrariwise,
Curls up into a ball, pretending death
For fright at my approach: the two ways please.
But what would move my choler more than this,
That either creature counted on its life
To-morrow and next day and all days to come,
Saying, forsooth, in the inmost of its heart,
"Because he did so yesterday with me,
And otherwise with such another brute,
So must he do henceforth and always."—Ay?

212| MS:before, I ate i' the shade— *P1864a:* before, I slept i' the shade: 214| MS:Dug *P1864a:* 'Dug 215| MS:All turned <> stone: *P1864a:* And turned <> stone. 217| MS:tell you how *P1864a:* tell me how 219| MS:the Isle *P1864a:* isle 220| MS:Some fly afar, some *P1864a:* Some flee afar, some 221| MS:why, it pleases Him *P1864a:* why, they please Him 223| MS:wroth: *P1864a:* wroth. 224| MS:off *P1864a:* off, 225| MS:issue: 'doth <> himself— *P1864a:* issue. 'Doth <> himself: 227| MS:underneath his thumb *P1864a:* underneath my thumb, 228| MS:when he threats, bites *P1864a:* when I threat, bites 229| MS:that, contrariwise, *P1864a:* that contrariwise, 230| MS:ball pretending *P1864a:* ball, pretending 231| MS:at his approach <> please: *P1864a:* at my approach <> please. 232| MS:move his choler <> this *P1864a:* move my choler <> this, 235| MS:Saying forsooth in *1888:* Saying, forsooth, in 236| MS:me *P1864a:* me, 237| MS:such an other one *P1864a:* such another brute, 238| MS:must §over illegible erasure§ <> always"—Ay? §over illegible erasure§ *P1864a:* always."—Ay?

'Would teach the reasoning couple what "must" means!
'Doth as he likes, or wherefore Lord? So He.

'Conceiveth all things will continue thus,
And we shall have to live in fear of Him
So long as He lives, keeps His strength: no change,
If He have done His best, make no new world
To please Him more, so leave off watching this,—
If He surprise not even the Quiet's self
Some strange day,—or, suppose, grow into it
As grubs grow butterflies: else, here are we,
And there is He, and nowhere help at all.

'Believeth with the life, the pain shall stop.
His dam held different, that after death
He both plagued enemies and feasted friends:
Idly! He doth His worst in this our life,
Giving just respite lest we die through pain,
Saving last pain for worst,—with which, an end.
Meanwhile, the best way to escape His ire
Is, not to seem too happy. 'Sees, himself,
Yonder two flies, with purple films and pink,
Bask on the pompion-bell above: kills both.
'Sees two black painful beetles roll their ball
On head and tail as if to save their lives:
Moves them the stick away they strive to clear.

Even so, 'would have Him misconceive, suppose
This Caliban strives hard and ails no less,

239| MS:'Would teach §over illegible word§ <> means. *P1864a:* means! *1888:* Would *1889:* Would §emended to§ 'Would §see Editorial Notes§ 241| MS:thus *P1864a:* thus, 243| MS:keeps §over illegible erasure§ <> change— *P1864a:* change, 245| MS:him *P1864a:* please Him 246| MS:quiet's *P1864a:* the Quiet's 248| MS:we *P1864a:* we, 249| MS:and never help *P1864a:* and nowhere help
250| MS:Believeth <> stop: §over illegible erasure§ *P1864a:* 'Believeth <> stop. 251| MS:different—that *P1864a:* different, that 252| MS:He plagued His enemies *P1864a:* He both plagued enemies 253| MS:Idly! He does his worst <> life *P1864a:* Idly! He doth His worst <> life, 254| MS:lest it stop through *P1864a:* lest we die through 255| MS:Saving the last for *P1864a:* Saving last pain for 256| MS:his *P1864a:* escape His 257| MS:happy: sees *P1864a:* happy. Sees *1868:* happy. 'Sees 258| MS:and brown, *P1864a:* and pink, 259| MS:both: *P1864a:* both. 260| MS:Sees *P1864a:* 'Sees 262–63| MS:§no ¶§ *P1864a:* §¶§

And always, above all else, envies Him;
Wherefore he mainly dances on dark nights,
Moans in the sun, gets under holes to laugh,
And never speaks his mind save housed as now:
Outside, 'groans, curses. If He caught me here,
O'erheard this speech, and asked "What chucklest at?"
'Would, to appease Him, cut a finger off,
Or of my three kid yearlings burn the best,
Or let the toothsome apples rot on tree,
Or push my tame beast for the orc to taste:
While myself lit a fire, and made a song
And sung it, "*What I hate, be consecrate*
To celebrate Thee and Thy state, no mate
For Thee; what see for envy in poor me?"
Hoping the while, since evils sometimes mend,
Warts rub away and sores are cured with slime,
That some strange day, will either the Quiet catch
And conquer Setebos, or likelier He
Decrepit may doze, doze, as good as die.

[What, what? A curtain o'er the world at once!
Crickets stop hissing; not a bird—or, yes,
There scuds His raven that has told Him all!
It was fool's play, this prattling! Ha! The wind

265| MS:And, always above <> else, evies Him. *P1864a:* And always, above <> else, envies Him. *1868:* envies Him; 267| MS:gets into holes *P1864a:* gets under holes 268| MS:save caved as *P1864a:* save housed as 269| MS:curses: if He caught him now, *P1864a:* curses. If He caught me now, *CP1864a(Yale):* now, §crossed out§ here, §in R margin§ *1864a:* here, 271| MS:Would <> off; *P1864a:* 'Would <> off, 272| MS:of his three *P1864a:* of my three 273| MS:toothsome §inserted above§ apples rot upon the §last two words over illegible erasure§ tree, *P1864a:* rot on tree, 274| MS:push his tame <> taste: §over illegible erasure§ *P1864a:* push my tame 275| MS:While himself lit *P1864a:* While myself lit 276–78| MS:§no italics called for§ *CP1864a(Berg):* §italics called for§ *1864a:* §italic type§ 278| MS:For Thee, what *P1864a:* For Thee; what 280| MS:Warts die away, and *P1864a:* Warts rub away, and *1868:* away and 281| MS:day, or else the quiet catch *P1864a:* day, will either the Quiet catch 282| MS:he *P1864a:* likelier He 283| MS:Decrepit will doze, doze, or wholly die. *P1864a:* Decrepit may doze, doze, as good as die. 283–84| *P1864a:* §rule§ *1888:* §no rule; ¶ lost. Emended to restore ¶. See Editorial Notes§ 284| MS:There, see! A curtain *P1864a:* [What, what? A curtain 285| MS:hissing—not *P1864a:* hissing; not 286| MS:scuds his raven having told *P1864a:* scuds His raven that hath told *1888:* that has told 287| MS:prattling! See! The *P1864a:* prattling! Ha! The

Shoulders the pillared dust, death's house o' the move,
And fast invading fires begin! White blaze—
A tree's head snaps—and there, there, there, there, there,
His thunder follows! Fool to gibe at Him!
Lo! 'Lieth flat and loveth Setebos!
'Maketh his teeth meet through his upper lip,
Will let those quails fly, will not eat this month
One little mess of whelks, so he may 'scape!]

289| MS:And the invading *P1864a:* And fast invading 290| MS:and, there *P1864a:* and there *CP1864a(Berg):* §comma after ***and*** called for and then deleted§ 291| MS:follows: fool *P1864a:* follows! Fool 292| MS:See! 'Lieth *P1864a:* Lo! 'Lieth 293| MS:Maketh <> lip— *P1864a:* 'Maketh <> lip, 294| MS:fly—will *P1864a:* fly, will 295| MS:'scape! *P1864a:* 'scape!]

CONFESSIONS

I

What is he buzzing in my ears?
"Now that I come to die,
Do I view the world as a vale of tears?"
Ah, reverend sir, not I!

II

What I viewed there once, what I view again
Where the physic bottles stand
On the table's edge,—is a suburb lane,
With a wall to my bedside hand.

III

That lane sloped, much as the bottles do,
From a house you could descry
O'er the garden-wall: is the curtain blue
Or green to a healthy eye?

IV

To mine, it serves for the old June weather
Blue above lane and wall;
And that farthest bottle labelled "Ether"
Is the house o'ertopping all.

V

At a terrace, somewhere near the stopper,
There watched for me, one June,
A girl: I know, sir, it's improper,
My poor mind's out of tune.

CONFESSIONS 2| MS:—"Now *P1864a:*"Now 3| MS:a Vale of Tears?" *P1864a:*vale of tears?" 4| MS:reverend Sir *P1864a:*sir 5| *P1864a:*again, *1868:*again 7| MS:lane *P1864a:*lane, 16| MS:o'er-topping *1888:*o'ertopping 17| MS:terrace—somewhat near its stopper— *P1864a:*terrace, somewhat <> stopper, *1868:*near the stopper, *1888:*terrace, somewhere near 19| MS:know, Sir *P1864a:*sir

VI

Only, there was a way . . . you crept
Close by the side, to dodge
Eyes in the house, two eyes except:
They styled their house "The Lodge."

VII

What right had a lounger up their lane?
But, by creeping very close,
With the good wall's help,—their eyes might strain
And stretch themselves to Oes,

VIII

Yet never catch her and me together,
As she left the attic, there,
By the rim of the bottle labelled "Ether,"
And stole from stair to stair,

IX

And stood by the rose-wreathed gate. Alas,
We loved, sir—used to meet:
How sad and bad and mad it was—
But then, how it was sweet!

21| MS:way . . crept *P1864a:*Ouly, there *1864b:*Only, there *1888:*way . . . crept 24| MS:house, "The *P1864a:*house "The 25| MS:had loungers up *P1864a:*had a lounger up 30| MS:attic—there, *P1864a:*attic, there, 33| MS:gate— alas, *P1864a:*gate. Alas, 34| MS:loved, Sir *P1864a:*sir 36| MS:then, how §inserted above§ it was so §crossed out§ sweet!

MAY AND DEATH

I

I wish that when you died last May,
    Charles, there had died along with you
Three parts of spring's delightful things;
    Ay, and, for me, the fourth part too.

II

A foolish thought, and worse, perhaps!
    There must be many a pair of friends
Who, arm in arm, deserve the warm
    Moon-births and the long evening-ends.

III

So, for their sake, be May still May!
    Let their new time, as mine of old,
Do all it did for me: I bid
    Sweet sights and sounds throng manifold.

IV

Only, one little sight, one plant,
    Woods have in May, that starts up green
Save a sole streak which, so to speak,
    Is spring's blood, spilt its leaves between,—

MAY AND DEATH §*MS1857* at Armstrong Browning Library; see Editorial Notes§
1| *MS1857:* last May *1857:* last May, 3| *MS1857:* of Spring's *P1864a:* spring's
4| *MS1857:* and for me the *1857:* me, the MS:and, for 5| *MS1857:* thought and *1857:* thought, and 8| *MS1857:* Moon's birth and the late evening-ends. *1857:* the long evening-ends. MS:Moon-births and 9| *MS1857:* So for their sake, prove May *1857:* So, for MS:sakes, be May *1868:* sake 10| *MS1857:* Let the new time, like mine *1857:* Let their new MS:time, as mine 11| *MS1857:* Do as it <> me; I *1857:* Do all it MS:me: I 13| *MS1857:* Only, a little sight, a plant *1857:* Only, one little sight, one plant MS:plant, 15| *MS1857:* Except a streak, which MS:Save a sole streak which 16| *MS1857:* Is Spring's blood spilt *1857:* blood, spilt *P1864a:* spring's

V

That, they might spare; a certain wood
    Might miss the plant; their loss were small:
But I,—whene'er the leaf grows there,
    Its drop comes from my heart, that's all.

17| *MS1857:* spare—a *1857:* spare: a MS:spare; a 18| *MS1857:* Might lose the plant; the loss *1857:* plant; their loss MS:Might miss the 19| *MS1857:* And I whene'er the leaf is there *1857:* And I,—whene'er the plant is MS:But I,—whene'er the leaf grows there,

PROSPICE

Fear death?—to feel the fog in my throat,
The mist in my face,
When the snows begin, and the blasts denote
I am nearing the place,
The power of the night, the press of the storm,
The post of the foe;
Where he stands, the Arch Fear in a visible form,
Yet the strong man must go:
For the journey is done and the summit attained,
And the barriers fall,
Though a battle's to fight ere the guerdon be gained,
The reward of it all.
I was ever a fighter, so—one fight more,
The best and the last!
I would hate that death bandaged my eyes, and forbore,
And bade me creep past.
No! let me taste the whole of it, fare like my peers
The heroes of old,
Bear the brunt, in a minute pay glad life's arrears
Of pain, darkness and cold.
For sudden the worst turns the best to the brave,
The black minute's at end,
And the elements' rage, the fiend-voices that rave,
Shall dwindle, shall blend,
Shall change, shall become first a peace out of pain,
Then a light, then thy breast,
O thou soul of my soul! I shall clasp thee again,
And with God be the rest!

PROSPICE [6]| MS:foe— *P1864a:* foe; [7]| MS:stands the *P1864a:* stands, the [8]| MS:go, *P1864a:* go: [13]| MS:more *P1864a:* more, [16]| MS:past: *P1864a:* past. [20]| MS:cold: *P1864a:* cold. [25]| MS:peace, then a joy, *1868:* peace out of pain, [26]| MS:breast *P1864a:* breast, [27]| MS:soul, I *P1864a:* soul! I

YOUTH AND ART

I

It once might have been, once only:
We lodged in a street together,
You, a sparrow on the housetop lonely,
I, a lone she-bird of his feather.

II

Your trade was with sticks and clay,
You thumbed, thrust, patted and polished,
Then laughed "They will see some day
Smith made, and Gibson demolished."

III

My business was song, song, song;
I chirped, cheeped, trilled and twittered,
"Kate Brown's on the boards ere long,
And Grisi's existence embittered!"

IV

I earned no more by a warble
Than you by a sketch in plaster;
You wanted a piece of marble,
I needed a music-master.

V

We studied hard in our styles,
Chipped each at a crust like Hindoos,
For air looked out on the tiles,
For fun watched each other's windows.

YOUTH AND ART 2| MS:to-gether, *P1864a:* together, 7| MS:see one day *P1864a:* see one §crossed out§ some §in R margin§ day 8| MS:demolished. *P1864a:* demolished." 19| MS:air, looked *1888:* air looked 20| MS:fun, watched each others *P1864a:* other's *1888:* fun watched

VI

You lounged, like a boy of the South,
Cap and blouse—nay, a bit of beard too;
Or you got it, rubbing your mouth
With fingers the clay adhered to.

VII

And I—soon managed to find
Weak points in the flower-fence facing,
Was forced to put up a blind
And be safe in my corset-lacing.

VIII

No harm! It was not my fault
If you never turned your eye's tail up
As I shook upon E *in alt,*
Or ran the chromatic scale up:

IX

For spring bade the sparrows pair,
And the boys and girls gave guesses,
And stalls in our street looked rare
With bulrush and watercresses.

X

Why did not you pinch a flower
In a pellet of clay and fling it?
Why did not I put a power
Of thanks in a look, or sing it?

22| MS:too— *P1864a:* too; 26| MS:facing— *P1864a:* facing, 30| MS:eyes' *1888:* eye's 31| MS:upon E. *in alt., P1864a:* upon E *in 1888:in alt,*

XI

I did look, sharp as a lynx,
    (And yet the memory rankles)
When models arrived, some minx
    Tripped up-stairs, she and her ankles.

XII

But I think I gave you as good!
    "That foreign fellow,—who can know
How she pays, in a playful mood,
    For his tuning her that piano?"

XIII

Could you say so, and never say
    "Suppose we join hands and fortunes,
And I fetch her from over the way,
    Her, piano, and long tunes and short tunes?"

XIV

No, no: you would not be rash,
    Nor I rasher and something over:
You've to settle yet Gibson's hash,
    And Grisi yet lives in clover.

XV

But you meet the Prince at the Board,
    I'm queen myself at *bals-paré*,
I've married a rich old lord,
    And you're dubbed knight and an R.A.

XVI

Each life unfulfilled, you see;
    It hangs still, patchy and scrappy:

41| MS:lynx *P1864a:* lynx, 44| MS:ancles. *P1864a:* ankles. 46| MS:—"That *P1864a:* "That 52| MS:Her, Piano *P1864a:* piano 59| MS:old Lord, *P1864a:* lord, 60| MS:dubbed Knight *P1864a:* knight 61| MS:life's *1868:* life 62| MS:hangs here, patchy *P1864a:* hangs still, patchy

We have not sighed deep, laughed free,
    Starved, feasted, despaired,—been happy.

XVII

And nobody calls you a dunce,
    And people suppose me clever:
This could but have happened once,
    And we missed it, lost it for ever.

66| MS:clever:— *P1864a:* clever:

A FACE

If one could have that little head of hers
Painted upon a background of pale gold,
Such as the Tuscan's early art prefers!
No shade encroaching on the matchless mould
Of those two lips, which should be opening soft
In the pure profile; not as when she laughs,
For that spoils all: but rather as if aloft
Yon hyacinth, she loves so, leaned its staff's
Burthen of honey-coloured buds to kiss
And capture 'twixt the lips apart for this.
Then her lithe neck, three fingers might surround,
How it should waver on the pale gold ground
Up to the fruit-shaped, perfect chin it lifts!
I know, Correggio loves to mass, in rifts
Of heaven, his angel faces, orb on orb
Breaking its outline, burning shades absorb:
But these are only massed there, I should think,
Waiting to see some wonder momently

A FACE §*MS1852a, MS1852b:* see Editorial Notes§ *Title*| *MS1852a: Written on Emily in her Album, from which it is torn* *MS1852b:* §untitled§ MS:A Face
2| *MS1852a:* gold *P1864a:* gold, 3| MS:prefers, *P1864a:* prefers!
4| *MS1852a:* —No *P1864a:* No 5| *MS1852a:* lips, that should MS:lips, which should
6| *MS1852a:* profile—not *P1864a:* profile; not 7| *MS1852a:* all—but <> as aloft MS:as if aloft *P1864a:* all: but 8| *MS1852a:* Some hyacinth she *MS1852b:* Some §crossed out and replaced above by§ Yon hyacinth MS:hyacynth, she *P1864a:* hyacinth
9| *MS1852a:* honey-colored studs to kiss, MS:honey-coloured buds to kiss
10| *MS1852a:* Or capture <> lips, apart *MS1852b:* twixt MS:And capture <> lips apart *P1864a:* 'twixt 13| *MS1852a:* fruit-shaped perfect MS:fruit- §over illegible erasure§ shaped, perfect 13-14| *MS1852a:* §¶§ *P1864a:* §no ¶§ 14| *MS1852a:* know Correggio <> mass in MS:know, Correggio <> mass, in 15| *MS1852a:* Of Heaven his angel-faces *MS1852b:* angel faces MS:Of Heaven, his *P1864a:* heaven
16| *MS1852a:* outline burning MS:outline, burning 17| *MS1852a:* only mustered, I *MS1852b:* mustered §replaced above by two words§ massed there

Grow out, stand full, fade slow against the sky
(That's the pale ground you'd see this sweet face by),
All heaven, meanwhile, condensed into one eye
Which fears to lose the wonder, should it wink.

19| *MS1852a:* fade off against MS:fade slow against 20| *MS1852a:* you see the sweet face by) MS:you'd see this sweet *P1864a:* by), 21| *MS1852a:* All Heaven meanwhile condensed MS:All Heaven, meanwhile, condensed *P1864a:* heaven
22| *MS1852a:* Which fears to lose a wonder should *MS1852b:* a §replaced below by§ the MS:That fears <> wonder, should *Signature*| *MS1852a:* Robert Browning— / London, Oct. 11. '52 *MS1852b:* I wrote the above poem for the album of Mrs Coventry Patmore—(the *first* Angel of his House)—and this copy was made from the rough draught by E. B. B. / Robert Browning / March 27. '74.

A LIKENESS

Some people hang portraits up
In a room where they dine or sup:
    And the wife clinks tea-things under,
And her cousin, he stirs his cup,
    Asks, "Who was the lady, I wonder?"
"'Tis a daub John bought at a sale,"
    Quoth the wife,—looks black as thunder:
"What a shade beneath her nose!
Snuff-taking, I suppose,—"
Adds the cousin, while John's corns ail.

Or else, there's no wife in the case,
But the portrait's queen of the place,
Alone mid the other spoils
Of youth,—masks, gloves and foils,
And pipe-sticks, rose, cherry-tree, jasmine,
    And the long whip, the tandem-lasher,
And the cast from a fist ("not, alas! mine,
    But my master's, the Tipton Slasher"),
And the cards where pistol-balls mark ace,
And a satin shoe used for cigar-case,
And the chamois-horns ("shot in the Chablais")
    And prints—Rarey drumming on Cruiser,
    And Sayers, our champion, the bruiser,
And the little edition of Rabelais:
Where a friend, with both hands in his pockets,
    May saunter up close to examine it,
    And remark a good deal of Jane Lamb in it,
"But the eyes are half out of their sockets;
That hair's not so bad, where the gloss is,
But they've made the girl's nose a proboscis:

A LIKENESS 3| MS:clinks §over illegible erasure§ 5| MS:wonder!" *P1864a:* wonder?" 8| MS:nose *P1864a:* nose! 9| MS:—Snuff-taking *P1864a:* Snuff-taking 17| MS:fist—"Not, alas, mine— *P1864a:* fist ("not, alas! mine, 18| MS:the Tipton Slasher" *P1864a:* the Tipton Slasher") *1888:* the Tipton Slasher"), 19| MS:And cards *P1864a:* And the cards 22| MS:prints—Rarey a-drumming on *P1864a:* prints—Rarey drumming on 24| MS:little §over illegible erasure§ edition 25| MS:And a *P1864a:* Where a 28| MS:—"But *P1864a:* "But 30| MS:proboscis— *P1864a:* proboscis:

Jane Lamb, that we danced with at Vichy!
What, is not she Jane? Then, who is she?"

All that I own is a print,
An etching, a mezzotint;
'Tis a study, a fancy, a fiction,
Yet a fact (take my conviction)
Because it has more than a hint
Of a certain face, I never
Saw elsewhere touch or trace of
In women I've seen the face of:
Just an etching, and, so far, clever.

I keep my prints, an imbroglio,
Fifty in one portfolio.
When somebody tries my claret,
We turn round chairs to the fire,
Chirp over days in a garret,
Chuckle o'er increase of salary,
Taste the good fruits of our leisure,
Talk about pencil and lyre,
And the National Portrait Gallery:
Then I exhibit my treasure.
After we've turned over twenty,
And the debt of wonder my crony owes
Is paid to my Marc Antonios,
He stops me—*"Festina lentè!*
What's that sweet thing there, the etching?"
How my waistcoat-strings want stretching,

---

[31]| MS:Jane Lamb that *P1864a:* Jane Lamb, that [36]| MS:fact—that's my conviction— *P1864a:* fact (take my conviction) [41]| MS:clever *P1864a:* clever. [46]| MS:garrett, *P1864a:* garret, [46–48]| MS:garrett, / Taste *P1864a:* §line 47 added§ [50]| MS:the National Portrait Gallery— *P1864a:* the National Portrait Gallery: [52]| MS:After §over illegible erasure§ we've [54]| MS:He pays to my Marcantonios, §over illegible erasure§ *P1864a:* Is paid to my Marc Antonios, [55]| MS:me—"Festina lentè! *P1864a:* me—*"Festina lentè!* [57]| MS:And my *P1864a:* How my

How my cheeks grow red as tomatos,
How my heart leaps! But hearts, after leaps, ache.

"By the by, you must take, for a keepsake,
That other, you praised, of Volpato's."
The fool! would he try a flight further and say—
He never saw, never before to-day,
What was able to take his breath away,
A face to lose youth for, to occupy age
With the dream of, meet death with,—why, I'll not engage
But that, half in a rapture and half in a rage,
I should toss him the thing's self—" 'Tis only a duplicate,
"A thing of no value! Take it, I supplicate!"

58| MS:For my <> tomatos. *P1864a:* How my <> tomatos, 59| MS:leaps—but *P1864a:* leaps! But 61| MS:of Volpato's:" *P1864a:* of Volpato's." 62| MS:fool! Would <> say *P1864a:* would *1868:* say— 63| MS:That he never *P1864a:* He never 64| MS:away *P1864a:* away, 65| MS:for, to wile away age *P1864a:* for, to occupy age

MR. SLUDGE, "THE MEDIUM"

Now, don't sir! Don't expose me! Just this once!
This was the first and only time, I'll swear,—
Look at me,—see, I kneel,—the only time,
I swear, I ever cheated,—yes, by the soul
Of Her who hears—(your sainted mother, sir!)
All, except this last accident, was truth—
This little kind of slip!—and even this,
It was your own wine, sir, the good champagne,
(I took it for Catawba, you're so kind)
Which put the folly in my head!

"Get up?"
You still inflict on me that terrible face?
You show no mercy?—Not for Her dear sake,
The sainted spirit's, whose soft breath even now
Blows on my cheek—(don't you feel something, sir?)
You'll tell?

Go tell, then! Who the devil cares
What such a rowdy chooses to . . .

Aie—aie—aie!
Please, sir! your thumbs are through my windpipe, sir!
Ch-ch!

Well, sir, I hope you've done it now!
Oh Lord! I little thought, sir, yesterday,

MR SLUDGE, "THE MEDIUM" 1| MS:don't, Sir! don't *P1864a:* don't sir! Don't *1870:* sir! don't 2| MS:swear, *P1864a:* swear,— 3| MS:—Look *P1864a:* Look 4| MS:swear,—I *P1864a:* swear, I 5| MS:her *P1864a:* Of Her 6| MS:truth *P1864a:* truth— 7| MS:—This *P1864a:* This 8| MS:sir—the good champagne— *P1864a:* sir, the good champagne, 9| MS:for Catawba,—you're *1868:* for Catawba, you're 10| MS:Which §over illegible word§ 11| MS:You'll still inflict on me §last two words inserted above§ that <> face? on me? §last two words and question mark crossed out§ *P1864a:* You still 12| MS:You'll show no mercy?—not for her *P1864a:* You show no mercy?—Not for Her 15| MS:then—who, the devil, cares *P1864a:* then! Who the devil cares 17| MS:Please, Sir Your thumbs <> Sir! *P1864a:* Please, sir! your <> sir! 18| MS:Ch—ch! Well, Sir—I *P1864a:* sir, I 19| MS:thought, Sir, yesterday *P1864a:* sir, yesterday,

When your departed mother spoke those words
Of peace through me, and moved you, sir, so much,
You gave me—(very kind it was of you)
These shirt-studs—(better take them back again,
Please, sir)—yes, little did I think so soon
A trifle of trick, all through a glass too much
Of his own champagne, would change my best of friends
Into an angry gentleman!

                                                  Though, 'twas wrong.
I don't contest the point; your anger's just:
Whatever put such folly in my head,
I know 'twas wicked of me. There's a thick
Dusk undeveloped spirit (I've observed)
Owes me a grudge—a negro's, I should say,
Or else an Irish emigrant's; yourself
Explained the case so well last Sunday, sir,
When we had summoned Franklin to clear up
A point about those shares i' the telegraph:
Ay, and he swore . . . or might it be Tom Paine? . . .
Thumping the table close by where I crouched,
He'd do me soon a mischief: that's come true!

Why, now your face clears! I was sure it would!
Then, this one time . . . don't take your hand away,
Through yours I surely kiss your mother's hand . . .
You'll promise to forgive me?—or, at least,

21| MS:you, Sir *P1864a:*sir 24| MS:Please, Sir <> think that §replaced above by§ so *P1864a:*sir 27| MS:wrong— *P1864a:*wrong. 28| MS:just:— *P1864a:*just: 29| MS:What ever put this §crossed out and replaced above by§ such *P1864a:*Whatever 30| MS:me: there's a thick, *P1864a:*me. There's a thick
31| MS:Dark, undeveloped spirit, I've observed, *P1864a:*Dusk, undeveloped spirit (I've observed) *1868:*Dusk undeveloped 33| MS:emigrant's,—yourself *P1864a:*emigrant's; yourself 34| MS:last Sunday, Sir— *P1864a:*sir,
36| MS:about your §crossed out and replaced above by§ those shares in the telegraph— *P1864a:*telegraph: *1870:*i' 37| MS:swore . . or <> Paine? *CP1864a(Yale):*be Tom Paine? . . *CP1864a(Berg):*be Tom Paine? . . . *1864a:*be Tom Paine? . . *1870:*be Tom Paine? . *1888:*swore . . . or <> Paine? . . . 39–40| MS:§¶§ *1888:*§no ¶; emended to restore ¶; see Editorial Notes§ 40| MS:clears—I *P1864a:*clears! I
41| MS:time . . don't <> away,— *P1864a:*away, *1888:*time . . . don't
42| MS:hand— *P1864a:*hand . . *1888:*hand . . . 43| MS:—You'll *P1864a:*You'll

Tell nobody of this? Consider, sir!
What harm can mercy do? Would but the shade
Of the venerable dead-one just vouchsafe
A rap or tip! What bit of paper's here?
Suppose we take a pencil, let her write,
Make the least sign, she urges on her child
Forgiveness? There now! Eh? Oh! 'Twas your foot,
And not a natural creak, sir?

Answer, then!
Once, twice, thrice . . . see, I'm waiting to say "thrice!"
All to no use? No sort of hope for me?
It's all to post to Greeley's newspaper?

What? If I told you all about the tricks?
Upon my soul!—the whole truth, and nought else,
And how there's been some falsehood—for your part,
Will you engage to pay my passage out,
And hold your tongue until I'm safe on board?
England's the place, not Boston—no offence!
I see what makes you hesitate: don't fear!
I mean to change my trade and cheat no more,
Yes, this time really it's upon my soul!
Be my salvation:—under Heaven, of course.
I'll tell some queer things. Sixty Vs must do.
A trifle, though, to start with! We'll refer
The question to this table?

How you're changed!
Then split the difference; thirty more, we'll say.

44| MS:this? Consider, Sir! *P1864a:* sir! 47| MS:paper's this? *P1864a:* paper's here? 48| MS:Suppose I §crossed out and replaced above by§ we take 49| MS:Make just a sign <> child §over illegible word§ *P1864a:* Make the least sign 52| MS:thrice . . see, I'm <> "thrice"— *P1864a:* thrice . . . see, I'm <> "thrice!" 54| MS:to Greely's Newspaper? *P1864a:* newspaper? *1864a(r):* to Greely's §altered to§ Greeley's §with *e* in L margin§ 63| MS:really it's §over illegible erasure§ upon 64| MS:under Providence §crossed out and replaced above by three words§ Heaven, of course. 65| MS:things: sixty V's must do— *P1864a:* things. Sixty Vs must do. 66| MS:with—we'll *P1864a:* with! We'll 68| MS:Then, split the difference—thirty <> say: *P1864a:* Then split the difference; thirty <> say.

Ay, but you leave my presents! Else I'll swear
'Twas all through those: you wanted yours again,
So, picked a quarrel with me, to get them back!
Tread on a worm, it turns, sir! If I turn,
Your fault! 'Tis you'll have forced me! Who's obliged
To give up life yet try no self-defence?
At all events, I'll run the risk. Eh?

Done!
May I sit, sir? This dear old table, now!
Please, sir, a parting egg-nogg and cigar!
I've been so happy with you! Nice stuffed chairs,
And sympathetic sideboards; what an end
To all the instructive evenings! (It's alight.)
Well, nothing lasts, as Bacon came and said.
Here goes,—but keep your temper, or I'll scream!

Fol-lol-the-rido-liddle-iddle-ol!
You see, sir, it's your own fault more than mine;
It's all your fault, you curious gentlefolk!
You're prigs,—excuse me,—like to look so spry,
So clever, while you cling by half a claw
To the perch whereon you puff yourselves at roost,
Such piece of self-conceit as serves for perch
Because you chose it, so it must be safe.
Oh, otherwise you're sharp enough! You spy
Who slips, who slides, who holds by help of wing,
Wanting real foothold,—who can't keep upright
On the other perch, your neighbour chose, not you:

69| MS:presence—else *P1864a:*presence! Else 70| MS:through that §crossed out and replaced by§ those: you 71| MS:So picked *P1864a:*So, picked 72| MS:turns, Sir! If *P1864a:*sir 73| MS:you that §crossed out and replaced above by§ 'll have 76| MS:sit, Sir *P1864a:*sir 77| MS:Please, Sir *P1864a:*sir 78| MS:you—nice *P1864a:*you! Nice 79| MS:side-boards—what *P1864a:*sideboards; what 81| MS:said! *1868:*said. 83| MS:Fol-lol-the-rido-liddle-iddle-ol! 84| MS:see, Sir *P1864a:*sir 85| MS:Its all <> gentlefolk, *P1864a:*It's all <> gentlefolk! 86| MS:spry,— *P1864a:*spry, 87| MS:clever, you can cling *P1864a:*clever, while you cling 89| MS:The special §last two words crossed out and replaced above by three words§ Such piece of self-conceit 90| MS:it—so *P1864a:*it, so 91| MS:enough, you *P1864a:*enough! You

There's no outwitting you respecting him!
For instance, men love money—that, you know
And what men do to gain it: well, suppose
A poor lad, say a help's son in your house,
Listening at keyholes, hears the company
Talk grand of dollars, V-notes, and so forth,
How hard they are to get, how good to hold,
How much they buy,—if, suddenly, in pops he—
"*I*'ve got a V-note!"—what do you say to him?
What's your first word which follows your last kick?
"Where did you steal it, rascal?" That's because
He finds you, fain would fool you, off your perch,
Not on the special piece of nonsense, sir,
Elected your parade-ground: let him try
Lies to the end of the list,—"He picked it up,
His cousin died and left it him by will,
The President flung it to him, riding by,
An actress trucked it for a curl of his hair,
He dreamed of luck and found his shoe enriched,
He dug up clay, and out of clay made gold"—
How would you treat such possibilities?
Would not you, prompt, investigate the case
With cow-hide? "Lies, lies, lies," you'd shout: and why?
Which of the stories might not prove mere truth?

95| MS:respecting that §crossed out and replaced above by§ his! *P1864a:* him!
96| MS:know— *1888:* know 99| MS:key-holes, hearing §altered to§ heard the §inserted above§ company *P1864a:* keyholes, hears 100| MS:V-notes and *P1864a:* V-notes, and 102| MS:What things §last two words crossed out and replaced above by two words§ How much they'll buy <> he *P1864a:* much they buy <> he— 103| MS:a V note *P1864a:* a V-note 104| MS:word that follows *P1864a:* word which follows 106| MS:finds, §word illegibly crossed out and replaced above by§ you, tries to fool *P1864a:* finds you, fain would fool 107| MS:the §over possibly *your*§ favourite §crossed out and replaced above by§ special piece <> Sir, *P1864a:* sir, 109| MS:he *P1864a:* list,—"He 111| MS:The President threw §crossed out and replaced above by§ flung <> by— *P1864a:* by, 112| MS:actress gave §crossed out and replaced above by§ trucked <> hair— *P1864a:* hair, 113| MS:shoe §next two words illegibly crossed out and replaced above by§ enriched— *P1864a:* enriched, 115| MS:How do §last word crossed out and replaced above by two words§ is it *P1864a:* How would you
116| MS:Would §crossed out and replaced by§ Do not *P1864a:* Would not
117| MS:you'd §altered to *you'*§ *P1864a:* you'd 118| MS:mere §over illegible erasure§

This last, perhaps, that clay was turned to coin!
Let's see, now, give him me to speak for him!
How many of your rare philosophers,
In plaguy books I've had to dip into,
Believed gold could be made thus, saw it made
And made it? Oh, with such philosophers
You're on your best behaviour! While the lad—
With him, in a trice, you settle likelihoods,
Nor doubt a moment how he got his prize:
In his case, you hear, judge and execute,
All in a breath: so would most men of sense.

But let the same lad hear you talk as grand
At the same keyhole, you and company,
Of signs and wonders, the invisible world;
How wisdom scouts our vulgar unbelief
More than our vulgarest credulity;
How good men have desired to see a ghost,
What Johnson used to say, what Wesley did,
Mother Goose thought, and fiddle-diddle-dee:—
If he break in with, "Sir, *I* saw a ghost!"
Ah, the ways change! He finds you perched and prim;
It's a conceit of yours that ghosts may be:
There's no talk now of cow-hide. "Tell it out!

119| MS:perhaps—that <> coin? *P1864a:* perhaps, that <> coin! 119–20| MS:§call for ¶ inserted and cancelled§ 120| MS:now, had §crossed and and replaced above by§ give <> him— *P1864a:* him! 121| MS:many of your §last two words inserted above§ rare philosophers of old §last two words crossed out§ *P1864a:* philosophers, 123| MS:Had faith §last two words crossed out and replaced above by§ Believed § made so §crossed out and replaced above by§ thus,—saw *P1864a:* thus, saw 125| MS:behaviour— §word illegibly crossed out and replaced above by§ while *P1864a:* behavior! While 127| MS:prize— *P1864a:* prize: 128| MS:In §word illegibly crossed out and replaced above by§ his case, <> execute *P1864a:* execute, 129| MS:breath,—so would all men *P1864a:* breath: so would most men 130| MS:as fine *P1864a:* as grand 132| MS:world, *P1864a:* world; 133| MS:—How <> vulgar disbelief *P1864a:* How <> vulgar unbelief 134| MS:vulgarest incredulity; *1875:* vulgarest credulity; 135| MS:ghost,— *P1864a:* ghost, 136| MS:say, §word illegibly crossed out and replaced above by§ what 137| MS:thought, the §crossed out and replaced above by§ and fiddle-diddle-dee, *P1864a:* fiddle-diddle-dee:— 138| MS:—If he then break *1888:* If he break 139| MS:change—he <> prim— §over illegible word§ *P1864a:* change! He <> prim; *1870:* prim *C1870:* prim; 140| MS:be— *P1864a:* be: 141| MS:cow-hide—"Tell it all §crossed out and replaced by§ out *P1864a:* cow-hide. "Tell it out!

Don't fear us! Take your time and recollect!
Sit down first: try a glass of wine, my boy!
And, David, (is not that your Christian name?)
Of all things, should this happen twice—it may—
Be sure, while fresh in mind, you let us know!"
Does the boy blunder, blurt out this, blab that,
Break down in the other, as beginners will?
All's candour, all's considerateness—"No haste!
Pause and collect yourself! We understand!
That's the bad memory, or the natural shock,
Or the unexplained *phenomena!*"

Egad,
The boy takes heart of grace; finds, never fear,
The readiest way to ope your own heart wide,
Show—what I call your peacock-perch, pet post
To strut, and spread the tail, and squawk upon!
"Just as you thought, much as you might expect!
There be more things in heaven and earth, Horatio,"..
And so on. Shall not David take the hint,
Grow bolder, stroke you down at quickened rate?
If he ruffle a feather, it's "Gently, patiently!
Manifestations are so weak at first!
Doubting, moreover, kills them, cuts all short,
Cures with a vengeance!"

There, sir, that's your style!
You and your boy—such pains bestowed on him,

142| MS:us. Take <> recollect— *P1864a:* us! Take <> recollect! 143| MS:first—try <> boy— *P1864a:* first: try <> boy! 144| MS:And, David—is <> name? *P1864a:* And, David, (is <> name?) 145| MS:should that §altered to§ this happen yet again, §last two words and comma crossed out and replaced above by§ twice—it may— 148| MS:in §word illegibly crossed out and replaced above by two words§ the other, <> will,— *P1864a:* will? 149| MS:considerateness! "No haste— *P1864:* considerateness—"No haste! 150| MS:yourself: we *P1864a:* yourself! We 152| MS:unexplained phenomena." §¶§ *P1864a: phenomena!*" §¶§ 153| MS:grace—finds *P1864a:* grace; finds 154| MS:to set §crossed out and replaced above by§ ope <> own §inserted above§ own heart ope §crossed out§ wide, 155| MS:post §over illegible erasure§ 156| MS:spread your tail *P1864a:* spread the tail 157| MS:expect,— *P1864a:* expect! 159| MS:on: shall *P1864a:* on. Shall 160| MS:quickened pace? §crossed out and replaced above by§ rate? 162| MS:first— *P1864a:* first! 164| MS:vengeance!" §¶§ There, Sir *P1864a:* sir

Or any headpiece of the average worth,
To teach, say, Greek, would perfect him apace,
Make him a Person ("Porson?" thank you, sir!)
Much more, proficient in the art of lies.
You never leave the lesson! Fire alight,
Catch you permitting it to die! You've friends;
There's no withholding knowledge,—least from those
Apt to look elsewhere for their souls' supply:
Why should not you parade your lawful prize?
Who finds a picture, digs a medal up,
Hits on a first edition,—he henceforth
Gives it his name, grows notable: how much more,
Who ferrets out a "medium"? "David's yours,
You highly-favoured man? Then, pity souls
Less privileged! Allow us share your luck!"
So, David holds the circle, rules the roast,
Narrates the vision, peeps in the glass ball,
Sets-to the spirit-writing, hears the raps,
As the case may be.

Now mark! To be precise—
Though I say, "lies" all these, at this first stage,
'Tis just for science' sake: I call such grubs
By the name of what they'll turn to, dragonflies.
Strictly, it's what good people style untruth;

167| MS:him in Greek §last two words crossed out and replaced above by§ apace, 168| MS:a person (—"Porson?" Thank you, Sir!) *P1864a:*a Person ("Porson?" thank you, sir!) 169| MS:in this §altered to§ the <> lies: *P1864a:*lies. 170| MS:lesson! Fire §over illegible word§ 171| MS:friends— *P1864a:*friends; 173| MS:Not §crossed out§ apt §altered to§ Apt to look elsewhere §inserted above§ for their souls' §inserted above§ supply to you: §last two words crossed out§ 174| MS:lawful §inserted above§ prize? §word and punctuation illegibly crossed out§ 177| MS:grows famous §crossed out and replaced above by§ notable—how *P1864a:*notable: how 178| MS:a "Medium"?—"David—yours, *P1864a:*a "medium?" "David's yours, *1888:*a "medium"? "David's 180| MS:privileged, allow <> luck! *P1864a:*privileged! Allow <> luck!" 181| MS:So David <> rules his roast, *P1864a:*So, David <> rules the roast, 182| MS:Narrates his vision, peeps into §altered to§ in his glass §inserted above§ ball, *P1864a:*Narrates the vision <> in the glass 183| MS:Began §crossed out and replaced by two words§ Sets to his spirit-writing, hears his raps, *P1864a:*Sets to the spirit-writing, hears the raps, *1870:*Sets-to 184| MS:mark—to *P1864a:*mark! To 187| MS:to—butterflies. *P1864a:*to, dragonflies. 188| MS:people call untruth— *P1864a:*people style untruth;

But yet, so far, not quite the full-grown thing:
It's fancying, fable-making, nonsense-work—
What never meant to be so very bad—
The knack of story-telling, brightening up
Each dull old bit of fact that drops its shine.
One does see somewhat when one shuts one's eyes,
If only spots and streaks; tables do tip
In the oddest way of themselves: and pens, good Lord,
Who knows if you drive them or they drive you?
'Tis but a foot in the water and out again;
Not that duck-under which decides your dive.
Note this, for it's important: listen why.

I'll prove, you push on David till he dives
And ends the shivering. Here's your circle, now:
Two-thirds of them, with heads like you their host,
Turn up their eyes, and cry, as you expect,
"Lord, who'd have thought it!" But there's always one
Looks wise, compassionately smiles, submits
"Of your veracity no kind of doubt,
But—do you feel so certain of that boy's?
Really, I wonder! I confess myself
More chary of my faith!" That's galling, sir!
What, he the investigator, he the sage,
When all's done? Then, you just have shut your eyes,

189| MS:And §crossed out and replaced above by§ But <> far, it's scarce §last two words crossed out and replaced above by§ not quite <> thing— *P1864a:* thing: 192| MS:And as he tells a story, §last six words and comma crossed out and replaced by§ The knack of story-telling, 193| MS:The dull *P1864a:* Each dull 194| MS:eyes *P1864a:* eyes, 195| MS:only sparks and streaks; and §crossed out§ tables do §inserted above§ *P1864a:* only spots and 196| MS:themselves—and *P1864a:* themselves: and 197| MS:knows when §crossed out and replaced above by§ if <> them and §crossed out and replaced above by§ or 198| MS:again, *P1864a:* again; 200| MS:important,— §word illegibly crossed out and replaced above by§ listen *P1864a:* important: listen 200–201| MS:§¶§ *1888:* §no ¶; emended to restore ¶; see Editorial Notes§ 201| MS:This way you *P1864a:* I'll prove, you 202| MS:shivering: here's *P1864a:* shivering. Here's 203| MS:Two thirds of them have heads *P1864a:* Two-thirds of them, with heads 204| MS:cry as you expect *P1864a:* cry, as you expect, 205| MS:it!"—but *P1864a:* it!" But 207| MS:doubt— *P1864a:* doubt, 210| MS:faith!"—that's galling, Sir! §over illegible word§ *P1864a:* faith!" That's galling, sir! 212| MS:done? Then §crossed out and replaced above by§ Why, you *P1864a:* done? Then, you

Opened your mouth, and gulped down David whole,
You! Terrible were such catastrophe!
So, evidence is redoubled, doubled again,
And doubled besides; once more, "He heard, we heard,
You and they heard, your mother and your wife,
Your children and the stranger in your gates:
Did they or did they not?" So much for him,
The black sheep, guest without the wedding-garb,
The doubting Thomas! Now's your turn to crow:
"He's kind to think you such a fool: Sludge cheats?
Leave you alone to take precautions!"

Straight
The rest join chorus. Thomas stands abashed,
Sips silent some such beverage as this,
Considers if it be harder, shutting eyes
And gulping David in good fellowship,
Than going elsewhere, getting, in exchange,
With no egg-nogg to lubricate the food,
Some just as tough a morsel. Over the way,
Holds Captain Sparks his court: is it better there?
Have not you hunting-stories, scalping-scenes,
And Mexican War exploits to swallow plump
If you'd be free o' the stove-side, rocking-chair,

213| MS:gulped this David *P1864a:* gulped down David 214| MS:You! §over illegible erasure§ Anything but §last two words crossed out and replaced above by§ Terrible were 215| MS:The evidence is redoubled, §word illegibly crossed out§ doubled *P1864a:* So, evidence 216| MS:more, he §over illegible erasure§ heard, we §over illegible erasure§ heard, *P1864a:* more, "He 218| MS:gates, *P1864a:* gates: 219| MS:not? So *P1864a:* not?" So 221| MS:doubting Thomas: §inserted above§ now's <> crow: "He's kind §punctuation and last two words crossed out§ *P1864a:* doubting Thomas! Now's 222| MS:"He's kind §in L margin§ To <> fool: David a §last two words crossed out and replaced above by§ Sludge cheat? §altered to§ cheats? *P1864a:* to 224| MS:chorus—Thomas *P1864a:* chorus. Thomas 226| MS:if it's harder shutting *P1864a:* if it be harder, shutting 227| MS:good §over illegible word§ company *P1864a:* good fellowship, 228| MS:Than §over illegible word§ going 231| MS:The §crossed out and replaced above by§ Our Captain holds his court—is *P1864a:* Holds Captain Sparks his court: is 233| MS:Mexican exploits to be swallowed plump *P1864a:* And Mexican War exploits to swallow plump 234| MS:of *1870:* o'

And trio of affable daughters?
                                                            Doubt succumbs!
Victory! All your circle's yours again!
Out of the clubbing of submissive wits,
David's performance rounds, each chink gets patched,
Every protrusion of a point's filed fine,
All's fit to set a-rolling round the world,
And then return to David finally,
Lies seven-feet thick about his first half-inch.
Here's a choice birth o' the supernatural,
Poor David's pledged to! You've employed no tool
That laws exclaim at, save the devil's own,
Yet screwed him into henceforth gulling you
To the top o' your bent,—all out of one half-lie!

You hold, if there's one half or a hundredth part
Of a lie, that's his fault,—his be the penalty!
I dare say! You'd prove firmer in his place?
You'd find the courage,—that first flurry over,
That mild bit of romancing-work at end,—
To interpose with "It gets serious, this;
Must stop here. Sir, I saw no ghost at all.
Inform your friends I made . . . well, fools of them,
And found you ready-made. I've lived in clover
These three weeks: take it out in kicks of me!"

235| MS:And love §crossed out and replaced above by§ trio of <> daughters? §¶§ He §crossed out and replaced above by§ Doubt succumbs— *P1864a:* succumbs! 237| MS:wits *P1864a:* wits, 240| MS:to go §crossed out and replaced above by§ set 242| MS:seven-feet-thick *1868:* seven-feet thick 243| MS:of the supernatural *P1864a:* supernatural, *1870:* o' 244| MS:Poor §in L margin§ That §crossed out§ David's <> tools *P1864a:* tool 245| MS:The law exclaims at *P1864a:* That laws exclaim at 246| MS:Yet §over illegible erasure§ <> henceforth fooling you *P1864a:* henceforth gulling you 247| MS:of your *1870:* o' 248| MS:You stay §crossed out and replaced above by§ hold, if there be half or a §inserted above§ hundredth *P1864a:* if there's one half 249| MS:be §inserted above§ 252| MS:romancing,— in good time §punctuation and last three words crossed out and replaced above by§ at an end,— *P1864a:* romancing-work at end,— 253| MS:with It's getting §last two words crossed out and replaced above by§ "It gets <> this— *P1864a:* this; 254| MS:stop §over illegible word§ here: Sir *P1864a:* here. Sir 255| MS:made . . well <> them *P1864a:* them, *1888:* made . . . well 256| MS:ready made,— I've *P1864a:* ready-made. I've 257| MS:weeks—take *P1864a:* weeks: take

I doubt it. Ask your conscience! Let me know,
Twelve months hence, with how few embellishments
You've told almighty Boston of this passage
Of arms between us, your first taste o' the foil
From Sludge who could not fence, sir! Sludge, your boy!
I lied, sir,—there! I got up from my gorge
On offal in the gutter, and preferred
Your canvas-backs: I took their carver's size,
Measured his modicum of intelligence,
Tickled him on the cockles of his heart
With a raven feather, and next week found myself
Sweet and clean, dining daintily, dizened smart,
Set on a stool buttressed by ladies' knees,
Every soft smiler calling me her pet,
Encouraging my story to uncoil
And creep out from its hole, inch after inch,
"How last night, I no sooner snug in bed,
Tucked up, just as they left me,—than came raps!
While a light whisked" . . . "Shaped somewhat like a star?"
"Well, like some sort of stars, ma'am."—"So we thought!
And any voice? Not yet? Try hard, next time,
If you can't hear a voice; we think you may:

258| MS:it! Ask <> conscience—let me know *P1864a:* it. Ask <> conscience! Let me know,. 259| MS:hence with *P1864a:* hence, with 260| MS:almighty Boston this short passage *P1864a:* almighty Boston of this passage 261| MS:taste of *1870:* o' 262| MS:fence, Sir! Sludge, the §crossed out and replaced above by§ your *P1864a:* sir 263| MS:They §crossed out and replaced above by§ I 264| MS:gutter and *P1864a:* gutter, and 265| MS:took the §altered to§ their 266| MS:Measured your §crossed out and replaced above by§ his 267| MS:Tickled you §crossed out and replaced above by§ him <> of your §crossed out and replaced above by§ his 268| MS:feather and next day found *P1864a:* feather, and next week found 269| MS:clean, stuffed with dainties, § two words illegibly crossed out and replaced above by§ dizened *P1864a:* clean, dining daintly §altered to§ daintily 270| MS:stool §two words illegibly crossed out and replaced above by§ buttressed 271| MS:Every sweet smile calling <> pet, §over illegible erasure§ *P1864a:* Every soft smiler calling 273| MS:hole inch *P1864a:* hole, inch 274| MS:"Of how last night, no <> snug §over illegible word§ *P1864a:* "How last night, I no 275| MS:me,—§word illegibly crossed out and replaced above by§ than the raps! *P1864a:* than came raps! 276| MS:whisked" §quotation marks inserted above§ —"shaped *P1864a:* whisked" . . "Shaped *1888:* whisked" . . . "Shaped 277| MS:stars, Ma'am"—"So *P1864a:* stars, ma'am."—"So 278| MS:hard next *P1864a:* hard, next 279| MS:voice: we <> may— *P1864a:* voice; we <> may:

At least, the Pennsylvanian 'mediums' did."
Oh, next time comes the voice! "Just as we hoped!"
Are not the hopers proud now, pleased, profuse
O' the natural acknowledgment?

Of course!
So, off we push, illy-oh-yo, trim the boat,
On we sweep with a cataract ahead,
We're midway to the Horseshoe: stop, who can,
The dance of bubbles gay about our prow!
Experiences become worth waiting for,
Spirits now speak up, tell their inmost mind,
And compliment the "medium" properly,
Concern themselves about his Sunday coat,
See rings on his hand with pleasure. Ask yourself
How you'd receive a course of treats like these!
Why, take the quietest hack and stall him up,
Cram him with corn a month, then out with him
Among his mates on a bright April morn,
With the turf to tread; see if you find or no
A caper in him, if he bucks or bolts!
Much more a youth whose fancies sprout as rank
As toadstool-clump from melon-bed. 'Tis soon,
"Sirrah, you spirit, come, go, fetch and carry,
Read, write, rap, rub-a-dub, and hang yourself!"

280| MS:the Pennsylvanian mediums did." *P1864a:* the Pennsylvanian 'mediums' did." 281| MS:voice—"just as they hoped!" *P1864a:* voice! "Just as *1864a:* as we hoped!" 282| MS:hopers §over illegible erasure§ proud now §last two words inserted above§ pleased, §erasure§ profuse §over illegible erasure§ *P1864a:* now, pleased 283| MS:Of the *1870:* O' 284| MS:So off *P1864a:* So, off 285| MS:a-head, *P1864a:* ahead, 286| MS:the Horse-shoe—stop who *P1864a:* the Horse-shoe: stop, who *1875:* can. DC,BrU:can, *1889:* can, 287| MS:The §over illegible word§ 289| MS:Spirits that §crossed out and replaced above by§ now 290| MS:the medium properly, *P1864a:* the "medium" properly, 292| MS:pleasure,—ask *P1864a:* pleasure. Ask 293| MS:of things §crossed out and replaced above by§ treats 296| MS:Among the females §last two words crossed out and replaced above by two words§ his mates on an §altered to§ a bright §inserted above§ April morn *P1864a:* morn, 297| MS:tread—see *P1864a:* tread; see 298| MS:him—if *P1864a:* him, if 299| MS:—Much more in §inserted above§ a man §crossed out and replaced above by§ youth *P1864a:* Much more a 300| MS:As a toad-stool clump in §altered to§ on a melon-bed: 'tis soon *P1864a:* As toadstool-clump from melon-bed. 'Tis soon, 302| MS:and thou be hanged §last three words crossed out and replaced by§ hang yourself!"

I'm spared all further trouble; all's arranged;
Your circle does my business; I may rave
Like an epileptic dervish in the books,
Foam, fling myself flat, rend my clothes to shreds;
No matter: lovers, friends and countrymen
Will lay down spiritual laws, read wrong things right
By the rule o' reverse. If Francis Verulam
Styles himself Bacon, spells the name beside
With a *y* and a *k*, says he drew breath in York,
Gave up the ghost in Wales when Cromwell reigned,
(As, sir, we somewhat fear he was apt to say,
Before I found the useful book that knows)
Why, what harm's done? The circle smiles apace,
"It was not Bacon, after all, you see!
We understand; the trick's but natural:
Such spirits' individuality
Is hard to put in evidence: they incline
To gibe and jeer, these undeveloped sorts.
You see, their world's much like a jail broke loose,
While this of ours remains shut, bolted, barred,
With a single window to it. Sludge, our friend,
Serves as this window, whether thin or thick,
Or stained or stainless; he's the medium-pane

303| MS:trouble, all's arranged, *P1864a:* trouble; all's arranged; 304| MS:Your §over illegible word§ <> business—I might §crossed out and replaced above by§ may *P1864a:* business; I 305| MS:an §inserted above§ epileptic Dervish, in *P1864a:* dervish in 306| MS:clothes §over illegible erasure§ to shreds,— *P1864a:* shreds; 307| MS:matter,—lovers *P1864a:* matter: lovers 308| MS:Lay down the spiritual *P1864a:* Will lay down spiritual 309| MS:rule of reverse; if *P1864a:* reverse. If *1870:* o' 310| MS:Styles §over illegible erasure§ 311| MS:in York *P1864a:* in York, 312| MS:And died §last two words crossed out and replaced by four words§ Gave up the ghost <> when Oliver §crossed out§ Cromwell 313| MS:(As, Sir <> say *P1864a:* sir <> say, 315| MS:smiles, that's all, §last two words and punctuation crossed out and replaced above by§ apace, 317| MS:understand—the trick's §three words illegibly crossed out and replaced above by§ but natural— *P1864a:* understand; the <> natural: 320| MS:sorts,— *P1864a:* sorts. 322| MS:shut, §inserted above§ barred, bolted fast, §last word crossed out and preceding two words marked for transposition§ 323| MS:it—Sludge *P1864a:* it. Sludge 324| MS:as its pane of glass, whether §last five words and comma crossed out and replaced above by three words§ this window,—whether *P1864a:* window, whether 325| MS:stainless,—he's the medium pane §over illegible word§ *P1864a:* stainless; he's the medium-pane

Through which, to see us and be seen, they peep:
They crowd each other, hustle for a chance,
Tread on their neighbour's kibes, play tricks enough!
Does Bacon, tired of waiting, swerve aside?
Up in his place jumps Barnum—'I'm your man,
I'll answer you for Bacon!' Try once more!"

Or else it's—"What's a 'medium'? He's a means,
Good, bad, indifferent, still the only means
Spirits can speak by; he may misconceive,
Stutter and stammer,—he's their Sludge and drudge,
Take him or leave him; they must hold their peace,
Or else, put up with having knowledge strained
To half-expression through his ignorance.
Suppose, the spirit Beethoven wants to shed
New music he's brimful of; why, he turns
The handle of this organ, grinds with Sludge,
And what he poured in at the mouth o' the mill
As a Thirty-third Sonata, (fancy now!)
Comes from the hopper as bran-new Sludge, nought else,
The Shakers' Hymn in G, with a natural F,
Or the 'Stars and Stripes' set to consecutive fourths."

Sir, where's the scrape you did not help me through,
You that are wise? And for the fools, the folk

326| MS:which, they peep to <> seen, §*they peep* marked for transposition to end of line; colon added§ 329| MS:waiting, duck his head— *P1864a:* waiting, swerve aside? 331| MS:Try once more!" §last three words over illegible erasures§ 332| MS:a medium? He's *P1864a:* a 'medium'? He's *1868:* a 'medium?' He's *1888:* a 'medium'? He's 334| MS:by—he *P1864a:* by; he 335| MS:their Sludge the same §last two words crossed out and replaced above by§ and drudge, 336| MS:him,—they <> peace *P1864a:* him; they <> peace, 337| MS:Or, wiselier, put up with §last three words over illegible erasure§ their knowledge *P1864a:* Or, else, put up with having knowledge 339| MS:Suppose the <> to spill §crossed out and replaced by§ shed *P1864a:* Suppose, the 340| MS:The music <> of—why *P1864a:* New music <> of; why 342| MS:what he §crossed out and replaced above by§ was poured *P1864a:* what he poured 343| MS:As the Thirty third Sonata . . fancy now! . . *P1864a:* As a Thirty-third Sonata, (fancy now!) 344| MS:hopper—as bran-new Sludge, §last four words over illegible erasure§ *P1864a:* hopper as 345| MS:in G. with <> F., *P1864a:* in G, with <> F, 346| MS:the "Stars and Stripes" set *P1864a:* the 'Stars and Stripes' set 346–47| MS:§¶§ *1888:* §no ¶; emended to restore ¶; see Editorial Notes§ 348| MS:wise?—And <> folks *P1864a:* wise? And *1864a:* folk

Who came to see,—the guests, (observe that word!)
Pray do you find guests criticize your wine,
Your furniture, your grammar, or your nose?
Then, why your "medium"? What's the difference?
Prove your madeira red-ink and gamboge,—
Your Sludge, a cheat—then, somebody's a goose
For vaunting both as genuine. "Guests!" Don't fear!
They'll make a wry face, nor too much of that,
And leave you in your glory.

"No, sometimes
They doubt and say as much!" Ay, doubt they do!
And what's the consequence? "Of course they doubt"—
(You triumph) "that explains the hitch at once!
Doubt posed our 'medium,' puddled his pure mind;
He gave them back their rubbish: pitch chaff in,
Could flour come out o' the honest mill?" So, prompt
Applaud the faithful: cases flock in point,
"How, when a mocker willed a 'medium' once
Should name a spirit James whose name was George,

349| MS:That came <> guests,—observe that word! *P1864a:* Who came <> guests, (observe that word!) 350| MS:Pray §over *Sir*§ do 351| MS:grammar or *P1864a:* grammar, or 352| MS:Why Then, §last two words marked for transposition§ your medium? What's *P1864a:* Then, why your "medium?" What's *1888:* "medium"? What's 353| MS:If §crossed out and replaced by§ Prove <> madeira §word illegibly word crossed out§ red-ink 354| MS:cheat—why, somebody's *P1864a:* cheat—then, somebody's 355| MS:genuine: "guests"!—dont fear— *P1864a:* genuine. "Guests!" Don't fear! 356| MS:Just §crossed out and replaced above by§ They'll make 357| MS:And §crossed out and replaced above by§ Then leave <> glory. §¶§ "Oh, sometimes, *P1864a:* And leave <> §¶§ "No, sometimes, *1864a:* sometimes 358| MS:do— *P1864a:* do! 359| MS:course you §crossed out and replaced above by§ they doubt"— 360| MS:(You §crossed out and replaced above by§ What §crossed out and replaced above by§ (You triumph)—"that <> once— *P1864a:* triumph) "that <> once! 361| MS:That §crossed out and replaced above by§ Doubt <> our medium—puddled <> mind,— *P1864a:* our 'medium,' puddled <> mind; 362| MS:He gives you §crossed out and replaced above by§ them back your §crossed out and replaced above by§ their rubbish—pitch *P1864a:* He gave them <> rubbish: pitch 363| MS:Does flour <> mill?" So, §inserted above§ prompt *P1864a:* Could flour 364| MS:faithful: §word illegibly crossed out§ cases flock §inserted above§ 365| MS:a medium once *P1864a:* a 'medium' once 366| MS:Should call §crossed out and replaced above by§ name

'James' cried the 'medium,'—'twas the test of truth!"
In short, a hit proves much, a miss proves more.
Does this convince? The better: does it fail?
Time for the double-shotted broadside, then—
The grand means, last resource. Look black and big!
"You style us idiots, therefore—why stop short?
Accomplices in rascality: this we hear
In our own house, from our invited guest
Found brave enough to outrage a poor boy
Exposed by our good faith! Have you been heard?
Now, then, hear us; one man's not quite worth twelve.
You see a cheat? Here's some twelve see an ass:
Excuse me if I calculate: good day!"
Out slinks the sceptic, all the laughs explode.
Sludge waves his hat in triumph!

Or—he don't.
There's something in real truth (explain who can!)
One casts a wistful eye at, like the horse
Who mopes beneath stuffed hay-racks and won't munch
Because he spies a corn-bag: hang that truth,
It spoils all dainties proffered in its place!
I've felt at times when, cockered, cosseted

367–69| MS:'James' §quotation marks crossed out; word underlined§ cried the medium,—'twas <> truth!" §¶§ / Does *P1864a:*'James' cried the 'medium,' 'twas <> truth!" / In <> more. §no ¶§ / Does 371| MS:The §over illegible erasure§ 373| MS:in § two words illegibly crossed out and replaced above by§ cheatery: this *P1864a:* in rascality: this 374| MS:house—from *P1864a:* house, from 375| MS:Who's brave <> a poor boy §last three words over illegible erasure§ *P1864a:* Found brave 376| MS:by §two words crossed out and replaced above by§ our §crossed out§ mere good faith! May this suffice? §last three words crossed out and replaced above by§ Have you been heard? *P1864a:* by our good 377| MS:hear me; one <> twelve: *P1864a:* hear us; one <> twelve. 378| MS:cheat? Here §crossed out and replaced above by two words§ Here's some twelve that §crossed out§ see 380| MS:explode, *1888:* explode. 381| MS:§¶§ Well §crossed out and replaced above by§ Or,—he don't: *P1864a:* Or—he don't. 382| MS:truth; explain who can, *P1864a:* truth (explain who can!) 383| MS:That §in L margin§ One casts a §crossed out§ wistful eyes at, like a horse *P1864a:* One casts a wistful eye at, like the horse 384| MS:That §crossed out and replaced above by§ Who mopes neath §altered to§ beneath or §crossed out§ stuffed §over illegible word§ *1870:* munch, *1875:* munch 385| MS:spies the corn-bag: hang the truth, *P1864a:* spies a corn-bag: hang that truth, 387| MS:I've felt at times §last four words over illegible erasure§ <> cossetted, *P1864a:* cossetted *1888:* cosseted

And coddled by the aforesaid company,
Bidden enjoy their bullying,—never fear,
But o'er their shoulders spit at the flying man,—
I've felt a child; only, a fractious child
That, dandled soft by nurse, aunt, grandmother,
Who keep him from the kennel, sun and wind,
Good fun and wholesome mud,—enjoined be sweet,
And comely and superior,—eyes askance
The ragged sons o' the gutter at their game,
Fain would be down with them i' the thick o' the filth,
Making dirt-pies, laughing free, speaking plain,
And calling granny the grey old cat she is.
I've felt a spite, I say, at you, at them,
Huggings and humbug—gnashed my teeth to mark
A decent dog pass! It's too bad, I say,
Ruining a soul so!

But what's "so," what's fixed,
Where may one stop? Nowhere! The cheating's nursed
Out of the lying, softly and surely spun
To just your length, sir! I'd stop soon enough:
But you're for progress. "All old, nothing new?
Only the usual talking through the mouth,
Or writing by the hand? I own, I thought
This would develop, grow demonstrable,
Make doubt absurd, give figures we might see,

389| MS:enjoy your bullying *P1864a:* enjoy their bullying 390| MS:o'er their §crossed out and replaced above by§ your shoulders §altered to§ shoulder spit <> man— *P1864a:* o'er their shoulders <> man,— 391| MS:child—but then, a *P1864a:* child; only, a 392| MS:That, §illegible word and *round* crossed out and replaced above by two words§ dandled soft 394| MS:wholesome dirt §crossed out and replaced above by§ mud <> be clean §crossed out and replaced above by§ sweet, 396| MS:ragged §word illegibly crossed out and replaced above by§ sons of *1870:* o' 397| MS:of *1870:* o' 399| MS:the old *P1864a:* the grey old 400| MS:you and them, *P1864a:* you, at them, 401| MS:§first word illegibly crossed out§ Huggings 402| MS:pass: it's *P1864a:* pass! It's 403| MS:Fooling a <> so! §¶§ But §over illegible word and quotation marks§ *P1864a:* Ruining a 405| MS:surely, spun *P1864a:* surely spun 406| MS:length, Sir <> enough.— *P1864a:* sir <> enough: 407| MS:progress—"All *P1864a:* progress. "All 408| MS:through your §crossed out and replaced above by§ the 409| MS:by your §crossed out and replaced above by§ the <> own I thought §over illegible erasure§ *P1864a:* own, I 411| MS:absurd—show §crossed out and replaced above by§ give *P1864a:* absurd, give

Flowers we might touch. There's no one doubts you, Sludge!
You dream the dreams, you see the spiritual sights,
The speeches come in your head, beyond dispute.
Still, for the sceptics' sake, to stop all mouths,
We want some outward manifestation!—well,
The Pennsylvanians gained such; why not Sludge?
He may improve with time!"

Ay, that he may!

He sees his lot: there's no avoiding fate.
'Tis a trifle at first. "Eh, David? Did you hear?
You jogged the table, your foot caused the squeak,
This time you're . . . joking, are you not, my boy?"
N-n-no!"—and I'm done for, bought and sold henceforth.
The old good easy jog-trot way, the . . . eh?
The . . . not so very false, as falsehood goes,
The spinning out and drawing fine, you know,—
Really mere novel-writing of a sort,
Acting, or improvising, make-believe,
Surely not downright cheatery,—any how,
'Tis done with and my lot cast; Cheat's my name:
The fatal dash of brandy in your tea

412| MS:touch: there's <> doubts your faith— §last two words crossed out and replaced above by§ you, Sludge! *P1864a:* touch. There's 413| MS:dreams, and §crossed out and replaced above by§ you 414| MS:come into §altered to§ in your head, no doubt. §last two words and period crossed out and replaced above by§ beyond dispute, *P1864a:* dispute. 416| MS:We want §last two words in L margin§ Some <> manifestation! Don't despair §last two words crossed out§—well, *P1864a:* some 417| MS:gained them, why *P1864a:* gained such; why 419| MS:lot—there's <> fate. §over illegible erasure§ *P1864a:* lot: there's 420| MS:first—"Eh, §over illegible word§ David, . . did *P1864a:* first. "Eh, David? Did 422| MS:This time §last two words in L margin§ And now §last two words crossed out§ you're . . joking *P1864a:* you're . . . joking 424| MS:easy §next two words illegibly crossed out and replaced above by§ jog-trot <> the . . eh? *P1864a:* the . . . eh? 425| MS:as lying goes, *P1864a:* as falsehood goes, 427| MS:Really 'twas novel-writing *P1864a:* Really mere novel-writing 428| MS:or §over illegible erasure§ <> make-believe— *P1864a:* make-believe, 429| MS:cheatery! Any *1868:* cheatery,—any 430| MS:cast—Cheat's *P1864a:* cast; Cheat's

Has settled what you'll have the souchong's smack:
The caddy gives way to the dram-bottle.

Then, it's so cruel easy! Oh, those tricks
That can't be tricks, those feats by sleight of hand,
Clearly no common conjuror's!—no indeed!
A conjuror? Choose me any craft i' the world
A man puts hand to; and with six months' pains
I'll play you twenty tricks miraculous
To people untaught the trade: have you seen glass blown,
Pipes pierced? Why, just this biscuit that I chip,
Did you ever watch a baker toss one flat
To the oven? Try and do it! Take my word,
Practise but half as much, while limbs are lithe,
To turn, shove, tilt a table, crack your joints,
Manage your feet, dispose your hands aright,
Work wires that twitch the curtains, play the glove
At end o' your slipper,—then put out the lights
And . . . there, there, all you want you'll get, I hope!
I found it slip, easy as an old shoe.

Now, lights on table again! I've done my part,
You take my place while I give thanks and rest.
"Well, Judge Humgruffin, what's your verdict, sir?

433| MS:dram bottle. *P1864a:*dram-bottle. 435| MS:tricks—those *P1864a:*tricks, those 436| MS:So clearly not a conjuror's!—no, indeed! *P1864a:*Clearly no common conjuror's *1888:*no indeed! 437| MS:Conjuror? Take §crossed out and replaced above by two words§ Choose me any honest §crossed out§ craft in the *P1864a:*A conjuror? Choose *1870:*i' 438| MS:puts will to, and <> pains, *P1864a:*puts hand to; and *1888:*pains 439| MS:He'll §crossed out and replaced in L margin by§ I'l play a dozen tricks impossible §crossed out§ extravagant *P1864a:*I'd play you twenty tricks miraculous *1864a:*I'll play 440| MS:To hands untaught *P1864a:*To people untaught 441| MS:biscuit §over illegible erasure§ 442| MS:watch §over illegible word§ 444| MS:much, with pliant §inserted above§ limbs, like these,— §last two words and punctuation crossed out§ *P1884a:*much, while Limbs are lithe, 445| MS:table—crack *P1864a:*table, crack 447| MS:the hand— §last word and dash crossed out and replaced above by§ glove 448| MS:of *1870:*o' 449| MS:And . . there <> want you've §altered to§ you'll got *P1864a:*And . . . there <> get 451| MS:again—I've *P1864a:*again! I've 452| MS:You'd §altered to§ You may succeed §last two words crossed out and replaced above by three words§ take my place <> rest— *P1864a:*rest. 453| MS:Well, §over illegible word§ <> what's the §crossed out and replaced above by§ your <> Sir? *P1864a:*sir?

You, hardest head in the United States,—
Did you detect a cheat here? Wait! Let's see!
Just an experiment first, for candour's sake!
I'll try and cheat you, Judge! The table tilts:
Is it I that move it? Write! I'll press your hand:
Cry when I push, or guide your pencil, Judge!"
Sludge still triumphant! "That a rap, indeed?
That, the real writing? Very like a whale!
Then, if, sir, you—a most distinguished man,
And, were the Judge not here, I'd say, . . . no matter!
Well, sir, if you fail, you can't take us in,—
There's little fear that Sludge will!"

Won't he, ma'am?
But what if our distinguished host, like Sludge,
Bade God bear witness that he played no trick,
While you believed that what produced the raps
Was just a certain child who died, you know,
And whose last breath you thought your lips had felt?
Eh? That's a capital point, ma'am: Sludge begins
At your entreaty with your dearest dead,
The little voice set lisping once again,
The tiny hand made feel for yours once more,
The poor lost image brought back, plain as dreams,
Which image, if a word had chanced recall,

454| MS:You, the best §last two words crossed out and replaced above by§ hardest
455| MS:here? Wait—let's see— *P1864a:* here? Wait! Let's see! 456| MS:sake— *P1864a:* sake! 457| MS:tilts— *P1864a:* tilts: 458| MS:it? Write—I'll <> hand— *P1864a:* it? Write! I'll <> hand: 459| MS:pencil, Judge §crossed out and replaced above by§ Sir!" *P1864a:* pencil, Judge!" 462| MS:And §crossed out§ Then, if, Sir, you *P1864a:* sir *1888:* sir you §emended to§ sir, you §see Editorial Notes§
463| MS:say,—no *P1864a:* say, . . no *1888:* say, . . . no 464| MS:Well, Sir <> fail, §two words crossed out and replaced above by two words§ you can't *P1864a:* sir
465| MS:fear §two words illegibly crossed out§ Sludge <> Ma'am? *P1864a:* fear that Sludge <> ma'am? 468| MS:And you *P1864a:* While you 469| MS:child that §crossed out and replaced above by§ who died, last year §last two words crossed out§ you
470| MS:§in L margin§ Whose latest §crossed out and replaced above by§ last *P1864a:* And whose 471| MS:point, Ma'am *P1864a:* ma'am 473| MS:set stammering §crossed out and replaced above by§ lisping once again, §over illegible word§
474| MS:yours again, §crossed out and replaced by two words§ once more,
476| MS:Which, if a careless word *P1864a:* Which image, if a word

The customary cloud would cross your eyes,
Your heart return the old tick, pay its pang!
A right mood for investigation, this!
One's at one's ease with Saul and Jonathan,
Pompey and Cæsar: but one's own lost child . . .
I wonder, when you heard the first clod drop
From the spadeful at the grave-side, felt you free
To investigate who twitched your funeral scarf
Or brushed your flounces? Then, it came of course
You should be stunned and stupid; then, (how else?)
Your breath stopped with your blood, your brain struck work.
But now, such causes fail of such effects,
All's changed,—the little voice begins afresh,
Yet you, calm, consequent, can test and try
And touch the truth. "Tests? Didn't the creature tell
Its nurse's name, and say it lived six years,
And rode a rocking-horse? Enough of tests!
Sludge never could learn that!"

He could not, eh?
You compliment him. "Could not?" Speak for yourself!

477| MS:The usual cloud <> your brow, you know, §last three words crossed out and replaced above by three words§ eyes, I think, *P1864a:* The customary cloud <> eyes,
478| MS:And §crossed out§ Your heart §word illegibly crossed out and replaced above by§ return <> tick, §word illegibly crossed out and replaced above by two words§ give the pang! §word and punctuation illegibly crossed out§ *P1864a:* tick, pay its pang!
479| MS:The right *P1864a:* A right 481| MS:and Cæsar—but <> own §over illegible erasure§ *P1864a:* and Cæsar: but 483| MS:grave-side, were you *P1864a:* grave-side, felt you 484| MS:funeral cloak *P1864a:* funeral scarf
485| MS:your hat-band? Then, <> course, *P1864a:* your flounces? Then *1888:* course
486| MS:That you were §last three words crossed out and replaced above by three words§ You should be <> stupid—then, how else? *P1864a:* stupid, then, (how else?)
487| MS:work— *P1864a:* work. 488| MS:now—such §over illegible erasure§ <> of such §over illegible erasure§ effects— *P1864a:* now, <> effects,
489| MS:begins again §crossed out§ afresh *P1864a:* afresh, 490| MS:And you, <> consequent, §over illegible erasure§ can §over illegible word§ tested §altered to§ test and §inserted above§ tried §altered to§ try, *P1864a:* Yet you, <> try
491| MS:touched §altered to§ touch the truth: tests? didn't *P1864a:* truth. "Tests? Didn't
493| MS:And had §crossed out and replaced above by§ rode <> tests— *P1864a:* tests!
494| MS:that! §¶§ *P1864a:* that!" §¶§ 495| MS:You §over illegible erasure§ <> him. §over illegible word§ <> not"? Speak *P1864a:* not?" Speak

I'd like to know the man I ever saw
Once,—never mind where, how, why, when,—once saw,
Of whom I do not keep some matter in mind
He'd swear I "could not" know, sagacious soul!
What? Do you live in this world's blow of blacks,
Palaver, gossipry, a single hour
Nor find one smut has settled on your nose,
Of a smut's worth, no more, no less?—one fact
Out of the drift of facts, whereby you learn
What someone was, somewhere, somewhen, somewhy?
You don't tell folk—"See what has stuck to me!
Judge Humgruffin, our most distinguished man,
Your uncle was a tailor, and your wife
Thought to have married Miggs, missed him, hit you!"—
Do you, sir, though you see him twice a-week?
"No," you reply, "what use retailing it?
Why should I?" But, you see, one day you *should*,
Because one day there's much use,—when this fact
Brings you the Judge upon both gouty knees
Before the supernatural; proves that Sludge

496| *P1864a:* know what man *CP1864a:* know the man 499| MS:know—sagacious sir! *P1864a:* know, sagacious soul! 500| MS:What do §over illegible erasure§ *P1864a:* What? Do 502| MS:find some §crossed our and replaced above by§ one <> your §over illegible erasure§ nose *P1864a:* nose, 503| MS:less, some §crossed out and replaced above by§ one *P1864a:* less?—one 504| MS:you §over illegible word§ 505| MS:was §two words and punctuation illegibly crossed out and replaced above by three words and punctuation§ somewhere, somewhen, somewhy— *P1864a:* was, <> somewhy? 506| MS:You §over illegible word§ <> folks <> me— *P1864a:* folk <> me! 509| MS:you." *P1864a:* you!"— 510| MS:—Do §over illegible erasure§ you, Sir *P1864a:* sir 511| MS:"Now" §altered to§ "No" you reply "what <> retailing this? *P1864a:* "No," you reply, "what <> retailing it? 512| MS:should I?" §over *you* erased§ 514| MS:upon his bended §crossed out and replaced above by§ gouty *P1864a:* upon both gouty 515| MS:supernatural, proves *P1864a:* supernatural; proves

Knows, as you say, a thing he "could not" know:
Will not Sludge thenceforth keep an outstretched face
The way the wind drives?

"Could not!" Look you now,
I'll tell you a story! There's a whiskered chap,
A foreigner, that teaches music here
And gets his bread,—knowing no better way:
He says, the fellow who informed of him
And made him fly his country and fall West
Was a hunchback cobbler, sat, stitched soles and sang,
In some outlandish place, the city Rome,
In a cellar by their Broadway, all day long;
Never asked questions, stopped to listen or look,
Nor lifted nose from lapstone; let the world
Roll round his three-legged stool, and news run in
The ears he hardly seemed to keep pricked up.
Well, that man went on Sundays, touched his pay,
And took his praise from government, you see;
For something like two dollars every week,
He'd engage tell you some one little thing
Of some one man, which led to many more,
(Because one truth leads right to the world's end)
And make you that man's master—when he dined

516| MS:Knows, sure enough, §last two words crossed out and replaced above by three words§ as you say, 516–17| MS:And once begin the traffic, never fear §line cancelled§ 517| MS:But §crossed out and replaced above by two words§ Will not Sludge will §crossed out§ henceforth keep <> face, *P1864a:* not Sludge thenceforth keep DC,BrU:face *1889:* face 518| MS:wind blows §crossed out and replaced above by§ drives! *P1864a:* drives? 519| MS:you something §crossed out and replaced by two words§ a story: there's *P1864a:* story! There's 522| MS:fellow that informed *P1864a:* fellow who informed 523| MS:fall West, DC,BrU:fall West *1889:* fall West 524| MS:cobbler that stitched <> sang *P1864a:* cobbler, sat, stitched <> sang, 526| MS:broadway §over illegible erasure§ all <> long, *P1864a:* their Broadway, all <> long; 528| MS:lifted head from lapstone—let *P1864a:* lifted nose from lapstone; let 530| MS:up: *P1864a:* up. 533| MS:week *P1864a:* week, 534| MS:engage answer questions—some one thing *P1864a:* engage tell you some one little thing 535| MS:man, leading to many many §last two words crossed out and replaced above by two words§ some few more, *P1864a:* man, which led to many more, 536| MS:end) *1864a:* end,) *1888:* end) 537| MS:And so become his master—when §over illegible word§ *P1864a:* And make you that man's master

And on what dish, where walked to keep his health
And to what street. His trade was, throwing thus
His sense out, like an ant-eater's long tongue,
Soft, innocent, warm, moist, impassible,
And when 'twas crusted o'er with creatures—slick,
Their juice enriched his palate. "Could not Sludge!"

I'll go yet a step further, and maintain,
Once the imposture plunged its proper depth
I' the rotten of your natures, all of you,—
(If one's not mad nor drunk, and hardly then)
It's impossible to cheat—that's, be found out!
Go tell your brotherhood this first slip of mine,
All to-day's tale, how you detected Sludge,
Behaved unpleasantly, till he was fain confess,
And so has come to grief! You'll find, I think,
Why Sludge still snaps his fingers in your face.
There now, you've told them! What's their prompt reply?
"Sir, did that youth confess he had cheated me,
I'd disbelieve him. He may cheat at times;
That's in the 'medium'-nature, thus they're made,
Vain and vindictive, cowards, prone to scratch.
And so all cats are; still, a cat's the beast
You coax the strange electric sparks from out,
By rubbing back its fur; not so a dog,
Nor lion, nor lamb: 'tis the cat's nature, sir!

539| MS:street: his <> was throwing *P1864a:* street. His <> was, throwing 540| MS:out like an anteater's <> tongue *P1864a:* out, like <> tongue, *1888:* ant-eater's 541| MS:moist, §over illegible word§ 543| MS:palate: §altered to§ palate. <> not" §quotation mark crossed out§ Sludge!" 544| MS:further and *P1864a:* further, and 545| MS:Once the foundation sunk its *P1864a:* Once the imposture plunged its 546| MS:In the weakness of <> natures; all *P1864a:* the rotten of <> natures, all *1870:* I' 547| MS:If <> drunk—and <> then— *P1864a:* (If <> drunk, and <> then) 550| MS:to-day's story §crossed out and replaced above by§ tale, how 551| MS:unpleasantly, till §last two words over illegible erasures§ 552| MS:grief,—you'll *P1864a:* grief! You'll 556| MS:him: true, he cheats at times— *P1864a:* him. He may cheat at times; 557| MS:the medium-nature, so they're *P1864a:* the 'medium'-nature, thus they're 558| MS:scratch, *P1864a:* scratch. 559| MS:Why, so <> are,—still a *P1864a:* And so <> are; still, a 561| MS:its §over illegible erasure§ fur—not *P1864a:* fur; not 562| MS:lamb,—'tis the beast's §crossed out and replaced above by§ cat's *P1864a:* lamb: 'tis

Why not the dog's? Ask God, who made them beasts!
D' ye think the sound, the nicely-balanced man
(Like me"—aside)—"like you yourself,"—(aloud)
—He's stuff to make a 'medium'? Bless your soul,
'Tis these hysteric, hybrid half-and-halfs,
Equivocal, worthless vermin yield the fire!
We take such as we find them, 'ware their tricks,
Wanting their service. Sir, Sludge took in you—
How, I can't say, not being there to watch:
He was tried, was tempted by your easiness,—
He did not take in me!"

Thank you for Sludge!
I'm to be grateful to such patrons, eh,
When what you hear's my best word? 'Tis a challenge
"Snap at all strangers, half-tamed prairie-dog,
So you cower duly at your keeper's beck!
Cat, show what claws were made for, muffling them
Only to me! Cheat others if you can,
Me, if you dare!" And, my wise sir, I dared—
Did cheat you first, made you cheat others next,
And had the help o' your vaunted manliness
To bully the incredulous. You used me?
Have not I used you, taken full revenge,
Persuaded folk they knew not their own name,

563| MS:not these too §last two words crossed out and replaced above by two words§ the dog's? Ask God who <> them all §crossed out and replaced above by§ beasts! *P1864a:* dog's? Ask God, who 566| MS:"He's <> medium? Bless *P1864a:* "—He's <> 'medium?' Bless *1888:* 'medium'? Bless 567| MS:half and halfs, *P1864a:* half-and-halfs, 568| MS:fire— *P1864a:* fire! 569| MS:We must take *1888:* We take 570| MS:service: Sir *P1864a:* service. Sir 571| MS:watch— §over illegible word§ *1864a:* watch: 572| MS:tried, was §inserted above§ 575| MS:word? §word illegibly crossed out and replaced above by§ 'Tis a challenge, *P1864a:* challenge; *1870:* challenge 576| MS:strangers, you half-tamed wild brute, §over illegible word§ *P1864a:* half-tamed prairie-dog, *1868:* strangers, half-tamed 577| MS:keeper's foot §crossed out§ nod! *1888:* keeper's beck! 578| MS:Show what those claws *P1864a:* Cat, show what claws 579| MS:me—cheat *P1864a:* me! Cheat 580| MS:sir, I could— *P1864a:* sir, I dared— 582| MS:of *1870:* o' 583| MS:the doubters. §crossed out and replaced above by§ incredulous. You made §crossed out§ use §altered to§ used of §crossed out§ me? 584| MS:you, had my §last two words crossed out and replaced above by§ taken full revenge! *P1864a:* revenge, 585| MS:—Persuaded folks <> names, *P1864a:* MS:Persuaded folk <> name,

And straight they'd own the error! Who was the fool
When, to an awe-struck wide-eyed open-mouthed
Circle of sages, Sludge would introduce
Milton composing baby-rhymes, and Locke
Reasoning in gibberish, Homer writing Greek
In noughts and crosses, Asaph setting psalms
To crotchet and quaver? I've made a spirit squeak
In sham voice for a minute, then outbroke
Bold in my own, defying the imbeciles—
Have copied some ghost's pothooks, half a page,
Then ended with my own scrawl undisguised.
"All right! The ghost was merely using Sludge,
Suiting itself from his imperfect stock!"
Don't talk of gratitude to me! For what?
For being treated as a showman's ape,
Encouraged to be wicked and make sport,
Fret or sulk, grin or whimper, any mood
So long as the ape be in it and no man—
Because a nut pays every mood alike.
Curse your superior, superintending sort,
Who, since you hate smoke, send up boys that climb
To cure your chimney, bid a "medium" lie
To sweep you truth down! Curse your women too,
Your insolent wives and daughters, that fire up
Or faint away if a male hand squeeze theirs,

586| MS:they §altered to§ they'd owned §altered to§ own the error; who <> fool, *P1864a:*error! Who *1864a:*fool 587| MS:When to an awe-struck, wide-eyed, open-mouthed *P1864a:*When, to *1868:*awe-struck wide-eyed open-mouthed 589| MS:baby-rhymes §over illegible word§ and *P1864a:*baby-rhymes, and 590| MS:gibberish—Homer *P1864a:*gibberish, Homer 591| MS:crosses, Asaph §over illegible erasure§ 594| MS:defying such a §last two words crossed out and replaced above by one word§ the set of fools— *P1864a:*the imbeciles— 596| MS:undisguised— *P1864a:*undisguised. 597| MS:right—the *P1864a:*right! The 598| MS:Suiting himself from an imperfect stock." §altered to§ stock" *P1864a:*Suiting itself from his imperfect stock!" 599| MS:me—for *P1864a:*me! For 602| MS:grin §over illegible erasure§ 603| MS:ape was §crossed out and replaced above by§ be 604| MS:pays §over illegible erasure§ 605| MS:superintending souls, *P1864a:*superintending sort, 606| MS:since they hate <> boys like me §last two words crossed out and replaced above by two words§ that climb *P1864a:*since you hate 607| MS:cure their chimney <> medium *P1864a:*cure your chimney <> "medium" 608| MS:To find them truth out: curse *P1864a:*To sweep you truth down! Curse *1888:*too. DC,BrU:too, *1889:*too,

Yet, to encourage Sludge, may play with Sludge
As only a "medium," only the kind of thing
They must humour, fondle . . . oh, to misconceive
Were too preposterous! But I've paid them out!
They've had their wish—called for the naked truth,
And in she tripped, sat down and bade them stare:
They had to blush a little and forgive!
"The fact is, children talk so; in next world
All our conventions are reversed,—perhaps
Made light of: something like old prints, my dear!
The Judge has one, he brought from Italy,
A metropolis in the background,—o'er a bridge,
A team of trotting roadsters,—cheerful groups
Of wayside travellers, peasants at their work,
And, full in front, quite unconcerned, why not?
Three nymphs conversing with a cavalier,
And never a rag among them: 'fine,' folk cry—
And heavenly manners seem not much unlike!
Let Sludge go on; we'll fancy it's in print!"
If such as came for wool, sir, went home shorn,
Where is the wrong I did them? 'Twas their choice;

611| MS:encourage Sludge may fondle §crossed out and replaced above by two words§ play with *P1864a:*encourage Sludge, may 612| MS:a medium, just §crossed out§ that mere §inserted above§ kind *P1864a:*a "medium," only the kind 613| MS:§first four words illegibly crossed out and replaced above by three words and comma§ They must humour, fondled §altered to§ fondle . . oh *1888:*fondle . . . oh
614| MS:—That were too foolish! But <> out— *P1864a:*Were too preposterous! But <> out! 615| MS:truth *P1864a:*truth, 616| MS:sate *P1864a:*sat
617| MS:forgive— *P1864a:*forgive! 619| MS:perhaps, *P1864a:*perhaps
620| MS:old pictures, this— §last two words and punctuation crossed out and replaced above by three words and punctuation§ prints, my dear. *P1864a:*dear!
621| MS:one he *P1864a:*one, he 622| MS:A city §crossed out and replaced above by§ metropolis 623| MS:trotting horses §crossed out and replaced above by§ roadsters—cheerful *P1864a:*roadsters,—cheerful 625| MS:front, all unconcerned <> not?— *P1864a:*front, quite unconcerned <> not? 626| MS:cavalier *P1864a:*cavalier, 627| MS:And not §crossed out and replaced above by§ never a rag among §inserted above ; next word and replacement above both crossed out§ them—"fine," folks cry,— *P1864a:*them: 'fine,' folk cry— 628| MS:manners may be §last two words crossed out and replaced above by one word§ are not much §inserted above§ *P1864a:*manners seem not 628–30| MS:unlike! / §¶ called for in margins§ If *P1864a:*unlike! / §no ¶§ Let Sludge go on; we'll fancy it's in print!" / If 630| MS:If some, that §last two words crossed out and replaced above by two words§ such as <> sir, §inserted above§ went home thus §crossed out§ shorn, 631| MS:choice— *P1864a:*choice;

They tried the adventure, ran the risk, tossed up
And lost, as some one's sure to do in games;
They fancied I was made to lose,—smoked glass
Useful to spy the sun through, spare their eyes:
And had I proved a red-hot iron plate
They thought to pierce, and, for their pains, grew blind,
Whose were the fault but theirs? While, as things go,
Their loss amounts to gain, the more's the shame!
They've had their peep into the spirit-world,
And all this world may know it! They've fed fat
Their self-conceit which else had starved: what chance
Save this, of cackling o'er a golden egg
And compassing distinction from the flock,
Friends of a feather? Well, they paid for it,
And not prodigiously; the price o' the play,
Not counting certain pleasant interludes,
Was scarce a vulgar play's worth. When you buy
The actor's talent, do you dare propose
For his soul beside? Whereas, my soul you buy!
Sludge acts Macbeth, obliged to be Macbeth,
Or you'll not hear his first word! Just go through
That slight formality, swear himself's the Thane,
And thenceforth he may strut and fret his hour,

633| MS:someone's <> games: *P1864a:* games; *1864a:* some one's 634| MS:fancied Sludge was <> lose §over illegible word§ *P1864a:* fancied I was 635| MS:Or use to <> eyes— *P1864a:* Useful to <> eyes: 636| MS:had he proved *P1864a:* had I proved 637| MS:They thought §crossed out and replaced above by§ hoped to <> pains, grown §crossed out and replaced above by§ grew *P1864a:* They thought to
639| MS:gain; the *P1864a:* gain, the 641| MS:it: they've *P1864a:* it! They've
642| MS:The self-conceit <> starved—what *P1864a:* Their self-conceit <> starved: what
643| MS:Like this, <> o'er their golden *P1864a:* Save this, <> o'er a golden
645| MS:The §crossed out§ friends §altered to§ Friends <> it *P1864a:* it,
646| MS:prodigiously—the *P1864a:* prodigiously; the 648| MS:worth; §altered to§ worth. when §altered to§ When 649| MS:talent, never §crossed out and replaced above by two words§ do you 650| MS:beside? Whereas, §inserted above§ my <> buy— §over illegible erasure§ *P1864a:* buy! *1888:* beside? Whereas my §emended to§ Whereas, my §see Editorial Notes§ 651| MS:acts Macbeth <> be Macbeth *P1864a:* acts Macbeth, <> be Macbeth, 652| MS:you will <> word: just go though §last three words over illegible erasure§ *P1864a:* word! Just go through *1868:* you'll 653| MS:The slight <> swear he's §altered to§ himself's *P1864a:* That slight

Spout, spawl, or spin his target, no one cares!
Why hadn't I leave to play tricks, Sludge as Sludge?
Enough of it all! I've wiped out scores with you—
Vented your fustian, let myself be streaked
Like tom-fool with your ochre and carmine,
Worn patchwork your respectable fingers sewed
To metamorphose somebody,—yes, I've earned
My wages, swallowed down my bread of shame,
And shake the crumbs off—where but in your face?

As for religion—why, I served it, sir!
I'll stick to that! With my *phenomena*
I laid the atheist sprawling on his back,
Propped up Saint Paul, or, at least, Swedenborg!
In fact, it's just the proper way to baulk
These troublesome fellows—liars, one and all,
Are not these sceptics? Well, to baffle them,
No use in being squeamish: lie yourself!
Erect your buttress just as wide o' the line,
Your side, as they build up the wall on theirs;
Where both meet, midway in a point, is truth
High overhead: so, take your room, pile bricks,
Lie! Oh, there's titillation in all shame!
What snow may lose in white, snow gains in rose!

655| MS:spawl or *P1864a:* spawl, or 655–57| MS:cares! / §¶ called for in margins§ / Enough *P1864a:* cares! / §no ¶§ Why hadn't I leave to play tricks, Sludge as Sludge? / Enough <> I've wiped §last two words over illegible erasure§ 659| MS:Like a Tom-Fool with your §inserted above§ *P1864a:* tom-fool *1868:* Like tom-fool 660| MS:And worn the patchwork your clean fingers *P1864a:* Worn patchwork your respectable fingers 661| MS:yes I've *P1864a:* yes, I've 662| MS:My pay and swallowed *P1864a:* My wages, swallowed 664| MS:it, Sir! *P1864a:* sir! 665| MS:A capital point! Doing these pretty tricks *P1864a:* I'll stick to that! With my *phenomena* 666| MS:back— *P1864a:* back, 667| MS:I propped §over illegible erasure§ Saint Paul up, or *P1864a:* And propped *1868:* Propped up Saint Paul, or 668| MS:the only way to stop §crossed out§ baulk *P1864a:* the proper way 671| MS:lie §over illegible erasure§ 673| MS:they run up the works §crossed out and replaced above by§ wall on theirs— *P1864a:* they've built up <> theirs; *1888:* they build up 674| MS:midway, in <> truth, *1864b:* midway in *1888:* truth 675| MS:High o'er our heads: so, <> room and build— *P1864a:* High overhead: so, <> room, pile bricks, 676| MS:in the shame,— *P1864a:* in all shame! 677| MS:What §in L margin§ The §crossed out§ <> white, it gains in rose: *1868:* rose! *1888:* white, snow gains

Miss Stokes turns—Rahab,—nor a bad exchange!
Glory be on her, for the good she wrought,
Breeding belief anew 'neath ribs of death,
Browbeating now the unabashed before,
Ridding us of their whole life's gathered straws
By a live coal from the altar! Why, of old,
Great men spent years and years in writing books
To prove we've souls, and hardly proved it then:
Miss Stokes with her live coal, for you and me!
Surely, to this good issue, all was fair—
Not only fondling Sludge, but, even suppose
He let escape some spice of knavery,—well,
In wisely being blind to it! Don't you praise
Nelson for setting spy-glass to blind eye
And saying . . . what was it—that he could not see
The signal he was bothered with? Ay, indeed!

I'll go beyond: there's a real love of a lie,
Liars find ready-made for lies they make,
As hand for glove, or tongue for sugar-plum.
At best, 'tis never pure and full belief;
Those furthest in the quagmire,—don't suppose
They strayed there with no warning, got no chance
Of a filth-speck in their face, which they clenched teeth,

679| MS:Glory §over*Blessings*§ <> she did, §crossed out§ wrought, 681| MS:Bringing the shameless sceptic §last four words crossed out and replaced above by four words§ Brow-beating now the unabashed *1888:* Browbeating 682| MS:Disposing of a §last three words crossed out and replaced in L margin by four words§ Ridding us of their <> life's hoarded §crossed out and replaced above by§ piled-up straws *P1864a:* life's gathered straws 683| MS:altar: why, of old *P1864a:* altar! Why, of old, 684| MS:spent all their lives §last three words crossed out and replaced above by three words§ years and years 685| MS:hardly §inserted above§ did §word illegibly crossed out§ it, then! *P1864a:* hardly proved it then: 688| MS:fondling Sludge but *P1864a:* fondling Sludge, but 689| MS:of cheatery, *P1864a:* of knavery,—well, 690| MS:it—don't *P1864a:* it! Don't 691| MS:blind eye §crossed out§ brow *P1864a:* blind eye 692| MS:saying . . what *1888:* saying . . . what 693| MS:was beaten? Ay *CP1864a:* beaten? §crossed out and replaced below by§ bothered? Ay *C1870:* bothered with? Ay 695| MS:ready made *P1864a:* ready-made 700| MS:which §inserted above§ they clenched the §crossed out§ teeth *P1864a:* teeth,

Bent brow against! Be sure they had their doubts,
And fears, and fairest challenges to try
The floor o' the seeming solid sand! But no!
Their faith was pledged, acquaintance too apprised,
All but the last step ventured, kerchiefs waved,
And Sludge called "pet": 'twas easier marching on
To the promised land; join those who, Thursday next,
Meant to meet Shakespeare; better follow Sludge—
Prudent, oh sure!—on the alert, how else?—
But making for the mid-bog, all the same!
To hear your outcries, one would think I caught
Miss Stokes by the scruff o' the neck, and pitched her flat,
Foolish-face-foremost! Hear these simpletons,
That's all I beg, before my work's begun,
Before I've touched them with my finger-tip!
Thus they await me (do but listen, now!
It's reasoning, this is,—I can't imitate
The baby voice, though) "In so many tales
Must be some truth, truth though a pin-point big,
Yet, some: a single man's deceived, perhaps—

701| MS:And §crossed out§ Bent the §crossed out§ brow on: oh, §last two words and comma crossed out and replaced above by three words and comma§ against: be sure, they *P1864a:* against! Be sure they 702| MS:fears and *P1864a:* fears, and 703| MS:floor of the §crossed out§ seeming <> sand—but *P1864a:* floor o' the seeming <> sand! But 704| MS:pledged, acquaintances appraised, *P1864a:* pledged, acquaintence too appraised, 705| MS:waved *P1864a:* waved, 706| MS:"pet"— §over illegible word§ 'twas *P1864a:* "pet:" 'twas *1888:* "pet": 'twas 707| MS:the §illegible word§ party for such §last four words crossed out and replaced above by five words and punctuation§ promised land, join those who, Thursday night *P1864a:* land; join <> Thursday next *1888:* next, DC:land, join BrU:land join *1889:* land join §emend to§ land; join §see Editorial Notes§ 708| MS:When §crossed out and replaced above by three words§ Join company with Shakespeare was expected; §last two words crossed out§ follow Sludge *P1864a:* Meant to meet Shakespeare; better follow Sludge— 709| MS:else? DC:else?— BrU:else— *1889:* else?— 710| MS:making §altered to§ make we §inserted above§ for <> mind-bog all *P1864a:* making for <> mind-bog, all 712| MS:the scuff o' the neck and *P1864a:* neck, and *1870:* flat. *C1870:* flat, *1888:* scruff 713| MS:these people talk, *P1864a:* these simpletons, 714| MS:my work begins, *P1864a:* my work's begun, 715| MS:Before I touch them <> finger-tip: *P1864a:* Before I've touched them <> finger-tip! 716| MS:me—do <> listen now— *P1864a:* listen, now! *CP1864a:* me §dash replaced by parenthesis§ (do 718| MS:though—"In *CP1864a:* though) §dash replaced by parenthesis§ "In 720| MS:Still, some: <> man §altered to§ man's may be §last two words crossed out§ deceived *P1864a:* Yet, some

Hardly, a thousand: to suppose one cheat
Can gull all these, were more miraculous far
Than aught we should confess a miracle"—
And so on. Then the Judge sums up—(it's rare)
Bids you respect the authorities that leap
To the judgment-seat at once,—why don't you note
The limpid nature, the unblemished life,
The spotless honour, indisputable sense
Of the first upstart with his story? What—
Outrage a boy on whom you ne'er till now
Set eyes, because he finds raps trouble him?

Fools, these are: ay, and how of their opposites
Who never did, at bottom of their hearts,
Believe for a moment?—Men emasculate,
Blank of belief, who played, as eunuchs use,
With superstition safely,—cold of blood,
Who saw what made for them i' the mystery,
Took their occasion, and supported Sludge
—As proselytes? No, thank you, far too shrewd!
—But promisers of fair play, encouragers
O' the claimant; who in candour needs must hoist
Sludge up on Mars' Hill, get speech out of Sludge
To carry off, criticize, and cant about!
Didn't Athens treat Saint Paul so?—at any rate,

721| MS:Hardly a *P1864a:* Hardly, a 722| MS:Gulls all of these, that §crossed out§ were *P1864a:* Can gull all these 723| MS:Than what would confess §last three words crossed out and replaced above by three words§ aught that constitutes a *P1864a:* aught we should confess a 724| MS:the Judge begins—(it's rare)— *P1864a:* the Judge sums up—(it's *1870:* rare) 725| MS:He bids you mark the *P1864a:* Bids you respect the 726| MS:why, don't *1868:* why don't 728| MS:honor *P1864a:* honour 731| MS:he says §crossed out and replaced above by§ finds 731–32| MS:§¶§ *1888:* §no ¶; emended to restore ¶; see Editorial Notes§ 732| MS:But §crossed out§ fools, §altered to§ Fools, these are: §inserted above§ ay, but §crossed out and replaced above by§ and 733| MS:did §over illegible erasure§ 734| MS:moment? Men emasculate *P1864a:* moment?—Men emasculate, 735| MS:Of all belief *P1864a:* Blank of belief 737| MS:Saw prompt what <> in the *P1864a:* Who saw what *1870:* i' 738| MS:occasion §over illegible word§ 740| MS:But *P1864a:* —But 741| MS:Of the claimant, who *P1864a:* claimant; who *1870:* O' 742| MS:get §word illegibly crossed out§ speech <> of him *P1864a:* of Sludge 743| MS:criticize and <> about— *P1864a:* criticize, and <> about! 744| MS:so?—at any rate, §last three words over illegible erasure§

It's "a new thing" philosophy fumbles at.
Then there's the other picker-out of pearl
From dung-heaps,—ay, your literary man,
Who draws on his kid gloves to deal with Sludge
Daintily and discreetly,—shakes a dust
O' the doctrine, flavours thence, he well knows how,
The narrative or the novel,—half-believes,
All for the book's sake, and the public's stare,
And the cash that's God's sole solid in this world!
Look at him! Try to be too bold, too gross
For the master! Not you! He's the man for muck;
Shovel it forth, full-splash, he'll smooth your brown
Into artistic richness, never fear!
Find him the crude stuff; when you recognize
Your lie again, you'll doff your hat to it,
Dressed out for company! "For company,"
I say, since there's the relish of success:
Let all pay due respect, call the lie truth,
Save the soft silent smirking gentleman
Who ushered in the stranger: you must sigh
"How melancholy, he, the only one
Fails to perceive the bearing of the truth

745| MS:at! *P1864a:* at. 745–46| MS:§¶§ *P1864a:* §no ¶§ 746| MS:other §inserted above§ picker-out §hyphen and *out* inserted above§ of the other §last two words crossed out§ pearl 747| MS:From dung heaps <> your poet, novelist, §last two words crossed out and replaced above by two words§ literary man *P1864a:* man, *1888:* dung-heaps 748| MS:Your literary man who §last four words crossed out and replaced above by seven words§ Who takes off his kid gloves to deal in Sludge *P1864a:* Who draws on his <> deal with Sludge 749| MS:a §word illegibly crossed out and replaced by§ dust 750| MS:Of <> flavours just, he *P1864a:* flavours thence, he *1870:* O' 751| MS:narrative, the *P1864a:* narrative or the 752| MS:sake and <> stare *P1864a:* sake, and <> stare, 753| MS:that's §word illegibly crossed out§ God's real §inserted above§ solid <> world: *P1864a:* God's sole solid <> world! 755| MS:the Master <> muck— *P1864a:* master <> muck; 756| MS:smooth the brown *P1864a:* smooth your brown 758| MS:stuff—when *P1864a:* stuff; when *1868:* recognise *1888:* recognize 759| MS:again you'll *P1864a:* again, you'll 760| MS:company! For company, *P1864a:* company! "For company," 761| MS:Observe,—for §inserted above and crossed out§ since §inserted above§ <> success— *P1864a:* I say, since <> success: 762| MS:When all pay their §crossed out and replaced above by§ due respects, call *P1864a:* Let all <> respect, call 763| MS:Save him, the silent <> gentleman, *P1864a:* Save the soft silent <> gentleman 764| MS:That ushered *P1864a:* Who ushered 765| MS:melancholy he *P1864a:* melancholy, he

Himself gave birth to!"—There's the triumph's smack!
That man would choose to see the whole world roll
I' the slime o' the slough, so he might touch the tip
Of his brush with what I call the best of browns—
Tint ghost-tales, spirit-stories, past the power
Of the outworn umber and bistre!

Yet I think
There's a more hateful form of foolery—
The social sage's, Solomon of saloons
And philosophic diner-out, the fribble
Who wants a doctrine for a chopping-block
To try the edge of his faculty upon,
Prove how much common sense he'll hack and hew
I' the critical minute 'twixt the soup and fish!
These were my patrons: these, and the like of them
Who, rising in my soul now, sicken it,—
These I have injured! Gratitude to these?
The gratitude, forsooth, of a prostitute
To the greenhorn and the bully—friends of hers,
From the wag that wants the queer jokes for his club,
To the snuff-box-decorator, honest man,
Who just was at his wits' end where to find

767| MS:gives birth to!" there's *P1864a:* gave birth to!"—There's 768| MS:That §crossed out and replaced above by§ The man <> world wallow *P1864a:* That man <> world roll 769| MS :In <> slough, if §crossed out and replaced above by§ so he might dip the *P1864a:* I' <> might touch the 770| MS:brush in what §over illegible erasure§ *P1864a:* brush with what 771| MS:ghost-tales, spirit- §crossed out and replaced above by§ phantom-stories *P1864a:* spirit-stories 772| MS:bistre. §¶§ *P1864a:* bistre! §¶§ 774| MS:social sage, the Solomon of saloons, *P1864a:* social sage's, Solomon of saloons 775| MS:The philosophic *P1864a:* And philosophic
776| MS:That wants the doctrine *P1864a:* Who wants a doctrine 778| MS:sense §word illegibly word crossed out and replaced above by§ is hacked and hewn §marked for transposition to§ hewn and hacked *P1864a:* sense he'll hack and hew
779| MS:In *1870:* I' 780| MS:patrons—them §altered to§ these <> of these, §altered to§ them *P1864a:* patrons: these 781| MS:sicken me,— *P1864a:* sicken it,—
784| MS:greenhorn, and the bully; §three words illegibly crossed out and replaced above by three words§ friends of hers, *P1864a:* greenhorn and the bully—friends *1870:* hers *C1870:* hers, 785| MS:And §crossed out and replaced above by§ From <> that lists §crossed out and replaced above by§ wants <> jokes at §crossed out and replaced above by§ for 786| MS:And §crossed out and replaced in L margin by§ To

So genial a Pasiphae! All and each
Pay, compliment, protect from the police:
And how she hates them for their pains, like me!
So much for my remorse at thanklessness
Toward a deserving public!

But, for God?

Ay, that's a question! Well, sir, since you press—
(How you do tease the whole thing out of me!
I don't mean you, you know, when I say "them":
Hate you, indeed! But that Miss Stokes, that Judge!
Enough, enough—with sugar: thank you, sir!)
Now for it, then! Will you believe me, though?
You've heard what I confess; I don't unsay
A single word: I cheated when I could,
Rapped with my toe-joints, set sham hands at work,
Wrote down names weak in sympathetic ink,
Rubbed odic lights with ends of phosphor-match,
And all the rest; believe that: believe this,
By the same token, though it seem to set
The crooked straight again, unsay the said,
Stick up what I've knocked down; I can't help that
It's truth! I somehow vomit truth to-day.
This trade of mine—I don't know, can't be sure

788| MS:A model for §last three words crossed out and replaced above by three words§ So genial a <> All these pay, *P1864a:*a <> All and each 789| MS:Make §crossed out and replaced above by§ And compliment <> police, *P1864a:*Pay, compliment *1888:*police: 789-90| MS:police, / Allow her privilege, try §two illegible words§ on her— §entire line crossed out§ 790| MS:them all, as I hate you! *P1864a:*them for their pains, like me! 791| MS:at having sinned *P1864a:*at thanklessness 792| MS:Against a respectable public! §¶§ *P1864a:*Toward a deserving public! §¶§ 793| MS:question! Well, Sir,—since *P1864a:*sir, since 794| MS:do get §crossed out and replaced above by§ teaze 795| MS:"them"— *P1864a:*"them:" *1888:*"them": 796| MS:that Miss Stokes, §two words illegibly crossed out and replaced above by§ that Judge! 797| MS:you, Sir!) *P1864a:*sir!) 798| MS:me. Sir? *P1864a:*me, though? 799| MS:confess—I *P1864a:*confess; I 800| MS:A single §inserted above§ word: of it. §last two words and period crossed out§ I 802| MS:Wrote the names *P1864a:*Wrote down names 803| MS:Drew §crossed out and replaced above by§ Made odic streaks §crossed out and replaced above by§ spots with *P1864a:*Rubbed odic lights with 807| MS:what I've thrown down—I <> that— *P1864a:*down; I <> that: *1870:*that *1888:*what I've knocked down 808| MS:truth—I <> to-day: *P1864a:*truth! I <> to-day.

But there was something in it, tricks and all!
Really, I want to light up my own mind.
They were tricks,—true, but what I mean to add
Is also true. First,—don't it strike you, sir?
Go back to the beginning,—the first fact
We're taught is, there's a world beside this world,
With spirits, not mankind, for tenantry;
That much within that world once sojourned here,
That all upon this world will visit there,
And therefore that we, bodily here below,
Must have exactly such an interest
In learning what may be the ways o' the world
Above us, as the disembodied folk
Have (by all analogic likelihood)
In watching how things go in the old home
With us, their sons, successors, and what not.
Oh yes, with added powers probably,
Fit for the novel state,—old loves grown pure,
Old interests understood aright,—they watch!
Eyes to see, ears to hear, and hands to help,
Proportionate to advancement: they're ahead,
That's all—do what we do, but noblier done—

810| MS:But there's §altered to§ there been §crossed out and replaced above by§ was <> all. *P1864a:* all! 811| MS:I §crossed out§ Really <> mind— *P1864a:* mind.
812| MS:what I want §crossed out and replaced above by§ mean 813| MS:true: first <> you, now?— *P1864a:* true. first <> you, sir? 816| MS:tenantry— *P1864a:* tenantry; 817| MS:And §crossed out and replaced above by§ That
818| MS:And §crossed out and replaced above by§ That all §word illegibly crossed out and replaced above by§ upon this our §crossed out§ world will soon pass §last two words crossed out and replaced above by one word§ travel there, *1868:* will visit there, 822| MS:the above §crossed out and replaced above by§ same unbodied folk *1864a:* the disembodied folk
823| MS:Have, by <> likelihood, *P1864a:* Have, (by <> likelihood,) *1864a:* Have (by <> likelihood) 824| MS:go in the §last three words over illegible erasure§ old world, *1864a:* world *1888:* old home 825| MS:successors and <> not— *P1864a:* successors, and <> not. 826| MS:Watching, with <> powers, probably, *P1864a:* Oh, yes, with *1864a:* powers probably, *1888:* Oh yes 827| MS:loves, grown §over illegible erasure§ *1864a:* loves grown 828| MS:aright, they watch, *P1864a:* aright,—they watch!
829| MS:and §inserted above§ 830| MS:Proportioned to the advancement <> a-head, *P1864a:* Proportionate to advancement <> ahead, 831| MS:but §over illegible word§

Use plate, whereas we eat our meals off delf,
(To use a figure).

Concede that, and I ask
Next what may be the mode of intercourse
Between us men here, and those once-men there?
First comes the Bible's speech; then, history
With the supernatural element,—you know—
All that we sucked in with our mothers' milk,
Grew up with, got inside of us at last,
Till it's found bone of bone and flesh of flesh.
See now, we start with the miraculous,
And know it used to be, at all events:
What's the first step we take, and can't but take,
In arguing from the known to the obscure?
Why this: "What was before, may be to-day.
Since Samuel's ghost appeared to Saul, of course
My brother's spirit may appear to me."
Go tell your teacher that! What's his reply?
What brings a shade of doubt for the first time
O'er his brow late so luminous with faith?
"Such things have been," says he, "and there's no doubt
Such things may be: but I advise mistrust
Of eyes, ears, stomach, and, more than all, your brain,
Unless it be of your great-grandmother,
Whenever they propose a ghost to you!"

832| MS:plate whereas <> delf *P1864a:* plate, whereas <> delf, 833| MS:—To <> figure. §¶§ Concede me that, I *P1864a:* (To <> figure.) §¶§ Concede that, and I *1888:* figure). 834| MS:Next—what *P1864a:* Next, what *1868:* Next what
835| MS:Between the men <> and the once-men *P1864a:* Between us men <> and those once-men 836| MS:the Bible in—then, history, *P1864a:* the Bible's speech; then, history 840| MS:it's our bone of bone & flesh of flesh: *P1864a:* it's found bone of bone and flesh of flesh. 841| MS:now,—we *P1864a:* now, we 842| MS:Knowing what §last two words crossed out and replaced above by three words§ And know it
843| MS:take *P1864a:* take, 845| MS:this—"What <> before may be to-day— *P1864a:* this: "What <> before, may be to-day. 846| MS:to Saul,—of course, *1864a:* course *1888:* to Saul, of 848| MS:that—What's <> reply, *P1864a:* that! What's <> reply? 849| MS:brings §over illegible erasure§ 850| MS:O'er the brow *P1864a:* O'er his brow 851| MS:he "and *P1864a:* he, "and
852| MS:be—but *P1864a:* be: but 853| MS:Of your eyes <> and most of all, your §last four words in R margin, marked for insertion after *and*§ brain, *P1864a:* Of eyes <> and, most *CP1864a:* most §altered to§ more of §altered to§ than

The end is, there's a composition struck;
'Tis settled, we've some way of intercourse
Just as in Saul's time; only, different:
How, when and where, precisely,—find it out!
I want to know, then, what's so natural
As that a person born into this world
And seized on by such teaching, should begin
With firm expectancy and a frank look-out
For his own allotment, his especial share
I' the secret,—his particular ghost, in fine?
I mean, a person born to look that way,
Since natures differ: take the painter-sort,
One man lives fifty years in ignorance
Whether grass be green or red,—"No kind of eye
For colour," say you; while another picks
And puts away even pebbles, when a child,
Because of bluish spots and pinky veins—
"Give him forthwith a paint-box!" Just the same
Was I born . . . "medium," you won't let me say,—
Well, seer of the supernatural
Everywhen, everyhow and everywhere,—
Will that do?

I and all such boys of course
Started with the same stock of Bible-truth;

857| MS:Tis *P1864a:*'Tis 858| MS:time—only, different— *P1864a:*time; only, different: 859| MS:What, when *CP1864a:*What, §crossed out and replaced in L margin by§ How, when 862| MS:by this teaching *P1864a:*by such teaching 863| MS:firm assurance §crossed out and replaced above by§ expectancy 864| MS:own endowment §crossed out and replaced above by§ allotment, his especial §over illegible word§ 865| MS:In *1870:*I' 867| MS:Since §over illegible word§ <> differ: there's the *P1864a:*For <> differ: take the *CP1864a:*For §crossed out and replaced in L margin by§ Since 869| MS:Whether the grass <> gred— §altered to§ red—"no eye *P1864a:*Whether grass <> red,—"No kind of eye 870| MS:you— while *P1864a:*you; while 871| MS:away the §crossed out and replaced above by§ even pebbles, while a *P1864a:*pebbles, when a 872| MS:bluish eyes §crossed out and replaced above by§ spots 874| MS:born . . "medium" *P1864a:*born . . . "medium" 875| MS:Well §over illegible erasure§ 877| MS:all the other boys *P1864a:*all such boys of course 878| MS:Started §over illegible erasure§ <> bible-truth, *P1864a:*bible-truth; *1870:*of Bible-truth;

Only,—what in the rest you style their sense,
Instinct, blind reasoning but imperative,
This, betimes, taught them the old world had one law
And ours another: "New world, new laws," cried they:
"None but old laws, seen everywhere at work,"
Cried I, and by their help explained my life
The Jews' way, still a working way to me.
Ghosts made the noises, fairies waved the lights,
Or Santa Claus slid down on New Year's Eve
And stuffed with cakes the stocking at my bed,
Changed the worn shoes, rubbed clean the fingered slate
O' the sum that came to grief the day before.

This could not last long: soon enough I found
Who had worked wonders thus, and to what end:
But did I find all easy, like my mates?
Henceforth no supernatural any more?
Not a whit: what projects the billiard-balls?
"A cue," you answer: "Yes, a cue," said I;
"But what hand, off the cushion, moved the cue?
What unseen agency, outside the world,
Prompted its puppets to do this and that,
Put cakes and shoes and slates into their mind,
These mothers and aunts, nay even schoolmasters?"
Thus high I sprang, and there have settled since.

879| MS:Ghost-stories,— §crossed out§ only, what in the rest §last three words inserted above§ you *P1864a:* Only,—what 881| MS:Taught them, betimes, the *P1864a:* This, betimes, taught them the 882| MS:And this of ours another: "new laws" cried they— *P1864a:* And ours another: "New world, new laws," cried they: 883| MS:—"None but the old, seen *P1864a:* "None but old laws, seen 884| MS:explained the world *P1864a:* explained my life 885| MS:me— *P1864a:* me. 887| MS:Old Santa Claus came down *P1864a:* And Santaclaus slid down *1864a:* Or Santaclaus slid *1888:* Or Santa Claus slid 890| MS:Of *1870:* O' 892| MS:had done all these things §last four words crossed out and replaced above by three words§ worked wonders thus 893| MS:mates, *P1864a:* mates? 896| MS:cue," they §crossed out and replaced above by§ you answered— §altered to§ answer—"Yes <> I, *P1864a:* answer: "Yes <> I; 897| MS:the cushion, §over illegible word§ edge §crossed out§ moved that? §crossed out and replaced above by two words§ the cue? 898| MS:the §over illegible word§ 899| MS:Prompted the puppets *P1864a:* Prompted its puppets 900–902| MS:mind?" §¶§ Thus *P1864a:* mind, §no ¶§ These <> schoolmasters?" / Thus 902| MS:So §crossed out and replaced by§ Thus < there I've Bcrossed out and replaced above by§ have

Just so I reason, in sober earnest still,
About the greater godsends, what you call
The serious gains and losses of my life.
What do I know or care about your world
Which either is or seems to be? This snap
O' my fingers, sir! My care is for myself;
Myself am whole and sole reality
Inside a raree-show and a market-mob
Gathered about it: that's the use of things.
'Tis easy saying they serve vast purposes,
Advantage their grand selves: be it true or false,
Each thing may have two uses. What's a star?
A world, or a world's sun: doesn't it serve
As taper also, time-piece, weather-glass,
And almanac? Are stars not set for signs
When we should shear our sheep, sow corn, prune trees?
The Bible says so.

Well, I add one use
To all the acknowledged uses, and declare
If I spy Charles's Wain at twelve to-night,
It warns me, "Go, nor lose another day,
And have your hair cut, Sludge!" You laugh: and why?

905| MS:of this life. *P1864a:* of my life. 907| MS:That either *P1864a:* Which either 908| MS:Of <> Sir *1870:* O' <> sir 909| MS:Myself, the whole <> reality. *P1864a:* Myself am whole <> reality 910| MS:and the §inserted above§ market-mob *P1864a:* and a market-mob 911| MS:it just to profit §last three words crossed out and replaced above by two words§ to advantage me— *P1864a:* it: that's the use of things. 912| MS:they §two words illegibly crossed out and replaced above by two words§ serve vast 913| MS:Live for their own grand selves: that's true or false— *P1864a:* Advantage their grand selves: be it true or false, 914| MS:Still, a thing may <> uses; what's *P1864a:* Each thing may *1864a:* uses. What's 915| MS:sun,—but none the less *P1864a:* sun: doesn't it serve 916| MS:Tis man's clock, §last three words and comma crossed out and replaced above by two words§ Our taper also <> weather-glass *P1864a:* As taper, also <> weather-glass, *1864a:* As taper also 917| MS:almanac—are *P1864a:* almanac? Are 918| MS:shear sheep <> corn, or prune *P1864a:* shear our sheep <> corn, prune 920| MS:To these acknowledged *P1864a:* To all the acknowledged 921| MS:spy Charles' Wain at nine to night, *P1864a:* spy Charles's Wain at twelve to-night, 923| MS:And get your <> laugh: but why? *P1864a:* And have your <> laugh: and why?

Were such a sign too hard for God to give?
No: but Sludge seems too little for such grace:
Thank you, sir! So you think, so does not Sludge!
When you and good men gape at Providence,
Go into history and bid us mark
Not merely powder-plots prevented, crowns
Kept on kings' heads by miracle enough,
But private mercies—oh, you've told me, sir,
Of such interpositions! How yourself
Once, missing on a memorable day
Your handkerchief—just setting out, you know,—
You must return to fetch it, lost the train,
And saved your precious self from what befell
The thirty-three whom Providence forgot.
You tell, and ask me what I think of this?
Well, sir, I think then, since you needs must know,
What matter had you and Boston city to boot
Sailed skyward, like burnt onion-peelings? Much
To you, no doubt: for me—undoubtedly
The cutting of my hair concerns me more,
Because, however sad the truth may seem,
Sludge is of all-importance to himself.
You set apart that day in every year
For special thanksgiving, were a heathen else:
Well, I who cannot boast the like escape,

924| MS:Is such *P1864a:* Were such 925| MS:No—but §inserted above§ Sludge is found §last two words crossed out and replaced above by§ seems <> such §over illegible erasure§ *P1864a:* No: but 926| MS:you, Sir—so you think—so *P1864a:* sir! So you think, so 930| MS:on Kings' *P1864a:* kings' 931| MS:me, Sir, *P1864a:* sir, 932| MS:Of such §crossed out and replaced above by§ plain interpositions! You, yourself, *P1864a:* Of such interpositions! How, yourself, *1864a:* How yourself 933| MS:How, missing, on <> day, *P1864a:* Once, missing *1864a:* day 937| MS:thirty three whom Providence o'erlooked— *P1864a:* thirty-three whom Providence forgot. 938| MS:tell and <> of that? *P1864a:* tell, and <> of this? 939| MS:Well, Sir <> since the truth §last two words crossed out and replaced above by two words, crossed out and replaced by§ you §inserted above§ *P1864a:* sir 940| MS:and all New York to *P1864a:* and Boston city to 941| MS:§first word illegibly crossed out§ Sailed §over illegible erasure§ skyward, Sir, §crossed out§ like burnt §inserted above§ 945| MS:of most- §crossed out and replaced above by§ all- 948| MS:who never had the *P1864a:* who cannot boast the

Suppose I said "I don't thank Providence
For my part, owing it no gratitude"?
"Nay, but you owe as much"—you'd tutor me,
"You, every man alive, for blessings gained
In every hour o' the day, could you but know!
I saw my crowning mercy: all have such,
Could they but see!" Well, sir, why don't they see?
"Because they won't look,—or perhaps, they can't."
Then, sir, suppose I can, and will, and do
Look, microscopically as is right,
Into each hour with its infinitude
Of influences at work to profit Sludge?
For that's the case: I've sharpened up my sight
To spy a providence in the fire's going out,
The kettle's boiling, the dime's sticking fast
Despite the hole i' the pocket. Call such facts
Fancies, too petty a work for Providence,
And those same thanks which you exact from me
Prove too prodigious payment: thanks for what,
If nothing guards and guides us little men?
No, no, sir! You must put away your pride,
Resolve to let Sludge into partnership!
I live by signs and omens: looked at the roof
Where the pigeons settle—"If the further bird,
The white, takes wing first, I'll confess when thrashed;
Not, if the blue does"—so I said to myself

949| MS:Suppose I said §crossed out and replaced above by§ say "I can't thank *P1864a:*I said "I don't thank 950| MS:gratitude"— *P1864a:*gratitude?" *1888:*gratitude"? 951| MS:you do owe much" you'd <> me *P1864a:*you owe as much"—you'd <> me, 953| MS:of *1870:*o' 954| MS:mercy,—all *P1864a:*mercy: all 955| MS:see!" Well, then, why *P1864a:*see!" Well, sir, why 957| MS:But, Sir <> can and will and *P1864a:*Then, sir <> can, and will, and 958| MS:as you did, §last two words and comma crossed out and replaced above by two words and comma§ is right,
961| MS:That's just the <> sharpened §over illegible word§ up my eyes *P1864a:*For that's the <> my sight 962| MS:To see §altered to§ spy 964| MS:pocket. Call these facts, *P1864a:*Call such facts 965| MS:Fancies—too petty, in short, for *P1864a:*Fancies, too petty a work for 966| MS:me, *1888:*me 967| MS:Were too <> what? *P1864a:*Prove too <> what, 967–69| MS:what? §¶§ No *P1864a:*what? §no ¶§ If, nothing <> men? / No 968| *CP1864a(Yale):*If nothing 969| MS:No, no, Sir—you *P1864a:*sir! You 972| MS:"if *P1864a:*settle—"If 973| MS:confess the trick— *P1864a:*confess when thrashed;

Last week, lest you should take me by surprise:
Off flapped the white,—and I'm confessing, sir!
Perhaps 'tis Providence's whim and way
With only me, i' the world: how can you tell?
"Because unlikely!" Was it likelier, now,
That this our one out of all worlds beside,
The what-d'you-call-'em millions, should be just
Precisely chosen to make Adam for,
And the rest o' the tale? Yet the tale's true, you know:
Such undeserving clod was graced so once;
Why not graced likewise undeserving Sludge?
Are we merit-mongers, flaunt we filthy rags?
All you can bring against my privilege
Is, that another way was taken with you,—
Which I don't question. It's pure grace, my luck:
I'm broken to the way of nods and winks,
And need no formal summoning. You've a help;
Holloa his name or whistle, clap your hands,
Stamp with your foot or pull the bell: all's one,
He understands you want him, here he comes.
Just so, I come at the knocking: you, sir, wait
The tongue o' the bell, nor stir before you catch
Reason's clear tingle, nature's clapper brisk,
Or that traditional peal was wont to cheer

975| MS:When you grew angry, took me by surprize— *P1864a:* Last week, lest you should take me by surprise: 976| MS:confessing, Sir! *P1864a:* sir! 978| MS:in the world—how *P1864a:* world: how *1870:* i' 979| MS:unlikely"—was *P1864a:* unlikely!" Was 982| MS:Precisely that chosen *P1864a:* Precisely chosen 984| MS:—Such <> clod if §crossed out and replaced above by§ was *P1864a:* Such 985| MS:not grace likewise *P1864a:* not graced likewise 985–87| MS:undeserving Sludge? §¶§ All *P1864:* undeserving Sludge? §no ¶§ Are <> rags? / All 988| MS:Is that <> way is taken *P1864a:* Is, that <> way was taken 989| MS:luck. *1888:* luck: 990| MS:I've got used to *P1864a:* I'm broken to 991| MS:need §over illegible erasure§ 992| MS:Call out §last two words crossed out and replaced above by one word§ Hollo his name, or whistle clap *P1864a:* Holloa his name or whistle, clap 993| MS:foot, or ring §crossed out and replaced above by§ pull *P1864a:* foot or 994| MS:he stands: *P1864a:* he comes. 995| MS:the whistle: you, Sir *P1864a:* the knocking: you, sir 996| MS:tongue §over illegible word§ of the bell nor <> catch §over illegible word§ *P1864a:* bell, nor *1870:* o' 997| MS:nature's §word illegibly crossed out and replaced above by§ summons brisk, *P1864a:* nature's clapper brisk, 998| MS:traditional omen §crossed out and replaced above by§ peal

Your mother's face turned heavenward: short of these
There's no authentic intimation, eh?
Well, when you hear, you'll answer them, start up
And stride into the presence, top of toe,
And there find Sludge beforehand, Sludge that sprang
At noise o' the knuckle on the partition-wall!
I think myself the more religious man.
Religion's all or nothing; it's no mere smile
O' contentment, sigh of aspiration, sir—
No quality o' the finelier-tempered clay
Like its whiteness or its lightness; rather, stuff
O' the very stuff, life of life, and self of self.
I tell you, men won't notice; when they do,
They'll understand. I notice nothing else:
I'm eyes, ears, mouth of me, one gaze and gape,
Nothing eludes me, everything's a hint,
Handle and help. It's all absurd, and yet
There's something in it all, I know: how much?
No answer! What does that prove? Man's still man,
Still meant for a poor blundering piece of work
When all's done; but, if somewhat's done, like this,
Or not done, is the case the same? Suppose
I blunder in my guess at the true sense

999| MS:heavenwards—short *CP1864a:* heavenward: short 1003| MS:that knew *P1864a:* that sprung *1888:* sprang 1004| MS:The noise <> partition-wall. *P1864a:* At noise <> partition-wall! 1004–06| MS:partition-wall. §¶§ Religion's *P1864a:* partition-wall! §no ¶§ I <> man. / Religion's 1006| MS:no smile *P1864a:* no mere smile 1007| MS:Of content §altered to§ contentment, §word illegibly crossed out§ <> aspiration, merely— *P1864a:* aspiration, sir— *1870:* O' 1008| MS:of *1870:* o' 1009| MS:Like its §crossed out§ whiteness, or its §crossed out§ lightness; Sir, its very §inserted above§ stuff *P1864a:* Like its whiteness or its lightness rather, stuff 1010| MS:Of <> life of our life itself, §altered to§ itself. *P1864a:* life of life, self of self. *1870:* O' <> of life, and self 1010–11| MS:Everywhere, whether recognized or no. §entire line crossed out§ 1011| MS:they will §crossed out and replaced above by§ do, 1012| MS:understand: for §crossed out§ I §word illegibly crossed out and replaced above by§ notice <> else, *P1864a:* understand. I *1888:* else: 1013| MS:I'm, eyes, and §crossed out§ ears, and §crossed out§ mouth of me, §last two words inserted above§ *P1864a:* I'm eyes 1014| MS:Nothing escapes §crossed out and replaced above by§ eludes *P1864a:* everything *CP1864a:* everything §altered to§ everything's 1017| MS:No telling! §crossed out and replaced above by§ answer! What 1018| MS:for just §inserted above§ a poor §crossed out§ blundering *P1864a:* a poor blundering 1020| MS:same? Suppose, *P1864a:* same? Suppose 1021| MS:my guesses at the sense *P1864a:* my guess at the true sense

O' the knuckle-summons, nine times out of ten,—
What if the tenth guess happen to be right?
If the tenth shovel-load of powdered quartz
Yield me the nugget? I gather, crush, sift all,
Pass o'er the failure, pounce on the success.
To give you a notion, now—(let who wins, laugh!)
When first I see a man, what do I first?
Why, count the letters which make up his name,
And as their number chances, even or odd,
Arrive at my conclusion, trim my course:
Hiram H. Horsefall is your honoured name,
And haven't I found a patron, sir, in you?
"Shall I cheat this stranger?" I take apple-pips,
Stick one in either canthus of my eye,
And if the left drops first—(your left, sir, stuck)
I'm warned, I let the trick alone this time.
You, sir, who smile, superior to such trash,
You judge of character by other rules:
Don't your rules sometimes fail you? Pray, what rule
Have you judged Sludge by hitherto?

Oh, be sure,
You, everybody blunders, just as I,
In simpler things than these by far! For see:
I knew two farmers,—one, a wiseacre
Who studied seasons, rummaged almanacs,

1022| MS:Of *1870:* O' 1023| MS:happens §altered to§ happen to be true? §crossed out and replaced above by§ right? 1025| MS:nugget? I save §crossed out and replaced above by§ gather 1026| MS:failure; pounce *P1864a:* failure, pounce 1026–28| MS:success. §¶§ When *P1864a:* success. §no ¶§ To <> laugh!) / When 1031| MS:I come to my *P1864a:* Arrive at my 1033| MS:patron, Sir *P1864a:* sir 1034| MS:this man?" I take two apple-pips, *P1864a:* this stranger?" I take apple-pips, 1035| MS:Stick each §crossed out and replaced above by§ one in either corner of *P1864a:* either *canthus* of *1888:* canthus 1036| MS:left, Sir *P1864a:* sir 1037| MS:I §altered to§ I'm lie big, §last two words and comma crossed out and replaced above by two words and comma§ warned, I 1040| MS:you? Pray what *P1864a:* you? Pray, what 1041| MS:Did you <> hitherto? §inserted above§ §¶§ *P1864a:* Have you 1043| MS:In §over illegible word§ <> far: for see— *P1864a:* far! For see: 1044| MS:wiseacre, *1868:* wiseacre 1045| MS:seasons, searched in almanacs, *P1864a:* seasons, rummaged almanacs,

Quoted the dew-point, registered the frost,
And then declared, for outcome of his pains,
Next summer must be dampish: 'twas a drought.
His neighbour prophesied such drought would fall,
Saved hay and corn, made cent. per cent. thereby,
And proved a sage indeed: how came his lore?
Because one brindled heifer, late in March,
Stiffened her tail of evenings, and somehow
He got into his head that drought was meant!
I don't expect all men can do as much:
Such kissing goes by favour. You must take
A certain turn of mind for this,—a twist
I' the flesh, as well. Be lazily alive,
Open-mouthed, like my friend the ant-eater,
Letting all nature's loosely-guarded motes
Settle and, slick, be swallowed! Think yourself
The one i' the world, the one for whom the world
Was made, expect it tickling at your mouth!
Then will the swarm of busy buzzing flies,
Clouds of coincidence, break egg-shell, thrive,
Breed, multiply, and bring you food enough.

I can't pretend to mind your smiling, sir!
Oh, what you mean is this! Such intimate way,

1046| MS:Measured the rain and registered *P1864a:* Quoted the dew-point, registered 1047| MS:declared, as outcome *P1864a:* declared, for outcome 1048| MS:Next §crossed out and restored in L margin§ summer would §crossed out and replaced above by§ must 1050| MS:made money, so want, §last three words crossed out and replaced above by three words and§ cent. per cent., thereby, *P1864a:* per cent. thereby, 1051| MS:proved the sage <> how grew §crossed out and replaced above by§ came his guess? *P1864a:* proved a sage <> "how <> his lore? *CP1864a:* §quotation marks crossed out§ 1052| MS:Because a brindled <> Spring, *P1864a:* Because one brindled <> spring, *CP1864a:* spring, §crossed out and replaced in R margin by§ March, 1053| MS:evenings—and *P1864a:* evenings, and 1054–56| MS:meant! §¶§ Such *P1864a:* meant! §no ¶§ I <> much: / Such 1058| MS:well—be *P1864a:* well. Be 1059| *P1864a:* anteater, *1888:* ant-eater, 1061| MS:and so be swallowed: think *P1864a:* and, slick, be swallowed! Think 1064| MS:busy little flies, *P1864a:* busy buzzing flies, 1065| MS:Coincidences, chop §crossed out and replaced above by§ break their egg-shell *P1864a:* Clouds of coincidence, break egg-shell 1066| MS:They §crossed out and replaced above by§ And §crossed out§ Multiply, they are §last two words crossed out and replaced above by two words§ and prove irrisistible! *P1864a:* Breed, multiply, and bring you food enough. 1067| MS:smiling, Sir! *P1864a:* sir! 1068| MS:this—the intimate *P1864a:* this! Such intimate

Close converse, frank exchange of offices,
Strict sympathy of the immeasurably great
With the infinitely small, betokened here
By a course of signs and omens, raps and sparks,—
How does it suit the dread traditional text
O' the "Great and Terrible Name"? Shall the Heaven of Heavens
Stoop to such child's play?

Please, sir, go with me
A moment, and I'll try to answer you.
The "*Magnum et terribile*" (is that right?)
Well, folk began with this in the early day;
And all the acts they recognized in proof
Were thunders, lightnings, earthquakes, whirlwinds, dealt
Indisputably on men whose death they caused.
There, and there only, folk saw Providence
At work,—and seeing it, 'twas right enough
All heads should tremble, hands wring hands amain,
And knees knock hard together at the breath
O' the Name's first letter; why, the Jews, I'm told,
Won't write it down, no, to this very hour,
Nor speak aloud: you know best if't be so.
Each ague-fit of fear at end, they crept
(Because somehow people once born must live)
Out of the sound, sight, swing and sway o' the Name,
Into a corner, the dark rest of the world,

1072| MS:sparks, *P1864a:* sparks,— 1073| MS:—How *P1864a:* How
1074| MS:Of <> the Heaven of §over illegible erasure§ Heavens §inserted§ *P1864a:* and Terrible Name?" *1870:* O' *1888:* Name"? 1075| MS:play? §¶§ Please Sir *P1864a:* sir *CP1864a:* child's-play *1870:* child's play *1888:* §¶§ Please, sir 1076| MS:moment and *P1864a:* moment, and 1078| MS:Well, folks began with that in *P1864a:* Well, folk began with this in 1079| MS:The only acts men recognized *P1864a:* And all the acts they recognized 1081| MS:caused: *P1864a:* caused. 1082| MS:only, they saw *P1864a:* only, folk saw 1083| MS:seeing thus, 'twas *P1864a:* seeing it, 'twas
1085| MS:knock fast §crossed out and replaced above by§ hard 1086| MS:Of <> letter—and §crossed out and replaced above by§ why, the *P1864a:* letter; why *1870:* O'
1088| MS:speak it aloud—you know, Sir, if 'tis so. *P1864a:* speak aloud: you know best if *1864a:* if 't be so. 1089| MS:Such ague-fit <> they crawled §crossed out and replaced above by§ crept *P1864a:* Each ague-fit 1090 | MS:somehow a man is §crossed out and replaced above by§ once born to §crossed out and replaced above by§ must *P1864a:* somehow people once 1091| MS:sway of the Name *P1864a:* the Name, *1870:* o' 1092| MS:corner—called §over illegible word§ the rest *P1864a:* corner, the

And safe space where as yet no fear had reached;
'Twas there they looked about them, breathed again,
And felt indeed at home, as we might say.
The current o' common things, the daily life,
This had their due contempt; no Name pursued
Man from the mountain-top where fires abide,
To his particular mouse-hole at its foot
Where he ate, drank, digested, lived in short:
Such was man's vulgar business, far too small
To be worth thunder: "small," folk kept on, "small,"
With much complacency in those great days!
A mote of sand, you know, a blade of grass—
What was so despicable as mere grass,
Except perhaps the life o' the worm or fly
Which fed there? These were "small" and men were great.
Well, sir, the old way's altered somewhat since,
And the world wears another aspect now:
Somebody turns our spyglass round, or else
Puts a new lens in it: grass, worm, fly grow big:
We find great things are made of little things,
And little things go lessening till at last
Comes God behind them. Talk of mountains now?
We talk of mould that heaps the mountain, mites
That throng the mould, and God that makes the mites.

---

dark rest 1093| MS:The §over illegible word§ safe <> had come §crossed out and replaced above by§ reached, *P1864a:* And safe <> reached; 1094| MS:And there <> breathed at length §last two words crossed out and replaced above by§ again, *P1864a:* 'Twas there 1095| MS:felt indeed §inserted above§ at home again, §crossed out§ 1096| MS:of common things that §crossed out and replaced above by§ which make up life, *P1864a:* things, the daily life, *1870:* o' 1097| MS:contempt—no *P1864a:* contempt; no 1098| MS:Man, from *P1864a:* Man from 1101| MS:That was man's proper business, and §crossed out and replaced above by§ far *P1864a:* Such was man's vulgar business 1102| MS:thunder: men said §crossed out and replaced above by§ repeated "small" *P1864a:* thunder: "small," folk kept on, "small," 1103| MS:those same days— *P1864a:* those great days! 1105| MS:despicable, Sir, §crossed out and replaced above by§ now as grass *P1864a:* despicable as mere grass, 1106| MS:of *1870:* o' 1107| MS:That fed there? They §altered to§ These *P1864a:* Which fed 1108| MS:Well, Sir *P1864a:* sir 1109| MS:world looks quite differently §last three words crossed out and replaced above by three words§ wears another aspect 1111| MS:it: little things, grow *P1864a:* it: grass, worm, fly grow 1114| MS:them: talk *P1864a:* them. Talk 1116| MS:mites *P1864a:* mites.

The Name comes close behind a stomach-cyst,
The simplest of creations, just a sac
That's mouth, heart, legs and belly at once, yet lives
And feels, and could do neither, we conclude,
If simplified still further one degree:
The small becomes the dreadful and immense!
Lightning, forsooth? No word more upon that!
A tin-foil bottle, a strip of greasy silk,
With a bit of wire and knob of brass, and there's
Your dollar's-worth of lightning! But the cyst—
The life of the least of the little things?

No, no!

Preachers and teachers try another tack,
Come near the truth this time: they put aside
Thunder and lightning: "That's mistake," they cry,
"Thunderbolts fall for neither fright nor sport,
But do appreciable good, like tides,
Changes o' the wind, and other natural facts—
'Good' meaning good to man, his body or soul.
Mediate, immediate, all things minister
To man,—that's settled: be our future text
'We are His children!'" So, they now harangue

1117| MS:The "Nomen" close §over illegible erasure§ *P1864a:*The Name comes close 1119| MS:lives, *P1864a:*lives 1120| MS:we suppose, §crossed out and replaced above by§ conclude, 1122| MS:small's become the <> and the great! *P1864a:*small becomes the <> and immense! *1888:*immense §emended to§ immense! §see Editorial Notes§ 1123| MS:Lightning §over illegible erasure§ forsooth? <> that— *P1864a:*Lightning, forsooth? <> that! 1124| MS:bottle, and §crossed out§ a <> of greasy §inserted above§ 1125| MS:And §crossed out and replaced above by two words§ With a 1126| MS:dollar's worth <> but the cyst,— *P1864a:*dollar's-worth <> But the cyst— 1130| MS:Whirlwind §crossed out and replaced above by§ Thunder and earth quake, §last two words crossed out and replaced above by§ lightning: "that's men stuff §last two words crossed out and replaced above by§ mistake" they *P1864a:*lightning: "That's mistake," they 1131| MS:Thunderbolts fall neither for §last two words marked for transposition§ <> sport: *P1864a:*sport, *CP1864a:*"Thunderbolts
1133| MS:of the moon, §crossed out and replaced above by§ wind *1870:*o'
1134| MS:And good means good <> soul; *P1864a:*'Good' meaning good <> soul.
1137| MS:"We <> children"—and §crossed out and replaced above by§ so they're preaching now *P1864a:*'We <> children!' So, they now harangue *CP1864a(Yale):*children!'" So *CP1864a(Berg):*"We <> children!'" So *1864a:*'We <> children!'" So

About the intention, the contrivance, all
That keeps up an incessant play of love,—
See the Bridgewater book.

Amen to it!

Well, sir, I put this question: I'm a child?
I lose no time, but take you at your word:
How shall I act a child's part properly?
Your sainted mother, sir,—used you to live
With such a thought as this a-worrying you?
"She has it in her power to throttle me,
Or stab or poison: she may turn me out,
Or lock me in,—nor stop at this to-day,
But cut me off to-morrow from the estate
I look for"—(long may you enjoy it, sir!)
"In brief, she may unchild the child I am."
You never had such crotchets? Nor have I!
Who, frank confessing childship from the first,
Cannot both fear and take my ease at once,
So, don't fear,—know what might be, well enough
But know too, child-like, that it will not be,
At least in my case, mine, the son and heir
O' the kingdom, as yourself proclaim my style.
But do you fancy I stop short at this?
Wonder if suit and service, son and heir
Needs must expect, I dare pretend to find?

1139| MS:up the incessant *P1864a:*up an incessant 1140| MS:the Bridgewater Book. §¶§ *P1864a:*book. §¶§ 1141| MS:Then, Sir, <> child— *P1864a:*Now, sir, <> child? *CP1864a:*Now §crossed out and replaced in L margin by§ Well 1142| MS:§line added§ word. *P1864a:*word: 1144| MS:mother, Sir *P1864a:*sir 1145| MS:you *P1864a:*you? 1148| MS:this, to-day *1870:*this to-day 1150| MS:it, Sir!) *P1864a:*sir!) 1151| MS:—"In brief, she may §last two words inserted above§ <> child of hers §last two words crossed out§ I am?" *P1864a:*"In <> am." 1152| MS:have I, *P1864a:*have I! 1153| MS:Who frank <> from §over illegible word§ *P1864a:*Who, frank 1154| MS:Could §crossed out§ not §altered to§ Cannot 1156| MS:know, too <> it cannot §crossed out and replaced above by two words§ will not *1864a:*know too 1158| MS:Of the <> proclaim §over illegible word§ *1870:*O' 1158–60| MS:style. §¶§ And yet you wonder that what sons and heirs *P1864a:*style. §no ¶§ But do you fancy I stop short at this / Wonder if suit and service, sons and heirs *CP1864a:*this? *C1870:*son and heir 1161| MS:find— *P1864a:*find?

If, looking for signs proper to such an one,
I straight perceive them irresistible?
Concede that homage is a son's plain right,
And, never mind the nods and raps and winks,
'Tis the pure obvious supernatural
Steps forward, does its duty: why, of course!
I have presentiments; my dreams come true:
I fancy a friend stands whistling all in white
Blithe as a boblink, and he's dead I learn.
I take dislike to a dog my favourite long,
And sell him; he goes mad next week and snaps.
I guess that stranger will turn up to-day
I have not seen these three years; there's his knock.
I wager "sixty peaches on that tree!"—
That I pick up a dollar in my walk,
That your wife's brother's cousin's name was George—
And win on all points. Oh, you wince at this?
You'd fain distinguish between gift and gift,
Washington's oracle and Sludge's itch
O' the elbow when at whist he ought to trump?
With Sludge it's too absurd? *Fine, draw the line*
Somewhere, but, sir, your somewhere is not mine!

Bless us, I'm turning poet! It's time to end.
How you have drawn me out, sir! All I ask
Is—am I heir or not heir? If I'm he,

1162| MS:That looking <> one *P1864a:* If, looking <> one, 1163| MS:And may not say they are §last six words crossed out and replaced above by five words§ I should dare perceive them *P1864a:* I straight perceive them 1164| MS:Concede, on the other hand, §word illegibly crossed out and replaced above by§ these signs may right, *P1864a:* Concede that homage is a son's plain right, 1166| MS:pure natural Supernatural *P1864a:* pure obvious supenatural 1167| MS:forward to instruct me: why *P1864a:* forward, does its duty: why 1170| MS:dead, I find. *P1864a:* dead I learn. 1171| MS:favourite now, *P1864a:* favourite long, 1174| MS:years: there's <> knock! *P1864a:* years; there's <> knock. *1888:* knock DC,BrU:knock. *1889:* knock §emended to conform to DC and BrU; see Editorial Notes§ 1175| MS:wager "Sixty *P1864a:* sixty 1178| MS:points—Oh <> this, *P1864a:* points. Oh <> this? 1181| MS:trump— *P1864a:* trump? 1182| MS:absurd! Fine §no italics called for§ *P1864a:* absurd? *Fine* 1183| MS:§no italics called for§ *P1864a:* §italic type§ 1184| MS:end! *P1864a:* end. 1185| MS:out, Sir *P1864a:* sir

Then, sir, remember, that same personage
(To judge by what we read i' the newspaper)
Requires, beside one nobleman in gold
To carry up and down his coronet,
Another servant, probably a duke,
To hold egg-nogg in readiness: why want
Attendance, sir, when helps in his father's house
Abound, I'd like to know?

Enough of talk!
My fault is that I tell too plain a truth.
Why, which of those who say they disbelieve,
Your clever people, but has dreamed his dream,
Caught his coincidence, stumbled on his fact
He can't explain, (he'll tell you smilingly)
Which he's too much of a philosopher
To count as supernatural, indeed,
So calls a puzzle and problem, proud of it,—
Bidding you still be on your guard, you know,
Because one fact don't make a system stand,
Nor prove this an occasional escape
Of spirit beneath the matter: that's the way!
Just so wild Indians picked up, piece by piece,
The fact in California, the fine gold
That underlay the gravel—hoarded these,

1187| MS:Please, Sir, remember that *P1864a:* Then, sir, remember, that 1188| MS:in newspapers) *P1864a:* in the newspaper) *1870:* i' 1189| MS:Requires beside one nobleman §over illegible erasure§ *P1864a:* Requires, beside 1192| MS:hold cigars in readiness—why *P1864a:* hold egg-nog in readiness: why 1193| MS:Service when servants in *P1864a:* Attendance, sir, when helps in 1195| MS:It's fault is that §over illegible erasure§ it's far too *P1864a:* My fault is that I tell too 1196| MS:which one out §last two words crossed out§ <> who say they §last two words inserted above§ 1197| MS:The clever *P1864a:* Your clever 1199| MS:(he tells §altered to§ he'll tell 1200| MS:Which §crossed out and replaced above by§ But he's *P1864a:* Which he's 1201| MS:supernatural indeed, *P1864a:* supernatural, indeed, 1202| MS:But §crossed out and replaced above by§ So calls <> problem—proud of it: *1864a:* problem, proud *1888:* it DC,BrU:it,— *1889:* it §emended to conform to DC and BrU; see Editorial Notes§ 1205| MS:Or §in L margin§ Prove possible §crossed out and replaced above by§ this the occasional *P1864a:* Nor prove this an occasional 1206| MS:Of the §crossed out§ spirit 1207| MS:so poor Indians <> up piece by piece *P1864a:* so wild Indians <> up, piece by piece, 1209| MS:gravel—§over illegible word§ <> these; *P1864a:* these,

But never made a system stand, nor dug!
So wise men hold out in each hollowed palm
A handful of experience, sparkling fact
They can't explain; and since their rest of life
Is all explainable, what proof in this?
Whereas I take the fact, the grain of gold,
And fling away the dirty rest of life,
And add this grain to the grain each fool has found
O' the million other such philosophers,—
Till I see gold, all gold and only gold,
Truth questionless though unexplainable,
And the miraculous proved the commonplace!
The other fools believed in mud, no doubt—
Failed to know gold they saw: was that so strange?
Are all men born to play Bach's fiddle-fugues,
"Time" with the foil in carte, jump their own height,
Cut the mutton with the broadsword, skate a five,
Make the red hazard with the cue, clip nails
While swimming, in five minutes row a mile,
Pull themselves three feet up with the left arm,
Do sums of fifty figures in their head,

1211| MS:Such wise man holds you §crossed out and replaced above by§ out in his hollow palm *P1864a:* So wise men hold out in each hollowed palm 1212| MS:His handful of experience, his §crossed out§ sparkling *P1864a:* A handful 1213| MS:He can't explain,—and since his rest *P1864a:* They can't explain; and since their rest 1214| MS:what proves the fact? §last three words crossed out and replaced above by three words§ proof in this? 1215| MS:take his fact, his grain *P1864a:* take the fact, the grain 1216| MS:away his dirty *P1864a:* away the dirty 1217| MS:this §over illegible word§ grain to the §inserted above§ 1218| MS:Of <> other §inserted above§ such §crossed out§ *P1864a:* other such *1870:* O' 1219| MS:Till §over illegible word§ 1220| MS:unexplainable *P1864a:* unexplainable, 1221| MS:proved the daily thing. §last two words crossed out and replaced above by one word and punctuation§ commonplace! 1224| MS:fiddle-fugues? *P1864a:* fiddle-fugues, 1224–25| MS:§fragment of line erased§ at billiards, put §illegible word inserted above§ ball in the black, §entirely crossed out§ 1225| MS:carte, I'd like to know, foil— §last word and dash crossed out§ *P1864a:* carte, jump their own height, 1226| MS:Cut the leg of mutton <> broadsword, fence, §last word and comma crossed out§ skate, *P1864a:* Cut the mutton <> broadsword, skate a five, 1227| MS:Learn to speak French in six weeks, §last seven words crossed out and replaced above by seven words§ Make the red hazard with the cue, do a §crossed out§ sum §altered to§ sums *P1864a:* cue, clip nails 1228| MS:Of fifty figures in their brain, swim, row, *P1864a:* While swimming, in five minutes row a mile, 1229| MS:themselves up, over head, with *P1864a:* themselves three feet up with 1230| MS:Trip §over illegible word§ on a tight-rope stretched §inserted above§ across the Falls *P1864a:* Do sums of fifty figures in their head,

And so on, by the scores of instances?
The Sludge with luck, who sees the spiritual facts
His fellows strive and fail to see, may rank
With these, and share the advantage.

Ay, but share
The drawback! Think it over by yourself;
I have not heart, sir, and the fire's gone grey.
Defect somewhere compensates for success,
Everyone knows that. Oh, we're equals, sir!
The big-legged fellow has a little arm
And a less brain, though big legs win the race:
Do you suppose I 'scape the common lot?
Say, I was born with flesh so sensitive,
Soul so alert, that, practice helping both,
I guess what's going on outside the veil,
Just as a prisoned crane feels pairing-time
In the islands where his kind are, so must fall
To capering by himself some shiny night,
As if your back-yard were a plot of spice—
Thus am I 'ware o' the spirit-world: while you,
Blind as a beetle that way,—for amends,
Why, you can double fist and floor me, sir!
Ride that hot hardmouthed horrid horse of yours,
Laugh while it lightens, play with the great dog,
Speak your mind though it vex some friend to hear,
Never brag, never bluster, never blush,—
In short, you've pluck, when I'm a coward—there!

1232| MS:luck, that sees the golden facts, *P1864a:* luck, who sees the precious facts, *1864a:* the spiritual facts, *1888:* facts 1233| MS:and strain to *P1864a:* and fail to 1234| MS:these, you see §last two words crossed out and replaced above by two words§ and share the advantage! §¶§ Ay *1868:* advantage. §¶§ Ay 1235| MS:yourself, *P1864a:* yourself; 1236| MS:not time, Sir <> gone out. *P1864a:* not heart, sir <> gone grey. 1237| MS:somewhere §inserted above§ 1238| MS:that,—oh <> Sir! *P1864a:* that! Oh <> sir! *1868:* that. Oh 1242| MS:Yes, I *P1864a:* Say, I 1244| MS:I know what's <> veil *P1864a:* I guess what's <> veil, 1246| MS:are, needs must *P1864a:* are, so must 1249| MS:So am <> of *P1864a:* Thus am *1870:* o' 1251| MS:me, Sir! *P1864a:* sir! 1252| MS:hot, hardmouthed, horrid *1868:* hot hardmouthed horrid 1254| MS:Speak your mind §last three words over illegible erasure§ 1255| MS:never lie,— *P1864a:* never blush,— 1256| MS:pluck, while I'm *P1864a:* pluck, when I'm

I know it, I can't help it,—folly or no,
I'm paralyzed, my hand's no more a hand,
Nor my head a head, in danger: you can smile
And change the pipe in your cheek. Your gift's not mine.
Would you swap for mine? No! but you'd add my gift
To yours: I dare say! I too sigh at times,
Wish I were stouter, could tell truth nor flinch,
Kept cool when threatened, did not mind so much
Being dressed gaily, making strangers stare,
Eating nice things; when I'd amuse myself,
I shut my eyes and fancy in my brain
I'm—now the President, now Jenny Lind,
Now Emerson, now the Benicia Boy—
With all the civilized world a-wondering
And worshipping. I know it's folly and worse;
I feel such tricks sap, honeycomb the soul,
But I can't cure myself: despond, despair,
And then, hey, presto, there's a turn o' the wheel,
Under comes uppermost, fate makes full amends;
Sludge knows and sees and hears a hundred things
You all are blind to,—I've my taste of truth,

1258| MS:paralysed *P1864a:*paralyzed 1259| MS:my head, a <> can laugh *P1864a:*can smile *1888:*my head a 1260| MS:cheek—your gift, this time. §last two words crossed out and replaced above by two words§ you see. *P1864a:*cheek. Your gift's not mine. 1262| MS:say! I, too, sigh *1864a:*say! I too 1263| MS:were stout, <> tell the truth nor flinch, §over illegible erasure§ *P1864a:*were stouter, <> tell truth 1264| MS:Were cool *P1864a:*Kept cool 1265| MS:dressed fine, making folks envy me, §last three words and comma crossed out and replaced above by four words and comma§ strangers stare at me, *P1864a:*dressed gaily, making <> stare, 1266| MS:when I amuse myself. *P1864a:*myself, *1864a:*when I'd amuse 1267| MS:eyes, and *1864a:*eyes and *1868:*brain, *1888:*brain 1268| MS:the President, now, Jenny *1888:*the President, now Jenny 1269| MS:Now, Emerson,—now, the *P1864a:*Now Emerson, now, the *1888:*Now Emerson, now the 1271| MS:worshipping! I <> worse— *P1864a:*worse: *1868:*worshipping. I <> worse; 1272| MS:These §over perhaps *This*§ §word illegibly crossed out and replaced above by§ same trick §altered to§ tricks that emasculate the *P1864a:*I feel such tricks sap, honeycomb the *1868:*soul: *1888:*soul, 1273| MS:myself, all but §last two words crossed out] and replaced above by§ despond, despair, *1888:*myself: despond 1274| MS:of the wheel *P1864a:*wheel, *1870:*o' 1275| MS:And under's uppermost <> makes full §inserted above§ amends, *P1864a:*Under comes uppermost <> amends; 1276| MS:knows §over illegible word§

Likewise my touch of falsehood,—vice no doubt,
But you've your vices also: I'm content.

What, sir? You won't shake hands? "Because I cheat!"
"You've found me out in cheating!" That's enough
To make an apostle swear! Why, when I cheat,
Mean to cheat, do cheat, and am caught in the act,
Are you, or, rather, am I sure o' the fact?
(There's verse again, but I'm inspired somehow.)
Well then I'm not sure! I may be, perhaps,
Free as a babe from cheating: how it began,
My gift,—no matter; what 'tis got to be
In the end now, that's the question; answer that!
Had I seen, perhaps, what hand was holding mine,
Leading me whither, I had died of fright:
So, I was made believe I led myself.
If I should lay a six-inch plank from roof
To roof, you would not cross the street, one step,
Even at your mother's summons: but, being shrewd,
If I paste paper on each side the plank
And swear 'tis solid pavement, why, you'll cross
Humming a tune the while, in ignorance
Beacon Street stretches a hundred feet below:
I walked thus, took the paper-cheat for stone.
Some impulse made me set a thing o' the move
Which, started once, ran really by itself;

1278| MS:And just the §crossed out and replaced above by§ my *P1864a:* Likewise my 1280| MS:What, Sir <> cheat,— *P1864a:* sir <> cheat! *1870:* cheat!" 1281| MS:You found me §last two words over illegible words§ *P1864a:* You've found *1868:* "You've found 1283| MS:§no italics called for§ *P1864a:* §italic type§ 1284| MS:§no italics called for§ or rather <> of *P1864a:* §italic type§ *1870:* o' *1888:* or, rather 1285| MS:verse, again <> somehow) *P1864a:* verse again <> somehow.) 1286| MS:then, I'm not sure,—I *P1864a:* sure! I *1868:* then I'm 1289| MS:question: answer *1870:* question; answer 1291| MS:fright, *1888:* fright: 1292| MS:So I *P1864a:* So, I 1294| MS:step *P1864a:* step, 1295| MS:summons: if, being *P1864a:* summons: but, being 1296| MS:I paste §over illegible word§ first paper <> side of the *P1864a:* If I paste paper *1870:* side the 1297| MS:swear §over illegible word§ 'twas §crossed out and replaced above by§ 'tis <> you'd §altered to§ you'll 1298| MS:Whistling a *P1864a:* Humming a 1299| MS:The broadway stretched §altered to§ stretches *P1864a:* Beacon Street stretches 1300| MS:walked and took *P1864a:* walked thus, took 1301| An §over illegible word§ impulse <> on *P1864a:* Some impulse *1870:* o' 1302| MS:itself— *P1864a:* itself;

Beer flows thus, suck the siphon; toss the kite,
It takes the wind and floats of its own force.
Don't let truth's lump rot stagnant for the lack
Of a timely helpful lie to leaven it!
Put a chalk-egg beneath the clucking hen,
She'll lay a real one, laudably deceived,
Daily for weeks to come. I've told my lie,
And seen truth follow, marvels none of mine;
All was not cheating, sir, I'm positive!
I don't know if I move your hand sometimes
When the spontaneous writing spreads so far,
If my knee lifts the table all that height,
Why the inkstand don't fall off the desk a-tilt,
Why the accordion plays a prettier waltz
Than I can pick out on the piano-forte,
Why I speak so much more than I intend,
Describe so many things I never saw.
I tell you, sir, in one sense, I believe
Nothing at all,—that everybody can,
Will, and does cheat: but in another sense
I'm ready to believe my very self—
That every cheat's inspired, and every lie
Quick with a germ of truth.

                                                  You ask perhaps
Why I should condescend to trick at all

1303| MS:flows §over perhaps *runs*§ <> syphon *CP1864a:* siphon 1304| MS:force: *P1864a:* force. 1305| MS:rot §over illegible erasure§ 1306| MS:a timely §last two words over illegible words§ <> it— *P1864a:* it! 1307| MS:beneath §altered above to§ underneath <> hen *P1864a:* hen, 1308| MS:deceived— *P1864a:* deceived, 1309| MS:come. I told *P1864a:* come. I've told 1310| MS:mine, *P1864a:* mine; 1311| MS:cheating, Sir, I'm positive. *P1864a:* sir, I'm positive! 1313| MS:spreads itself, *P1864a:* spreads so far, 1315| MS:fall §over perhaps *run*§ 1316| MS:prettier tune *P1864a:* accordion somehow plays *CP1864a:* somehow §crossed out§ *1864a:* prettier waltz 1317| MS:Than I pick *P1864a:* I can pick 1318| *P1864a:* than I first intend, *1868:* than I intend, 1319| MS:things I do not §last two words crossed out and replaced above by one word§ never see, *P1864a:* saw. 1320| MS: . . I tell you, Sir *P1864a:* I <> sir 1322| MS:Will and *P1864a:* Will, and 1324| MS:inspired, every *P1864a:* inspired, and every 1325| MS:In quick <> truth: §¶§ You'll *P1864a:* Quick <> truth. §¶§ You 1326| MS:trick §over illegible word§

If I know a way without it? This is why!
There's a strange secret sweet self-sacrifice
In any desecration of one's soul
To a worthy end,—isn't it Herodotus
(I wish I could read Latin!) who describes
The single gift o' the land's virginity,
Demanded in those old Egyptian rites,
(I've but a hazy notion—help me, sir!)
For one purpose in the world, one day in a life,
One hour in a day—thereafter, purity,
And a veil thrown o'er the past for evermore!
Well, now, they understood a many things
Down by Nile city, or wherever it was!
I've always vowed, after the minute's lie,
And the end's gain,—truth should be mine henceforth.
This goes to the root o' the matter, sir,—this plain
Plump fact: accept it and unlock with it
The wards of many a puzzle!

Or, finally,
Why should I set so fine a gloss on things?
What need I care? I cheat in self-defence,
And there's my answer to a world of cheats!

1327| MS:Since there's a <> why— *P1864a:* If I know a <> why! 1330| MS:end,—all prostitution, say, §last three words and comma crossed out and replaced above by§ isn't it Herodotus 1332| MS:gift of truth's virginity, *CP1864a(Yale):* truth's §crossed out and replaced above by two words§ the land's *CP1864a(Berg):* of the lan's §last two words over erasure; *the land's* in R margin§ *1870:* o' 1333| MS:Religious §crossed out and replaced above by§ Demanded in the old <> rite, *P1864a:* in those old <> rites, 1334| MS:me, Sir!) *P1864a:* sir!) 1336| MS:in that §altered to§ the day *1868:* in a day 1337| MS:And forgetfulness of the *P1864a:* And a veil thrown o'er the 1338–39| MS:§these two lines inserted§ 1338| MS:Well now *1888:* Well, now 1340| MS:the good end's <> mine, henceforth. *1864a:* mine henceforth. *1870:* the end's 1342| MS:I go to <> of <> Sir, the plain *P1864a:* This goes to <> sir, this plain *1870:* o' 1343| MS:and detect, §last word and comma crossed out and replaced above by§ unlock with §word illegibly crossed out and replaced above by§ it 1344| MS:The play §crossed out and replaced above by§ wards <> finally *P1864a:* finally, 1345| MS:—Why <> I put so fine a point on it? *P1864a:* Why <> I set so fine a gloss on *CP1864a:* on it §crossed out and replaced by§ things? 1347| MS:to a §crossed out and replaced above by§ your world of cheats. *P1864a:* to a world of cheats!

Cheat? To be sure, sir! What's the world worth else?
Who takes it as he finds, and thanks his stars?
Don't it want trimming, turning, furbishing up
And polishing over? Your so-styled great men,
Do they accept one truth as truth is found,
Or try their skill at tinkering? What's your world?
Here are you born, who are, I'll say at once,
Of the luckiest kind, whether in head and heart,
Body and soul, or all that helps them both.
Well, now, look back: what faculty of yours
Came to its full, had ample justice done
By growing when rain fell, biding its time,
Solidifying growth when earth was dead,
Spiring up, broadening wide, in seasons due?
Never! You shot up and frost nipped you off,
Settled to sleep when sunshine bade you sprout;
One faculty thwarted its fellow: at the end,
All you boast is "I had proved a topping tree
In other climes"—yet this was the right clime
Had you foreknown the seasons. Young, you've force
Wasted like well-streams: old,—oh, then indeed,
Behold a labyrinth of hydraulic pipes
Through which you'd play off wondrous waterwork;
Only, no water's left to feed their play.
Young,—you've a hope, an aim, a love: it's tossed

1348| MS:What? These are things when I am out of sorts, §entire line crossed out and replaced above by§ Cheat? To be sure, Sir! What's the world worth else, *P1864a:* sir <> else? 1349| MS:The §two illegible words§ helpless you'd believe. §entire line crossed out and replaced above by§ Who takes it as he finds and thanks his stars? *P1864a:* finds, and 1350| MS:up, *P1864a:* up 1351| MS:Polishing over <> men *P1864a:* And polishing over <> men, 1352| MS:as truth they §crossed out and replaced above by§ is 1353–54| MS:As you open eyes to it? I'll tell you, Sir. §entire line crossed out§ 1355| MS:One of the luckiest ones in *P1864a:* luckiest whether in *1870:* Of the *1888:* luckiest kind, whether 1356| MS:soul, and <> helps the same: *P1864a:* soul, or <> same. *1888:* helps them both. 1361| MS:wide in <> due: *P1864a:* wide, in <> due? 1364| MS:thwarts *P1864a:* thwarted 1365| MS:you can boast is, "I had proved a tree *1864a:* you boast <> proved a topping tree *1888:* is "I 1366| MS:climes"—and yet <> the clime *P1864a:* climes"—yet <> the right clime 1368| MS:well-stream §altered to§ well-streams under §crossed out and replaced above by *colon*§ <> then, indeed, *1864a:* then indeed, 1370| MS:water-work *P1864a:* water-work; *1868:* waterwork; 1371| MS:water left *CP1864a:* play! *1870:* play *1875:* play. *1888:* water's left 1372| MS:love, suppose: *P1864a:* love: it's tossed

And crossed and lost: you struggle on, some spark
Shut in your heart against the puffs around,
Through cold and pain; these in due time subside,
Now then for age's triumph, the hoarded light
You mean to loose on the altered face of things,—
Up with it on the tripod! It's extinct.
Spend your life's remnant asking, which was best,
Light smothered up that never peeped forth once,
Or the cold cresset with full leave to shine?
Well, accept this too,—seek the fruit of it
Not in enjoyment, proved a dream on earth,
But knowledge, useful for a second chance,
Another life,—you've lost this world—you've gained
Its knowledge for the next. What knowledge, sir,
Except that you know nothing? Nay, you doubt
Whether 'twere better have made you man or brute,
If aught be true, if good and evil clash.
No foul, no fair, no inside, no outside,
There's your world!

Give it me! I slap it brisk
With harlequin's pasteboard sceptre: what's it now?
Changed like a rock-flat, rough with rusty weed,

1373| MS:It's crossed <> on, the spark *P1864a:* And crossed <> on, some spark
1375| MS:Thru' cold and pain—these in due §two illegible words and *out* crossed out and replaced above by§ subside, *P1864a:* Through cold <> due time subside, *1864a:* pain; these
1376| MS:And now then for your triumph, §crossed out and replaced above by two illegible words, crossed out and replaced below by§ triumph *P1864a:* Now then for age's triumph
1377| MS:To let loose *P1864a:* You mean to loose 1378| MS:High on the triumphant §last four words crossed out and replaced above by five words§ Up with it on the <> extinct! *P1864a:* extinct. 1379| MS:Spend their §crossed out and replaced above by§ your
1381| MS:cold altar lamp §last two words crossed out and replaced above by one word§ cresset with full §inserted above§ <> shine! *P1864a:* shine? 1383| MS:enjoyment proved impossible §crossed out§ a *P1864a:* enjoyment, proved 1384| MS:knowledge useful *P1864a:* knowledge, useful 1386| MS:This knowledge <> next.—What <> Sir, *P1864a:* Its knowledge <> sir, *1888:* next. What 1387| MS:nothing?—Nay *P1864a:* nothing? Nay 1388| MS:better you had seen a §last three words crossed out and replaced above by three words§ were man or *1864a:* better have made you man
1389| MS:be real §crossed out and replaced above by§ true <> clash; *P1864a:* clash.
1390| MS:No real, no *P1864a:* No foul, no 1391| MS:me: I *CP1864a:* me! I
1393| MS:rock-flat with its rusty weed *P1864a:* rock-flat, rough with rusty weed,

At first wash-over o' the returning wave!
All the dry dead impracticable stuff
Starts into life and light again; this world
Pervaded by the influx from the next.
I cheat, and what's the happy consequence?
You find full justice straightway dealt you out,
Each want supplied, each ignorance set at ease,
Each folly fooled. No life-long labour now
As the price of worse than nothing! No mere film
Holding you chained in iron, as it seems,
Against the outstretch of your very arms
And legs i' the sunshine moralists forbid!
What would you have? Just speak and, there, you see!
You're supplemented, made a whole at last,
Bacon advises, Shakespeare writes you songs,
And Mary Queen of Scots embraces you.
Thus it goes on, not quite like life perhaps,
But so near, that the very difference piques,
Shows that e'en better than this best will be—
This passing entertainment in a hut
Whose bare walls take your taste since, one stage more,
And you arrive at the palace: all half real,
And you, to suit it, less than real beside,
In a dream, lethargic kind of death in life,
That helps the interchange of natures, flesh

1394| MS:of *1870:* o' 1395| MS:dry, dead, impracticable *1868:* dry dead impracticable 1398| MS:cheat you,—what's *P1864a:* cheat, and what's 1399| MS:Each man finds justice <> dealt to him, *P1864a:* You find full justice <> dealt you out, 1400| MS:want of his supplied, <> ignorance eased, *P1864a:* want supplied, <> ignorance set at ease, 1401| MS:folly further §crossed out§ fooled; no *P1864a:* fooled. No 1403| MS:you captive §crossed out and replaced above by§ chained 1405| MS:in *1870:* i' 1408| MS:Shakespeare advises, yes, and Bacon warns, §entire line crossed out and replaced above by§ Bacon advises, Shakespeare sings you songs, *P1864a:* Shakespeare writes you 1409| MS:you, *P1864a:* you. 1410| MS:So *CP1864a:* So §crossed out and replaced by§ Thus 1411| MS:near that *P1864a:* near, that 1412| MS:be! *P1864a:* be— 1414| MS:take our taste <> stage §crossed out and replaced above by§ stage *P1864a:* take your taste 1415| MS:And we arrive <> all so real, *P1864a:* And you arrive <> all half real, 1416| MS:And we, to <> it, grown unreal besides, *P1864a:* And you, to <> it, less than real besides, *1864a:* beside, 1417| MS:dream, half-lethargy, kind *P1864a:* dream, lethargic kind

Transfused by souls, and such souls! Oh, 'tis choice!
And if at whiles the bubble, blown too thin,
Seem nigh on bursting,—if you nearly see
The real world through the false,—what *do* you see?
Is the old so ruined? You find you're in a flock
O' the youthful, earnest, passionate—genius, beauty,
Rank and wealth also, if you care for these:
And all depose their natural rights, hail you,
(That's me, sir) as their mate and yoke-fellow,
Participate in Sludgehood—nay, grow mine,
I veritably possess them—banish doubt,
And reticence and modesty alike!
Why, here's the Golden Age, old Paradise
Or new Eutopia! Here's true life indeed,
And the world well won now, mine for the first time!

And all this might be, may be, and with good help
Of a little lying shall be: so, Sludge lies!
Why, he's at worst your poet who sings how Greeks
That never were, in Troy which never was,
Did this or the other impossible great thing!
He's Lowell—it's a world (you smile applause),
Of his own invention—wondrous Longfellow,

1419| MS:souls: oh, 'tis rare! *P1864a:* souls! Oh, 'tis choice! 1420| MS:bubble be blown too thin *P1864a:* bubble, blown too thin, 1421| MS:Seem §over illegible word§ <> you come to see *P1864a:* you nearly see 1422| MS:through this false *P1864a:* through the false 1423| MS:find yourself in *P1864a:* find you're in 1424| MS:Of <> genius, Sir, *P1864a:* genius, beauty, *1870:* O' 1425| MS:them, §altered to§ these, *1888:* these: 1427| MS:me, Sir) <> yoke fellow. *P1864a:* sir) <> yoke-fellow, *1870:* yoke-fellow. DC,BrU:yoke-fellow, *1889:* yoke-fellow, 1428| MS:grow yours, *P1864a:* grow mine, 1429| MS:You veritably *P1864a:* I veritably 1432| MS:new Eutopia! This is life indeed *P1864a:* Eutopia! Here is life indeed, *1888:* Here's true life 1433| MS:now, for *P1864a:* now, yours for *CP1864a(Yale):* yours §altered to§ found *1888:* now, mine for 1435| MS:so Sludge *P1864a:* so, Sludge 1436| MS:sings that Greeks *P1864a:* sings how Greeks 1437| MS:Who never *P1864a:* That never 1438| MS:thing, *P1864a:* thing! 1439| MS:He's Homer—it's a world, you smile and say, *P1864a:* He's Lowell—it's *1888:* world (you smile applause),

Surprising Hawthorne! Sludge does more than they,
And acts the books they write: the more his praise!

But why do I mount to poets? Take plain prose—
Dealers in common sense, set these at work,
What can they do without their helpful lies?
Each states the law and fact and face o' the thing
Just as he'd have them, finds what he thinks fit,
Is blind to what missuits him, just records
What makes his case out, quite ignores the rest.
It's a History of the World, the Lizard Age,
The Early Indians, the Old Country War,
Jerome Napoleon, whatsoever you please,
All as the author wants it. Such a scribe
You pay and praise for putting life in stones,
Fire into fog, making the past your world.
There's plenty of "How did you contrive to grasp
The thread which led you through this labyrinth?
How build such solid fabric out of air?
How on so slight foundation found this tale,
Biography, narrative?" or, in other words,
"How many lies did it require to make
The portly truth you here present us with?"
"Oh," quoth the penman, purring at your praise,
"'Tis fancy all; no particle of fact:

1441| MS:more, §comma crossed out§ than 1442| MS:more's *1868:* more
1443| MS:But §in L margin§ Why <> Poets *P1864a:* why <> poets 1444| MS:set each at *P1864a:* set these at 1445| MS:can he do without his helpful *P1864a:* can they do without their helpful 1446| MS:of *1870:* o' 1447| MS:have these—finds <> fit— *P1864a:* have them, finds <> fit, 1449| MS:out, and ignores *P1864a:* out, quite ignores 1450| MS:history of the world, the lizard age, *P1864a:* a History of the World, the Lizard Age, 1451| MS:early *P1864a:* The Early
1452| MS:whatsoever §over illegible erasure§ 1453| MS:All §over illegible word§ <> author would have it *P1864a:* author wants it 1454| MS:You thank and <> stones *P1864a:* You pay and <> stones, 1457| MS:through the labyrinth? *P1864a:* through this labyrinth? 1458| MS:build this solid *P1864a:* build such solid 1459| MS:on such slight *P1864a:* on so slight 1460| MS:Biography, description?"—in other words *P1864a:* words, *CP1864a:* description §crossed out and replaced above by§ narrative?"—§dash crossed out§ or, §inserted above§ 1461| MS:to tell *CP1864a:* to make
1463| MS:"Oh" quoth *P1864a:* "Oh," quoth 1464| MS:'Twas fancy all—no <> fact— *P1864a:* 'Tis fancy all; no <> fact: *CP1864a:* " 'Tis §quotation marks inserted§

I was poor and threadbare when I wrote that book
'Bliss in the Golden City.' I, at Thebes?
We writers paint out of our heads, you see!"
"—Ah, the more wonderful the gift in you,
The more creativeness and godlike craft!"
But I, do I present you with my piece,
It's "What, Sludge? When my sainted mother spoke
The verses Lady Jane Grey last composed
About the rosy bower in the seventh heaven
Where she and Queen Elizabeth keep house,—
You made the raps? 'Twas your invention that?
Cur, slave and devil!"—eight fingers and two thumbs
Stuck in my throat!

Well, if the marks seem gone
'Tis because stiffish cock-tail, taken in time,
Is better for a bruise than arnica.
There, sir! I bear no malice: 'tisn't in me.
I know I acted wrongly: still, I've tried
What I could say in my excuse,—to show
The devil's not all devil . . . I don't pretend,
He's angel, much less such a gentleman
As you, sir! And I've lost you, lost myself,
Lost all-l-l-l- . . .

No—are you in earnest, sir?
O yours, sir, is an angel's part! I know

1466| MS:"Life in <> City"—I *P1864a:*'Bliss in <> City.' I 1467| MS:We poets paint *P1864a:*We writers paint 1468| MS:"Ah *1868:*"—Ah 1469| *1888:*craft!' DC,BrU:craft!" *1889:*craft!" 1472| MS:verses Lady Jane Gray late composed *P1864a:*Grey last composed 1475| MS:raps? All your <> that?" *P1864a:*raps? 'Twas your <> that? 1476| MS:Beast, slave §over perhaps *cur*§ <> devil! eight *P1864a:*Cur, slave <> devil!—eight 1477| MS:marks are gone *P1864a:*marks seem gone, *1888:*gone 1479–80| MS:§¶§ *1870:*§no ¶§ 1480| MS:There, Sir *P1864a:*There. sir *CP1864a:*There, sir 1481| MS:wrongly—still I've *P1864a:*wrongly: still, I've 1483| MS:all devil—I don't pretend *P1864a:*devil . . . I don't pretend, 1484| MS:He's §crossed out§ An angel DC,BrU: He's angel *1889:*He's angel 1485–86| MS:you, Sir! §¶§ No—are <> Sir? *P1864a:*you, sir! And I've lost you, lost myself, / Lost all, l-l-l-. . . . §¶§ No—are *1888:*all-l-l-l- . . . §¶§ 1487| MS:O, your's, Sir *P1864a:*sir *1888:*O yours

What prejudice prompts, and what's the common course
Men take to soothe their ruffled self-conceit:
Only you rise superior to it all!
No, sir, it don't hurt much; it's speaking long
That makes me choke a little: the marks will go!
What? Twenty V-notes more, and outfit too,
And not a word to Greeley? One—one kiss
O' the hand that saves me! You'll not let me speak,
I well know, and I've lost the right, too true!
But I must say, sir, if She hears (she does)
Your sainted . . . Well, sir,—be it so! That's, I think,
My bed-room candle. Good-night! Bl-l-less you, sir!

R-r-r, you brute-beast and blackguard! Cowardly scamp!
I only wish I dared burn down the house
And spoil your sniggering! Oh what, you're the man?
You're satisfied at last? You've found out Sludge?
We'll see that presently: my turn, sir, next!
I too can tell my story: brute,—do you hear?—
You throttled your sainted mother, that old hag,
In just such a fit of passion: no, it was . . .
To get this house of hers, and many a note
Like these . . . I'll pocket them, however . . . five,

1488| MS:prejudice is, and what the *P1864a:*prejudice must be, what *1870:*prejudice prompts, and what's the 1489| MS:ruffled vanity— *P1864a:*ruffled self-conceit: 1491| MS:No, Sir <> much—it's *P1864a:*sir <> much; it's 1492| MS:little—the *P1864a:*little: the 1493| MS:What twenty <> more, §word illegibly crossed out and replaced above by *for*, crossed out and replaced by§ and <> too? *P1864a:*What? Twenty <> too, 1494| MS:to Greely *1864a(r):*Greely §altered to§ Greeley 1495| MS:Of *1870:*O' 1496| MS:know—and I've §over *now*§ <> right—too *P1864a:*know, and <> right, too 1497| MS:say, Sir <> hears—she does— *P1864a:*sir <> hears (she does) 1498| MS:sainted . . Well, Sir,—better §altered to§ best so *P1864a:*sainted . . . Well, sir,—be it so 1499| MS:candle—Good night,—and §crossed out and replaced by dash§ bless you, Sir! *P1864a:*candle. Good night! Bl-l-less you, sir! 1499–1500| MS:§¶§ *P1864a:*§rule§ 1500| MS:Aie, you brute, beast *P1864a:*R-r-r, you brute beast *CP1864a:*brute-beast 1502| MS:your shocking §crossed out and replaced above by§ sniggering! Oh, what *1888:*Oh what 1504| MS:turn, Sir *P1864a:*sir 1507| MS:was *P1864a:*was . . . 1509| MS:these . . I'll <> them however . . five, *P1864a:*these . . . I'll <> them, however . . . five,

Ten, fifteen . . . ay, you gave her throat the twist,
Or else you poisoned her! Confound the cuss!
Where was my head? I ought to have prophesied
He'll die in a year and join her: that's the way.

I don't know where my head is: what had I done?
How did it all go? I said he poisoned her,
And hoped he'd have grace given him to repent,
Whereon he picked this quarrel, bullied me
And called me cheat: I thrashed him,—who could help?
He howled for mercy, prayed me on his knees
To cut and run and save him from disgrace:
I do so, and once off, he slanders me.
An end of him! Begin elsewhere anew!
Boston's a hole, the herring-pond is wide,
V-notes are something, liberty still more.
Beside, is he the only fool in the world?

1510| MS:fifteen, . . ay, <> twist *P1864a:*fifteen . . . ay, <> twist, 1513| MS:way, *P1864a:*way. 1513–14| MS:Since to succeed, the niggers say, who knows? §entire line crossed out; ¶§ *1888:*§no ¶; emended to restore ¶. See Editorial Notes§ 1514| MS:what have I *CP1864a:*have §altered to§ had 1515| MS:said he'd poisoned her *P1864a:*her, *1864a:*said he poisoned 1517| MS:quarrel, and §crossed out§ bullied 1519| MS:mercy—prayed *P1864a:*mercy, prayed 1520| MS:from §over illegible word§ 1521| MS:me! *P1864a:*me. 1522| MS:him, we'll begin <> anew: *P1864a:*him! Begin <> anew! 1523| MS:herring pond *P1864a:*herring-pond 1524| MS:still §over illegible word§ more; *P1864a:*more. 1525| MS:Besides *P1864a:*Beside

APPARENT FAILURE

"We shall soon lose a celebrated building."

Paris Newspaper

I

No, for I'll save it! Seven years since,
I passed through Paris, stopped a day
To see the baptism of your Prince;
Saw, made my bow, and went my way:
Walking the heat and headache off,
I took the Seine-side, you surmise,
Thought of the Congress, Gortschakoff,
Cavour's appeal and Buol's replies,
So sauntered till—what met my eyes?

II

Only the Doric little Morgue!
The dead-house where you show your drowned:
Petrarch's Vaucluse makes proud the Sorgue,
Your Morgue has made the Seine renowned.
One pays one's debt in such a case;
I plucked up heart and entered,—stalked,
Keeping a tolerable face
Compared with some whose cheeks were chalked:
Let them! No Briton's to be baulked!

III

First came the silent gazers; next,
A screen of glass, we're thankful for;
Last, the sight's self, the sermon's text,
The three men who did most abhor

APPARENT FAILURE *Epigraph*| MS:building—" / Paris, Newspaper. *P1864a:*building." / *Paris Newspaper.* [1]| *1870:*since *1888:*since, [4]| MS:bow and *P1864:*bow, and [13]| MS:has made §over illegible erasure§ [14]| MS:case, *P1864a:*case; [16]| MS:face, *P1864a:*face [17]| MS:cheeks grew chalked: *P1864a:*cheeks were chalked:

Their life in Paris yesterday,
So killed themselves: and now, enthroned
Each on his copper couch, they lay
Fronting me, waiting to be owned.
I thought, and think, their sin's atoned.

IV

Poor men, God made, and all for that!
The reverence struck me; o'er each head
Religiously was hung its hat,
Each coat dripped by the owner's bed,
Sacred from touch: each had his berth,
His bounds, his proper place of rest,
Who last night tenanted on earth
Some arch, where twelve such slept abreast,—
Unless the plain asphalte seemed best.

V

How did it happen, my poor boy?
You wanted to be Buonaparte
And have the Tuileries for toy,
And could not, so it broke your heart?
You, old one by his side, I judge,
Were, red as blood, a socialist,
A leveller! Does the Empire grudge
You've gained what no Republic missed?
Be quiet, and unclench your fist!

VI

And this—why, he was red in vain,
Or black,—poor fellow that is blue!
What fancy was it turned your brain?
Oh, women were the prize for you!
Money gets women, cards and dice
Get money, and ill-luck gets just

31| MS:bed *P1864a:* bed, 45| MS:quiet and §over illegible erasure§ *P1864a:* quiet, and 46| MS:vain *P1864a:* vain, 48| MS:it, turned *1888:* it turned 51| MS:ill luck *P1864a:* ill-luck

The copper couch and one clear nice
    Cool squirt of water o'er your bust,
The right thing to extinguish lust!

VII

It's wiser being good than bad;
    It's safer being meek than fierce:
It's fitter being sane than mad.
    My own hope is, a sun will pierce
The thickest cloud earth ever stretched;
    That, after Last, returns the First,
Though a wide compass round be fetched;
    That what began best, can't end worst,
Nor what God blessed once, prove accurst.

EPILOGUE

FIRST SPEAKER, *as David*

I

On the first of the Feast of Feasts,
The Dedication Day,
When the Levites joined the Priests
At the Altar in robed array,
Gave signal to sound and say,—

II

When the thousands, rear and van,
Swarming with one accord
Became as a single man
(Look, gesture, thought and word)
In praising and thanking the Lord,—

III

When the singers lift up their voice,
And the trumpets made endeavour,
Sounding, "In God rejoice!"
Saying, "In Him rejoice
Whose mercy endureth for ever!"—

IV

Then the Temple filled with a cloud,
Even the House of the Lord;
Porch bent and pillar bowed:
For the presence of the Lord,

EPILOGUE MS:First Speaker. *P1864a:*§italic type§ *1864a(r):First Speaker.* §small caps called for; period altered to comma§ as David. §italics called for on last two words§ 7| MS:accord, *1888:*accord 8| MS:man, *1888:*man 9| MS:—Look <> word— *P1864a:*(Look <> word)

In the glory of His cloud,
Had filled the House of the Lord.

SECOND SPEAKER, *as Renan*

Gone now! All gone across the dark so far,
Sharpening fast, shuddering ever, shutting still,
Dwindling into the distance, dies that star
Which came, stood, opened once! We gazed our fill
With upturned faces on as real a Face
That, stooping from grave music and mild fire,
Took in our homage, made a visible place
Through many a depth of glory, gyre on gyre,
For the dim human tribute. Was this true?
Could man indeed avail, mere praise of his,
To help by rapture God's own rapture too,
Thrill with a heart's red tinge that pure pale bliss?
Why did it end? Who failed to beat the breast,
And shriek, and throw the arms protesting wide,
When a first shadow showed the star addressed
Itself to motion, and on either side
The rims contracted as the rays retired;
The music, like a fountain's sickening pulse,
Subsided on itself; awhile transpired
Some vestige of a Face no pangs convulse,
No prayers retard; then even this was gone,
Lost in the night at last. We, lone and left
Silent through centuries, ever and anon
Venture to probe again the vault bereft
Of all now save the lesser lights, a mist
Of multitudinous points, yet suns, men say—
And this leaps ruby, this lurks amethyst,
But where may hide what came and loved our clay?

21–22| MS:Second Speaker. *P1864a:*§italic type§ *1864a(r):Second Speaker.* §small caps called for; period altered to comma§ as Renan. §italics called for on last two words§
27| MS:a face §altered to§ a Face 49| *1870:*clay *1875:*clay?

How shall the sage detect in yon expanse
    The star which chose to stoop and stay for us?
Unroll the records! Hailed ye such advance
    Indeed, and did your hope evanish thus?
Watchers of twilight, is the worst averred?
    We shall not look up, know ourselves are seen,
Speak, and be sure that we again are heard,
    Acting or suffering, have the disk's serene
Reflect our life, absorb an earthly flame,
    Nor doubt that, were mankind inert and numb,
Its core had never crimsoned all the same,
    Nor, missing ours, its music fallen dumb?
Oh, dread succession to a dizzy post,
    Sad sway of sceptre whose mere touch appals,
Ghastly dethronement, cursed by those the most
    On whose repugnant brow the crown next falls!

THIRD SPEAKER

I

Witless alike of will and way divine,
How heaven's high with earth's low should intertwine!
Friends, I have seen through your eyes: now use mine!

II

Take the least man of all mankind, as I;
Look at his head and heart, find how and why
He differs from his fellows utterly:

III

Then, like me, watch when nature by degrees
Grows alive round him, as in Arctic seas
(They said of old) the instinctive water flees

50–53| MS:§first pair of lines§ Unroll <> / <> thus? §marked for transposition with second pair of lines§ How <> / <> us? 61| MS:dumb. *P1864a:*dumb? 65–66| MS:Third Speaker. *P1864a:*§italic type§ *1864a(r):*§small caps called for§ 67| MS:How Heaven's *1870:*heaven's 68| MS:mine. *1868:*mine!

IV

Toward some elected point of central rock,
As though, for its sake only, roamed the flock
Of waves about the waste: awhile they mock

V

With radiance caught for the occasion,—hues
Of blackest hell now, now such reds and blues
As only heaven could fitly interfuse,—

VI

The mimic monarch of the whirlpool, king
O' the current for a minute: then they wring
Up by the roots and oversweep the thing,

VII

And hasten off, to play again elsewhere
The same part, choose another peak as bare,
They find and flatter, feast and finish there.

VIII

When you see what I tell you,—nature dance
About each man of us, retire, advance,
As though the pageant's end were to enhance

IX

His worth, and—once the life, his product, gained—
Roll away elsewhere, keep the strife sustained,
And show thus real, a thing the North but feigned—

X

When you acknowledge that one world could do
All the diverse work, old yet ever new,
Divide us, each from other, me from you,—

79| MS:blackest §over illegible erasure§ 93| MS:real a <> feigned,— *P1864a:* real, a *1870:* feigned—

XI

Why, where's the need of Temple, when the walls
O' the world are that? What use of swells and falls
From Levites' choir, Priests' cries, and trumpet-calls?

XII

That one Face, far from vanish, rather grows,
Or decomposes but to recompose,
Become my universe that feels and knows.

98| MS:From the §crossed out§ Levites' 99| MS:And one <> grows *P1864a:* That one <> grows, 100| MS:recompose *P1864a:* recompose, 101| MS:And be my <> knows! *P1864a:* Become my *1888:* knows. *P1864a(Yale):* §dated§ *London,* / April 12, 1864. *P1864a(Berg):* §no date; see Editorial Notes, 428-29 below§

§This page reproduces the preface that B provided for *A Selection from the Works of Robert Browning,* published by Edward Moxon in 1865.§

It is the wish of Messrs. Chapman & Hall, who now publish my poems, that a little gathering from the lightest of these should be tied together after the pretty device of my old publishers, Messrs. Moxon. Not a single piece here belongs to the Selection already issued by the former gentlemen, which was, perhaps, a fair sample of the ground's ordinary growth; this, such as it may prove, contentedly looks pale beside the wonderful flower-show of my illustrious predecessor—dare I say? my old friend: who will take it, all except the love in the gift, at a mere nosegay's worth.

R. B.

London,
March 21, 1865

§MS and proof at Texas; see Editorial Notes§ MS:Moxon: nor does a P:§altered to§ Moxon. Not a MS:belong P:§altered to§ belongs MS:gentlemen. That was a P:§altered to§ gentlemen, which was, perhaps, a MS:of my ordinary growth P:§altered to§ of the ground's ordinary growth §last word cancelled and restored§ MS:may be, P:§altered to§ may prove, MS:gift, as a nosegay's P:§altered to§ gift, at a mere nosegay's

§This page reproduces the preface that B provided for *A Selection from the Poetry of Elizabeth Barrett Browning,* published by Chapman and Hall in 1866.§

It has been attempted to retain and to dispose the characteristics of the general poetry, whence this is an abstract, according to an order which should allow them the prominency and effect they seem to possess when considered in the larger, not exclusively the lesser works of the poet. A musician might say, such and such chords are repeated, others made subordinate by distribution, so that a single movement may imitate the progress of the whole symphony. But there are various ways of modulating up to and connecting any given harmonies; and it will be neither a surprise nor a pain to find that better could have been done, as to both selection and sequence, than, in the present case, all care and the profoundest veneration were able to do.

R. B.

London, November, 1865

§Proof at Texas; see Editorial Notes§ P:*R. B.* §period inserted after *B*§

§This and the following pages reproduce the title page, B's dedication and notes, and the table of contents of his 1868 collected edition. The 1870 edition replicated the preliminary pages of 1868 except for the dates on the title pages. These six-volume editions did not have detailed tables of contents in each volume; what is given below derives from the general index at the end of the sixth volume.§

THE POETICAL WORKS
OF
ROBERT BROWNING,
M.A.,
HONORARY FELLOW OF BALLIOL COLLEGE, OXFORD

VOL. I

PAULINE—PARACELSUS—STRAFFORD

LONDON:
SMITH, ELDER, & CO., 15 WATERLOO PLACE
1868

§Dedication as 1863 and 1865, above. The following prefatory note appears in Volume I only.§

The poems that follow are printed in the order of their publication. The first piece in the series, I acknowledge and retain with extreme repugnance, indeed purely of necessity; for not long ago I inspected one, and am certified of the existence of other transcripts, intended sooner or later to be published abroad: by forestalling these, I can at least correct some misprints (no syllable is changed) and introduce a boyish work by an exculpatory word. The thing was my earliest attempt at "poetry always dramatic in principle, and so many utterances of so many imaginary persons, not mine," which I have since written according to a scheme less extravagant and scale less impracticable than were ventured upon in this crude preliminary sketch—a sketch that, on reviewal, appears not altogether wide of some hint of the characteristic features of that particular *dramatis persona* it would fain have reproduced: good draughtsmanship, however, and right handling were far beyond the artist at that time.

R. B.

London, December 25th, 1867.

§The following note appears in Volume III, preceding *Dramatic Lyrics.*§

In a late edition were collected and redistributed the pieces first published in 1842, 1845 and 1855, respectively, under the titles of "Dramatic Lyrics," "Dramatic Romances," and "Men and Women." It is not worthwhile to disturb this arrangement.

Part of the Poems were inscribed to my dear friend John Kenyon: I hope the whole may obtain the honour of an association with his memory.

R. B.

CONTENTS

VOLUME I

PAULINE
PARACELSUS
STRAFFORD

VOLUME II

SORDELLO
PIPPA PASSES

VOLUME III

KING VICTOR AND KING CHARLES

DRAMATIC LYICS:

CAVALIER TUNES
I. MARCHING ALONG
II. GIVE A ROUSE
III. BOOT AND SADDLE
THE LOST LEADER
"HOW THEY BROUGHT THE GOOD NEWS FROM GHENT TO AIX"
THROUGH THE METIDJA TO ABD-EL-KADR
NATIONALITY IN DRINKS
GARDEN FANCIES
I. THE FLOWER'S NAME
II. SIBRANDUS SCHAFNABURGENSIS
SOLILOQUY OF THE SPANISH CLOISTER
THE LABORATORY
THE CONFESSIONAL
CRISTINA
THE LOST MISTRESS
EARTH'S IMMORTALITIES
MEETING AT NIGHT
PARTING AT MORNING
SONG
A WOMAN'S LAST WORD
EVELYN HOPE
LOVE AMONG THE RUINS
A LOVERS' QUARREL
UP AT A VILLA—DOWN IN THE CITY
A TOCCATA OF GALUPPI'S
OLD PICTURES IN FLORENCE
"DE GUSTIBUS—"

HOME-THOUGHTS, FROM ABROAD
HOME-THOUGHTS, FROM THE SEA
SAUL
MY STAR
BY THE FIRESIDE
ANY WIFE TO ANY HUSBAND
TWO IN THE CAMPAGNA
MISCONCEPTIONS
A SERENADE AT THE VILLA
ONE WAY OF LOVE
ANOTHER WAY OF LOVE
A PRETTY WOMAN
RESPECTABILITY
LOVE IN A LIFE
LIFE IN A LOVE
IN THREE DAYS
IN A YEAR
WOMEN AND ROSES
BEFORE
AFTER
THE GUARDIAN-ANGEL—A PICTURE AT FANO
MEMORABILIA
POPULARITY
MASTER HUGUES OF SAXE-GOTHA

THE RETURN OF DRUSES

VOLUME IV

A BLOT IN THE 'SCUTCHEON

COLOMBE'S BIRTHDAY

DRAMATIC ROMANCES:

INCIDENT OF THE FRENCH CAMP
THE PATRIOT—AN OLD STORY
MY LAST DUCHESS—FERRARA
COUNT GISMOND—AIX IN PROVENCE
THE BOY AND THE ANGEL
INSTANS TYRANNUS
MESMERISM
THE GLOVE
TIME'S REVENGES
THE ITALIAN IN ENGLAND
THE ENGLISHMAN IN ITALY—PIANO DI SORRENTO
IN A GONDOLA

WARING
THE TWINS
A LIGHT WOMAN
THE LAST RIDE TOGETHER
THE PIED PIPER OF HAMELIN; A CHILD'S STORY
THE FLIGHT OF THE DUCHESS
A GRAMMARIAN'S FUNERAL
THE HERETIC'S TRAGEDY—A MIDDLE AGE INTERLUDE
HOLY-CROSS DAY
PROTUS
THE STATUE AND THE BUST
PORPHYRIA'S LOVER
"CHILDE ROLAND TO THE DARK TOWER CAME"

VOLUME V

A SOUL'S TRAGEDY

LURIA

CHRISTMAS-EVE AND EASTER-DAY

MEN AND WOMEN:

'TRANSCENDENTALISM:' A POEM IN TWELVE BOOKS
HOW IT STRIKES A CONTEMPORARY
ARTEMIS PROLOGIZES
AN EPISTLE CONTAINING THE STRANGE MEDICAL EXPERIENCE OF KARSHISH, THE ARAB PHYSICIAN
JOHANNES AGRICOLA IN MEDITATION
PICTOR IGNOTUS
FRA LIPPO LIPPI
ANDREA DEL SARTO
THE BISHOP ORDERS HIS TOMB AT SAINT PRAXED'S CHURCH
BISHOP BLOUGRAM'S APOLOGY
CLEON
RUDEL TO THE LADY OF TRIPOLI
ONE WORD MORE

VOLUME VI

IN A BALCONY

DRAMATIS PERSONAE:

JAMES LEE'S WIFE
GOLD HAIR: A STORY OF PORNIC

THE WORST OF IT
DÎS ALITER VISUM; OR, LE BYRON DE NOS JOURS
TOO LATE
ABT VOGLER
RABBI BEN EZRA
A DEATH IN THE DESERT
CALIBAN UPON SETEBOS; OR, NATURAL THEOLOGY IN THE ISLAND
CONFESSIONS
MAY AND DEATH
DEAF AND DUMB: A GROUP BY WOOLNER
PROSPICE
EURYDICE TO ORPIHEUS: A PICTURE BY LEIGHTON
YOUTH AND ART
A FACE
A LIKENESS
MR. SLUDGE, "THE MEDIUM"
APPARENT FAILURE
EPILOGUE

DEAF AND DUMB

Text edited by John C. Berkey
Annotations by Allan C. Dooley and Susan E. Dooley

DEAF AND DUMB

A GROUP BY WOOLNER

Only the prism's obstruction shows aright
The secret of a sunbeam, breaks its light
Into the jewelled bow from blankest white,
    So may a glory from defect arise:
Only by Deafness may the vexed Love wreak
Its insuppressive sense on brow and cheek,
Only by Dumbness adequately speak
    As favoured mouth could ever, through the eyes.

DEAF AND DUMB. A GROUP BY WOOLNER §Subsequent placement: *1868:* DP§ MS1862:§see Editorial Notes§ [3]| MS1862:white; *1888:* white, [5]| MS1862:vext *1868:* vexed

Editorial Notes

MEN AND WOMEN, Volume II

Emendations to the Text

The following emendations have been made to the 1889 copy-text:

Before, l. 12: The double quotation marks at the end of the line, required to close the quotation, disappeared in 1888; the error was not corrected in 1889. The 1863-75 reading is restored.
Saul, l. 173: In 1888, the last word of the line was mis-set as *heigh;* B corrected this in DC and BrU to *height,* restoring the P-1875 reading. In 1889, the compositors did not insert the comma B requested; the P-1875 and DC-BrU reading is restored.
Saul, l. 328: From P through 1868, the eighth word in this line was *off.* During the printing of 1868, however, the upper portion of the second *f* broke away, leaving something like a *t.* In the 1870 resetting, the compositors dutifully but erroneously set the word as *oft,* and the error was never corrected. The P-1868 reading is restored.
Cleon, l. 301: The comma at the end of this line was correctly set in 1888, but during printing it began to decay; by the 1889 impression, the comma had disappeared from most copies. The P-1888 reading is inserted.
One Word More, l. 159: The mistake B made when correcting a compositor's error in 1888 is discussed at length in Section V of the Preface to this volume. The P-1875 reading is restored.
Composition, publication, sources] For information about the general background of *Men and Women,* see Volume 5 of the present edition, pp. 356-59.

Text

Since the publication of *Men and Women I* in Volume 5, the textual authority of the 1870 typesetting and the 1875 corrected impression of the *Poetical Works* has been established (see *Preface,* sections II and III above). Our collations now include these texts, and additional variants for *Men and Women I* from these texts will appear in the final volume of this edition. It may be noted that the most common effect of collating these additional texts is to change the date of a variant reading, not its substance; a variant that would have been dated 1888 actually appeared in 1870 or 1875.

We have also included in our variant list the pencilled-in alterations B made in Volumes 5 and 6 of a copy of the 1870 *Poetical Works* (in the 1872 impression). Exactly when, and for what immediate purpose, B made these changes is not known, but their correspondence with readings in the 1875 corrected impression suggests that B used these volumes (now in the Gordon Ray collection in the Pierpont Morgan Library, New York; see *Reconstruction,* E378.1) as work-sheets for the list of changes he asked for in 1875. Because the eleven pencil corrections (coded *C1870* in our variant lists) in the Morgan volumes appear to have been done between 1872 and 1875, they lie very close to the line of textual development, and merit inclusion in our collations.

There are three bodies of textual alterations which we do not include in our collations and variant lists: B's hand corrections in the proofs of the first edition of *Men and Women II;* a list of changes to this same volume, included in a letter from B to D. G. Rossetti; and changes made to certain poems from *Men and Women* when they appeared in a volume of selected poems B helped to prepare in 1865. These we consider to be secondary materials; despite their obvious interest to the scholar, they stand apart from the direct line of textual descent that results in the 1888-89 copy-text. Each deserves some comment here.

The printed readings in the proofs of the 1855 first edition of *Men and Women* (now in the Henry E. Huntington Library in California and labelled *P1855* in our variant lists) represent the earliest state of the texts of most of the poems in the two volumes (*Reconstruction,* E253). An extensively altered set of these proofs, not known to survive, went back to B's printers as a crucial step in the creation of the first edition. But B's hand corrections in Volume II of the Huntington proofs did not go to his printers; they correspond fairly closely to the changes B listed in his letter to Rossetti, and were probably written on the Huntington proofs after the first edition of *Men and Women* had been printed. Indeed, they could have been entered on the Huntington proofs at any time between 1855 and 1863, when most of these changes were made to the text, or even later. There is no evidence that these corrections, though in B's hand, had any direct influence on the development of his printed texts (see also Allan C. Dooley, "Further Notes on the *Men and Women* Proofs." *Studies in Browning and His Circle* 5 (1977): 52-54).

Shortly before the publication of *Men and Women* (and apparently after the sheets had been printed), B included in a letter to D. G.

Rossetti a list of sixteen changes he wished to have made in Volume II (see Hood, 42). Of these alterations, fourteen were made in 1863 (the next time the poems were printed), almost exactly as listed in the letter. Again, this list is of interest, but it had no direct impact on the printing of B's text; the changes he made in the 1863 *Poetical Works* include this list, for the most part, but there are hundreds more changes that B made through some other vehicle, probably a marked up copy of the first edition sent to his printers.

As for the *Selections* of 1865, a set of proofs for this volume, with corrections in B's hand, survives in fragments (see *Reconstruction*, E432). The importance of this volume in the rise of B's reputation in the 1860s cannot be overstated, but its textual importance is not established by its success with Victorian readers. If it were known that a copy of the *Selections* was used to prepare a later collected edition, it would be imperative to include it in our collations; but there is no evidence that the *Selections* volume stands within the line of textual descent in this way. The variant readings, both printed and hand written, in the proofs and printed edition of the *Selections* are secondary materials. The final volume of this edition will contain readings from a wide range of secondary materials, including those discussed here.

ANDREA DEL SARTO

Composition] DeVane's assertions about the origins and composition of "Andrea del Sarto" (*Hbk.*, 245) have been convincingly challenged by Julia Markus (*SBHC* 2 [1973], 52-55), but it is nonetheless likely that the poem dates from early 1853, when B was "digging at Vasari" (see Betty Miller, *Robert Browning, A Portrait* [New York, 1953], 187) and working on poems he described as having "more music and painting in them" (see Irvine and Honan, 335).
Sources] B relied on Vasari for facts and some judgments about Andrea Del Sarto, using the lives of Andrea and of Raphael (Vasari, 2.303-25 and 221-49) from both the first edition of *Le Vite de' Più Eccelenti Architetti, Pittori, et Scultori Italiani* (1550) and the annotated Le Monnier edition (Florence, 1846-57) based on the 1568 revision by Vasari. His view of his subject was strongly influenced by Anna Brownell Jameson's treatment of Andrea del Sarto in her *Memoirs of Early Italian Painters* (1845); for details of B's use of these materials, see Allan C. Dooley, "Andrea, Raphael, and the Moment of 'Andrea del Sarto,'" *MP* 81 (1983), 38-46. A play about Andrea by Alfred de Musset has been suggested as an auxiliary source. [PT]

To these written sources must be added B's own extensive exposure to and interest in Italian art. During his first two journeys to Italy in 1838 and 1844, his appetite for painting and sculpture was so keen that he must have inevitably seen some works by Andrea del Sarto. Back in London, he could have studied several Andreas at the National Gallery and in the private collections to which Jameson could provide access. Once arrived in Florence, B surely saw most of the works of Andrea that were publicly displayed at the time: fourteen in the Chiostro dello Scalzo, sixteen in the Pitti Palace, five in the Santissima Annunziata, and eight original paintings, along with numerous copies and drawings, in the Uffizi Gallery. The particular painting which is associated with the poem, a portrait of an artist and his wife, is in the Pitti Palace. That the persons there pictured are Andrea and Lucrezia has been doubted since at least 1835 (see S. J. Freedberg, *Andrea del Sarto* [Cambridge, MA, 1963], 223), but B believed they were. Julia Markus argues persuasively that the marital situation of the painter William Page (1811-85) informs "Andrea del Sarto" and may have been a stimulus for it composition. Page was a member of the American expatriate colony in Rome in the 1850s, where the Bs knew him well; Page painted B's portrait in 1854. See Markus, 197-206.

Title] Andrea (1486-1531) was born in Florence into the Lanfranchi family and was later called "del Sarto" because his father Agnolo di Francesco was a tailor. As one of the most talented members of the generation after Leonardo and Michelangelo, Andrea felt the rivalry with Raphael that B implies; Andrea was highly respected in Florence and beyond, but Raphael's fame and talent were so great that he easily won many of the most important commissions in Rome. A passing reference to this rivalry is made in Vasari (3.77), whose account of Andrea's life and career is now thought to be somewhat inaccurate and biased (for a brief, more authoritative life see J. Shearman, *Andrea del Sarto* [Oxford, 1965], 1.1-120).

Subtitle] The ironies that hover around this subtitle come from Browning rather than Vasari, who describes Andrea's paintings, not their creator, as faultless (2.155). The phrase "Il pittore senza errore" often has been applied to Andrea in guidebooks and by art historians in recognition of his technical skill.

2] *Lucrezia* Andrea married Lucrezia del Fede (?1490-1570) in 1517; she had modelled for him some years earlier. A modern scholar notes: "Vasari's squalid account of the private life of Andrea del Sarto in the first edition of the *Vita* has been enormously influential; factually, a good deal of it is untrue" (J. Shearman, *op. cit.* above, 1.9). But Browning accepted Vasari's characterization of Lucrezia as greedy, cold-hearted, and manipulative, and added to it the charge of infidelity which seems to have originated with Jameson. William Page's wife Sarah was notoriously unfaithful, as B knew well (see *Sources* above).

6-7] *Treat his . . . own price* Vasari asserts several times that Andrea was willing to paint whatever a buyer wanted, and that he "always put a low value on his things" (2.322-23).

15] *Fiesole* Ancient and picturesque hilltop village about 4 mi. NE of the center of Florence. The Bs passed near or through Fiesole many times on their travels; EBB described a family visit there in May 1853 (see *EBB: Letters to Her Sister, 1846-1859,* ed. Leonard Huxley [London, 1929], 184).

23-25] *you must serve . . . a model* Vasari claims that Andrea "never painted a woman without using her [i.e., Lucrezia] as his model" (2.312).

34-35] *our harmony . . . silvers everything* Mid-nineteenth century painters, including B's friend William Page, were very interested in discovering what they called scientific laws of color and form, specifically the principles of color harmony. Page believed that a subdued gray linked diverse colors, and this idea may be hinted at here (see Markus, 197-99). Mrs. Jameson espoused a notion of a harmony within the artistic temperament, balancing technical prowess with intellectual and moral strength (*Memoirs of Early Italian Painters* [Boston, 1896], 177-78). But it is also true that Andrea achieved a silvered effect in some of his works, and that the lines are more reflective than descriptive.

57-59] *that cartoon . . . Madonna* Andrea was justly famed for his drawings, both as studies for paintings and as finished works. Hundreds of these survive; B does not appear to have a specific one in mind.

65] *Legate's talk* A Legate is an emissary representing the Pope in secular matters, and thus a person of importance or influence.

66] *they . . . France* In 1518, Andrea was recruited by King Francis I to the French royal court at Fontainebleau, where he found immediate success. Vasari reports that Andrea was a favorite with not only the King but also the entire court, earning large commissions immediately upon his arrival (2.312-13).

76] *Someone* Michelangelo; see ll. 184-93 and nn.

93] *Morello's outline* Mt. Morello is a peak in the Appenines, about 7 mi. N of Florence; as viewed from the city, it rises above the nearer foothills and lower peaks.

105] *The Urbinate . . . ago* The Renaissance painter Raphael (Raffaello Sanzio, 1483-1520), was born in Urbino, N of Rome. He had executed important paintings by the age of nineteen; at twenty-five he was so esteemed that Pope Julius II commissioned him to paint extensive frescoes in the Vatican. The reference to Raphael's death places the action of "Andrea del Sarto" in 1525; for discussion of this dating and Raphael's relationship with Andrea, see the article by Dooley cited in *Sources* above.

106] *'Tis copied . . . Vasari* Giorgio Vasari (1511-74), now ranked as the first important historian of Italian Renaissance art, was in his time renowned as a painter. In his youth he studied with Michelangelo, who sent him to Andrea in 1525 for further training. Vasari became a prolific artist and a skilled copyist of masterpieces, including works by Raphael and by Andrea himself (Vasari, 4.54-55, 133, 259).

108] *kings and popes* Raphael's patrons were the popes Julius II and his successor Leo X. Princes and kings competed for opportunities to obtain his works, and as a sign of special regard, Leo X commissioned in 1518 two major paintings by Raphael to be presented to Francis I of France.

119] *Rafael* An alternate spelling; see l. 105n. above.

130] *Agnolo* A short form of the name of Michelangelo Buonarroti (1475-1564), painter, sculptor, architect, and poet, who, along with Leonardo da Vinci (see l. 263n., below) and Raphael might fairly be ranked as the finest artists of the Florentine Renaissance.

136] *What wife . . . Agnolo* Raphael, described by Vasari as a man who enjoyed his pleasures and the company of women, never married. According to an early biographical tradition, he did become fascinated with a woman named Margherita, nicknamed *La Fornarina,* and mentioned in his will. Michelangelo never married a woman, but he characterized himself as wedded to his art, his works being his children (Vasari, 2.241, 247; 4.177). [PT]

143] *I am something underrated* All of the published sources B may have used place Andrea in the second rank of Florentine painters. Jameson, echoing Vasari's harsh comments, blames Andrea's marriage to Lucrezia for a decline in his talent. See *Sources* above.

145-46] *I dared not . . . the Paris lords* According to Vasari (and his followers), Andrea was sent back to Florence in 1519 with a substantial sum of King Francis's money, to be used for purchasing works of art for the royal collections; Andrea is accused by Vasari of spending this money on "building and pleasures." This accusation lacks corroborating evidence, but B accepted it, as he did the unattested tale that Andrea once hid from emissaries of the French king. See Shearman, op. cit, and Dooley, both cited above.

149-50] *Francis . . . Fontainebleau* Andrea left for the French court in May or June of 1518, and was back in Florence by October, 1519.

151] *leave the ground* The phrase appears in the 1550 edition of

Vasari and is quoted in a footnote in the Le Monnier edition B used. The passage specifically blames Lucrezia and her supposedly avaricious family for Andrea's sense of futility: "He saw that he could never lift himself from the earth; though perpetually toiling, he did so to no purpose" (Vasari, trans. Mrs. Jonathan Foster [London, 1887], 4.204n.).

161] *my hand kept plying* Though Vasari says that Andrea did numerous paintings for the French nobility at Fontainebleau, only one work certainly painted by Andrea there is known to survive—the "Caritas" now in the Louvre in Paris.

166] *had you . . . restless* Andrea had been married to Lucrezia del Fede for only a few months before going to France. Though there is no direct evidence that Lucrezia summoned Andrea back to Florence, Vasari and Jameson take the view that had it not been for her demands, Andrea would have risen to even greater successes at Fontainebleau.

177] *The Roman's* The reference is to Raphael, who lived in Rome during his most productive years, from 1508 to his death in 1520.

179] *other's . . . wife* See ll. 23-25n. above.

184-93] *Said one day . . . brow of yours* Michelangelo's remark to Raphael is first reported in Francesco Bocchi's *Le Bellezze della Città di Fiorenza* (1591), but B could have found the story in a footnote to Vasari's life of Andrea in the Le Monnier edition. The note may be translated as follows: "Bocchi reported in his book *Bellezze di Firenze* that Michelangelo, while discussing with Raphael the merit of eminent artists, said to him: 'In Florence there is a little guy (meaning Andrea) who, if he were employed in great projects as you are, would bring a sweat to your brow.' "

186-87] *flaming out . . . to see* Between 1508, when he arrived in Rome, and 1511, Raphael executed the vast series of seventeen frescoes on the walls of the Stanze della Segnatura in the Vatican Palace.

209] *Morello* See l. 93n. above.

210] *cue-owls* The "pew" call of the diminutive scops owl, *Otus scops,* is rendered as "chiu" (pronounced "cue") in Italian. [PT]

212-13] *little house / We built* An elaboration of Vasari's charge that Andrea appropriated the French King's money to himself; see ll. 145-46n. above.

214] *Francis may forgive me* This hope was nursed by Andrea, according to Vasari (2.315-16).

241] *thirteen scudi* The *scudo* was a silver Italian coin of the 16th to the 19th century; the name was also applied to an earlier gold coin. The sum of money here was modest, but more than a trifle.

250-51] *My father . . . want* In fact Andrea's parents were financial-

ly secure. In the first edition of *Le Vite,* Vasari says that Andrea neglected to support his parents in their old age. In the second edition this story, apparently unfounded, is toned down (2.309).
256] *my two hundred pictures* The number represents not an exact count but simply a large output. Modern catalogues of Andrea's works list 100 signed paintings and nearly 200 drawings; in B's time the number of attributed paintings was larger still.
261-62] *Four great walls . . . angel's reed* See Rev. 21:9-21 for the description of the New Jerusalem, the eternal abode of those spared in the Last Judgment.
263] *Leonard, Rafael, Agnolo* For Raphael and Agnolo see 105n. and 130n. above. Leonardo da Vinci (1452-1519), universal genius of the Italian Renaissance, preceded Andrea as a court painter at Fontainebleau. These three artists, in this order, are presented by Vasari as an ascending hierarchy, with Michelangelo at the pinnacle of Italian art.

BEFORE

Composition] Exactly when B composed this and the companion poem "After" is unknown, but they present two views of a subject about which B and EBB had strong feelings. Duelling over points of honor in Britain of the 1840s was so rife that a society for its suppression was formed in 1842. In April 1846, press reports of a duel in Paris (and the subsequent trial) prompted a misunderstanding and dispute between B and EBB, then a little more than a year into their courtship. B defended duelling as sometimes necessary, while EBB abhorred it. Their correspondence between 4 and 8 April 1846 (Kintner, 587-608; *Correspondence,* 12.211-28), reveals both disagreement and B's willingness to reassess his position. The pair of poems suggests that B recognized more than one viewpoint, despite the vehemence of his initial remarks. See Markus, 41-45.
8] *entoilment* The state of being entrapped; the *OED* cites only this example of the word.
10] *caps* Salutes by tipping or removing a hat; a B coinage in this sense.
18] *grape-trees* An alternate term for grape vines, presumably closely pruned and trained upward over supports (*OED,* s.v. "grape," sense 9).
21] *leopard-dog-thing* This and the previous reference to the "sly mute thing" in the garden suggest B may be remembering that the devil Mephistopheles first appears to Goethe's Faust as a dog (*Faust, Part I,* 1147-1250). Mysterious, threatening, leopard-like beasts also appear in Dan. 7:6 and Rev. 13:2.

31] *chicane* That is, chicanery—subterfuge or legal trickery.
32] *provisos . . . saving-clauses* Legalistic conditions to protect a party to a contract; the "fine print."

AFTER

3] *rights of a man* In his letters to EBB during their dispute about duelling, B repeatedly sought to assert some rational basis for the persistence of the practice, and this phrase glances ironically at the philosophic notion of natural rights. EBB sardonically invokes a rational principle for executions in her letter of 7 April 1846 (Kintner, 595-96; *Correspondence,* 12.216-18).

IN THREE DAYS

23] *As early . . . gold* Medieval painters and manuscript illuminators often used gold leaf as backgrounds in their works. The artists made the color of the gold darker but richer by using a tinted adhesive behind the leaf and by burnishing the surface with a hard implement. B may be echoing the painter William Page's belief that some Renaissance paintings were dark-toned by design, not as a result of time, dirt, and varnish (see "Andrea del Sarto," *Sources,* above, and Markus, 197-98).

OLD PICTURES IN FLORENCE

Date] As another product of B's engagement with Florentine art and Vasari's accounts of Italian painting, the poem surely dates from the early 1850s. B was an enthusiastic if impecunious collector of old paintings when they could be bought cheap enough; some of his finds are mentioned in EBB's letter to Anna Jameson, 4 May 1850 (*Letters of EBB,* 1.448). The reference to *Casa Guidi Windows* in l. 260 suggests a date around 1851, when EBB's poem was published; but parts of *Casa Guidi Windows* were composed as early as 1847, and the title had been adopted by 1849. The political content of "Old Pictures," as well as numerous shared topographical and literary references, tie it closely to EBB's poem (see the edition of *Casa Guidi Windows* by Julia Markus [Barre, MA, 1977], *passim*). DeVane feels that "Old Pictures" is one of the poems about music and painting that B was writing in early 1853 (*Hbk.,* 251; Irvine and Honan, 335).
Sources] For historical facts about the painters mentioned in *Old Pictures,* B relied on Vasari, in particular on the annotated Le Monnier edition of *Le Vite* (Florence, 1846-57; see *Reconstruction,* A.2379), which contained engraved portraits of many of the artists covered. These por-

traits, created by Vasari himself for the 1568 second edition of *Le Vite,* have been reproduced in many editions of Vasari from the 18th century to the present. Some of B's views on ancient and early Renaissance art are clearly influenced by Anna Jameson's writings on art, which the Bs knew and owned (see David DeLaura, "The Context of Browning's Painter Poems: Aesthetics, Polemics, and Historics," *PMLA* [1980], 367-88; "Some Notes on Browning's Pictures and Painters," *SBHC,* 8:2 [1980], 7-16; *Reconstruction,* A1301-1303). But the judgments and characterizations of the works of the artists are B's own, stemming from his ceaseless exploration of Florence and its monuments. His adventures and discoveries are described in detail in Korg, 98-106, who notes that Rossetti held B's knowledge of early Italian art to exceed even Ruskin's.

Title] In the proofs of the first edition of *Men and Women,* the poem is entitled "Opus Magistri Jocti." Korg (99) takes *Jocti* to be a Latinized form of "Giotto," and the rejected title to be "The Work of Master Giotto"; an alternate translation as "*A* Work of Master Giotto," would connect the title to the work alluded to in l. 24.

3] *aloed arch* The gate may be shaded by a variety of the Aloe family of succulents or by a lign-aloes tree (*Aquilaria agallocha*).

12] *magic crystal ball* The mid-Victorian popular mania for spiritualism led to a revival of the belief that some persons can see distant scenes and foretell events by staring into a polished sphere of rock-crystal. In 1852, the Bs witnessed a demonstration of this power by Lord Stanhope, who claimed to show spirits in a crystal ball (see *Letters of EBB,* 2.79). For a time the Bs were very interested in spiritualist phenomena; see the Editorial Notes to *Men and Women I,* "A Lovers' Quarrel" and "Mesmerism" (5.359, 5.360-61, 5.373-74) and particularly to "Mr. Sludge, 'the Medium,'" in the present volume.

15] *bell-tower Giotto raised* Giotto di Bondone (c.1266-1337), the Florentine artist sometimes called the father of Renaissance art, designed the bell-tower (or campanile) for the cathedral of Florence. Construction began in 1334, but the campanile remained unfinished at Giotto's death. His design was never completed; the original plans called for a steeple on the tower, but in 1359 a nearly flat roof was put on.

24] *a Giotto . . . rest* The line refers to specific instances of official indifference to Giotto's works in B's time. In the 1840s, the Church of Santa Croce rented out its refectory as a carpet factory; the looms obscured from view several important frescoes by Giotto and Taddeo Gaddi (see l. 205-7n. below). Frescoes that Vasari attributed to Giotto, containing scenes from Dante's *Divine Comedy,* had been whitewashed over when the chapel of the Bargello Palace was subdivided for use as a prison. B's friend Seymour Kirkup, who shared his enthusiasm for early Renaissance art, led a campaign to rescue the Dante frescoes; the Bargello was completely restored in 1857 (see Korg, 105; also alluded to in *Casa Guidi Windows,* 1.628-33).

27] *sharp-curled . . . shed* The olive tree (*Olea europa*) is an evergreen; its lance-shaped leaves are replaced singly rather than in a general fall.

37-39] *chapter-room . . . crypt* All these locations in a monastery provided spaces which were often decorated with frescoes.

44] *One* Either the ghost of the long-dead artist or the sympathetic speaker of the poem.

47] *lion . . . ass's kick* This image of an absurd attack on the noble by the ignoble derives from a fable attributed to Aesop, "The Old Lion." An aged lion is attacked in his weakness by a boar, a bull, and finally an ass, which kicks him in the head. The lion laments his disgrace and dies (*The Fables of Aesop and Others,* ed. E. Rhys [London, 1958], 85).

51] *the Michaels and Rafaels* I. e., Michelangelo and Raphael; see "Andrea del Sarto," ll. 105n., 130n. above.

64] *Da Vincis . . . Dellos* For Da Vinci, see "Andrea del Sarto," l. 263n. above. Dello di Niccolo Delli (1404-c.1470), a forgotten Florentine painter who, according to Vasari, "was not a very good draughtsman, but was among the earliest to discover the importance of a just representation of the muscles of naked bodies" (1.221).

69-72] *Stefano . . . Vasari* One of Giotto's finest students, Stefano (1301-50) was praised by Vasari as "so excellent that . . . he did surpass all the artists who had studied the arts before him" (1.94). Vasari's 1568 illustration (1.140) shows Stefano as an old bearded man with a very high forehead. The nickname "Nature's Ape" appears in Vasari (1.95), and the Le Monnier edition (2.17) cites the source of the phrase as Cristoforo Landino, in the "Apology" to his *Commentary on Dante* (1481). B's description of Stefano as "the world's despair" reflects a sad situation: a few of his works survived until Vasari's day, but nothing known to be by him has come down to modern times.

76] *sic transit* From the Latin tag *Sic transit gloria mundi,* "So passes away the glory of this world." The phrase appears in Thomas à Kempis, *The Imitation of Christ* (c.1427), 3.6, but may be much older.

81] *deal your dole* Pay what you owe (in this case, respect).

83] *Greek Art . . . goal* From Roman times to the present, many commentators have held that the architecture, sculpture, and painting of Athens in its Classical period (during the fifth and fourth centuries B.C.) represent an unequalled pinnacle in the history of art.

84] *in fructu* Latin for "as [the] fruit," an old financial term meaning "as profit."

91] *Olympus* The mountain home of the ancient Greek gods.
98] *Theseus* Legendary hero and king of Athens in ancient Greece. B had seen a magnificent classical semi-reclining figure in the British Museum, as part of the sculptures from the Parthenon known as the Elgin marbles; this figure was long identified as Theseus, though scholars today believe it may represent the god Dionysus.
99-100] *Son of Priam . . . knees' use* Priam, the legendary king of Troy, had more than one son, and which one B means here is not completely clear. Because of a desire to make the allusions in this passage refer consistently to sculptures, early annotators chose Paris (also called Alexander); a figure of Paris as a kneeling archer had been excavated at Aegina in Greece in 1811, though there is no sign that B knew this work. PT makes the persuasive suggestion that B alludes to Hector, Priam's eldest son and the greatest Trojan warrior, whom Apollo gives strong and agile knees when Hector is running away from Achilles (Homer, *Iliad,* 22.204).
101] *slay . . . Apollo* The Greek god Apollo, son of Zeus and Leto, killed the huge snake called Python at Delphi, and promptly established his own cult and oracle there. In 1880, B wrote that the line refers specifically to the Apollo Belvedere in the Vatican Museum; this Roman copy of a Greek statue shows the god just after releasing the arrow that slew the serpent (letter printed in P-C, 4.372). Both myth and statue are described by Byron in an apposite passage in *Childe Harold's Pilgrimage* (4.156, ll. 1441-49), a poem that is alluded to several times in EBB's *Casa Guidi Windows.*
102] *Niobe* In Greek myth, Niobe's fourteen daughters and sons were killed by Apollo and Artemis after their mother Leto was offended by Niobe's boasting about her children. After weeping herself to death, Niobe was transformed into a stone (Homer, *Iliad,* 24.605-17). B had seen the Roman sculptures of the grieving Niobe in the Sala della Niobe, a large room in the Uffizi Gallery in Florence.
103] *Racers' frieze* I. e., the section of the Parthenon frieze which captures horsemen and charioteers in vigorous movement; it is another component of the Elgin marbles in the British Museum.
104] *dying Alexander* The final illness and death of Alexander the Great (356-323 B.C.), described in minute detail by Arrian and other early biographers, are always treated with great solemnity in the popular romances about him. A sculpted head in the Uffizi was identified as "the dying Alexander" in B's day.
129] *lump be leaven* "Purge out therefore the old leaven, that ye may be a new lump, as ye are unleavened" (1 Cor. 5:7).
133-135] *Giotto . . . "O!"* Vasari reports that Giotto demonstrated

his artistic skill by drawing a perfect circle with one continuous stroke of his pencil (1.72).

136] *Thy . . . finish* See l. 15n. above.

156] *quiddit* Archaic form of *quiddity,* a trifling point; a quibble.

162-68] *when this . . . all* Theories of reincarnation were widely discussed in the mid-nineteenth century. B would have encountered the idea in the works of Shelley, Goethe, and Carlyle; soul migration also figures in Swedenborgianism, which the Bs studied in the 1850s. See also "Evelyn Hope" in *Men and Women I,* 5.174.

175] *There . . . God* Heb. 4:9.

179] *Nicolo the Pisan* Nicola Pisano (c.1220-c.1283), praised highly by Vasari (1.40-46), is still regarded by some experts as the father of modern sculpture. He designed and carved magnificent marble pulpits in the bapistry at Pisa and the Cathedral at Siena. The Bs saw the baptistry when they lived at Pisa in 1846-47, and they toured the cathedral of Siena in 1850 (*Letters of EBB,* 1.324, 1.462).

180] *Cimabue* Vasari gives Giovanni Cimabue, whose real name was Cenni de Peppe (c.1240-1302), pride of place as the first painter discussed in *Le Vite.* He is said to have taught Giotto and to have "achieved hardly less than the resurrection of painting from the dead" (1.26). Most of the works once attributed to Cimabue, including those in the Uffizi, are now assigned to other artists, but a cycle of frescoes in the Upper Church at Assisi (visited by the Bs in November 1853) is thought to display his great abilities. EBB praises Cimabue in *Casa Guidi Windows,* 1.331-73.

182] *Ghiberti and Ghirlandajo* Lorenzo Ghiberti (1378-1455) spent over fifty years making two sets of magnificent bronze doors for the baptistry at Florence. Domenico Bigordi, called Ghirlandaio, (c.1448-1494), continued the early naturalistic style in painting; B owned a Ghirlandaio altarpiece (see *Reconstruction,* H9). B sees these artists as among the last masters of the old style (once the new style) that preceded the work of Raphael and Michelangelo.

187] *Blocked . . . whitewashed o'er* See l. 24n. above.

190] *Works . . . clime* It has been suggested that B here echoes a passage in one of Jameson's works (DeLaura, *SBHC,* cited under *Sources* above). But B's sardonic point would seem to be that only because they are painted directly on the plaster walls can the frescoes escape the English mania for collecting Italian art.

192] *quick-lime* The caustic solution of calcium oxide and magnesia used as a whitewash.

201] *Bigordi* See l. 182n. above.

202] *Sandro . . . bellicose* Alessandro di Mariano Filipepi (1445-

1510), called Sandro Botticelli, whose genius was not widely recognized in his own day. B would have seen some of Botticelli's most famous paintings, including "The Allegory of Spring," "The Birth of Venus," and "The Adoration of the Magi" in the Uffizi Gallery. Why B characterized Botticelli as "chivalric" is not obvious, but Vasari portrays him as a practical joker who could be "bellicose" (2.88). [PT]

203] *the wronged Lippino* Filippino Lippi (c.1457-1504) son of Fra Filippo Lippi and his mistress Lucrezia Buti (see "Fra Lippo Lippi" in *Men and Women I,* 5.183 and nn.). Lippino had a great reputation as a painter in his time, and executed frescoes in the church of Santa Maria Novella in Florence. Mrs. Orr (210n.) says that B called Lippino "wronged" because "others were credited with some of his best work."

204] *Frà Angelico* Guido di Pietro (c.1400-1455) was called Fra Angelico. His reputation was very high in the mid-nineteenth century; B praises his naturalism to EBB in September 1845 (Kintner, 190; *Correspondence,* 11.70). B would have seen Fra Angelico's altarpieces and frescoes in the Convent of San Marco in Florence.

205-7] *Taddeo Gaddi . . . sad eye* Taddeo Gaddi (c.1300-c.1366) was a follower of Giotto in style. *Intonaco* is the final layer of plaster on which fresco painting is done. B owned a painting of St. Jerome which he attributed to Taddeo Gaddi, though later scholars have assigned it successively to Masolino and then Toscani (see DeLaura, *SBHC,* cited in *Sources* above).

208] *Lorenzo Monaco* Piero di Giovanni (c.1370-1425), a follower of Giotto and Taddeo Gaddi was called Lorenzo Monaco. Scenes from saints' lives were the subjects of many of his paintings which B would have seen in Florence.

209-12] *the ghost . . . draughtsman* Antonio Pollaiuolo (c.1432-1498) of Florence was "twice a craftsman" because he began as a goldsmith, learning painting from his brother Piero (c.1441-1496) later in life (Vasari, 2.79-81). The 1568 Vasari illustration of Pollaiuolo shows the painter in a hat like a fez, and the red fez was frequently worn by Florentines (see Vasari, 2.87). The "muscular Christ" refers to a painting the Bs had in Casa Guidi; this work, now in Harewood House, at Harewood near Leeds in England, was probably not by Pollaiuolo, despite B's hopes (see DeLaura, *SBHC,* cited in *Sources* above). Photographs of this painting and the St. Jerome mentioned in l. 207 are reproduced in *Reconstruction,* plate 16.

213-15] *No Virgin . . . Baldovinetti* Baldovinetti (c.1426-1499) worked in Florence as a painter and maker of mosaics. B is following Vasari (1.359-60) in mentioning Baldovinetti's meticulous attention to detail and his failed attempt to create an improved tempera. According

to a note in *Browning Society Papers* (London, 1881-91:2.169), B owned a Madonna by Baldovinetti as well as the Crucifixion by Margarito mentioned in the next stanza.
217-22] *Margheritone of Arezzo . . . donor* Margarito of Arezzo, a thirteenth-century painter, according to Vasari, "died at the age of seventy-seven, regretting, it is said, that he had lived long enough to see the changes of the age and the honours accorded to the new artists [i.e. Giotto and his school]" (1.65). EBB alludes to the same materials in *Casa Guidi Windows,* 1.379-88. Vasari's 1568 portrait of the artist shows an angry looking old man glaring at the viewer. B renders this figure's headcloth as the "swaddling barret" and its plain cloak as "grave-clothes garb." "Poll-clawed parrot" recalls Shakespeare's *2 Henry IV,* 2.4.259. For the Crucifixion, see l. 213-15n. above; the practice of honoring a patron or donor by putting him into the scene of a religious painting was a common one (see "Fra Lippo Lippi," l. 375 and n., in *Men and Women I,* 5.195 & 368).
225] *panels* Before artists of the fifteenth century began using canvas, almost all paintings (except frescoes) were done on thin wooden panels.
230] *calm as Zeno* Zeno of Citium in Cyprus (c.333-262 B.C.) founded the Stoic school of philosophy, which urged the suppression of the emotions.
232] *some . . . Carlino* Carlo Dolci (1616-86), called Carlino, was a prolific Florentine painter of sentimental religious subjects; "clay-cold" describes a certain lifelessness in Carlino's work.
233] *Giotto* see l. 15n.
236-40] *a certain . . . at last* The matter of this painting's disappearance is described by Vasari: "that church [Ognissanti] contained a small panel painted in tempera by Giotto, representing the Death of Our Lady . . . . The work has been much praised by artists, and especially by Michelagnolo Buonarotti . . . . This picture . . . has been carried away" (1.79). In 1886, B wrote that "The 'little tablet' was a famous 'Last Supper,' mentioned by Vasari, and gone astray long ago from the Church of S. Spirito: it turned up, according to report, in some obscure corner, while I was in Florence, and was at once acquired by a stranger. I saw it,—genuine or no, a work of great beauty" (see H. Corson, *An Introduction to the Study of Robert Browning's Poetry* [Boston, 1889], facsimile following [ii]). B's recollection of the painting's subject disagrees with Vasari, and he confuses the San Spirito church with the Ognissanti, as the next lines of the poem suggest he did before. But he seems to be remembering an actual incident of his days in Florence.

241] *San Spirito* This large church has many early Renaissance paintings; San Spirito stands just around the corner from Casa Guidi, where the Bs lived in Florence.
242] *Ognissanti* The Church of All Saints, across the Arno River from Casa Guidi; it contains paintings by Ghirlandaio, Gaddi, Botticelli, and Raphael.
244] *Detur amanti* Latin for "let it be given to the one who loves [it]."
245] *Koh-i-noor* A huge diamond (whose name means "mountain of light" in Persian) now part of the crown jewels of Great Britain. It was presented to Queen Victoria after the annexation of the Punjab region of India to the British Empire in 1849.
246] *Jewel . . . eye* In Byron's *The Giaour* (1813), Leila's eye is described as "bright as the jewel of Giamschid" (l. 479). [PT] Giamschid or Jamshid was a legendary king of Persia who had amongst his treasures an immense ruby. The nineteenth-century kings of Persia took the title *Sophy* in recognition of the surname of the ruling house of the sixteenth through eighteenth centuries.
249-88] *When the hour . . . am I* These stanzas are marked by a romantic nationalism B and EBB shared. Both poets strongly supported the goal of a united Italy free from foreign domination. During the uprisings and revolutions of 1848-49 (and again in the period of the Risorgimento, 1859-61), EBB's letters are filled with intense commentaries on the ebb and flow of political events in Italy and elsewhere.
249] *a certain dotard* Count Joseph Radetzky (1766-1858), commander of the Austrian troops in Italy, 1832-49, and governor of Lombardy and Venetia, 1850-57. Radetzky was in command when the Austrian army defeated the army of the Piedmont at the battle of Novara, 23 March 1849, effectively crushing the nationalist movement for nearly a decade. Radetzky might be termed a "dotard" for being in his eighties when "Old Pictures" was composed, but not because of any lack of intelligence or military skill. See also *Casa Guidi Windows,* 2.352ff.
251] *Mont Saint Gothard* A peak in the Alps which at one time marked part of the border between Italy and Switzerland; the Bs crossed the Alps at St. Gothard in June of 1851.
255] *Radetzky* See l. 249n. above.
256] *Morello* See "Andrea del Sarto," l. 93n. above.
258] *display . . . Dante* A stone in the Piazza del Duomo in Florence marks a place where the great poet Dante Alighieri (1265-1321) is said to have sat and watched the construction of the cathedral. Because of Dante's fervent patriotism, this spot would be a fitting location for

nationalistic demonstrations. EBB had used the image similarly in *Casa Guidi Windows,* 1.601-19.
259] *Witanagemot* From OE *witan,* "wise men" + *gemót,* "a meeting": the national assembly of Britain in Anglo-Saxon times.
260] (*Ex: "Casa Guidi," quod videas ante*) A self-mocking acknowledgment, in scholarly form, of B's indebtedness to EBB's *Casa Guidi Windows.* "Ex:" is learned shorthand for "see the following example," and "*quod videas ante*" is scholarly Latin for "refer back to this previous discussion."
263] *hated house . . . Loraine's* When the ancient duchy of Lorraine in eastern France was dissolved in 1735 by the treaty of Vienna, its duke, Francis III, was given the duchy of Tuscany as compensation for his dispossession. Francis and his descendants in the house of Lorraine thus ruled Florence almost continuously from 1737 to 1859.
264] *days of Orgagna* Andrea di Cione (c.1308-1368), nicknamed Orcagna (meaning "archangel" in Florentine slang), was a famed painter, sculptor, and architect. According to Vasari, who praises him highly, Orcagna was also a poet (1.145). With his phrase B refers to an admirable period in Florentine history when (despite the Black Death in 1348) the city grew in power and wealth, in which artists and craftsmen shared (see Christopher Hibbert, *Florence* [New York, 1993], 35-73). Orcagna is also mentioned in *Casa Guidi Windows,* 1.328.
268] *want of the age* A reference to a dismissive commonplace in discussions of Italy's failure to free itself from foreign control—namely, that something was lacking in the Italian spirit in modern times.
269] *fructuous and sterile eras* Cyclical theories of history gained some important adherents in the nineteenth century, despite the age's devotion to the idea of progress. The concept of historical periodicity put forth by Claude Henri Saint-Simon (1760-1825) was widely discussed; B may first have heard of these ideas (which can be traced back to Giambattista Vico [1668-1744]) through the writings and conversation of Thomas Carlyle.
270-71] *uncouth cub . . . Chimæra's* European folk-tales assert that bear cubs are born as shapeless lumps that are licked into proper form by the mother. The fire-breathing Chimaera, a monster in Greek myth, had the head of a lion, the body of a goat, and the tail of a snake (Homer, *Iliad,* 6.178-83).
273] *curt Tuscan* The dialect of Italian spoken in Tuscany—or, more exactly, the dialect of Florence itself—has been for the last several centuries the standard literary language of Italy. Tuscans view their language as being more elegant, direct, and precise than other dialects.

274] *scarcely an "issimo"* That is, stripped of exaggerated rhetoric using adjectives in the superlative degree, which are marked in Italian by the suffix *issimo.*
275] *half-told . . . Cambuscan* B alludes here to Milton's "Il Penseroso," ll. 109-10, where the poet wishes that the spirit of Melancholy might "call up him that left half-told / The story of Cambuscan bold" (*The Works of John Milton* [New York, 1931-40], 1.43), referring in turn to "The Squire's Tale" in *The Canterbury Tales.* "The Squire's Tale," which breaks off after 672 lines, is an Oriental romance whose hero, Cambyuskan, may be based on Gengis Khan or Kublai Khan.
276] *alt to altissimo* "High" to "highest" (Italian).
277] *beak . . . beccaccia* The Eurasian Woodcock (*Scolopax rusticola*), called the *beccaccia* in Italian, has a long, slender bill.
278] *Campanile . . . Duomo* See l. 15n. above; the bell-tower stands next to the Duomo, or cathedral, of Florence.
279] *in gold . . . braccia* Vasari reports that "the campanile should have received a pointed top or quadrangular pyramid over the existing structure, 50 braccia [about 115 feet] in height" (1.80), but the notion that this spire would be gold is apparently B's own. A parallel use of the campanile as a patriotic symbol can be found in *Casa Guidi Windows,* 1.68.
285] *"God and the People"* The political motto of the republican leader Giuseppi Mazzini (1805-72), whom B may have met through the Carlyles as early as 1844; Mazzini called upon the Bs in 1852 (Irvine and Honan, 137, 299).
286] *new tricolor* The red, white, and green flag was the symbol of a united Italy, the goal of the several nationalist movements of the nineteenth century. B calls it "new" because the original tricolor was created by Napoleon I in 1805, when he formed a united Italy under French hegemony.

IN A BALCONY

Composition and date] According to the half-title in 1868 (6.[i]), *In a Balcony* was written at Bagni di Lucca in 1853. The Bs left Florence (because of the heat) on 15 July 1853 and returned 14 October. B may have written the play very quickly; on 9 September 1853 EBB wrote: "Not a stroke has he drawn since he came here—not a line has he written!" Yet a month later she claims that "Robert especially has done a great deal of work, and will have his volume ready for the spring without fail he says" (*EBB's Letters to Mrs. David Ogilvy, 1849-61,* ed. P.

Heydon and P. Kelley [New York, 1973], 103; Landis and Freeman, 200). In the editions from 1855 to 1865, the play was divided into three parts, with the divisions falling at ll. 339-40 and 605-6. Though the play was not written directly for the stage, as some of B's earlier plays were, it was given at least one performance during his life, on 28 November 1884 under the auspices of the Browning Society.

92] *'Faith* The apostrophe stands for *In,* thus creating the interjection *In faith,* "Truly."

109-12] *The fight . . . flowers and fruit* This catalogue of subjects for paintings and tapestries probably owes something to B's memories of de Lairesse (see "'Childe Roland to the Dark Tower Came,'" *Composition and Sources* n., in *Men and Women I,* 5.375). Some of the more specific references, however, are suggestive of Renaissance paintings B saw in Florence and Rome, such as Raphael's frescoes in the Stanze della Segnatura (see "Andrea del Sarto," ll. 186-87n. above).

130] *Rubens* Peter Paul Rubens (1577-1640), Flemish artist, standing here as a master of naturalistic representation.

192] *telegraphs* In the sense of "a message communicated by symbols or code," the word dates from 1792 (*OED*).

208] *ring . . . feet* Falcons trained to hunt wear leather thongs, called jesses, tied around each leg. To the jess is affixed a swivel ring to which a leash may be attached.

255] *Muse . . . lyre* Erato, the muse of lyric and love poetry, has the lyre as her primary symbolic attribute.

256] *Nymph . . . fawn* As companions to the goddess Diana, nymphs are portrayed in mythology and art as hunters.

Silence . . . rose B may have a particular work of art in mind; the rose is sometimes emblematic of silence, though more often of secrecy.

342] *Mercifullest Mother* An epithet for the Virgin Mary.

412] *baladine's* A female public dancer; this line is the only citation in the *OED*.

503-33] *See, I am old . . . does not—he* Of this passage B wrote to F. J. Furnivall in 1884:

> The great obstacle, in the Queen's mind, to the possibility of her awakening love, in the case of a young and handsome man, is her consciousness of being neither young nor handsome,—and she seeks for an instance where, in default of these qualities, the desired effect may be produced all the same. And this applies equally, or even more forcibly, to the second instance she gives—when driven to an extremity,—that, though all other attractions fail, men will find them in loving—not youth and beauty—but soul—phantasy—even that poorest one of *rank*—which she *curses* in recognition of its being the very poorest.

(See William S. Peterson, ed., *Browning's Trumpeter: The Correspondence of Robert Browning and Frederick J. Furnivall* [Washington, D.C., 1979] 102.).

516] *Triton's . . . Nymph's* The mythological merman Triton (as well as nymphs) is frequently portrayed in elaborate fountains. A common attribute is the conch shell, mentioned in l. 518.

558] *cuts the knot* A reference to the cutting of the Gordian knot by Alexander the Great, as a metaphor for the instant resolution of a seemingly insoluble problem.

677] *Rubens* See l. 130n. above.

688-89] *star / Transfiguring my brow* A star upon the brow is emblematic of divine power, both in Greek mythology and Christian iconography.

712] *Graces . . . dance* The three Graces of Greek myth—Aglaia, Thalia, and Euphrosyne—personified grace and beauty. They were portrayed in classical and Renaissance art as dancing.

837] *eye-flower* Probably referring to Eyebright (*Euphrasia officinalis*), a low-growing wildflower. The name of this plant had personal associations for B. He punningly called a close friend, Euphrasia Fanny Haworth, "Eyebright" in 1838, and inserted a reference to her into *Sordello* (3.967; the present edition, 2.227 and n.).

908] *centre of the labyrinth* In Greek myth, Theseus killed the Minotaur, a monster half bull and half human, which King Minos of Crete had hidden at the center of a maze called the Labyrinth. Until Ariadne assisted Theseus, no one had ever escaped from the Labyrinth.

SAUL

Composition and Text] What are now the first ninety-six lines of "Saul" appeared in *Bells and Pomegranates,* Number VII, published on 6 November 1845 (see the present edition, 4.246, 389). B alludes to the poem in manuscript in a letter of 3 May 1845 (Kintner, 55; *Correspondence,* 10.201). DeVane's observation (*Hbk.,* 254) that the half-line presentation, which EBB found objectionable (*New Poems,* 159), originated in the space-saving double-column format of *Bells and Pomegranates* seems plausible, but the persistence of this arrangement in 1849 must raise doubts. In these printings, each line was divided after the third metrical foot (following either the eight or ninth syllable); the breaks are almost always marked by punctuation. The second part of the line was indented and its initial letter capitalized. If the half-lines were forced on B in 1845, he could have changed to longer lines in 1849, where the page-width is adequate for all but the overrun lines of later editions. The layout of *Men and Women II* (and later editions) saves little space, since almost every line runs over into the next line space, the overrun words being set flush right. But as the variants show, B hardly revised the text at all in 1849, despite EBB's urging from the beginning that he "finish 'Saul'" eventually (Kintner, 508; *Correspondence,* 12.123). When B completed "Saul" for *Men and Women,* he revised the first part throughout and took EBB's advice about the line length, altering capitalization and punctuation to suit. DeVane (*Hbk.,* 256) believes that B revised and completed the poem in 1852-53, but no direct evidence is available. One could argue equally for an earlier date by connecting the poem to *Christmas-Eve and Easter-Day* or for a later one by relating it to "Bishop Blougram's Apology" or "An Epistle of Karshish."

Sources] To the discussion of literary sources and analogues in Volume 4 of the present edition (389) may be added Byron's similar view of David and the power of music in "The Harp the Monarch Minstrel Swept," in *Hebrew Melodies* (1815). B's expansion of the incident in 1 Sam. 16:14-23 draws on diverse biblical materials, particularly the Book of Psalms. As a singer and harpist, David is associated with seventy-three of the Psalms, some of which are echoed in "Saul." David as the prophet or even ancestor of the Messiah is a large theme in the Bible, and a messianic tone can be detected in Pss. 16, 70, 72, 110, and others linked to David. B's dramatic lyric draws on both literary and biblical traditions; see *A Dictionary of Biblical Tradition in English Literature,* ed. D. L. Jeffrey (Grand Rapids, MI, 1992), s.v. "David."

1] *Abner* Saul's cousin and captain of his armies (1 Sam. 14:50). The Bible account does not specify Abner's presence in the incident the poem relates. Though a friend, Abner became David's rival for power after Saul's death (2 Sam. 2:8-3:21).

12] *lilies . . . blue* When EBB asked "whether you had authority for the 'blue lilies' . . rather than white," B eventually responded: "lilies are of all colours in Palestine—one sort is particularized as *white* with a dark blue spot and streak—the water lily, lotos, which I think I meant, is *blue* altogether" (Kintner, 508, 539; *Correspondence,* 12.123, 154). As usual, B's botany is quite accurate, allowing for a certain amount of historical confusion in nomenclature. The true lily (which does appear in many colors) does not commonly grow in the area of Palestine, but what the Bible often means by the name *lily* is the poppy anemone, which grows freely in Palestine in a range of colors from white to blue. The "water lily, lotos" to which B refers is either *Nymphaea caerulea* or *Nymphaea stellata,* both common in the Middle East and both blue.

20] *foldskirts* Apparently a B coinage for the overlapping flaps that form the entrance of a tent.
27] *Then a sunbeam . . . showed Saul* EBB singled out this image for special praise but objected to the original wording of the line: "Then a sunbeam burst thro' the *blind* tent-roof / Showed Saul." She wrote: "Now, will you think whether[,] to enforce the admirable effect of your sudden sunbeam, this first line should not be rendered more rapid by the removal of the clogging epithet 'blind'—which you repeat, too, I believe, farther on in the next page. What if you tried the line thus—'Then a sunbeam that burst through the tent-roof— / Showed Saul!' " (*New Poems,* 158).
30-33] *caught . . . spring-time* B alludes to a folk-belief that snakes gain new strength and vitality by shedding their skins. Shakespeare uses the image similarly in *Henry V,* 4.1.20-23.
36] *the tune all our sheep know* In his youth, David was a shepherd (1 Sam.:11-13).
53] *balm-seeds* Seeds of the shrubs (perhaps *Balsamodendron*) that exude the aromatic resin called balm in the OT. Balm was valued as a perfume, a cosmetic, and a medicine (Jer. 51:8).
57] *the great march* Possibly B is recalling the most impressive "dead march" in Handel's oratorio *Saul* (1739).
60] *Levites . . . altar* In some parts of the OT, Levites are priests; elsewhere they are servants of priests. B refers to the former, since the servant Levites were prohibited from approaching the altar (Num. 4:20; see also 1 Chron. 23:24-32).
65] *male-sapphires, and rubies courageous* A sapphire that is a very dark rich blue was termed "male" (*OED,* s.v. "male," sense B.3). Among other things, the sapphire symbolizes truth and virtue, and the ruby zeal and power.
72] *hunt of the bear* In 1 Sam. 17:34-37, while pleading with Saul to let him fight Goliath, David recounts his success in killing a bear.
74] *dates . . . gold dust* Dates are picked from the tree just as they begin to ripen; at this stage they are a soft golden color.
75] *locust-flesh . . . pitcher* For use as food, locusts are boiled in brine and dried; they are rehydrated in water or date wine before serving.
80-81] *thy father . . . reward* Saul was the son of Kish, "a mighty man of power" (1 Sam. 9:1). It was the prophet Samuel, however, not Saul's father, that managed the selection of Saul as champion and king of the Israelites. When Saul won a great victory against the Ammonites, he was made king as his "glorious reward" (1 Sam. 9-11).
89] *boyhood of wonder and hope* Saul was "a choice young man, and a goodly: and there was not among the children of Israel a goodlier

person than he" (1 Sam. 9:2). Saul was destined by Jehovah for kingship, and when he was annointed by Samuel he suddenly found himself with the gift of prophecy (1 Sam. 9:15-10:13).

101] *cherubim-chariot* See Ezek. 10:1-17, 2 Kings 2:11.

150] *branch . . . fruit* The image appears in Prov. 11:30, Matt. 12:33, and elsewhere in the Bible.

155-56] *dates . . . sorrow* The juice and pulp of dates are fermented to make a strong wine. Prov. 31:6-7 advises, "Give strong drink unto him that is ready to perish, and wine unto those that be of heavy hearts. Let him drink, and forget his poverty, and remember his misery no more."

158] *nor be known in their place* Echoing Job 7:10, "He shall return no more to his house, neither shall his place know him any more."

179] *First King* Saul was the first king of Israel.

188] *paper-reeds* The papyrus reed, from which paper was made in the ancient Middle East.

prophet-winds In the Bible, divine actions, particularly destructive ones, are often accompanied by strong winds. See, for example, 1 Kings 19:11, Job 1:19, and Hos. 13:15.

193] *my shield and my sword* A recollection of Deut. 33:29.

197] *mighty to save* Isaiah 63:1, "I that speak in righteousness, mighty to save."

203] *Hebron* Ancient city in Palestine, about 18 mi. SW of Jerusalem. Hebron lies in a high valley 3000 ft. above the western coastal plain of Judea. David was annointed king of Israel in Hebron (2 Sam. 2:1-4).

204] *Kidron* A stream flowing through Jerusalem; David led his people across the Kidron to escape the rebellion of Absalom (2 Sam. 15:23).

211] *girds now his loins* In variant forms, a stock phrase in the Bible; it appears in David's hymn in 2 Sam. 22:40 and Ps. 18:39.

213-14] *ere error . . . communion* Saul's crucial error was his failure to slaughter utterly the Amalekites, as Jehovah had commanded. Jehovah and the prophet Samuel, Saul's mentor, turned against him after this transgression, and David was secretly annointed as the new king of Israel. It was Saul's despair at this rejection that David came to cure with his singing, so these lines remind the reader that David speaks his poem not as a servant of Saul, but as his unrevealed successor (see 1 Sam. 15-16).

240] *pronounced . . . handiwork* The first verse of Psalm 19, a Psalm of David, reads: "The heavens declare the glory of God; and the firmament showeth his handiwork."

263-64] *doors . . . flew ope* The opening of doors as a metaphor

for spiritual revelation appears frequently in the Bible. In the messianic context of the latter part of "Saul," the most relevant instance is Psalm 24, a Davidic Psalm, which evokes "everlasting doors" through which "the King of glory shall come in" (Ps. 24:7, 9).
288] *In the first is the last* Drawing upon Isa. 44:6 and Rev. 1:11.
291] *Sabaoth* The armies of Jehovah; see Rom. 9:29, James 5:4.
292] *atoms* An anachronism, though B may have thought of the Greek philosopher Democritus and his theory of atoms (developed in the 4th century B.C.) and the reign of Saul (c. 1000 B.C.) as roughly contemporaneous.
299] *my service is perfect* See Heb. 9:9 and the Anglican *Book of Common Prayer,* "Morning Prayer: a Collect for Peace."
307] *strongest . . . most weak* See 2 Sam. 3:1; 1 Cor. 1:25.
312] *Christ* A New Testament touch; the OT term is always "messiah," the Hebrew word meaning "the annointed one." The NT employs the Greek word which gives us "Christ"; it also means "the annointed one," but is not in the OT, which is written mainly in Hebrew.

"DE GUSTIBUS"

Date] Probably 1849; the political references in the second section, as well as the cicala and cypress of ll. 22-23, connect the poem with "Up at a Villa—Down in the City," (in *Men and Women I,* 5.177), a poem of the same period.
Title] From the Latin proverb, *De gustibus non est disputandam,* "There is no use in arguing about tastes."
16] *wind-grieved Apennine* The Apennine mountains run down the center of Italy; they are whipped by fierce winds, particularly in winter.
35-37] *the king . . . arm* Ferdinand II (1810-1859), a descendant of the Bourbon dynasty, reigned as king of the Two Sicilies from 1830 to 1859. Ferdinand's despotic rule (the *Encyclopaedia Britannica* termed him "bigoted, cruel, mean, treacherous, though not without a certain *bonhomie*" [11th ed., 10.268]) earned him the enmity of the Italian people, who conferred on him the name "King Bomba" after he ordered the shelling of the main cities of Sicily. There were several attempts on Ferdinand's life. The *liver-wing* is the right arm, so called because the liver of a game bird is placed under the right wing when it is dressed for serving.
40-44] *Queen Mary . . . "Italy."* Queen Mary I of England (1516-1588) felt the loss of Calais (which had been held by the English for

over two centuries) to the French very deeply. Tradition has it that Mary said that if she were opened up after her death the name "Calais" would be found carved into her heart.

WOMEN AND ROSES

Composition and date] Reputedly written in Paris on either 1 or 2 January 1852, though the date is somewhat disputed (see *Men and Women I, Composition,* 5.357-58). According to B in 1887, he wrote the poem in response to a basket of roses sent to EBB (Lillian Whiting, *The Brownings: Their Life and Art* [Boston, 1911], 261).
46-47] *I will . . . his mind* Despite the mention of the Biblical Eve, probably a reference to the legend of Pygmalion, the sculptor who carved his ideal of female beauty and then fell in love with the statue (Ovid, *Metamorphoses,* 10.243-98).

PROTUS

Date] DeVane (*Hbk,* 259) suggests that B got the idea for the poem during the Bs visit to Rome (22 November 1853-28 May 1854).
Sources] Protus is an imaginary ruler, but B is recalling a story from late Roman history. In 476, the barbarian leader Odoacer (c.433-93) deposed the boy emperor Romulus Augustulus (whose father had in fact usurped the title for him), effectively ending the Western Roman Empire. Odoacer spared the boy, gave him a pension, and sent him to live with his relatives in a region of southern Italy called Campania. His subsequent fate is unknown. Though busts of Roman emperors abounded in Florence, Paris, and London, the Bs could also have seen a splendid display of them in the Pinacotheca in the Vatican while they were in Rome.
2] *Half-emperors and quarter-emperors* Diocletian and Maximian ruled jointly over the Roman empire from 286 to 292 and could be called "half-emperors." From 292 until 305 the leadership of the empire was divided among four quasi-emperors.
4] *Loric . . . breast* The *lorica* (the form without the *a* is apparently B's invention) was a Roman soldier's leather breastplate. The Gorgons were mythical monsters with hideous faces and serpents writing about their heads; one look at them turned a living creature to stone. Roman soldiers bore images of Gorgons on their shields and breastplates in imitation of the hero Perseus, who cut off the head of the Gorgon Medusa and used it to petrify his enemies.
8-9] *a period . . . god* That is, beginning with Augustus (63 B.C.-

A.D. 14), the first Roman emperor, who was declared a god in the Roman religion at his death.

10] *porphyry chamber at Byzant* Byzantium, later called Constantinople and now Istanbul, was the capital of the Eastern Roman Empire. B may be remembering that the Eastern Emperor Constantine VII (905-959) was called "Porphyrogenitus" because he was born in a porphyry-lined delivery room in the imperial palace. This Constantine was a patron of the arts in a period of splendor, as B suggests in ll. 22-29.

22-23] *young . . . reconciled* Later Greek sculpture, represented by Praxiteles (364-330 B.C.), aimed at portraiture, whereas the earlier classical style of Phidias (fl. 5th century B.C.) idealized the human form and face.

36] *John the Pannonian* Odoacer (see *Sources* above) was born in the Roman province of Pannonia, which included parts of modern Austria, Hungary, and Yugoslavia. Several of the later Roman emperors rose to power as military leaders in Pannonia, which was much besieged by northern invaders.

40] *Huns* A bellicose nomadic people who invaded the northern parts of the Roman empire in the 4th and 5th centuries.

45-46] *Some think . . . away* See *Sources* above.

53] *Thrace* A mountainous district NE of modern Greece; its chief city was Byzantium (see l. 10n. above).

HOLY-CROSS DAY

Date] A date of late 1853 or early 1854 for "Holy-Cross Day" is suggested by two events. First, the Bs were in Rome, where the poem takes place, at that time—though not on Holy-Cross Day. Second, by 19 December 1853, B had read a book which may have drawn his attention to the poem's subject. In a letter to his sister, B refers to *Six Months in Italy* (New York, 1853) by G. S. Hillard, a travel memoir which contains a brief account of the compulsory sermons (*New Letters,* 68; DeVane, *Hbk.,* 260).

Source] Hillard's account (2.51) claims that although the compulsory sermons were officially abolished in 1846, the practice was still enforced several times a year in Rome; Korg (133) cites W. W. Story's report that some Jews in Rome were forced into Christian churches every Sunday. If so, then B could have seen such an occasion himself, or heard of the practice from Story, whom the Bs knew.

Title] Holy-Cross Day is 14 September; it is the festival of the Exaltation of the Cross.

Subtitle] The compulsory sermons seem to have been more frequent than once a year; see Hillard, 2.51 and Korg, 133.

Prefactory Note] *a crumb . . . dogs* Alluding to Matt. 15:27.

restif "Refusing to go forward; resisting control of any kind" (*OED*).

He Saith . . . in From Jesus's parable of the Great Supper in Luke 14:23.

though not . . . glory With ironic reference to 1 Cor. 10:31.

Diary . . . 1600 An imaginary work.

1] *Fee, faw, fum* For B's use of this phrase elsewhere in *Men and Women* to signify a threatening noise, see "A Lover's Quarrel," l. 133n., and "'Childe Roland to the Dark Tower Came,'" *Title and Subtitle* n., in the present edition, 5.361 and 5.376.

bubble and squeak In Cockney slang, "bubble and squeak" is the name of a dish made by frying cold boiled potatoes and greens together; they first bubble in the boiling water, then squeak in the skillet.

2] *Blessedest . . . the week* The Wednesday, Friday, and Saturday surrounding Holy Cross Day are declared "Ember days" by the Roman Catholic Church and are occasions for prayer and fasting; thus on Thursday celebrants would break their fast.

10] *handsel . . . shaving-shears* To *handsel* is to inaugurate the use of, to be the first to try. The removal of the beard was sign of conversion to Christianity (see ll. 39-41 below).

20] *acorned hog* That is, one well-fed on his favorite food; a similar phrase appears in Shakespeare's *Cymbeline* 2.5.16.

23] *chine* Back or flank.

24] *laps . . . swine* Before a pig is roasted whole, with its skin left on to retain juices, it is singed with a flame to remove the hair.

27] *purse . . . knob* Probably the maniple, an embroidered and decorated strip of cloth worn over the left forearm of the priest celebrating mass.

28] *gown . . . thingumbob* The priest's chasuble, the decorated outer vestment worn during mass.

38] *mount to a Turk* Bitterly ironic, in that the medieval church saw the Turks (a generalized term meaning any Muslims) as a far greater threat than the Jews to Christianity.

39-41] *selfsame . . . grace* See l. 10 n. above.

42] *hanging-face* "Having a downward cast of countenance; gloomy-looking" (*OED*, s.v. "hanging," ppl., sense 4, which cites the term in *Measure for Measure* 4.2.33-34 and "Fra Lippo Lippi" l. 307).

47] *the worst of trades* Usury, condemned in the OT and by the Christian church.

51-52] *It began . . . the Corso* Beginning in 1468, Roman Jews were made to run down the Corso, a major N-S street in central Rome, to be jeered at by the Christian citizens; after 1668, Jews could avoid this humiliation by paying a special tax (Korg, 134).

54] *To usher . . . Lent* That is, the Jews were forced to play the part of "penitents" in the solemn procession marking the beginning of Lent on Ash Wednesday.

61] *scapegoats leave our flock* A complex reference: the first significance is merely that the "volunteers" for spurious conversion have been taken away to begin the process. But the actual scapegoat was a feature of the Jewish Day of Atonement, the climactic day of the ritual cleansing of a congregation of its sins. After the sacrifice of one goat, another was designated as scapegoat. The sins of the people were ritually transferred to the scapegoat, which was then driven away into the wilderness. Thus B multiplies the ironies attaching to the notions of sin, forgiveness, penance, and justice in his poem.

66] *Ben Ezra's Song of Death* Abraham Ben Meir Ibn Ezra (c.1090-1164), poet, philosopher, and scholar, wrote important commentaries on the OT. During his wanderings across Europe he wrote many poems, but this "Song of Death" is B's own creation. Of the rest of the poem and its call to steadfast resistance to Christianity, B wrote in 1888: "in *Holy Cross Day,* Ben Ezra is not supposed to acknowledge Christ as the Messiah because he resorts to the obvious argument 'even on your own showing, and excepting for the moment the authority of your accepted Lawgiver, you are condemned by His precepts—let alone ours' " (Hood, 287-88). See also "Rabbi Ben Ezra" in *Dramatis Personae* in the present volume.

73-78] *The Lord . . . saith* This passage closely parallels Isa. 14:1.

73] *Jacob* The third Hebrew patriarch, but here, by extension, the decendants of Jacob, i.e., the Jewish people.

74] *his border . . . set* The patriarchs Abraham, Isaac, and Jacob established the land of Canaan as Israel's homeland. See Gen. 15:18, 17:8, 28:13-14, 37:1.

75] *Judah . . . Jerusalem* Judah, founder of the Tribe of Judah, was the fourth son of Jacob and Leah; Judah conquered Jerusalem, making it part of Israel (Judg. 1:8).

77] *Gentiles* In OT parlance, the term means simply "non-Hebrews."

78] *Prophet* I.e., Isaiah.

79] *children . . . race* 1 Chron. 16:13.

85-90] *God spoke . . . cock-crow* The language is derived from Mark 13:33-36.

89] *By . . . set* In Jehovah's covenant with Israel, given through Moses, there is no direct mention of a messiah (Exod. 34:10-11). But in Deut. 18:15-22, Jehovah speaks through Moses, promising to "raise up unto thee a Prophet from the midst of thee . . . unto him ye shall hearken." Acts 3:17-24 applies this passage to Jesus.
92] *starlight* The birth of Jesus was accompanied by the appearance of a new star (Matt. 2:2, 7, 9).
94] *martyr-gash* That is, the wound in the side inflicted on Jesus by a Roman soldier (John 19:33-34).
102] *maintain . . . in deed* See 1 John 3:18.
104] *Barabbas* A murderer and revolutionary who was released from prison by Pilate at the trial of Jesus, in response to the demands of the mob. Modern scholarship suggests that his full name was Jesus Bar-Abbas, and thus Pilate's question to the mob about their preference was "which Jesus do you want released?" (Matt. 27:15-23).
108] *Rome . . . Calvary* That is, let the Roman Catholic Church—rather than the Jews, who have suffered enough—do penance for the death of Jesus at the place called Calvary (Luke 23:33).
111] *Ghetto's plague* Though the term *ghetto* has become generalized, it once meant specifically a street or district where Jews were forced to live. The Roman Ghetto was established by Pope Paul IV in 1556, so the restrictions would be sharply felt by the speaker of "Holy-Cross Day." The appalling Roman Ghetto, which still existed in B's time, was located in a swamp and rife with infectious diseases.

the garb's disgrace In order that Christians might avoid inadvertant contact with a Jew, the Fourth Lateran Council (1215) required that Jews wear at all times a specified article of dress (which varied in different countries from a small badge to a garment of a particular color). This edict was enforced for many centuries.
112] *badge of shame* See l. 111n. above.

felon's place The restrictions on Jews were in fact more severe than those on some kinds of criminals. In the popular mind, to be a Jew was to be a felon—a "Christ-killer."
113] *branding-tool* During the frequent outbursts of violent anti-Semitism that mark the religious history of the Middle Ages, those Jews who were not killed outright were subjected to various tortures, including branding their flesh with crosses.
120] *South . . . Land* See Jer. 3:18-19.
Postscript] In texts prior to 1888, B identified the abolisher as "the present Pope," i.e., Pius IX; but it was his immediate predecessor Gregory XVI who ended the "bad business" just before his death in 1846.

THE GUARDIAN-ANGEL

Composition and Date] The poem was written in late July 1848, when the Bs travelled to the towns of Fano and Ancona on the Adriatic Sea. For a detailed discussion, see DeVane, *Hbk.*, 261-63.

Title and Subtitle] The painting described is "L'Angelo Custode," in the Church of San Agostino at Fano. The artist, Gian-Francesco Barbieri (1591-1666), was called Guercino (see l. 36), "the squinter." The Bs admired this painting so much that they went to see it each of the three days they were in Fano. In Paul Turner's description of the painting, "Guercino's angel stands with wings outspread over a child half-kneeling on a tomb, his left arm round the child's shoulders, and his right hand on the child's left forearm, as if showing him how to raise his hands in prayer." [PT] The painting and its subject may have captured the Bs attention for several reasons. EBB was in the early stages of pregnancy with the Bs' son; their journey was proving to be uncomfortable; and B was suffering from influenza, which had brought a recurrence of the headaches which frequently plagued him throughout his life. B may also have remembered another painting of a guardian angel which he and Alfred Domett (see l. 37) had seen years before in the Dulwich College picture gallery, which also contained pictures by Guercino. [PT]

4] *performed . . . ministry* A recollection of Coleridge's "Frost at Midnight," l. 1, another poem about the protection of an innocent child.

18] *bird of God* So the angel who appears to Dante on his way to Purgatory is called (*Purgatorio,* 2.29).

36] *Guercino* See *Title* above.

37] *Alfred* Alfred Domett (1811-87) was a very close friend of B in his youth. They lost touch for many years after Domett emigrated to New Zealand in 1842. Domett, of whom B had written in "Waring" (see the present edition, 3.228 and nn.), became Prime Minister of New Zealand in 1863; in 1872 he returned to London and renewed his acquaintance with B.

46] *My angel* EBB.

50-51] *he did not . . . some wrong* Modern critics would agree with B that Guercino's work was uneven, his early paintings being much livelier than his late ones. The "wrong" Guercino suffered came at the hands of Anna Brownell Jameson (see "Andrea del Sarto," *Sources,* above), who rated him rather low, and Ruskin, who condemned him in *Modern Painters.*

55] *Wairoa* More commonly Wairau, a small river in the NE part of the South Island of New Zealand. The place became infamous because of the massacre of 22 Europeans by Maori natives on 17 June 1843. As a leader among the colonists, Domett would probably have been present at the gathering that escalated into a massacre, but he was prevented from doing so by an injury to his leg (see *Diary of Alfred Domett,* ed. E. A. Horsman [Oxford, 1953], 15-16). Thus bad luck became good luck, and B might well have considered that a guardian angel was looking out for his old friend.
56] *Ancona* See *Composition and Date* above.

CLEON

Composition and Sources] In the absence of any direct evidence about the composition of the poem, A. W. Crawford's suggestion that "Cleon" was prompted by Matthew Arnold's "Empedocles on Etna" has gained some critical acceptance ("Browning's *Cleon,*" *JEGP* [1927]:485-90). Clearly the Bs had read some of Arnold's poetry by May 1853, as indicated by EBB's reference to "a volume of poems by Dr. Arnold's son, ('by A')" in a letter (Landis and Freeman, 184). But whether this was Arnold's *Empedocles* volume (published 27 October 1852) or his earlier *Strayed Reveller* (of February 1849) is not certain. "Empedocles" and "Cleon" have little in common in either form or content, except that they are both about ancient Greek intellectuals, whose stories occur 400 years apart. "Cleon" is set in Greece around 50 A.D., since St. Paul's visit to Greece (alluded to in the epigraph) took place on his second missionary journey between 49 and 52 A.D.
Epigraph] Acts 17:28 reads: "for in him [the Lord] we live, and move, and have our being; as certain also of your own poets have said, 'For we are also his offspring.'" Paul quotes the 4th century B.C. Greek poet Aratus, *Phaenomena,* 5. Acts 17:15-34 describes Paul's visit to Athens alluded to at the end of "Cleon."
1] *Cleon* The artist/philosopher, as well as the tyrant Protus, are creations of B's imagination, though both names are found in ancient history. Byron, in "Childish Recollections," gave the name Cleon to a college friend of noble character (ll. 325-40).

sprinkled isles a literal translation of the Greek *Sporades,* the name of a group of islands in the Aegean Sea.
4] *Protus in his Tyranny* Though Protus's reign is called a tyranny, he need not have been a tyrant in the modern sense of the word, with its implications of cruelty and oppression. In ancient Greece one who

held unconditional sovereignty was called "tyrant," the term being a quasi-official title.

12-13] *chequer-work / Pavement* A favorite decorative motif in later classical architecture.

15] *crocus vest* A loose tunic the color of crocuses—purple.

16] *sea-wools* Woolen cloth dyed with sea-purple, a dye derived from secretions of shellfish of the *Murex* and *Purpura* genera. [PT] See "Popularity" below.

17] *strainer . . . cup* Ancient Greek wine was thickened and flavored with various additives; when served the wine was diluted with water and strained into the drinking vessel.

41-42] *Zeus . . . calm* As Homer put it, "the gods themselves have no sorrows" (*Iliad* 24.526, Lattimore trans.).

51] *sun-god* Phoebus Apollo, the Greek god of the sun.

phare a lighthouse; perhaps B alludes to the Pharos at Alexandria, one of the seven wonders of the ancient world.

53-54] *Poecile . . . painting* Cleon refers to a *stoa,* or columned portico; "Poecile" is short for *stoa poikile,* Greek for "painted portico." There were stoas decorated with narrative paintings in several ancient cities, including Olympia and Athens.

55-56] *true proportions . . . woman also* Ancient aestheticians argued about the nature and relationships of those anatomical features which combined to produce ideal beauty (but Cleon may be indulging in self-mockery here).

60] *the moods* That is, *modes,* the arrangements of the tones selected for various scales. Ancient Greek music made use of numerous modes, including the major and the minor scales of modern Western music.

63] *seventeen islands* Only an approximate number, since the Sporades (see l. 1 above) included more islands than this in ancient times.

99-111] *little water . . . properties* This simple but impressive demonstration, in which the heat of the hands of the person manipulating the glass sphere causes the trace of water within to evaporate into the contained air, is still a fixture of basic instruction in simple physics.

132] *suave* "Pleasing or agreeable to the senses or the mind; sweet" (*OED,* sense 1).

savage-tasted drupe The harsher tasting wild fruit. As usual, B's botanizing is accurate—the European plum (*Prunus domestica*) was first cultivated about 2000 years ago.

139] *chanted verse like Homer* The great epics of Homer (? fl. 8th century B.C.), *The Odyssey* and *The Iliad,* were composed orally and were chanted by bards for many generations before they were written down. B adored Homer; for his retrospective view on his life-long reading of Homer, see "Development," in *Asolando* (the present edition, Vol. 17).

140] *swept . . . Terpander* Terpander (fl. 7th century B.C.) was the greatest musician of ancient Greece; he was traditionally credited with the invention of the seven-stringed *kithara,* the Greek lyre.

140-41] *carved / And painted . . . friend* Phidias (fl. 5th century B.C.) was one of the foremost sculptors of ancient Athens; he supervised the building of the Parthenon. In light of the reference to painting here, and to the *stoa poikile* in l. 53 above, the most likely candidate for "his friend" would be Polygnotus, believed in B's time to be Phidias's teacher. B saw works by Phidias (or copies of them) in London, Paris, and Rome.

148] *Rose-blood* A coinage, presumably indicating a liquid extract from rose flowers or rose-hips.

210] *third thing* In philosophy, the term *tertium quid* (the Latin rendering of the Greek for "third thing") means a distinct but undefined entity related to two defined entities.

231-36] *pleasure-house . . . perish there* See Tennyson's "The Palace of Art" for the potentially fatal pleasure-house, and "The Lady of Shalott" for the dangerous tower elevated above ordinary life. The Bs knew Tennyson personally from about 1846. His 1842 volume of poems, containing revised versions of the two poems mentioned above, was a great favorite of EBB's; B very seldom commented on Tennyson's poetry, but he disapproved of the 1842 revisions (see Kintner, 19).

288] *Phoebus* Apollo as sun-god; see l. 51 and n. above.

304] *Sappho* Poet of the island of Lesbos who lived in the later 7th century B.C.; though only fragments of her work have survived, Sappho's fame as a poet was unsurpassed in the ancient world. In 1850 EBB included in her *Poems* a translation from Sappho, with whom she was sometimes compared in her own lifetime.

305] *Æschylus* Greek tragedian (525-456 B.C.), author of the *Oresteia* trilogy and one of the B's favorite authors. EBB translated Aeschylus's *Prometheus Bound* in 1833, and B produced his version of Aeschylus's *Agamemnon* in 1877.

331-33] *Freed . . . his wings* See Dante, *Purgatorio* 10.124-29. [PT]

340] *Paulus* St. Paul (see *Composition and Sources* and *Epigraph* nn. above).

343] *mere barbarian Jew* The contemptuousness of this reference is intensified by the fact that St. Paul was born and raised in the city of Tarsus, a distinctly Hellenistic city. Though indeed born a Jew, Paul grew up in a sophisticated Greek culture, and could hardly be called a barbarian.

THE TWINS

Composition and Date] The poem was first published on 19 April 1854, with EBB's "A Plea for the Ragged Schools of London," in a pamphlet entitled *Two Poems*. The pamphlet was prepared by the Bs' publisher Edward Chapman for sale at a charity bazaar organized by EBB's sister Arabel. Both poems were probably written shortly after 4 March, when EBB wrote Arabel agreeing to her request for poems (see DeVane and Knickerbocker, 71; and *EBB: Letters to Her Sister, 1846-1859,* ed. L. Huxley [London, 1929], 203). The fair-copy MS of "The Twins" collated in this edition is in the Pierpont Morgan Library, New York.
Source] The anecdote that the poem relates appears in *The Table-Talk or Familiar Discourse of Martin Luther,* tr. W. Hazlitt, (London, 1848), parable 316. Though it seems likely that B encountered the story there, it is much older, deriving in part from St. Paul in Heb. 13:2.
Subtitle] Taken from Luke 6:38.
1-2] *Martin . . . fables* Martin Luther (1483-1546), leader of the Protestant Reformation in Germany; the *Table-Talk* volume contains many anecdotes and fables used as parables.
16] *Date and Dabitur* The Latin version of Luke 6:38 in the Vulgate is *"Date, et dabitur vobis."*

POPULARITY

Date] There is disagreement about the date of this poem. R. Altick sees the poem as a response to the biography of Keats published by Richard Monckton Milnes in 1848 ("Memo to the Next Annotator of Browning," *VP* 1 [1963], 65-66). DeVane (*Hbk.,* 267) believes the stimulus for the poem was the Bs' visit to Rome during the winter of 1853-54 when they visited various sites associated with Keats. B admired Keats and his poetry enormously throughout his life, quoting him repeatedly in letters to EBB during their courtship in 1845-46. B received a copy of Monckton Milnes's book from Edward Moxon (*Reconstruction,* A1603), the publisher of the biography (as well as an edition of Keats in 1846) and of B's poetry from 1840 to 1849. But it is also true that B was thinking deeply about popularity in 1853, shown in his now-famous remark to Milsand: "I am writing a sort of first step toward popularity" (Irvine and Honan, 335 and n.).
18-20] *Others give . . . till now* Drawn from John 2:10; the passage

describes the occasion when Jesus turned water into wine at the wedding in Cana.

24] *Tyre* Ancient seaport of Phoenecia; now called Sur and in Lebanon.

26-30] *Tyrian shells . . . merchant sells* The most famous product of ancient Tyre was Tyrian purple, a dye extracted from the secretions of shellfish of the genera *Murex* and *Purpura.* The shellfish do not literally "enclose the blue"; the secretion is clear. When diluted and spread on fabrics which are then exposed to sunlight, it imparts a permanent deep purple tint.

29] *Astarte* Astarte (Asherah, Ishtar, Ashtoreth), the Great Mother goddess of fertility in her Semitic name; a major temple of Astarte was at Tyre. Why B thought Astarte's eyes were blue is not at all clear, but he may have been punning on *aster,* a flower which is blue in many of its varieties.

33] *pall* Cloak.

35] *ball* That is, the orb, a symbol of kingship like the sceptre and crown.

38] *whelks* The common name for marine snails, including the *Murex* and *Purpura.*

41-45] *Solomon . . . shone* King Solomon's cedar-house is described in 1 Kings 6-7. The religious articles in it were made of gold (7:48-49), but Solomon's robes are not described, nor are any blue or purple hangings mentioned. The *Spouse* is the daughter of the Egyptian Pharoah (1 Kings 3:1, 7:8) who was one of Solomon's several wives.

53] *refine to proof* Distill to full strength.

58] *Hobbs . . . Nokes* Such ringing of the changes on typical English names is common in 19th-century writing; see, for example, chapter 40 of Dickens's *Bleak House,* where one meets the aristocrats Coodle and Doodle.

64] *murex* See ll. 26-30n. above.

65] *John Keats* A favorite poet of B's (see *Date* above). Certainly imitators of Keats in B's time made more profit ("porridge") from poetry than did Keats (1795-1821), who died in poverty.

THE HERETIC'S TRAGEDY

Composition and Sources] Date of composition unknown, though DeVane (*Hbk.,* 268) speculates that the poem may date from a period in

1851-52 when the Bs were in Paris, where the poem is set. Possible sources include the *Biographie universelle,* often relied on by B, and a popular work by G. G. Addison, *The History of the Knights Templars* . . . (1842), which appeared in a third edition in 1852.

Headnote] *Rosa . . . floribus:* "The rose of the world; or, prop me up with flowers." The Latin here and elsewhere in this headnote is inelegant and sometimes grammatically shaky, in keeping with B's comment about distortion in the second paragraph. *Ypres* (Flemish *Ieper*), a town in SW Belgium near the French border, had considerable political and cultural importance in the 14th century, when the poem is set. *Cantuque, Virgilius:* "and in song, a Virgil." *Hock-tide:* the second Monday and Tuesday after Easter (called "Hock Monday and Hock Tuesday"), once an occasion for rough sports and fund-raising for charity. *Gavisus eram, Jessides:* "I had rejoiced, the son of Jesse." A bungled quotation of Ps. 122:1, attributed to David, the son of Jesse. [PT] *Jacques du Bourg-Molay* (c. 1243-1314) was the last Grand Master of the Order of the Knights Templars, an international organization of knights which rose to great power and fame during the crusades of the 12th and 13th centuries. Wealthy, influential, and loyal to none outside their order, the Templars came to be seen as a threat to national sovereignty by several European rulers in the early 14th century. Accusations of corruption were circulated against the knights, and in 1307-8, with Pope Clement V and Philip IV of France leading the campaign to suppress the order, the Templars were arrested throughout Europe. Molay, arrested in 1307 and imprisoned thereafter, first confessed to several crimes, then retracted, then pled guilty again, throwing himself on the mercy of the Pope. However, Clement V decided to complete the suppression of the Templars, and on 18 or 19 March 1314, Molay and others of the order were sentenced to life imprisonment. At this Molay and the others in Paris once again retracted their confessions and were burned at the stake that same day.

3-4] *He knows . . . turning* The Abbot (or Master Gysbrecht, who supposedly wrote these words) seems to have forgotten that these words are drawn from the epistle of James (1:17), not from St. Paul.

8-9] *plagal-cadence* A particular chord structure having the chord on the subdominant tone (IV) followed by the tonic chord (I) at the end of a composition. The plagal cadence is also known as the "Amen" cadence because of its traditional use at the end of hymns.

10] *Temple of God* The Templars were so named because their headquarters in Jerusalem were located near the site of the old Jewish Temple.

12-13] *he bought . . . Saladin* One of the charges brought against the Templars was that they had betrayed the Christian cause and entered into a secret alliance with the Muslims. This charge might be loosely termed a species of simony, the buying and selling of church offices. But Master Gysbrecht is lost in his history, since there seems never to have been an Emperor Aldabrod, and Saladin, the Sultan of Egypt and Syria and capturer of Jerusalem, died in 1193, fifty years before Molay was born.
14] *Pope Clement* See *Headnote* n. above. It was King Philip IV of France who forced the execution of Molay; the Pope's representatives were willing to try him again, in light of his recantation.
17-18] *clavicithern* A harpsichord with a vertical body.
28] *bavins* Bundles of sticks used for kindling.
32] *in a chafe* In a state of fury.
33] *hog to scorch* See "Holy-Cross Day," l. 24n. above.
35] *Sing "Laudes"* That is, sing the hymns of praise to God, based on Ps. 145-48 and 150, all of which begin in the Vulgate with a form of Latin *laudare,* "to praise."
36] *Laus Deo* "Praise be to God" (Latin).
48] *Salvâ reverentiâ* "Saving reverence," a ritual Latin phrase interjected here as a pious response to the mention of "the Flesh," the Host.
50] *Turks* In medieval Christian terminology, any Muslim—since all followers of Islam were viewed as enemies of the Church.
60] *Sharon's rose* See the Song of Solomon, 2:1, "I am the rose of Sharon." The speaker follows the tradition of OT commentators in interpreting the Song of Solomon as an allegory of the love of God for the chosen people, though verse 2:1 is spoken by the bride of the Song, who represents Israel, not God.
66] *devil's-dung* Literally, the folk name for the foul-smelling resins of certain plants; B may be recalling Professor Teufelsdröckh (meaning "devil's-dung" in German) from Carlyle's *Sartor Resartus* (1833-34).
67-69] *Paul once . . . no less* See Acts 24:25, which describes the confrontation of St. Paul and Antonius Felix, governor of Judaea, during Paul's trial on charges of fomenting civil discord.

TWO IN THE CAMPAGNA

Date] The poem probably was written in the spring of 1854, when the Bs were in Rome and having "some exquisite hours on the Campagna upon picnic excursions" (*Letters of EBB,* 2.165).
Title] The Campagna was a vast unpopulated region S of Rome,

where ancient ruins, sheep, and not much else abounded in the 19th century. Excursions into the Campagna were recommended as picturesque day-trips by the guidebooks.

A GRAMMARIAN'S FUNERAL

Date] The poem was probably written after the Bs returned to Florence in mid-1854, a period when B wrote: "I am trying to make up for wasted time in Rome and setting my poetical house in order" (Hudson, 33).

Source] There has been much speculation about possible models for the Grammarian, but he is a type, not a specific individual. In his extensive and sometimes arcane reading, B had encountered any number of scholarly drudges, heroic or otherwise.

Subtitle] The poem is set in the early Renaissance, probably in the first half of the 15th century.

33-34] *thy face . . . Apollo* The Greek god Apollo, patron of poetry and music (thus "lyric") among other things, is represented in classical art as the ideal form of male beauty.

71] *steel . . . quartz* Given the metaphor, this reference is not to kindling a fire with flint and steel, but to the sparks thrown out when steel excavating tools strike hard rock.

86] *Calculus* Latin medical term meaning kidney or bladder stones.

88] *Tussis* Latin medical term meaning a persistent cough.

95] *soul-hydroptic* Being unquenchably thirsty in his soul; a B coinage, cited in *OED,* s.v. "hydroptic."

126] *Ground he at grammar* B may be remembering a vivid passage about pedants in Carlyle's *Sartor Resartus* (1833-34), Pt. 2, Ch. 3: "How can an inanimate, mechanical Gerund grinder . . . foster the growth of anything; much more of Mind, which grows, not like a vegetable (by having its roots littered with etymological compost), but like a spirit, by mysterious contact of Spirit . . . ? How shall *he* give kindling, in whose own inward man there is no live coal, but all is burnt-out to a dead grammatical cinder?"

129-31] *settled Hoti's . . . De* *Hoti, Oun,* and *De* are B's transliterations of three Greek particles. Ὅτι acts as a conjunction meaning "that" or "because"; Οὖν means "then" in the sense of "therefore"; and Δε means "towards." B was asked to explain this passage more than once. He wrote to Tennyson in 1863: "I wanted the grammarian 'dead from the waist down' . . . to spend his last breath on the biggest of the littlenesses: such an one is the '*enclitic δε*' " (see *The Brownings to the Tennysons,* ed. T. J. Collins, *Baylor Browning Interests* 22 (1971), 29-

30). Later he defended his fine point about Greek grammar to the editor of the London *Daily News,* citing an authority for the use of Δε to mean "towards," adding: "That this is not to be confounded with the accentuated 'De, meaning *but*' was the 'Doctrine' which the Grammarian bequeathed to those capable of receiving it" (Hood, 164).

ONE WAY OF LOVE

3] *Pauline* Perhaps recalling the idealized beloved of B's first published poem, *Pauline* (1833); see the present edition, 1.7-52.

ANOTHER WAY OF LOVE

19] *Eadem semper* Latin for "always the same"; B may be quoting Lucretius, *De Rerum Natura,* 3.945, *eadem sunt omnia semper,* "all things continue the same forever." Matthew Arnold used the same passage in "On the Modern Element in Literature" (1857) to illustrate the feeling of *ennui* (*Complete Prose Works,* ed. R. H. Super [Ann Arbor, MI, 1961-77], 1.33).

"TRANSCENDENTALISM: A POEM IN TWELVE BOOKS"

Date] It should be possible to date the composition of this poem exactly, given that B left such a tantalizing clue about it. In 1866 he wrote to Edward Dowden about the erroneous identification of Boehme as "Swedish" in the early editions of the poem: "The first blunder you point out is enormous—only explicable to myself—and hardly that—from the circumstances under which I well remember having written the poem, *Transcendentalism.* I was three parts thro' it, when called to assist a servant to whom a strange accident, partly serious, partly ludicrous, had suddenly happened; and after a quarter of an hour's agitation, of a varied kind, I went back to my room and finished what I had begun" (Hood, 103-4). Presumably the "strange accident" happened to either the Bs' maid Elizabeth Wilson or their manservant Ferdinando Romagnoli, and since the Bs frequently described the everyday events of their household in their letters to various family members, it is surprising that there is no mention of such an occasion in the published letters between 1846 and 1855. But the mystic Boehme (see ll. 22-24n. below) was connected in the Bs' experience with Swedenborg (perhaps accounting for B's mistaken epithet "Swedish" for Boehme), whom EBB read enthusiastically in Rome in 1853-54 (*Letters of EBB,* 2.145-46, 156). Other events of that period which may connect to the poem include EBB's intense interest in spiritualism (which developed rapidly

in 1853) and the publication of several widely-noticed "transcendental" works (see *Title* below); all in all, a date of 1853-54 seems most probable.
Title] B satirizes such lengthy "epic" (as suggested by "Twelve Books") and quasi-mystical works as Philip James Bailey's sprawling *Festus* (1839), Sydney Dobell's *Balder* (1853), and Alexander Smith's *A Life Drama* (1853). Smith's poem, which made a great sensation on its first appearance, strongly impressed EBB. There is perhaps a note of self-mockery here, since B's long, difficult early poems *Paracelsus* and *Sordello* had been classed by some with "Spasmodic" works like *Festus*.
4] *sights and sounds* B recommends his own plan, which he described to Milsand in 1853 as writing poems "with more music and painting than before, so as to get people to hear and see" (Irvine and Honan, 335).
12-13] *The six-foot . . . to Alp* That is, the Alpenhorn, a giant trumpet-like instrument, made of wood and wrapped with birch bark, used for signalling by herdsmen and villagers in the Alps.
22-24] *German Boehme . . . speak* B says in his letter to Dowden (see *Date* above) that he had read the German mystic Jacob Boehme (1575-1624), though there is no proof that Boehme's writings were in his or his father's library. He wrote "I knew something of Boehme, and his autobiography, and how he lived." DeVane suggests that B encountered Boehme when doing his extensive reading for *Paracelsus* in 1834, and this seems very likely. The incident of the speaking plants is narrated by Boehme's early biographers, quoted at length by DeVane (*Hbk.*, 273-74).
26] *daisy . . . eye indeed* The daisy's name comes from OE *daeges eage,* "day's eye," denoting the flower's similarity to the sun.
27] *Colloquized . . . cowslip* Here B has succumbed to a folk etymology: *cowslip* is not "cow's" + "lip," but "cow" + OE *slyppe,* meaning "the sloppy stuff from the cow," i.e., cow dung. The flower has a propensity to grow in moist, well-fertilized pastures.
28] *Jacob* I. e., Boehme.
36] *subtler . . . roses say* Perhaps refering to the Rosicrucians, a mystical brotherhood of the early 17th century linked to Boehme and Swedenborg by tradition. The Rosicrucians interpretations of their central symbol, the rose, are even more arcane than Boehme's.
37-38] *stout Mage . . . about* B may have come across the medieval German magician Johann Semeca, called Teutonicus, of Halberstadt in Nathaniel Wanley's *Wonders of the Little World* (1667), one of his favorite books as a child.
39] *vents . . . rhymes* Pronounces a magic formula.

40] *there breaks . . . herself* Teutonicus was credited by early writers with several impressive acts of magic, though not with creating flowers. Orr (212) suggests that this was a common enough trick amongst medieval magicians.

MISCONCEPTIONS

11] *regal dalmatic* A ceremonial robe used in royal coronation rituals.

ONE WORD MORE

Composition and Date] According to the date on MS, "One Word More" was completed on 22 Sept. 1855, while *Men and Women* was being printed and proofed. The Bs were in London from 12 July to 17 Oct., and memories of their three-week journey from Florence via Paris were clear in B's mind, as the poem shows. "One Word More" was added to the fifty poems of *Men and Women* when the printing was well along, and the poem reflects on the entire process of composing and publishing the volumes.
Manuscript] The MS of "One Word More"—the only piece of printer's copy surviving for the first edition of *Men and Women*—is now in the Pierpont Morgan Library in New York. It bears the title "A Last Word. / To E.B.B.," and consists of six leaves containing 201 lines, showing some degree of composition and revision. It seems likely that the Morgan MS is not the original draft; B's problems in adding and numbering the section divisions in the surviving MS suggest that he was copying from a previous version, redividing the poem as he went. For example, in the Morgan MS the section numbered 5 by B runs from l. 32 through l. 52. B has called for a new section, to be numbered 6, before l. 50. He apparently made this decision as he was writing out the printer's copy, since he labelled the next section (beginning with line 53) with an Arabic 7, consistent with the revised section division. The last leaf of the MS contains ll. 172 through the end of the poem, with two section divisions (at ll. 180 and 187) that appear in the printed texts. But these sections are numbered 16 and 17, repeating numbers already used on leaf 5 and corresponding to none of the printed texts. B may have simply made a numbering error in copying, or leaf 6 may come from an earlier draft consisting of only 17 sections. The haste with which B and his publisher were working in the autumn of 1855 is indicated by printer's marks assigning the six leaves of MS in five takes for at least three compositors. This shows that the typesetting of "One

Word More" was being done as quickly as possible, and the job must have been done before the Bs arrived in Paris on October 17th.

Title] Paul Turner speculates that B changed the poem's title in proof because the MS's "A Last Word" undesirably echoed "A Woman's Last Word" (in *Men and Women I,* 5.181), and given B's habit of pairing poems by parallel titles elsewhere, it is possible that he wished to prevent such a link here. Elvan Kintner and others have proposed that the replacement title looks back to a crucial use of the phrase by EBB during the Bs' courtship. On 30 August 1845, B passionately declared his love for EBB: "Let me say now—*this only once*—that I loved you from my soul, and gave you my life, so much of it as you would take" (Kintner, 176; *Correspondence,* 11.52). EBB responded the next day: "Your life! . . if you gave it to me & I put my whole heart into it; what should I put but anxiety, & more sadness than you were born to? . . . Therefore we must leave this subject—& I must trust you to leave it without one word more" (Kintner, 179; *Correspondence,* 11.54). "One Word More" was written (and re-titled) very near to the tenth anniversary of B's declaration, when the Bs were back in London, at a time when B was finally putting out a book reflecting his married life—a book in which the majority of poems have to do with the varieties of love and relationship. If B did recall EBB's use of the phrase, he resurrected it in the new context of a poem which testifies to the success of the love which EBB had sought to silence. There is an apposite use of the phrase in Shakespeare's *The Tempest,* 1.2.450, when Prospero decides to create impediments to the love of Ferdinand and Miranda.

5-6] *Raphael . . . volume* Surprisingly, this story is not in Vasari, though B could have encountered it in Filippo Baldinucci's *Delle Notizie de' professori del disegno da Cimabue in qua,* a book B knew and used (see Frederick Page, *TLS,* 25 May 1940, 255). It is equally plausible that he heard this story from Anna Brownell Jameson, who was a great enthusiast for Raphael (see "Andrea del Sarto," *Sources* and l. 105n. above). No volume of poems by Raphael survives, but he is known to have written sonnets, three of which (and a portion of a fourth) appear on the backs of Raphael's cartoons for his fresco "The Disputa." See ll. 27-31n. below.

8] *Madonnas* Raphael was something of a specialist in Madonnas, having painted at least fifty of them.

9-10] *one . . . you ask* The "one" is Raphael's beloved, a woman named Margherita (nicknamed "La Fornarina," "the baker's daughter") who served as a model for some of his Madonnas, including two mentioned later in the poem (see Vasari, 2.237). By the 19th century a biographical tradition had developed that Raphael's three surviving sonnets were addressed to her (see M. F. Sweetster, *Artist Biographies* [Boston, 1877], 1.60).

21-24] *Madonnas . . . Louvre* These famous Madonnas by Raphael, known today respectively as the *Sistine Madonna,* the *Madonna di Foligno,* the *Madonna del Granduca,* and *La Belle Jardinière,* were in public galleries in the 19th century, and B probably saw the latter three, among many other Raphael Madonnas. (In 1887 B commented on these identifications in a letter to W. J. Rolfe, later published in *The Nation,* 17 Feb. 1919, 159.) Margherita is portrayed in the *Madonna di Foligno* and the *Madonna del Granduca,* as well as in portraits in Rome and Florence that B may have seen.

27-31] *Guido Reni . . . vanished* According to Baldinucci's *Notizie,* the volume of sonnets by Raphael disappeared after the death in Bologna of the painter Guido Reni (1575-1642), who had owned the book and willed it to his heir. But Reni's biographer Carlo Malvasia (1616-1693) wrote that what disappeared was a book of a hundred drawings, not poems. Guido's heir got less than he deserved, says Malvasia, and "there would have been more too if the famous book containing a hundred drawings, all by Raphael, that Guido bought in Rome . . . had not all been fraudulently taken from the estate" (Carlo Cesare Malvasia, *The Life of Guido Reni,* tr. C. and R. Enggass [University Park, PA, and London, 1980], 106). See ll. 5-6n. above.

32-49] *Dante . . . my painting* In his *Vita Nuova,* ch. 35, Dante Alighieri (1265-1321) narrates an incident which occurred on the first anniversary of the death of his beloved Beatrice Portinari. On this occasion in 1291, the poet was drawing an angel on a tablet while thinking about Beatrice. He ceased his drawing when interrupted by the "people of importance," and resumed it after they left. B has embellished this tale by connecting those who interrupted Dante with figures the poet placed in Hell in the *Inferno.* And though Dante says he was drawing angels, B has him painting—which Dante certainly could have done, having had lessons from Cimabue (see "Old Pictures in Florence," l. 180n. above, and DeVane, *Hbk.,* 277).

35-41] *a pen . . . Florence* By alluding here to the moment in the *Inferno* when Dante grabs the hair of Bocca degli Abati (32.97-110), B implies that the poet was already working on the *Divine Comedy* in 1291, but scholars have always placed its composition after 1305.

57] *Bice* A short, affectionate form for *Beatrice.*

74] *He who smites . . . water* Moses. The miracle of bringing forth water from the rock is narrated in both Ex. 17:1-7 and Num. 20:2-13, with enough differences in detail to suggest that Moses performed this feat twice—the first time by himself, and the second time in company with his brother Aaron.

80] *he smote before* B takes the two accounts of Moses' smiting the rock as reflecting two separate events, and thus pictures here the Moses of Num. 20:2-13 as thinking back to first occasion on which he performed the miracle.

81-84] *When they stood . . . pleasant* The Israelites were frequently quick to complain about Moses' leadership, and to challenge his ability to relieve their difficulties on the exodus. See Ex. 15:22-17:7; 32:1-35.

92-95] *the 'customed . . . better* See Ex. 15:22-25; 16:2-3.

97] *Sinai-forehead's cloven brilliance* B's phrase accurately reflects the Hebrew Bible's description of Moses when he came down from Mt. Sinai with the second set of tablets bearing the Ten Commandments. As a sign of the divine revelation he had received, Moses had rays of light shining from his forehead. In the King James translation this is rendered less specifically as "the skin of his face shone" (Ex. 33:18-23; 34:29-30).

101-2] *Jethro's daughter . . . bondslave* The contrast here is based on an interpretation by B of OT texts which may suggest that Moses married first the Midianite woman Zipporah, daughter of the priest Jethro (alternate name Raguel), and later an unnamed Ethiopian woman. Some scholars hold that the same woman is meant in both narratives. See Ex. 2:16-21, Ex. 3:1, Ex. 18:1-4, and Num. 12:1.

120] *the last time* B means that he does not expect to speak again in his own voice in his poetry, but it is worth noting that while most of the poems in *Men and Women* underwent considerable correction and revision in later editions, B made very few changes to "One Word More" after the first edition.

121] *hair-brush* That is, a miniaturist's paintbrush, nearly as fine as a single hair, to do the delicate work in the margin of a missal (l. 125).

136] *Karshish, Cleon, Norbert* In the MS, B wrote *Karshook* for *Karshish,* thus referring to "Ben Karshook's Wisdom," which he wrote in 1854 and published in 1856 in *The Keepsake* (see "Ben Karshook's Wisdom" in the present volume). Though DeVane (*Hbk.,* 276) sees this as a "mere slip of the pen," it is reasonable to speculate that B had at least considered including "Ben Karshook's Wisdom" in *Men and Women. Cleon* refers to the poem of that title, and *Norbert* is from "In a Balcony," both in the present volume.

138] *Lippo, Roland, or Andrea* From, respectively, "Fra Lippo Lippi" and "'Childe Roland to the Dark Tower Came'" in *Men and*

Women I (vol. 5 of the present edition), and "Andrea del Sarto," in the present volume.
145] *Here . . . Florence* The Bs left Florence on 20 June 1855, travelled by way of Leghorn, Marseilles, and Paris, arriving in London on 12 July.
146] *thrice-transfigured* The moon had gone through three cycles between the time the Bs left Florence and the time of writing in September. The phrase may echo Shakespeare's *As You Like It,* 3.2.2, where the moon is termed "thrice-crowned."
148] *Fiesole* See "Andrea del Sarto," l. 15n. above.
150] *Samminiato* The Basilica of San Miniato al Monte stands on a hill in SE Florence, about a quarter mile from Casa Guidi.
157] *nothing . . . noteworthy* Perhaps recalling Shakespeare's *Antony and Cleopatra* 4.15.67-68, "And there is nothing left remarkable / Beneath the visiting moon."
158-60] *moon could love . . . mythos* The myth of the moon-goddess's love for a mortal youth exists in many versions with many cognates. The basic outline of the story (which B may be taking from *Endymion* by Keats, mentioned in l. 165) is that the virginal goddess of the moon—Selene, Luna, Diana, or Artemis by name—normally coldhearted and indifferent to love, is overwhelmed by the beauty of the young shepherd Endymion while he is asleep. The moon-goddess casts a spell on Endymion so that he sleeps eternally, never aging, retaining his beauty, but also never awakening to know his divine lover. The fact that B has Endymion awaken (l. 166) indicates that he is following Keats's elaboration of the myth.
163] *Zoroaster* The Persian prophet and teacher of the 6th century B.C. who founded the religion bearing his name. In Zoroastrianism, the sun, moon, planets, and stars are manifestations of Ormazd, god of light and goodness. The ancient Greeks and early Christians attributed the invention of astrology to Zoroaster.
164] *Galileo* The Italian astronomer Galileo Galilei (1564-1642), having made an immense improvement in the magnifying power of the telescope, discovered in 1609-10 that the surface of the moon was marked by craters and other irregularities. Galileo's observations of the moon from Fiesole are refered to in Milton's *Paradise Lost* (1.287-89), a passage alluded to by EBB in *Casa Guidi Windows* 1.1127, 1181-82.
165] *Homer . . . Keats* Among the Greek "Homeric Hymns" (once ascribed to Homer but now to Hesiod) are two songs addressed to goddesses of the moon: number 9 praises Artemis, and number 32 is a hymn to Selene. The latter was translated by Shelley with the title

"Homer's Hymn to the Moon," first published in the collected edition of 1839; B received a copy of the 1847 printing of this collection from the publisher Moxon (see *Reconstruction,* A2111). Keats's *Endymion* (1818) is an extended treatment of the myth of the moon-goddess's love for a mortal (see ll. 158-60n. above).

172-79] *paved work . . . saw God* Drawn from Ex. 24:9-11; in this shared vision on Mt. Sinai, Jehovah stands on (or above) a sapphire-blue pavement.

198-99] *Rafael . . . Inferno* See ll. 5-8, 32-49, and nn. above.

BEN KARSHOOK'S WISDOM

Publication and Date] "Ben Karshook's Wisdom" made its only appearance on p. 16 of the 1856 issue of *The Keepsake,* an annual edited by Marguerite A. Power and published in London from 1851 to 1857. The Bs contributed several poems to *The Keepsake,* including "May and Death" and part of "James Lee's Wife," both in *Dramatis Personæ,* below. In the 1856 *Keepsake,* "Ben Karshook's Wisdom" is dated "Rome, April 27, 1854"; this was near the end of the Bs' sojourn in Rome in the winter of 1853-54. P. Kelley and R. Hudson record one letter from B to Marguerite Power during the relevant period, dated 26 February 1855 (*The Browning's Correspondence, A Checklist* [New York, 1978], 414). If this letter (which has not been located) had to do with sending the poem for Power's annual, we may surmise that B had already removed "Ben Karshook's Wisdom" from *Men and Women*—if, indeed, he ever considered including it (see "One Word More, l. 136n., above). B never reprinted the poem in any of his collected editions.

Source] Though Karshook is imaginary, he appears to be based on Rabbi Eliezer ben Hyrkanos, though it is not known exactly how B came to know of him. DeVane (*Hbk.,* 558) proposes that the matter of the second stanza of the poem derives from a story in J. Knowles's edition of the *Life and Writings of H. Fuseli* (1831), a work B owned (*Reconstruction,* A1004); but neither the arguments nor the rhetoric of the two passages are truly parallel.

Title] Karshook's name, B said, meant "a thistle" in Hebrew (Hood, 196).

1] *rod* That is, the rod of divine punishment, as in 2 Sam. 7:14 and Isa. 10:5.

9] *Sadducee* The Sadducees were theologically conservative Jews in the period 100 B.C. to A.D. 100 who held that only the written Law was valid; thus they denied the existence of spirits, angels, and resurrection. Within Judaism, the sadducees were opposed by the Pharisees; they figure as enemies of Jesus in Matt. 3 and 16 and in Acts 4 and 5, contending with St. Paul in Acts 23:6-10.

17-18] *Hiram's-Hammer . . . column* The Tyrian master metalworker Hiram cast two gigantic decorated pillars for the entrance to Solomon's temple; the left column he named *Jachin,* meaning "It shall stand," and the right one *Boaz,* "In strength" (1 Kings 7:13-22, 2 Chron. 3:15-17).

EDITORIAL NOTES

DEDICATION AND ADVERTISEMENT TO EBB'S "LAST POEMS" (1862)

Composition and publication] References in his letters indicate that B composed these preliminaries for EBB's *Last Poems* in January of 1862 (Hudson, 95-96; McAleer, 93). The volume was published by Chapman and Hall on 20 March 1862.

The dedication echoes the inscription on a plaque placed by the city of Florence on Casa Guidi; the Italian inscription, composed by Niccolò Tommaseo, reads: "Here wrote and died / Elizabeth Barrett Browning / Who in her woman's heart reconciled / A scholar's learning and a poet's spirit / And whose poems forged a golden ring / Between Italy and England / Grateful Florence / Sets this memorial / 1861" (see McAleer, 95, 101, 144 and nn.).

Several references in the Advertisement require further explanation:

last June] M. Foster reports that after EBB's death on 29 June 1861, B "had her own list of everything she had written since her last collected edition" (*Elizabeth Barrett Browning, A Biography* [London, 1988], 369).

intended . . . friend] The "projected work" was an illustrated "Classical Album" with engravings of ancient gems, edited by Anne Thompson, whose acquaintance EBB made through mutual friends. Thompson solicited EBB's translations of various classical authors in the spring of 1845, but the work was never published. See G. Taplin, *The Life of Elizabeth Barrett Browning* (New Haven, 1957), 154; *Correspondence,* 10.157-58, 171, 327.

two . . . have subsequently appeared] The two poems had been published in EBB's *Poems* (1850); see *Reconstruction,* A8, D1207, D1257).

recent version] That is, EBB's translations from Heine, subtitled by B as "The Last Translation" and dated "Rome, 1860."

ADVERTISEMENT TO EBB'S "THE GREEK CHRISTIAN POETS AND THE ENGLISH POETS"

Composition and publication] Though this little preface is not signed, it was certainly written by B. As the custodian of EBB's writings and reputation, he was the only candidate to compose this introductory note to a compilation of EBB's early essays, and the "Advertisement" is executed in B's inimitable prose style. The oblique last paragraph refers to EBB's inclusion of B's own name among the promising young poets. B's sense of the need to tend EBB's literary legacy is feelingly expressed in several letters written in the months just before this volume came out; the language of the Advertisement echoes these letters (see McAleer, 142, 149). Chapman and Hall published the volume in March 1863.

POETICAL WORKS (1863 AND 1865)

Dedication] John Forster (1812-76), man of letters and literary entrepeneur, made numerous efforts to promote B's literary career in the 1830s, helping him with introductions and well-placed positive reviews. The relationship continued throughout Forster's life, though it was occasionally stormy; the fallings-out were always followed by reconciliations, one of which prevailed for some years after B returned to England in 1861. For an excellent sketch of the friendship, see *Correspondence,* 11.329-31; see also Irvine and Honan, 58-61, 63-68.

Notes to Volume I] B may have met John Kenyon (1784-1856), a cousin of EBB's and an old schoolmate of Robert Browning Sr.'s, as early as 1837. Both poets formed strong attachments to Forster, who encouraged them in every way. It was Kenyon who asked EBB if she wished to meet B, while simultaneously urging B to write to EBB. His assistance to the two poets went far beyond this, and he left them handsome sums of money in his will. For a sketch of Kenyon and his relationship with the Bs, see *Correspondence,* 3.316-18; see also Irvine and Honan, chapters 11-13.

The footnote, with its insistence on the distance between the poet and his speakers, is of great importance despite the failure of many readers and critics to absorb it.

EURYDICE TO ORPHEUS

Composition and date] The occasion for the poem was the exhibition of a painting entitled "Orpheus and Eurydice" by B's friend Frederic Leighton (1830-96). An unsigned manuscript of the poem was offered for sale by Anderson Galleries in 1920, and a signed manuscript dated 5 April 1864 was offered by Sotheby's in 1955; the present whereabouts of these MSS are unknown (see DeVane, *Hbk.,* 316; *Reconstruction,* E116, E117). The text appeared as a prose piece, signed "Robert Browning, A Fragment," in the Catalogue for the 1864 Royal Academy Exhibition, where the picture was shown. The Exhibition opened on 3 April 1864, thus providing a precise date for first publication. By the date of the abovementioned manuscript, the proofing of *Dramatic Personæ* was nearly finished, and B apparently made no effort to add "Eurydice to Orpheus" to the volume at that time. But the poem did appear in the 1865 *Selections* volume, and it was officially added to B's collected works as part of *Dramatis Personæ* in 1868. Leighton's "Orpheus and Eurydice" is now in Leighton House, London, its frame bearing B's lines. A discussion of the relation of poem and painting can be found in Catherine Maxwell, "Robert Browning and Frederic Leighton: 'Che Farò Senza Euridice?'" *RES* 44 (1993), 362.

Title] In Greek mythology the poet Orpheus married the nymph Eurydice. After her death from a snake bite, Orpheus went to the Underworld to seek her. Orpheus was granted permission to bring Eurydice back to the land of the living, so long as he did not look back at her as she followed him. But Orpheus did look back at his beloved, who thereupon vanished forever.

DRAMATIS PERSONÆ

Emendations to the Text

The following emendations have been made to the 1889 text:

James Lee's Wife, l. 217: The 1889 text lacks an apostrophe after *o,* present in all other texts; the apostrophe is restored.

The Worst of It, l. 26: All texts from MS through 1875 end this line with an exclamation point. The probable compositor's error eliminating any punctuation here creates an ungrammatical run-on sentence. The MS-1875 reading is restored.

Dîs Aliter Visum, l. 85: The MS ends this line with a single quotation mark, which correctly marks the end of an imagined speech. None of the printed texts includes this necessary punctuation; the MS reading is restored.

A Death in the Desert, l. 32: 1888-89 has damaged or missing punctuation at the end of the line. The colon present in MS-1875 is restored.

A Death in the Desert, l. 364: 1888-89 has a lower case *h* in the pronoun *he,* which refers to Jesus. Since all similar pronouns in this poem are capitalized, the P1864a-1875 reading *He* is inserted.

Caliban upon Setebos, l. 59: Since all other pronouns referring to Setebos are capitalized, the lower case *h* in *he* in this line is inconsistent. The MS-1868 reading *what He* is restored.

Caliban upon Setebos, l. 239: An apostrophe standing for an elided *he* at the beginning of this line disappeared in 1888, thus depriving the sentence of its implied subject. The MS-1875 reading is restored.

Caliban upon Setebos, ll. 283-84: P1864a-1875 have a rule between these lines to establish a shift in Caliban's discourse. 1888-89 has no rule, and

a page break eliminates any visible disjunction between the two lines. A paragraph space is inserted.
Mr. Sludge, "The Medium," ll. 39-40: A paragraph division appears between these lines, MS-1875. The paragraph was lost in 1888-89 and is restored.
Mr. Sludge, "The Medium," ll. 200-201: A paragraph division appears between these lines, MS-1875. The paragraph was lost in 1888-89 and is restored.
Mr. Sludge, "The Medium," ll. 346-47: A paragraph division appears between these lines, MS-1875. The paragraph was lost in 1888-89 and is restored.
Mr. Sludge, "The Medium," l. 462: The comma after *sir* is missing in 1888-89, though space for it remains. The MS-1875 reading is restored.
Mr. Sludge, "The Medium," l. 650: MS-1875 have a comma after *Whereas,* but there is no punctuation here in 1888-89. The comma is restored.
Mr. Sludge, "The Medium," l. 707: P1864a-1888 have a semicolon after *land;* in DC, B changed the printed semicolon to a comma. Misrecording the 1888 reading as a comma, B "corrected" by removing the punctuation entirely, and 1889 has none. Since the syntax requires some punctuation, the semicolon is restored.
Mr. Sludge, "The Medium," ll. 731-32: A paragraph division appears between these lines, MS-1875. The paragraph was lost in 1888-89 and is restored.
Mr. Sludge, "The Medium," ll. 1122: MS-1875 end this line with an exclamation point. 1888 shows the fragmentary remains of a punctuation mark, and 1889 has no punctuation here. The exclamation point is restored.
Mr. Sludge, "The Medium," ll. 1174: P1864a-1875 end this line with a period; there is no punctuation here in 1888. Both DC and BrU call for a period, but the correction was not made in 1889. The line is emended to conform to DC-BrU.
Mr. Sludge, "The Medium," ll. 1202: MS-1875 have a colon at the end of this line. 1888 has no punctuation; DC and BrU call for a comma and a dash. The copy-text is emended to conform to DC and BrU.
Mr. Sludge, "The Medium," ll. 1513-14: A paragraph division appears between these lines, P1864a-1875. The paragraph was lost in 1888-89 and is restored.

Text and Publication

The textual history of *Dramatis Personæ* is perhaps the most elaborate in the B corpus; there are eleven distinct stages of composition or revision for the entire volume (MS, P1864a, CP1864a, 1864a, 1864a(r), 1864b, 1868, 1870, 1875, 1888, 1889), with additional manuscripts and prior publications of some poems and parts of poems. The major steps in the development of the text are discussed below.

The Morgan Manuscript (MS) The printer's-copy manuscript of *Dramatis Personæ,* presented by B to Frederick Chapman after publication and now housed in the Pierpont Morgan Library (*Reconstruction,* E101), was probably assembled—except for the "Epilogue"—early in 1863. It consists of 217 leaves of faintly lined paper and is written in ink on one side only. The leaves are numbered erratically, often in B's hand and at other times by someone else; B supplied half-titles for all of the poems and sequential numbers for all but the last two. Page divisions and the names of compositors assigned to set the types appear throughout the MS. Some of the pieces were fair-copied from earlier drafts ("A Face") and others from previously published fragments ("James Lee's Wife," "May and Death"). Considered as a whole, the Morgan MS is characterized by a regularity of penmanship and ink color strongly suggesting that much of it was executed in a short time under consistent circumstances. But "Mr. Sludge, 'The Medium'" is heavily revised throughout, and the presence of numerous small alterations elsewhere indicates that B had time to go over the entire MS again.

The Yale and Berg Proofs (*P1864a*) There was time for B to polish his MS because the publication of *Dramatis Personæ* was purposely delayed for over a year. A volume of selections from his earlier works, prepared by his old friends John Forster and Bryan Procter in 1862, proved successful enough for Chapman and Hall to produce a new collected edition (the three-volume *Poetical Works* of 1863). This was the beginning of a most gratifying advance in B's British reputation and readership. Frustrated for years by what he saw as obtuse and offensive criticism, he reflected on the literary world's recent change of heart: "Seriously, now that I care not one whit about what I never cared for too much, people are getting goodnatured to my poems. There's printing a book of 'Selections from RB' . . . which is to popularize my old things: & so & so means to review it, and somebody or [other] always was looking out for such an occasion, and what's his name always said he admired me, only he didn't say it, though he said something else every week of his life in some Journal. The breath of man!" (Hudson, 101). But while the new edition was in press, *Dramatis Personæ* was held back: "My old books are getting printed, and so slowly that I shall not be able to bring out the new book till Autumn," he complained in March of 1863 (McAleer, 128). It was in fact well into the new year before the volume came out; typesetting and proofing were probably done after B's return from France in October 1863.

Two sets of proofs of the first English edition of *Dramatis Personæ* —identical in every printed detail but one—survive today; one set is in the Tinker Library at Yale University, the other in the Berg Collection of the New York Public Library (see *Reconstruction,* A419 and E102). The two sets represent a very late stage of proofing, but each contains some alterations in B's hand; neither is the set which actually went back to Chapman's printers (Clowes and Co.) bearing B's final revisions. The only difference between the printed readings in these two documents is the presence of the words "London, April 12, 1864," printed at the end of the last page of the Yale proofs. This date does not appear in the MS or in the first English edition; B probably wrote it at the end of a previous set of proofs to signify his readiness to go to press. The date does appear at the end of the American first edition, authorized but not proofed by B and published simultaneously with the English first by Osgood and Company of Boston. The set of proofs which B sent to his old friend James T. Fields for use in setting up the American edition must have been a duplicate of the Yale proofs, date and all. The Yale proofs themselves are most likely the set B kept for a record of his revisions, as indicated by the fact that they were eventually presented by B to his sister Sarianna. The Berg proofs were produced slightly later, and with a specifiic purpose: B's acquaintance Moncure Daniel Conway had arranged to review *Dramatis Personæ* in several journals immediately upon publication. It is likely that B, unwilling to give up his own set of proofs, arranged for a fresh set to be struck off, and in the process ordered the removal of the essentially meaningless date, the inclusion of which may have been a compositor's mistake. B sent the fresh proofs, with hand alterations almost identical to those on the Yale set, to Conway to 26 April 1864 (DeVane and Knickerbocker, 160); these proofs are now in the Berg Collection. Printed readings from these proofs are coded *P1864a* in the variant listings; B's corrections to them are coded *CP1864a.*

The First English Edition (*1864a*) Chapman and Hall published *Dramatis Personæ* on 28 May 1864; the book was bound in maroon pebble-grain cloth and priced rather high at seven shillings. The text of this edition incorporates all but one of the changes Browning made to the Yale proofs; two of the revisions were made differently in the first edition. Despite their recent successes with B's poems, Chapman and Hall proceeded cautiously with the new book, and kept the size of the first impression of *Dramatis Personæ* down, probably to fewer than a thousand copies. But for the first time in his career, and with the help of numerous good reviews, B's work was popular enough to sell out a first printing. By August 1864, a second print run of *Dramatis Personæ* was in process, giving B another opportunity to revise his text.

The Second English "Edition" (1864b) B revised his poems by entering his changes in a copy of the existing edition; this was a common practice among successful Victorian authors. The copy that he used for this purpose survives today; it too is in the Tinker Library at Yale (see *Reconstruction,* E103). The numerous small alterations are all in B's hand, done very carefully and with clear instructions to the printers; he has added the proud words "Second Edition" to the title page. The major textual development was the addition of three stanzas to "Gold Hair" (see below); these B wrote in a space at the end of the poem on page thirty-four, marking the lines for insertion on page thirty-two. Use of the Hinman Collator shows that all of his revisions were worked into the types left standing from the first edition. B's hand-written revisions in this copy of 1864a are coded *1864a(r)* in the variant listings.

To make the most of Browning's surprising marketability, Chapman and Hall differentiated their so-called second edition of *Dramatis Personæ* as much as they could from the first, while still using the same types to print from. The title-page may say "Second Edition" (and this was accurate enough by the standards of the Victorian book trade), but bibliographically speaking this was a revised second impression of the original typesetting. Still, the differences between the two impressions are plain to see. Small revisions were made throughout the text, and the additional stanzas in "Gold Hair" required resetting in two gatherings; pagination, however, was not affected. The second impression was bound in blue cloth, contrasting with the dull red of the first; the date on the title-page remained 1864. Demand for *Dramatis Personæ* was not sustained, and when B parted company with Chapman and Hall in 1866, he acquired a number of copies of the unbound sheets of the second impression in settling with the publisher. The Smith, Elder account books show that B was paid for these by his new publisher, who at some point bound up the sheets, still bearing Chapman's name on the title page, in blue boards with "Smith, Elder & Co." at the foot of the spine.

Collected Editions The poems of *Dramatis Personæ* were included in B's collected editions from 1868 onward, with "Eurydice to Orpheus" and "Deaf and Dumb" becoming part of *Dramatis Personæ* at that time. In this and the subsequent collected editions, B conducted his usual process of careful, minor revision and correction. Variant readings from all these editions are included in our collations, as are the scattered corrections (coded *C1870*) he made in a copy of the 1870 *Poetical Works* (discussed in *Men and Women II, Text,* above).

Among uncollated texts are "Gold Hair," "Prospice," and lines 152-231 of "James Lee's Wife," as published in the *Atlantic Monthly* in 1864 (13:79, 596-99; 13:80, 694 and 737-38). These publications derived from the set of proofs B had sent to James T. Fields and were essentially promotional material for the forthcoming American edition of *Dramatis Personæ* (DeVane, *Hbk.*, 284, erroneously characterizes these as piracies). There is no evidence that B in any way controlled these magazine texts, or that he ever reused or consulted them later; they branch off from the proof texts he had approved earlier. Also uncollated are the texts of parts or all of seven poems from *Dramatis Personæ* as republished in *A Selection from the Works of Robert Browning* (London: Moxon, 1865). B unquestionably did read proof of this volume (see *Reconstruction,* E432) and even provided a brief preface for it, which we include in the present volume. But again, these texts of the poems are offshoots of the 1864 editions, not steps connecting them to the next collected edition. Such materials as these, while of inherent scholarly interest, lack the textual authority necessary to be included in our collations of variant readings. They either lie outside the line of textual descent or were not produced under B's supervision.

Title

Memorable though the title of B's 1864 volume may be, he apparently was inclined to reuse the title *Men and Women* in some way for his next collection. As far back as January of 1859, EBB employed the phrase in worrying over B's dilatory attentions to his writing while they were in Rome: "He is plunged into gaieties of all sorts . . . . So plenty of distraction, and no Men and Women" (*Letters of EBB* 2.303). And in late 1862, when B expected his book to come out the following spring, he wrote: "I hope to print a new book of "Men & Women" (or under some such name) in April or May" (McAleer, 128). To mimic his earlier collection was still tentatively in his thoughts in September 1863: "I bring out two volumes of new things (men & women—but under some other name, to please the publisher)" (Hudson, 130). Precisely when and why B changed his mind are unknown, but perhaps adopting a new title had something to do with his desire to break with the past as he expressed it to the Storys in August 1861: "I want my new life to resemble the last fifteen years as little as possible" (Hudson, 77).

Composition

Some of the work that finally appeared in the 1864 volume was composed as early as 1836 (the first stanza of section 8 of "James Lee's Wife"); some poems were written in the late 1850s ("May and Death," "Caliban upon Setebos"); while others ("Mr. Sludge, 'The Medium,'" "Epilogue") joined the collection in 1863. B was living through a period of great change and accomplishment in these latter years. The change was drastic, painful, and permanent: on 29 June 1861, EBB died in Florence, and on 1 August B left Italy for England, where he made his home until the last year of his life. His return to London was attended by a rapid rise in his literary reputation, but emotionally and poetically he was paralyzed for months. By August of 1862 he had begun to write again, "whether I like it or no" (McAleer, 119). He began to add new poems to a collection that had been slowly growing. In 1865 B said of the poems in *Dramatis Personæ* that "most have been written a long time ago—some were seen by Ba" (McAleer, 212). A fair amount must have been done before EBB's death, since B told Isa Blagden that "most of what you saw at Siena [in the summer of 1860] will be brought out" in *Dramatis Personæ* (McAleer, 180). In March 1861, EBB had written that though B had not been working regularly at writing, "he has the material for a volume" (*Letters of EBB,* 2.436). Still, a fair number of the poems in *Dramatis Personæ* unquestionably reflect or derive from B's visits to France in 1862 and 1863. Scholars have also argued that "A Death in the Desert" and "Mr. Sludge, 'The Medium'" were composed mainly after EBB's death, but if we subtract those works and the French poems, there could hardly have been enough "material for a volume" in 1861. As his remarks to Isa Blagden show (see *Title* n., above), B himself thought of the collection as substantially complete by late 1862, though he seems to have decided to include "Mr. Sludge" after this. The heterogeneous nature of *Dramatis Personæ* illustrates the wide variety of experiences and emotions B underwent in his middle years. Additional information about the composition of individual poems appears in the notes below.

JAMES LEE'S WIFE

Composition and date] The poem as we find it today is the result of a process of amalgamation and revision that began in the 1830s. The earliest component of the text is lines 152-81, now stanzas 1-6 of section 6. These lines appeared under the title "Lines" in the *Monthly Repository*

10:112 (April 1836), 270-71, bearing the signature "Z" which B had used on previous publications in the same journal. Over twenty years passed before the next discernable stage of composition. In August of 1857 B sent a manuscript of ll. 244-69 (now stanza 1 of section 8) entitled "Study of a Hand, by Lionardo" to Marguerite Power, editor of *The Keepsake* annual (where B had published "Ben Karshook's Wisdom" in 1856). This MS apparently accompanied MSS of "May and Death" (see below) and two poems by EBB, "Amy's Cruelty" and "My Heart and I," all to be considered by Power for publication; the four MSS are now housed in the ABL (*Reconstruction,* E203, E246, D31, D559). "May and Death" and "Amy's Cruelty" were published in *The Keepsake* in 1857, but not this piece of "James Lee's Wife" or EBB's "My Heart and I." Another MS of this passage, dated 23 May 1860, is reported to have been put up for sale in 1935 (see *Reconstruction,* E204), but its present location is unknown. When B constructed the poem in the Morgan MS, he used only roman numerals to identify each part; the very effective section titles were added during the proofing process.

DeVane (*Hbk.,* 284-85) rightly observes that the poem evokes the scenery of coastal Brittany, where B stayed for many weeks in the summers of 1861-63, and some details in the poem come directly from places he saw (W. H. Griffin and H. C. Minchin, *The Life of Robert Browning* [New York, 1910], 229). The bleak isolation of the area proved harmonious with the mood of the poet after the death of EBB, and during his second stay in Brittany he wrote to Isa Blagden "[I] mean to keep writing, whether I like it or no" (McAleer, 119). The pre-existing fragments were incorporated into "James Lee's Wife" by the spring of 1863, when the printer's copy MS of *Dramatis Personæ* was assembled; there the poem bore the title "James Lee." This MS does not include any of the section titles, which B added while proofing the first English edition. The titles for sections 1 and 6 were altered for the second impression of the first edition. In the 1868 *Poetical Works,* B's next opportunity for revision, lines 270-330 (comprising all of stanza 2 and most of stanza 3 in section 8) were added, and the speaker of the poem was clearly indicated by changing the title to "James Lee's Wife." With this the poem finally achieved its full, stable state of being, the usual revisions in punctuation and spelling being made in the collected editions of 1870, 1875, and 1888-89.

B expressed his view of the poem's situation in a letter to Julia Wedgwood shortly after the publication of *Dramatis Personæ:* "I meant them [to be] people newly-married, trying to realize a dream of being sufficient to each other, in a foreign land . . . and finding it break up,

—the man being *tired* first,—and tired precisely of the love" (*Robert Browning and Julia Wedgwood,* ed. R. Curle [New York, 1937], 109).

73-74] *magpie . . . rebuff* A rare lapse in B's knowledge of natural history: the magpie (*Pica pica*) does not migrate.

104-6] *To watch . . . Book assures* Olive oil and wine are emblematic of plenty and prosperity in the Bible; see, for example, Deut. 8:7-10, Joel 2:24, and II Kings 18:32.

137] *warhorse . . . chanfroned* In medieval armory, *bard* is leather armor for the body of a horse, and a *chamfron* (which B's "chanfroned" derives from) is the headpiece.

138-39] *quixote-mage . . . all right* B is recalling the passage in Part 1, Chapter 3 of Cervantes' *Don Quixote* (1605) in which Don Quixote is told that wounded knights may get help from "some sage magician to aid them at once by fetching through the air on a cloud some damsel or dwarf with a vial of water of such power that by tasting one drop of it they were cured" (*Don Quixote,* ed. J. R. Jones and K. Douglas [New York, 1981], 35).

152-211] *Still . . . assigns* The book referred to in the title of this section must be the *Monthly Repository* for 1836, where B had published stanzas 1-6. Thus the commentary on the poet who wrote these lines and that poet's bitter knowledge gained in later years (ll. 182-211) is a sardonic piece of self-interpretation on B's part.

227-28] *grave . . . palms* Is. 49:16.

237] *sea-lark* Probably the Shore Lark (*Eremophila alpestris,* known as the Horned Lark in North America) which winters on shingle beaches in SE England and Brittany.

244] *As like . . . Hand* B may be alluding to his own work again; ll. 311-12 of "Saul" read "a Hand like this hand / Shall throw open the gates of new life to thee!"

270-71] *clay cast . . . live once* Though not a direct allusion, the image calls to mind Harriet Hosmer's casting of the clasped hands of B and EBB. See *Reconstruction,* H538.

300] *Da Vinci* Leonardo da Vinci (1452-1519) was a master of detailed and evocative line drawings of the human figure.

311-19] *Learning . . . sole sake* Da Vinci developed his anatomical expertise through intense study with a physician. According to Vasari, Leonardo "filled a book with drawings in red crayons, outlined with the pen, all copies made with the utmost care from bodies dissected by his own hand. In this book he set forth the entire structure, arrangement, and disposition of the bones, to which he afterwards added all the nerves, in their due order, and next supplied the muscles" (2.163).

GOLD HAIR: A STORY OF PORNIC

Composition and date] The poem certainly derives from B's stay on the Breton coast near Pornic in August and September of 1862; this was his first of several visits to the village of Sainte Marie, and by March 1863 he was thinking of *Dramatis Personæ* as a book ready for publication (see *Dramatic Personæ, Composition* above). In a letter of 18 August 1862, B wrote that he "wrote a poem yesterday of 120 lines," and of the poems in *Dramatis Personæ,* "Gold Hair" seems the most likely candidate for this description (McAleer, 119). In its earliest surviving state, a fair copy in the Morgan MS, "Gold Hair" contains 135 lines in twenty-six stanzas of five lines each. The proof and published forms of the first edition contained numerous revisions to punctuation and wording, but the major change in "Gold Hair" occurred after the first impression of the first edition had been issued. DeVane (*Hbk.,* 286) records an anecdote about the inclusion of three new stanzas in the poem for the second impression. It is said that B called upon George Eliot and G. H. Lewes at their London home on a Sunday in 1864. The novelist pointed out that "Gold Hair" as it stood did not adequately account for the presence of the gold coins in the girl's coffin. B took Eliot's copy of *Dramatis Personæ* home and composed the three additional stanzas of explanation, which became lines 101-15 of the poem. These stanzas B wrote into Eliot's book, and they also appear on page thirty-four of the copy of the first edition which he altered as copy for the second impression. The story comes from *Literary Anecdotes of the Nineteenth Century,* ed. W. R. Nicoll and T. J. Wise (London, 1895) 1.377. Though the only visit by B to the Priory that Eliot recorded during the relevant period occurred on 10 November 1864 (a Thursday), B was a regular in the Sunday literary gatherings that Eliot and Lewes hosted in the 1860s (*The George Eliot Letters,* ed. G. Haight [New Haven, CT, 1954-78], 4.167-68; F. R. Karl, *George Eliot: Voice of a Century,* [New York, 1995], 391).

Source] Mrs. Orr (303) reports that the story of "Gold Hair" was believed in Pornic to be historical, and that it was commonly told in 19th century guidebooks.

2] *Pornic* A small harbor town on the coast of Brittany, about 30 miles W of Nantes. B visited this region repeatedly on summer holidays from the 1860s onward. He mentioned Saint Gilles church, referred to in l. 54, in a letter of 18 August 1862 and recorded its destruction when he was visiting again in 1865 (McAleer, 119, 219).

3] *Loire* The longest river in France, rising in the S and flowing N and W, ending in a large estuary just N of Pornic.

4] *Brittany* A large region of W France, reaching into the Atlantic S of the British Isles.
16] *flix* Soft, downy hair.
72] *pavement* The stone floor of the church.
84] *pelf* A contemptuous term for money.
86-87] *O cor . . . caeca* "Oh human heart, blind souls." Derived from Lucretius, *De Rerum Natura (On the Nature of Things)*, 2.14.
90] *double Louis d'or* A valuable gold coin, issued in France from the reign of Louis XIII through Louis XVI.
127-30] *price of sin . . . Potter's Field* In Matt. 27:3-10, the repentant Judas gives the thirty pieces of silver he got for betraying Jesus back to the priests, who use it to purchase a burial for strangers called "the potter's field."
143-45] *Essays-and-Reviews . . . Colenso's words* A collection of articles on religion by seven authors was published in 1860 under the title *Essays and Reviews.* Echoing the Higher Critics, the essays temperately argued for a more liberal and less literal interpretation of the Bible; the book met with ferocious opposition, and two of its authors were convicted of heresy by an ecclesiastical court. Before this controversy had abated, John William Colenso (1814-83), Bishop of Natal, published the first of the seven parts of *The Pentateuch and Book of Joshua Critically Examined* (1862-79), a work which challenged scriptural authority and also got its author accused of heresy. EBB took note of the *Essays and Reviews* controversy in 1861 (*Letters of EBB,* 2.426-27), and B takes up the subject at length in "A Death in the Desert" (see below).
149] *Original Sin* The uniquely Christian doctrine which asserts that because all humans are descended from Adam, all share in the guilt of Adam's fall into sin. Thus even the newly-born are guilty of Original Sin, from which they may be absolved by baptism.

THE WORST OF IT

39] *myrrh* An aromatic resin which was wrapped in with the body of Jesus before his burial and resurrection (John 19:39).
40] *Shall . . . borne* Deriving from the vision of heaven in Rev. 7:9.
69] *loop* An obsolete term for a narrow window in a fortification.

DÎS ALITER VISUM

Date] Details of the setting (ll. 9, 19-22, 26-30, 42) suggest that the poem draws on B's visits to the coast of Brittany in 1861-63.

Title] The title comes from Virgil, *Aeneid* 2.428, and means "the gods see things differently" or "the gods thought otherwise."
Subtitle] The French subtitle means "the Byron of our time," and depends for its irony on B's ambivalent attitudes towards Bryon. While admiring him, B also felt that Byron's artistic energy, personal courage, and defiance of convention were undercut by his persistent cynicism and pettiness. EBB adored Byron (see *Letters of EBB,* 1.115); for B's views, see Irvine & Honan, 13-16, 226-27; W. H. Griffin and H. C. Minchin, *The Life of Robert Browning* [New York, 1910], 42 & nn.
26] *the church* B may be recalling either Pornic church (see "Gold Hair," 2n. above) or the nearby church at Sainte Marie; see McAleer, 119, 219, 223.
36] *Schumann's our music-maker* Robert Schumann (1810-56), German composer. After his death, his widow Clara (1819-96) began a series of concert tours which significantly raised her husband's reputation as a composer. In 1861 B acquired a collection of piano music that included works by Schumann (*Reconstruction,* A1699), and he vividly described the playing of Schumann's "Carnaval" in *Fifine at the Fair* (1872).
37] *march-movement* Several of Schumann's collections of character pieces include march movements or sections.
38] *Ingre's . . . paints* Jean August Ingres (1780-1867), "the most generally admired French painter of his day and . . . one of the most influential" (*Oxford Companion to Art,* s.v. "Ingres"). Ingres shunned public display of his work after 1834, but he was lured out of seclusion in 1855 by the promise of a gallery devoted entirely to his work at the Paris International Exposition. The Bs were in Paris 24 June-11 July 1855 and returned there 17 October, staying until 29 June 1856.
40] *Heine* Heinrich Heine (1797-1856), German poet, satirist and journalist who became quite popular in England in the 1850s and 1860s. George Eliot published a long article on Heine in the *Westminster Review* in January 1856, and Matthew Arnold's essay on Heine appeared in the August 1863 issue of *The Cornhill Magazine,* a journal B knew well. B also included EBB's adaptation of some stanzas from Heine in her *Last Poems* (London, 1862).
42] *votive-frigate* A model ship hung from the ceiling of a church as a pious offering for the protection of mariners or as thanks for a safe voyage.
58] *Sure . . . Arm-chair* The armchair is emblematic of a place in the French Academy, which is limited to forty members.
64] *the Three per Cents* Famously safe investments in government securities yielding three percent per year.

102] *Norman* In the style of English and French church architecture of the 11th and 12th centuries.
138] *Rose-jacynth* Rosy-orange in color; several orange semi-precious stones were once called "jacinth."

TOO LATE

75-76] *rat belled the cat* This derives from a fable attributed to Aesop called "The Mice in Council," in which a mouse suggests tying a bell around the neck of the cat to warn the mice of her approach (*The Fables of Aesop and Others,* ed. E. Rhys [London, 1958], 50).
87-88] *your pink of poets* Though *pink* is usually glossed as "the best or most exquisite," the derision expressed in the following lines suggests a sarcastic usage. More than half of the definitions of *pink* offered in the *OED* bear a negative connotation of triviality.
93] *Tekel* *Tekel* is one of the words written on the wall at Belshazzar's feast; Daniel interprets the word as "Thou art weighed in the balances, and art found wanting" (Dan. 5:27).
96] *tagging* Stringing together; see *OED,* s.v. "Tag," v.1, 3b.
112] *prog* Food obtained by scrounging or begging.
138] *summum jus* Latin for "the most thorough exercise of justice."

ABT VOGLER

Composition and sources] B's knowledge of Vogler dates from his youth, when he was trained by a musician who followed Vogler's approach to teaching and playing. Though there is no direct clue as to the poem's date of composition, its similarities to the "poems with more music and painting" that B included in *Men and Women* suggest that it may have been written early enough to be one of the poems that EBB considered "the material for a volume" in 1861 (see "Andrea del Sarto," *Composition* and *Dramatis Personæ, Composition,* both above). B was an enthusiastic and accomplished keyboard musician with strong views on musical taste (see "A Toccata of Galuppi's" and "Master Hugues of Saxe-Gotha" in *Men and Woman I,* 5.197, 285, and nn.; see also J. Maynard, *Browning's Youth* [Cambridge, MA, 1977], 140-43).
Title] Georg Joseph Vogler (1749-1814), usually known as Abbé or Abt Vogler, was born in Germany, but his court positions and travels took him all over Europe. His students were numerous; Browning's piano teacher John Relfe (1763-1837) was a disciple of Vogler's teaching method (J. Maynard, *Browning's Youth* [Cambridge, MA, 1977], 142-43; 423, n. 54; 424, n. 58). The "instrument of his own invention" in the

subtitle is the orchestrion, a portable organ designed by Abt Vogler. This remarkable instrument had four keyboards of five octaves each, and a pedal board of thirty-six keys, all packed into a three foot high cube (P-C, 5.308).

3-5] *Solomon . . . fly* The attribution to Solomon of the power to summon demons and spirits derives from extra-biblical sources with which B was quite familiar. Such diverse ancient writings as *The Wisdom of Solomon, The Testament of Solomon, The Koran,* the *Antiquities* of Josephus, and the *Arabian Nights* all credit Solomon with magical powers deriving from his possession of a magic seal ring inscribed with the secret name of God. Which of these, or what other works, may have served as B's sources is unknown. See *A Dictionary of Biblical Tradition in English Literature,* ed. D. L. Jeffrey (Grand Rapids, MI, 1992), s.v. "Solomon."

7] *ineffable name* The "unspeakable name of God" (P-C, 5.309).

19] *rampired* Strengthened by piling up materials, as in the construction of ramparts.

22-23] *great illumination . . . Rome's dome* The great dome of the basilica of St. Peter in Rome was illuminated on special occasions; DeVane asserts that Browning witnessed this at Easter-time in 1854 (*The Shorter Poems of Robert Browning* [New York, 1934], 369).

34] *Prototplast* Original from which copies are made, or the creator of original forms.

39] *What . . . shall be* Adapted from the "Gloria Patri" in the *Book of Common Prayer.*

66] *Builder . . . hands* Derived from 2 Cor. 5:1.

72] *perfect round* Though such ring imagery is commonplace in B's poetry, it is worth note that EBB used this phrase in quotation marks in a letter to B of 19 May 1846 (Kintner, 714).

82] *fulness of the days* See Eph. 1:10.

91] *common chord* A name for the major triad, the three-note chord consisting of the root, major third, and fifth.

93] *ninth* A four note chord consisting of the root and the third, fifth, and ninth intervals. The dissonances of a ninth chord strongly demand resolution into the tonic chord.

95] *dared and done* Closely echoing the final line of Christopher Smart's "Song to David" (1763), a poem B admired so much that he memorized it (J. Maynard, *Browning's Youth* [Cambridge, MA, 1977], 317 and n.).

96] *C Major* The final, resolving tonic chord in the cadence Abt Vogler has been playing

RABBI BEN EZRA

Composition and Sources] Though it is not known which works of Rabbi Ben Ezra B knew, as a young man he studied Hebrew seriously enough to read Genesis in the original (J. Maynard, *Browning's Youth* [Cambridge, MA, 1977], 312-13). B had a lifelong interest in Hebrew literature and Judaica, as did EBB; his father's library contained works in this field, including a translation with commentary of *The Itinerary of Benjamin of Tudela* which B certainly read (*Reconstruction,* A194; *Robert Browning and Julia Wedgwood,* ed. R. Curle [New York, 1937], 41). He had referred to Rabbi Ben Ezra in "Holy Cross Day" (see above), published in 1855. DeVane's conjecture that "Rabbi Ben Ezra" is a response to FitzGerald's *Rubáiyát of Omar Khayyám* (*Hbk,* 293) cannot be verified from B's letters, but the chronology is suggestive. Fitzgerald's poem was almost completely ignored by the public when it was first published in 1859. In 1861, D. G. Rossetti began to promote the work, some copies of which he had found in a book shop. B's acquaintance with Rossetti dated from at least 1847, and in the early 1860s the two poets met frequently (see DeVane and Knickerbocker, 128n., 150; McAleer, 98, 106, 136, 138). It is plausible, then, that B encountered the *Rubáiyát* through Rossetti, and it is possible that "Rabbi Ben Ezra" was written thereafter; but the circumstances alone do not firmly establish a date of composition.

Title] Abraham Ben Meir Ibn Ezra (c.1092-1167), born at Toledo in Spain, was a poet, philosopher, and scholar who wrote important commentaries on the OT. He also made an important contribution in philology by laying the foundations of Hebrew grammar.

5-6] *whole I planned . . . nor be afraid* Perhaps echoing Is. 54:4.

11] *Jove* The planet Jupiter, "Jove" being the Latin name for the god; in astrology, Jupiter and Mars symbolize contrasting destinies.

150] *wheel . . . shaped* The figure of humans, particularly the Israelites, as clay in the hands of God the potter is used frequently in the OT; see, for example, Is. 64:8 and Jer. 18:6.

161] *was . . . be* See "Abt Vogler," l. 39n., above.

190] *My times be in Thy hand* See Ps. 31:15.

A DEATH IN THE DESERT

Composition and Sources] In the absence of direct evidence, it is impossible to fix the date of this poem precisely. Those scholars who argue, as DeVane does (*Hbk,* 295-96), for a later date emphasize B's reading of E. Renan's *La Vie de Jésus* in November of 1863 (McAleer, 180). But others, including W. O. Raymond (*The Infinite Moment* [Toronto, 1965], 19-37), argue that B had been interested in the issues raised by the Higher Criticism since at least 1850, when he published *Christmas-Eve and Easter-Day* (see the present edition, 5.49-133 and nn.). A hint that the poem was composed early in the history of *Dramatis Personæ* may lie in B's view of the volume as substantially complete by the winter of 1861-62 (see *Dramatis Personæ, Title* and *Composition,* above).

Whether or not B had read Renan by the time he wrote "A Death in the Desert," he was familiar with numerous works involved in the mid-century debates about scriptural history and authority, as his references to *Essays and Reviews* and Bishop Colenso in "Gold Hair" demonstrate (see "Gold Hair," ll. 143-45n. above). The wide range of works which B may have known is treated at length in Makio Yoshikado's Master's thesis, "Browning and Higher Criticism in 'A Death in the Desert' " (Baylor University, 1986), which proposes D. F. Strauss's *Das Leben Jesu* (1835-36), L. Feuerbach's *Das Wesen des Christentums* (1841), and the works of F. C. Baur as influences. B's own familiarity with problems of textual transmission and corruption, a result of his long study of ancient languages and literatures, enhanced his appreciation of the mixture of scholarly and religious difficulties raised by the Higher Critics.

A direct source for many phrases in the poem is the body of biblical material attributed to John, including the Gospel of John, three Epistles, and the Book of Revelation. Though biblical scholars have long concluded that the apostle John, the author of the Gospel of John, and the author of the Book of Revelation were at least three different people, B treats them all as one person.

Text] In the Morgan MS, each of the irregular verse-paragraphs is consecutively numbered, from 1 through 28, in a hand which may be B's; these arabic numerals are not to be found in any printed text of the poem.

1] *Pamphylax the Antiochene* The Greek name *Pamphylax* means "all-guarding"; this purported possessor of the scrolls is an imaginary resident of Antioch. Two ancient cities named Antioch were the sites of early Christian settlements. The one in Syria became a center of early Christianity, but since the other Antioch was in a district of SW Asia Minor called Pamphylia, this latter one is probably what B intends. The poem presumably takes place in neither Antioch, but rather in Ephesus (see l. 361n.), where according to tradition John died c. AD 100.

4] *Episilon . . . Mu* The fifth and twelfth letters of the Greek alphabet, here marking sections of the manuscript.

7] *Xi* The fourteenth letter of the Greek alphabet.
8] *Xanthus* An imaginary follower of John; B used this name the same way in *Sordello,* 3.996 (see the present edition, 2.228 and n).
23] *decree* Presumably an order for the suppression of Christianity, perhaps issued by Trajan, who was Emperor of Rome when John is said to have died.
30] *Valens* Another imaginary character.
36] *Bactrian* Bactria is the ancient name for a region in N Iran.
39] *quitch* A particularly tenacious weedy grass.
50] *nard . . . perfume* Spikenard (*Nardostachys jatamansi*) is a plant which was distilled to make a perfume highly prized in the ancient world.
64] *I am . . . Life* John 11:25
69] *lone desert-bird that wears the ruff* Probably the Egyptian Vulture (*Neophron percnopterus*), which has a ruff of feathers at its neck and is of solitary habit.
73-74] *James . . . John* The apostles James and John were brothers, and were also fishermen, as were the apostle Peter and his brother Andrew. John, James, and Peter formed an inner circle around Jesus and were present at the transfiguration of Jesus and at the garden of Gethsemane.
82-104] *This is the doctrine . . . Theotypas* The doctrine of the tripartite soul is more Platonic than Christian. Theotypas is fictional, and the uncertainty about who is speaking these lines mimics the problems of textual authority confronted by the Higher Criticism. A *glossa* is an explanatory note.
115] *James . . . death* The apostles James and Peter were executed around AD 44 and AD 64, respectively.
122-23] *head . . . stars* Rev. 1:14-16.
131-32] *Saw . . . hands* 1 John 1:1
135-37] *whom . . . saw* See 1 John 1:1-3.
140-41] *Patmos . . . write* Rev. 1:9-11. *Patmos* is the island in the Aegean to which John was banished because of his testimony about Jesus. In a cave on Patmos John had the vision recorded in the book of Revelation.
147-48] *taught . . . believe* 2 John 3-6 concerns the commandment to love one another.
149] *letter to a friend* Like 2 John, 3 John is a letter to a fellow Christian; the former is addressed to an "elect lady," and the latter to a man named Gaius.
158] *Antichrist* An antagonist of Christ in John's vision, the hideous

"beast" of Rev. 13 and 17, is given the name *antichrist* in 1 John 2:18, 2:22, and 4:3, and in 2 John 7.

160] *Jasper* The name of the young skeptic who asks for proof in l. 162.

163] *call down fire* See Luke 9:54-55.

165] *Pick up . . . serpent* See Luke 10:19.

177] *Where . . . coming* 2 Peter 3:4.

186] *whole earth . . . wickedness* See 1 John 5:19.

215-16] *Uprise . . . throne* The image of the resurrected Jesus seated at the right hand of God appears first in Mark 16:19 and becomes a repeated feature in Paul's epistles; see Acts 7:56, Rom. 8:34, Col. 3:1, etc.

227-34] *optic glass . . . so clear* Though it may seem anachronistic to the modern reader, ancient peoples were aware of optical lenses and their powers. B may have assumed such knowledge from scattered references in ancient authors, or he may well have known of the discovery in Assyria of a rock crystal magnifier by A. H. Layard, an archaeologist whose works B read.

279-80] *fable of Prometheus . . . Jove's fiery flower* In Greek myth, the titan Prometheus defied the will of Zeus (called *Jove* in Latin) by stealing fire from heaven and bringing it to humans for the first time.

283] *sophist* Referring to group of ancient Greek intellectuals who were accused of scepticism, cynicism, and moral relativism.

284-85] *myth of Æschylus . . . satyrs of his play* The Greek tragedian Aeschylus (525-456 B.C.) portrayed Prometheus as the heroic defender of humankind in *Prometheus Bound.* EBB translated Aeschylus's *Prometheus Bound* in 1833. Aeschylus was considered by the ancients to be the master of the satyr-play, but only fragments of two of these survive. B may be alluding to a lost satyr-play called *Prometheus the Fire-Kindler,* sometimes attributed to Aeschylus, of which fewer than forty lines survive.

293] *gold and purple* Here symbolic of wealth and power (from the color of royal robes).

304] *transfigured* The transfiguration, witnessed by Peter, James, and John, is described in Matt. 17:1-8, Mark 9:2-8, and Luke 9:28-35.

305] *trod the sea and brought the dead to life* Jesus walks on the water in Matt. 14:25-26, Mark 6:48-49, and John 6:19; the dead are brought to life in Luke 7:12-15, Luke 8:49-56, and John 11:1-44.

310] *forsook and fled* See Matt. 26:56, and Mark 14:50.

328] *glozing* Specious commentary.

329] *Ebion . . . Cerinthus* Cerinthus, who lived in Asia Minor around AD 100, was condemned as a heretic by the church fathers. Because his writings were suppressed, the exact nature of his teachings is shadowy, but he questioned the divinity of Jesus and shared some unorthodox beliefs with the Gnostics. His importance in early gospel controversies (and thus in the Higher Criticism) is established by the existence of a group of 2nd century Christians in Asia Minor who claimed Cerinthus had written the Gospel of John. Cerinthus also influenced the Ebionites, another vaguely Gnostic sect of the 2nd century. Accounts of the Ebionites sometimes mentioned a founding figure called Ebion, but there is no historical testimony to his existence. Among the numerous lost Gnostic gospels are a Gospel of Cerinthus and a Gospel of the Ebionites. One of B's direct sources of information about these heretics was probably Edward Gibbon's *Decline and Fall of the Roman Empire* (1776-88). Gibbon specifically states the opposition of St. John to the Ebionites, describes how Cerinthus attempted to reconcile Ebionism with Gnosticism to strengthen his defiance of the church fathers, and includes in a footnote the story of an accidental meeting between St. John and Cerinthus at Ephesus (see Ch. 15, 21, and 47).

331-32] *I stated . . . misdelivered* Biblical scholars have long agreed that John's account of the life and works of Jesus differs significantly from that of the other three gospels, which may share a common source.

340-48] *if a babe . . . apprehend amiss* The analogy recalls Plato's parable of the cave in the seventh book of the *Republic.*

361] *Ephesus* One of twelve cities in the ancient Greek district of Ionia (in what is now Turkey), Ephesus was known in antiquity for its sacred shrines, including the Temple of Diana, which was one of the seven wonders of the world. In the first century AD St. Paul founded a Christian community in Ephesus; it became one of the most important settlements in early Christian history. One tradition has it that St. John came to Ephesus, after his banishment ended, to write the gospel and the three epistles credited to him. Ephesus was abandoned in the fifth century; the excavations of its "blank heaps of stone" by J. T. Wood of the British Museum were widely reported in the press in 1863.

362-63] *And no one asks . . . His coming* See l. 177n. above.

392-93] *charioteer's yoked steeds . . . down the west* In Greek mythology the sun is personified as a charioteer in a golden chariot drawn by fiery horses. The original sun-god was Helios, but his function was later transferred to Apollo.

404-5] *The sun . . . stood still* Divine power is sometimes manifested in the Bible by the eclipsing of the sun or by alteration of its motion; see Josh. 10:12, Isa. 38:8, Amos 8:9, Luke 23:45.

416] *Jove . . . Juno* The Roman names for, respectively, the Greek gods Zeus and Hera, the supreme gods of Olympus.

459-62] *I cried . . . could cure* The miraculous power of Jesus to restore sight to the blind is reported several times in the NT, at length in John 9; but nowhere is it claimed that John himself performed miracles.
530-36] *heathen bard's . . . on earth* That is, is John's proclamation of Jesus's divinity any more believable than Aeschylus's elevation of Prometheus as humanity's savior? When he stole fire from heaven, Prometheus brought it to humans in a stalk of fennel (see also ll. 284-85n., above).
537] *Titan* Prometheus.
565] *Atlas* In Greek mythology Atlas was a Titan, charged with guarding the pillars of heaven, which hold up the sky. After taking part in the revolt of the Titans, Atlas's punishment was to take the place of the pillars, holding up the sky by his own strength.
625-28] *pattern on the mount . . . replaced* The phrasing derives from Ex. 25:40, where Moses is being instructed to make lamps for his tabernacle; the language is echoed in Heb. 8:5.
646] *Ephesus.* The period at the end of this line is faintly present in most copies of 1888, but it must have been invisible in the example that B inspected while compiling the Brown University list of corrections. He calls for a period to be inserted, and the printers did insert a new piece of type, which yielded a darker point in the 1889 second impression. The Dykes Campbell copy of 1888 (see Section III of the *Preface,* above) has a distinct period, but whether it was so printed or was expertly darkened by B is not discernible.
649] *Bactrian* See l. 36n.
653] *Phoebas* An imaginary character.
654-58] *many look . . . his book* Referring to the erroneous belief that John had been granted immortality, described in John 21:23.
664] *Lies . . . God* See John 13:23. B apparently accepted the conjecture that John was the unnamed "beloved disciple" of the fourth gospel.
677-78] *should His coming . . . twelve years* Some early Christians believed that Jesus's prophesied return to Earth would occur before many years had passed, though the NT is ambiguous on this point. At the end of the Book of Revelation appears the repeated prediction, "I come quickly" (Rev. 22:7, 12, 20).
684] *Groom for each bride* The union of God and his followers is repeatedly expressed in the Bible with the imagery of marriage. In the NT Jesus is portrayed metaphorically as a groom in Matt. 25:1-13, Mark 2:19-20, and John 3:29, and similar imagery appears in Rev. 19:7 and 21:2.

CALIBAN UPON SETEBOS

Composition and Sources] C. R. Tracy persuasively argues for a composition date of 1859-60, based on striking similarities between concepts in the poem and the ideas of the American preacher Theodore Parker (1810-60), whom the Bs met in Rome in the winter of 1859-60 ("'Caliban upon Setebos,'" *Studies in Philology* 35 [1938], 487-99; *Letters of EBB,* 2.355). Such a date is also supported by the almost universal assumption that the poem is a response to the controversies about the origins of humankind provoked by Darwin's *On the Origin of Species,* which appeared in November 1859. But it is also true that B had been thinking about evolution and the place of humans in nature for many years, and the concept the poem embodies owes a considerable debt to earlier works on the philosophy of nature, including the *Bridgewater Treatises* (1833-40), R. Chambers's *Vestiges of Creation* (1844), and W. Paley's *A View of the Evidences of Christianity* (1794), a book B owned (*Reconstruction,* A1795). B did not find Darwin particularly shocking, and even argued that he had anticipated some of the evolutionary arguments of the 1860s in *Paracelsus* (1835). In an 1881 letter to F. J. Furnivall, B expressed his overall view of Darwinism, confidently proposing that the evolutionary view of nature was not incompatible with his own ideas about God and creation (Hood, 198-200).

B takes his title character and some details of setting from Shakespeare's *The Tempest,* but the argument of the poem is thoroughly embedded in 19th-century thought. B later argued that he had not diverged from Shakespeare widely (Hood, 228).

Title] *Caliban* is the "savage and deformed slave," "A freckled whelp hag-born[,] not honor'd with / A human shape," who performs menial tasks for Prospero in Shakespeare's *The Tempest.* His name is glossed by Shakespeare scholars as an anagram of "cannibal." *Setebos* is the god worshipped by Caliban's mother Sycorax (*Tempest* 1.2.284-85, 373). The phrase "Natural Theology" appears in the titles of many 19th-century works on nature and religion, one of the most influential being W. Paley's *Natural Theology, or Evidences of the Existence and Attributes of the Deity collected from the Appearances of Nature* (1802). *Island* refers to the place where the action of *The Tempest* occurs.

Epigraph] *Thou thoughtest . . . thyself* Ps. 50:21.

5] *eft-things* Small lizard-like animal, such as a newt.

7] *pompion plant* Pumpkin vine.

16] *whom his dam called God* I. e. Setebos; see above.

20] *Prosper and Miranda* Ten years before the action of Shakespeare's *The Tempest* begins, Prospero's brother had usurped the Dukedom of

Milan and banished Prospero and his young daughter Miranda. The two were abandoned on the ocean in a small boat, eventually being shipwrecked on the unnamed island referred to in B's title. Prospero rules the island with the aid of his magical powers.

24] *Setebos* See *Title* n. above.

50] *pie . . . tongue* *Pie* is usually short for "magpie," but the Latin root for this usage is *picus,* "woodpecker," birds which have long tongues and feed on insects.

51] *oakwarts* Oak-galls, swellings on an oak branch caused by gall flies.

71] *froth rises bladdery* In the manner of an inflated bladder.

79] *great comb . . . hoopoe's* The Hoopoe (*Upupa epops*), a bird of the Mediterranean and N. Africa, has a large crest of feathers which, when erected, is comb-like.

83] *grigs* An obscure dialectal word for grasshoppers or crickets.

148] *hips* Rose-hips.

150] *Prosper at his books* Prospero consults a book of magic spells; when he renounces magic he says "I'll drown my book" (*Tempest,* 5.1.57).

154] *wand* In imitation of Prospero's magic staff (*Tempest,* 5.1.54).

156] *oncelot* Apparently B's variant spelling of *ocelot,* a name which has been applied to more than one spotted ("eyed") tropical cat, including the jaguar.

157] *ounce* A name given at different times to various spotted cats, including the lynx, the snow leopard, and the cheetah.

161] *Ariel* In *The Tempest,* an "airy spirit," indentured to Prospero.

177] *orc* A vague term for a monster or an ogre.

259] *pompion-bell* Flower on the pumpkin vine.

269] *curses* Shakespeare's Caliban shouts at Prospero, "You taught me language, and my profit on 't / Is, I know how to curse" (*The Tempest,* 1.2.363-64).

274] *orc* see 177n. above.

287-291] *wind . . . thunder* The rising storm is presumably the tempest with which Shakespeare's play begins.

CONFESSIONS

Date] In 1860 EBB used a phrase which seems to derive from this poem, thus strongly suggesting that "Confessions" was one of the poems she had seen in Florence (see *Dramatis Personæ, Composition and Text,* above). Writing to Anna Brownell Jameson on 22 February 1860, EBB anticipates a hostile reaction to her forthcoming *Poems Be-*

fore Congress ("my thin slice of wicked book") with an unrepentent glee identical to that of the last two lines of "Confessions": "Say it's mad, and bad, and sad; but *add* that somebody did it who meant it" (*Letters of EBB,* 2.361-62).
3] *vale of tears* An expression with a long history and an obscure origin. It may derive from a misconstruction of Ps. 84:6, which in the Vulgate contains the phrase *valle lacrymarum,* translated in the Wycliffe Bible as "valei of teris"; or from an 11th century Latin hymn beginning "*Salve, regina, mater misericordiae,*" which contains the same phrase. A somewhat more immediate source may be the *Imitation of Christ* by Thomas à Kempis, 4.2.6, which in most English translations employs the words "vale of tears" in its discussion of the Eucharist. Several English poets before Browning had used the phrase as well.
28] *Oes* the seldom-seen plural of the letter *O,* here figurative of watching eyes (cf. Tennyson's "The Epic," [1842], l. 50).

MAY AND DEATH

Date and Text] "May and Death" first appeared in *The Keepsake* annual for 1857; B sent an MS of the poem (now in the ABL; *Reconstruction,* E246) to Marguerite Power, the editor of *The Keepsake,* on 1 August 1857 (McAleer, 3, 5). DeVane speculates that the poem was written shortly after the event it commemorates, the death of B's cousin (and best man at the wedding of B and EBB) James Silverthorne in May of 1852. If the phrase "you died last May" in the first line does signify that the poem was composed during the year that followed Silverthorne's death, then "May and Death" is a leftover from the period when most of the poems in *Men and Women* were written. But since B has changed his cousin's name from James to Charles, he may also have altered his time-frame for artistic purposes, and the "last May" of the opening line establishes a particular phase of mourning, not necessarily an exact date of composition. Indeed, "May and Death" could have been written in 1857 to meet a request from Power, who had published "Ben Karshook's Wisdom" in 1856.

Presumably B kept a copy of "May and Death" when he sent the ABL MS to Power, but it appears that when B assembled *Dramatis Personæ,* he copied the poem from the *Keepsake.* The readings in the Morgan MS are distinctly closer to the text published in 1857 than to the ABL MS. This suggests that the differences between the ABL MS and the text as printed in *The Keepsake* result from changes B made in proof at the time.
2] *Charles* See *Date and Title* above.

13-16] *one plant . . . spring's blood* Folklore has it that the Spotted Persicaria (*Polygonum persicaria*) grew beneath the cross, and received its purple splotches from the blood of Jesus dripping down on it.

PROSPICE

Date] There can be little doubt that "Prospice" was written in the autumn of 1861, after the death of EBB. The poem is often seen as autobiographical, arising from mixed desolation and resolve which B expresses to his friend Isa Blagden after leaving Italy: "I go round in the same order of ideas, & arrive always at the same conclusion, but I don't feel the miserable contrast between then & now, as when first coming on the old Paris nights"; "I am better in many respects: I should not count it 'better' to be with one regret the less,—nor shall I ever be"; "And now the past & present & future, pleasure & pain & pleasure, for the last taste of all, are mixed up like ingredients of a drink" (McAleer, 82, 86, 87).

The poem's title is Latin for "look forward."

YOUTH AND ART

Date] Several internal references suggest that "Youth and Art" derives from B's experiences in Rome in 1859-60, when he joined the painter Valentine Prinsep on excursions into a world of aspiring artists like that of the poem. The Bs first met Gibson (ll. 8 & 55) in 1853-54, and they were visited by him in 1859 when they returned to Rome after five years; they found him and others of their old acquaintance much changed in the interval. The shocking sense of change which can occur upon revisiting a youthful haunt might have triggered the ironic comparisons of past and present in "Youth and Art." B dined with the Prince of Wales in Rome on 25 February 1859, an event which may lie behind line 57 (see Mrs. Sutherland Orr, *Life and Letters of Robert Browning* [London, 1891], 234-36; Hudson, 272; Landis and Freeman, 212; *Letters of EBB*, 2.310; McAleer, 24, 39n.).

8] *Smith . . . Gibson* While *Smith* is imaginary, *Gibson* was John Gibson (1790-1866), a prominent English sculptor who worked and taught in Rome.

11] *Kate Brown* The imaginary speaker of the poem.

12] *Grisi* The Italian opera singer Giulia Grisi (1811-69) was one of the leading sopranos of the 19th century.

31] *shook upon E in alt* Trilled on high E.

32] *chromatic scale* A scale sung in half-tones.

57] *Prince at the Board* See *Date* above.
58] *bals-paré* A dress ball.
60] *R. A.* Member of the Royal Academy of Art, as Gibson was.

A FACE

Composition and date] A manuscript at the ABL signed "Robert Browning—London, Oct. 11. '52" (*Reconstruction,* E123), establishes the poem's date. The title at the head of this MS, termed MS1852a in the variant listings, alludes to the circumstances of composition, "Written on Emily in her Album, from which it is torn." The "Emily" was Emily Andrews Patmore (1824-62), wife of the poet Coventry Patmore and occasional model for pre-Raphaelite artists. The date on the MS was the day before the Bs left England, where they had spent much of the summer, to return to Florence. That this document constitutes the original MS (the "rough draught" B refers to in his note on EBB's transcript, discussed below) is questionable only in that the MS is very clean. The absence of cancellations or alterations suggests that B worked from an earlier draft; his even pen strokes and the regular spacing of words and lines suggest copying, not composition. This MS was published in 1900 in Basil Champneys, *Memoirs and Correspondence of Coventry Patmore.*

An untitled transcript of the poem in EBB's hand also survives in the ABL, and B's annotation of it explains its importance. On the second leaf of the transcript, termed MS1852b in the variant listings, is the following: "I wrote the above poem for the album of Mrs. Coventry Patmore—(the *first* Angel of his House)—and this copy was made from the rough draught by E. B. B. Robert Browning[,] March 27. '74." This MS, which initially followed MS1852a in almost every respect, bears later revisions in B's hand which correspond with the text in the Morgan MS. B eventually gave the EBB transcript to Mrs. FitzGerald (see *Reconstruction,* E122).

The most likely sequence of events seems to be this: on 11 October 1852 B wrote the poem on a page in Emily Patmore's album and tore it out (or vice-versa), thus accounting for the title. This MS remained in the Patmore family until at least 1900, when Champneys published it. But EBB had immediately made a transcript to preserve the poem, and this copy B kept until 1874 or after. When preparing "A Face" for *Dramatis Personæ* in 1862-63, B started with the EBB transcript, made a few revisions on it, and then fair-copied it into the Morgan MS, revising further as he went.

2-3] *Painted . . . Tuscan's early art* The artists of Tuscany in the

12th and 13th centuries still made use of gilding techniques common in medieval and Byzantine art. See "In Three Days," l. 23n. above.
14] *Correggio* Antonio Allegri (c.1489-1534) took the name Correggio from the town in N Italy where he was born. By 1518 he was in Parma, where his greatest works were commissioned. The Bs journeyed to Parma in 1851 largely to see the domes painted by Corregio in the church of St. Giovanni Evangelista and the Parma Cathedral (*Letters of EBB*, 2.9).

A LIKENESS

Date] Topical references within the poem establish that "A Likeness" could not have been written before the late 1850s: B acquired a copy of *The Art of Taming Horses* by John Rarey (l. 22) in 1858; the National Portrait Gallery (l. 50) opened in 1859 (though B could not have visited it until his return to England after EBB's death in 1861); Tom Sayers (l. 23) won the English boxing title in 1857 and held it until 1860. The catalogue of manly pastimes in ll. 14-24 reflects B's effort in the years after EBB's death to develop his son Pen's masculinity. In 1863-64 he wrote to friends with pride about Pen's aptitude for fencing, boxing, and riding (McAleer, 183; Hudson, 142).
14] *masks . . . foils* Fencing equipment.
15] *pipe-sticks* Stems for a tobacco pipe, made of different woods to impart various flavors to the smoke.
16] *tandem-lasher* A particularly long whip used to control horses harnessed one in front of the other, pulling a two-wheeled carriage built for speed.
18] *Tipton Slasher* William Perry, called "The Tipton Slasher" after the midlands village he came from, was the English boxing champion in 1850.
21] *chamois-horns . . . Chablais* The chamois is a small antelope of mountainous regions such as the *Chablais*, a district in the French Alps near Lake Geneva.
22] *Rarey . . . Cruiser* Opposite p. 153 of J. S. Rarey's once-standard work *The Art of Taming Horses* (London, 1858) appears a picture of a whip-brandishing man riding a horse, presumably Cruiser. B asked his publisher Chapman to send him a copy of Rarey's book in July 1858 (DeVane and Knickerbocker, 107).
23] *Sayers . . . bruiser* When Tom Sayers (see *Date* above) lost the English boxing championship in the spring of 1860, EBB sarcastically referred to the taste of the English public, which preferred boxing to her poetry (*Letters of EBB*, 2.387). To call Sayers a "bruiser" after he

lost the title fight may be doubly ironic, since he stood 5′8″ and weighed only 154 pounds.

24] *the little edition of Rabelais* François Rabelais (1494?-1553) was one of B's favorite authors. He owned a "little" (i.e., three volume) edition of the works of Rabelais, dated 1820 (*Reconstruction,* A1919).

27] *Jane Lamb* An imaginary woman.

30] *Vichy* A resort city in central France, whose mineral springs and fine hotels made it a favorite spa of the English.

42-43] *prints . . . portfolio* B complained to EBB about people who treated pictures this way (Kintner, 27).

50] *National Portrait Gallery* The British national collection of portraits of eminent people, which opened in Great George Street on 15 January, 1859. After several relocations, the collection found its present home in St. Martin's Place, behind the National Gallery.

54] *Marc Antonios* Marcantonio Raimondi (c.1480-c.1534), an Italian engraver whose speciality was reproducing paintings by Raphael and other great artists of the Italian Renaissance. B saw a collection of Raimondi's prints in 1846 (Kintner, 694).

55] *Festina lente* A Latin catch phrase meaning "make haste slowly," deriving from an earlier Greek proverb.

61] *Volpato* The Italian engraver Giovanni Volpato (1733-1803) produced an engraving of Caravaggio's frescoes of scenes from the Perseus legend; B extracted Volpato's rendering of "Perseus and Andromeda" from his father's portfolio and hung it above his desk in the 1840s (Kintner, 27). For further discussion about the importance of this subject and picture to B, see Irvine and Honan, 34 and 46; and J. Maynard, *Browning's Youth* (Cambridge, MA, 1977), 150-51, 425n., 160-61 which reproduce Volpato's engraving.

MR. SLUDGE, "THE MEDIUM"

Composition and sources] The poem derives from the Bs' involvement with the spiritualist movement of the 1850s, particularly from a seance conducted by D. D. Home in 1855 and attended by the Bs. Exactly what occurred at the seance in Ealing has been much discussed and disputed; a detailed account can be found in Markus, 229-38. The Bs contact with spiritualism and mediums was intense and sustained; several of the friends and acquaintances who made up the Browning circle in Florence and Rome in the 1850s were committed believers who claimed "mediumistic" powers. (For a full treatment of the subject, see Katherine H. Porter, *Through a Glass Darkly: Spiritualism in the Browning Circle* [Lawrence, KS, 1958].) EBB accepted on trust what others told her about spiritualism, and believed in the reality of phenomena like spirit-writing and table-turning. B appears to have been initially curious and open-minded, but he came to despise those who ingratiated themselves with EBB by encouraging her belief in mediums. Certainly B thought that Home was an utter fraud who had hoodwinked EBB. His frustration and anger at EBB's fascination with spiritualism far exceeded his willingness to express himself about it, and his temporizing can be detected in remarks reported by EBB. In one of her most enthusiastic letters about spiritualism, EBB writes: "Robert, who is a sceptic—observed of himself the other day, that we had received as much evidence of these spirits as of the existence of the town of Washington" (*Letters of EBB* 2.117). References to specific events suggest that B wrote a substantial portion of "Mr. Sludge" in 1859-60, and an early version of it may have been what EBB referred to in May 1860 as "a long poem which I have not seen a line of" (*Letters of EBB,* 2.388). The poem's vehemence about spiritualists and their dupes provides reason enough for B not have shown it to EBB, who would have found it offensive in matter and manner. It should be noted, however, that the two poets did not habitually read each other's work in progress.

If "Mr. Sludge" was conceived in 1859-60, it was reworked a few years later. The poem is by far the most heavily revised portion of the Morgan MS; the impression one gets is that B set out to produce a fair-copy, but soon found himself cancelling and replacing words and phrases. During this revision, most of the paragraph breaks in Sludge's recitation were added with lines across the MS or marginal notations. That B thought of this effort as completing the poem is indicated by his ending the MS with the incantatory letters "L. D. I. E." (*Laus Deo in excelcis*), which he habitually attached as a celebratory closing when he finished a work. Further changes were made in proofing for the first edition.

Spiritualism was often in B's mind in the years after EBB's death; as public interest in it waned, and as closer scrutiny exposed the fradulent practices of mediums, he looked ruefully back on the whole awkward situation (see Hudson, 102-3, McAleer, 135, 201). During the leisurely preparation of *Dramatis Personæ,* he added his long satiric attack to the manuscript; later in 1863 he wrote to Isa Blagden about Frederick Tennyson: "Poor F. T. and his 'mediumship'! I can quite fancy how it all comes about. . . . His verses are meant for fun. Those of mine, by the way, which you inquire about, shall be printed with my new things" (McAleer, 176). "Mr. Sludge," then, had existed long enough for Isa to be aware of the poem and inquire about it; B's sense of the severity of his work is shown in the way he contrasts it to verses "meant for fun."

Both the inclusion of the poem and the revisions may have been a consequence of the appearance in early 1863 of Home's book *Incidents in My Life* [First Series]. Though B wrote to Isa Blagden on 19 April 1863 "I never read Hume's book,—avoid looking at an extract from it," he was aware of the work, and two months earlier he had suffered the very unpleasant experience of accidentally meeting Home at a dinner. "I went to a party at Lady Salisbury's and came right upon *him*—though I could not believe my eyes: presently the Marchioness' sister asked me, 'what I thought of him?'—I said my say, as briefly as possible—'Why, he's gone!' said she—& so he had,—I can't help flattering myself, that the announcement of my name did him no good" (McAleer, 160, 154).

Title] Mr. Sludge is based on Daniel Dunglas Home (1833-86), the most famous spiritualist medium of B's time. Of Scottish birth, Home (who sometimes spelled and pronounced his name "Hume") was swept up in the American spiritualist movement of the 1840s when he lived in New York. He came to England in 1855 and became a celebrity through a series of spectacular séances. The Bs heard about these séances while they were still in Florence, and as soon as they arrived in London in July 1855, it was arranged that they should attend a Home séance. EBB was impressed with the occasion and the phenomena, but B was not, and his scepticism caused Home to refuse to allow the Bs to attend another seance; as Markus puts it, "he had missed the only opportunity he'd have to expose Home" (Markus, 234). Home's fame continued unabated through the 1860s, and B never relented in his dislike and distrust of the man, despite Home's repeated attempts to win B over. His hatred of Home is repeatedly expressed in his letters over the years (see, for example, DeVane and Knickerbocker, 199). A full account of Home, his techniques, and some of his séances can be found in F. Podmore, *Modern Spiritualism* (London, 1902), 2.223-43.

9] *catawba* Wine produced mainly in Ohio and New York, from a native American grape in both sparkling and still varieties; a far less sophisticated drink than the champagne Sludge gets.

35] *Franklin* While he was United States ambassador to France, Benjamin Franklin (1706-90) was asked to investigate an early spiritualist phenomenon called "animal magnetism." The spirit of Franklin, a thorough-going rationalist, was one of the ghosts most frequently conjured up by 19th-century mediums (see Podmore, *op. cit.* above, 1.54-55, 192, 268).

36] *telegraph* Spiritualists claimed to be able to send and receive messages without wires, calling the phenomenon "spiritual telegraphy"; one of the early instances took place when an American medium interviewed the spirit of Franklin, who gave her an electric shock.

Plans were in fact made to set up regular commercial services to exploit this "gift" (see Podmore, *op. cit.* above, 1.252-53 and nn.).

37] *Tom Paine* In 1852, the American medium Rev. C. Hammond published a book about the after-life which the author claimed had been dictated to him by the spirit of Thomas Paine (1737-1809), another hero of Revolutionary days whose ghost was often called up in séances (Podmore, *op. cit.* above, 1.269-71).

47] *rap or tip* Knocking noises and the tilting of tables were two of the most common phenomena claimed to be the manifestations of spirits.

54] *Greeley's newspaper* That is, *The New York Tribune,* founded in 1841 by Horace Greeley (1811-72).

65] *Sixty Vs* A *V* is a five-dollar bill, so the sum named by Mr. Sludge is $300, a considerable sum.

72] *Tread on a worm, it turns* An adaptation of *3 Henry VI,* 2.2.17, where (as here) *worm* means "snake."

81] *nothing lasts, Bacon came and said* An American book on spiritualism published in 1853 included messages dictated by the spirit of the English philosopher Sir Francis Bacon (1561-1626); see Podmore, *op. cit.* above, 1.271-72. One of Bacon's famous essays is entitled "Of Vicissitude of Things."

100] *V-notes* See l. 65n. above.

108] *parade-ground* A place for ceremonial displays and drills.

117] *cow-hide* I. e., a leather whip.

121-24] *rare philosophers . . . made it* The search for a method to turn lead into gold was a preoccupation of medieval alchemists like Paracelsus, the subject of B's second published poem (in the present edition, 1.59ff.). The arcane works (*plaguy books*) of Paracelsus were in B's father's library (*Reconstruction,* A1807-1808).

136] *Johnson . . . Wesley* One of the most famous early cases of "spirit disturbances" occurred at the Parsonage in Epworth, where the religious leader John Wesley (1703-91) was born. In the winter of 1716-17, the Wesley family was plagued by a poltergeist that rapped, groaned, disturbed household articles, and broke glassware. John Wesley did not witness any of these "manifestations," but he did assemble an account of the events in 1726 (see Podmore, *op. cit.* above, 1.32-40). Samuel Johnson (1709-84) had a complicated attitude toward reports of the supernatural; in 1762 he had taken pleasure in exposing the "Cock-Lane Ghost" of London as a fraud, but in *Rasselas* (Ch. 31) he places an argument for the plausibility of ghosts in the mouth of the wise poet Imlac. Boswell firmly states that Johnson never believed in spirit visitations, but maintained a sceptical interest in them. B may be remembering a specific passage in Boswell's *Life* where Johnson comments with laughter on John Wesley's solemn account of another encounter he had with a ghost in 1768 (see *Boswell's Life of Johnson,* ed. G. B. Hill, rev. L. F. Powell [Oxford: 1934, 1964], 1.343, 405-7; 3.230, 297-98; 4.97).

137] *Mother Goose* The volume known as the *Mother Goose Tales* is a translation of French folk tales published by Charles Perrault in 1697.

144] *David* The experiences of the imaginary lad, who is both a projection of Mr. Sludge and an alternative to him, partially parallel D. D. Home's account of himself.

158] *There be more things . . . Horatio* Mr. Sludge misquotes the words of Hamlet after his first encounter with his father's ghost (*Hamlet* 1.5.166).

168] *a "Porson"* I. e., as good a student of Greek as the English classical scholar Richard Porson (1759-1808), who produced authoritative editions of Greek tragedies, two of which were owned by EBB (*Reconstruction,* A892, A894).

181-83] *David holds the circle . . . hears the raps* These lines present a catalogue of the activities in a séance. To begin, the participants sit at a round table and join hands; the medium contacts a familiar spirit or enters a visionary trance; ghostly faces or distant prospects may be viewed in a crystal or glass ball; spirits cause the entranced medium to write out their messages to the living; ghosts announce their presence by sharp noises. Home's séances featured such events, all of which are mentioned or discussed in EBB's letters from 1851 onward; she and her friend Sophie Eckley (whom B came to hate) experimented with "automatic writing" in 1858-59 (see Markus, 276-94). To *rule the roast* is to have complete control or authority; this version of the catchphrase precedes its common bucolic equivalent, "rule the roost," by several centuries.

218] *stranger in your gates* See Deut. 5:14.

220] *guest . . . garb* Alluding to Jesus's parable of the marriage feast, specifically to Matt. 22:11-12.

221] *doubting Thomas* The disciple Thomas who was not present at the Resurrection, and refused to believe that Jesus had risen from the dead until he could see the wounds on Jesus's body for himself (John 20:24-29).

231-33] *Captain Sparks . . . Mexican war* Sparks is imaginary, but his tedious war stories are about the territorial dispute between Mexico and the United States in 1846-48.

238] *chink gets patched* Metaphorically, the little flaws or holes in his self-presentation get filled in.

246-47] *gulling you . . . your bent* Echoing *Hamlet,* 3.2.384.
261] *taste o' the foil* First experience with fencing.
263-71] *I got up . . . her pet* At the age of seventeen, Home was taken up by high society in America, residing as a guest at one house after another for five years (Podmore, *op. cit.* above, 2.224-5).
265] *canvas-backs* A large American duck, *Aythya valisineria.*
280] *Pennsylvanian 'mediums'* The American spiritualist movement of the 19th century began in 1847 in New York state, quickly spreading through New England; in 1851 there were a hundred mediums at work in New York City, and fifty or sixty more in Philadelphia, Pennsylvania. B maybe referring more specifically to the utopian communities of the Rappites and the Shakers, both of which had spiritualist tendencies and formed settlements in Pennsylvania.
286] *the Horseshoe* The cataracts called Niagara Falls include Horseshoe Falls, on the boundary of the state of New York and Canada.
307] *lovers . . . countrymen* Conflated from *Julius Caesar,* 3.2.13 and 3.2.73.
309-12] *Francis Verulam . . . when Cromwell reigned* Francis Bacon (see l. 81n. above) was made Baron Verulam in 1618. He was born in York House in London, not the city of York; he died in London (not Wales) in 1626 more than twenty-five years before the Protectorate of Oliver Cromwell (1599-1658), which lasted from 1653 to 1658. This kind of factual blunder was a frequent cause of embarrassment to mediums, and something of this kind occurred when Sophie Eckley contacted EBB's dead relations, who proceeded to send spirit-messages expressed in a distinctly American brand of English (Markus, 292-93).
328] *Tread . . . kibes* Borrowed from *Hamlet,* 5.1.141.
330] *Barnum* Phineas Taylor Barnum (1810-91) was an American showman who came to fame after purchasing Scudder's American Museum, where he exhibited such "wonders" as the dwarf Charles Stratton (General Tom Thumb) and the Siamese twins Chang and Eng. Barnum had a sensational tour in England with General Tom Thumb in 1844.
339-43] *Beethoven . . . Thirty-third Sonata* Ludwig van Beethoven (1770-1827), one of B's favorite composers, wrote his thirty-second and last piano sonata (*op.* 111 in C minor) in 1823.
345-46] *Shaker's Hymn . . . fourths* A complex passage which imagines several musical oddities: a hymn of the Shakers in the key of G, when all Shaker hymns were in the key of C; a scale in the key of G with a natural F, when the scale requires F sharp; and "The Star-Spangled Banner" (here miscalled "Stars and Stripes") arranged for harmony in parallel (*consecutive*) fourths instead of the harmony based on thirds which is standard in Western music.

353] *madeira red-ink and gamboge* The fortified sweet wine from the Madeira Islands is of a red-amber color, which could be simulated by adding coloring agents (like red ink and *gamboge,* a resin used as a pigment and cathartic) to a cheap sweet wine.
417] *Pennsylvanians* See l. 280n. above.
445-48] *To turn . . . end o' your slipper* Another catalogue of spiritualist phenomena, this including the confession that some of these effects were produced by conjurors' tricks. B imputed this kind of trickery to Home (see P-C, 5.315).
453] *Judge Humgriffin* The fictional host of the imaginary séance described in the preceeding lines.
461] *Very like a whale* See Shakespeare's *Hamlet,* 3.2.382.
480-81] *Saul . . . Caesar* The allusion is to two instances in which an older man brings down a younger kinsman. In the Bible, King Saul repeatedly opposed and threatened his son Jonathan (I Sam. 19 and 20). The Roman general Pompey the Great married the daughter of Julius Caesar, his friend and fellow triumvir. As Caesar rose to imperial power he turned against his son-in-law, pursuing him into Greece and defeating him at Pharsalia, in 48 B.C.
523] *fall West* I. e., escape westward to the United States.
526] *their Broadway* Presumably the Via Cavour, a large principal street in Rome.
528] *lapstone* A large stone, held in a shoemaker's lap, was used to beat leather until it was soft enough to make into shoes.
576] *prairie-dog* B seems to have associated this name with a wild canine rather than the rodent of the plains; perhaps he meant to refer to the coyote.
589-91] *Milton . . . quavers* A collection of ridiculous occurences. The earliest poetry of John Milton (1608-74) dates from his sixteenth year and is already mature in manner. The reasoning of John Locke (1632-1704), author of *An Essay Concerning Human Understanding* (1690), is always clear and cogently expressed. The epic poet Homer was illiterate, and the biblical musician Asaph (1 Chron. 16:4-7) lived centuries before any system of musical notation had been developed.
595] *pothooks* Illegible writing.
620-27] *old prints . . . among them* Perhaps recalling some of the old Italian prints in B's father's collection; see "A Likeness," ll. 42-43, 54, 61 and nn., above.
651] *Macbeth* The title character of Shakespeare's popular tragedy, *Macbeth.*
654] *strut and fret his hour* See *Macbeth,* 5.5.25.
655] *spawl* Spit.

667] *St. Paul . . . Swedenborg* Mr. Sludge is claiming that his spiritualism strengthens religious belief, if not the orthodox Christianity of St. Paul, then at least the mysticism of Emanuel Swedenborg (1688-1772). The Bs were well-acquainted with the doctrines of Swedenborg, having studied his *Conjugal Love* early in their marriage and decided to raise their son Pen according to Swedenborgian principles. EBB did, however, object to having her poetry characterized as Swedenborgian. See Markus, 219; Porter, *op. cit.* above, 43; Landis and Freeman, 207, 216.

678-83] *Miss Stokes turns—Rahab . . . from the altar* During a séance, the imaginary Miss Stokes apparently becomes the vehicle for the spirit of the harlot Rehab, who assisted Joshua's spies before the battle of Jericho. In recompense for her assistance, the Israelites allowed Rehab and her family to escape from Jericho when it was burned. She serves as an example of faith in the NT (Josh. 2:1-21, 6:22-25; Heb. 11:31). The metaphor of a piece of visionary knowledge as a live coal derives from Is. 6:6.

691-93] *Nelson . . . he was bothered with* The well-known story of Admiral Horatio Nelson's stratagem for refusing an order to break off a battle was popularized in Robert Southey's *Life of Nelson* (1813). At the Battle of Copenhagen in 1801, Nelson was told that his commander had run up the signal to retire; Nelson raised his telescope to his blind right eye, claimed to see no such signal, and fought on.

708] *Shakespeare* The ghost of Shakespeare was one of the ancient worthies frequently summoned up by mediums.

726] *judgment-seat* Mr. Sludge may be attempting to link his accusers to Pontius Pilate, who sat in the judgment seat when he condemned Jesus (Matt. 27:19, John 19:13).

742-44] *Mars' Hill . . . Saint Paul* When he was preaching in Athens, Paul was brought before the court of the Areopagus, which was on Mars' Hill, to be questioned by philosophers. The Athenians mocked Paul's beliefs (Acts 17:19-33).

745] *new thing* Acts 17:21 reports that the Athenians went to Mars' Hill "either to tell or to hear some new thing."

774] *Solomon* The OT King Solomon was proverbially famous for his wisdom.

779] *'twist the soup and fish* That is, between one course of a dinner and the next.

788] *Pasiphae* Pasiphaë's reputation for unnatural sexual appetites is hardly just, since in Greek mythology Poseidon punished her husband King Minos by inflicting on Pasiphaë a desire for a bull which Minos spared after promising to sacrifice it to the god. The "decorator" of l. 786 apparently wants to engage the prostitute (l. 783) to pose for an erotic illustration on a snuff box.

801-3] *Rapped . . . phosphor-match* A list of tricks used by mediums. Early investigators of spiritualism soon discovered that "spirit-rappings" were easily produced by cracking the joints of the toes or fingers (Podmore, *op. cit.* above, 1.185). By removing a hand from the circle and replacing it with a dummy, a medium could be free to operate deceptive devices. *Sympathetic ink* is a 19th-century term for ink that remains colorless until chemically activated. Mr. Sludge confesses that he uses the luminescence of phosphorus-scrapings to create ghostly lights during a séance. Such lights were called *odic* because they were produced by an insubstantial fluid force called "odyl" by Karl von Reichenbach in his *Researches on Magnetism;* EBB reported that she could see odic light (Kintner, 640).

805-6] *set the crooked straight* A well-known phrase from Is. 40:4 and 45:2, but the more apposite use is in Eccles. 1:15, "That which is crooked cannot be made straight."

832] *Use plate . . . delf* That is, use silver or gold dishes instead of cheap pottery.

846] *Samuel's ghost appeared to Saul* The Witch of Endor, at Saul's request, calls up the ghost of Samuel, who proceeds to rebuke Saul for disagreeing with Jehovah's commands (I Sam. 28:7-19).

868-69] *ignorance . . . green or red* That is, because he is color-blind.

921] *Charles's Wain* An old name for the constellation of stars in the N hemisphere known as the Great Bear or the Big Dipper. The constellation looks somewhat like a wagon (*wain*), and the *Charles* refers to Charlemagne.

929] *powder-plots prevented* A reference to the Gunpowder Plot of 1605, when Guy Fawkes was caught before carrying out a plan to blow up the Houses of Parliament.

932-37] *yourself . . . forgot* In 1861, on his way back to England after EBB's death, B himself had nearly boarded a train which subsequently crashed with great loss of life (Landis and Freeman, 275).

959] *hour . . . infinitude* The phrasing is reminiscent of ll. 3-4 of William Blake's "Auguries of Innocence," first published in A. Gilchrist's *Life of William Blake* (1863), a copy of which was presented to B by Mrs. Gilchrist, who finished the work (*Reconstruction,* A1035). The Bs knew Blake's poetry as early as 1848 (McAleer, 202n.2).

1024-25] *tenth shovel-load . . . nugget* Veins of gold are often found in quartz deposits.

1050] *cent. per cent.* A one hundred percent profit.

1074] *Great and Terrible Name* See Ps. 99:3.

1074] *Heaven of Heavens* A phrase used frequently in the OT; see Deut. 10:14, 1 Kings 8:27, 2 Chron. 2:6, etc.

1077] *Magnum et terribile* Latin for "great and terrible."

1124-26] *tin-foil bottle . . . lightning* The components of a Leyden jar, a large electrical capacitor from which impressive sparks may be drawn.

1140] *Bridgewater book* The will of the 8th Earl of Bridgewater (1756-1829) provided £8000 to support the writing of treatises "On the Power, Wisdom and Goodness of God, as manifested in the Creation." Eight Bridgewater treatises on "natural theology" were published between 1833 and 1840.

1180] *Washington's oracle* The spirit of George Washington was often summoned by American mediums in order to consult him about national affairs.

1224-30] *Bach's fiddle-fugues . . . their head* This catalogue of accomplishments ranges from the difficult to the absurd. To *"Time" with the foil in carte* in fencing means to parry at the advantageous moment, with the foil in a specified position; to *skate a five* means to cut the figure five into the ice in one continuous movement; and to *make the red hazard* is to sink the red ball in pocket billiards.

1268-69] *President . . . Benicia Boy* The list is graded from the famous to the forgotten: Abraham Lincoln (1809-65) was president from 1860 until his assassination; *Jenny Lind* (1820-87) was a world-famous Swedish soprano who toured extensively in America; B read the works of the American thinker Ralph Waldo *Emerson* (1803-82) and met him in 1872; the *Benicia Boy* was John Heenan, an American boxer from Benicia, Calif., who fought the last bare-knuckle prize fight in England, resulting in a draw with Tom Sayers (see "A Likeness," l. 23n. above).

1299] *Beacon Street* A principal street of Boston, Mass.

1305-6] *lump . . . leaven* Adapted from 1 Cor. 5:6-8.

1330-39] *Herodotus . . . Nile* Mr. Sludge's ignorance is glaringly shown here. The Greek historian Herodotus (c.490-c.425 B.C.) obviously did not write in Latin; and though he wrote much about Egypt, the custom Sludge refers to is attributed by Herodotus to the Babylonians, who lived far from any city on the Nile (see Herdotus, *The Histories,* 1.199).

1350] *turning* To get more wear out of a garment, it would be taken apart and "turned"—putting the inside face of the fabric out.

1392] *harlequin's pasteboard sceptre* Harlequin, a character in French and English comic pantomime, carries a wooden sword, not a pasteboard scepter.
1408-9] *Bacon . . . Mary Queen of Scots* Francis Bacon (see l. 81n. above) wrote a "Letter of Advice to Queen Elizabeth" while he was in Parliament; Shakespeare's comedies, often performed at court, contain many songs; Mary Stuart (1542-87) cousin and rival of Elizabeth I, reigned as Queen of Scotland 1542-67. Such famous people were often called up in séances.
1432] *Eutopia* From Greek, meaning "good place," often confused with "Utopia," which means "no place." "A region of ideal happiness" (*OED*).
1436-37] *Poet who sings . . . never was* The historical existence of both the Greek epic poet Homer and the city of Troy of his *Iliad* were brought into question in the 19th century. Much later in his life, B. mused about his own encounter with scepticism about Homer in "Development," published in *Asolando* (1889).
1439] *Lowell* The American poet James Russell Lowell (1819-91) was a friend of the Bs and rented their apartment in Casa Guidi while they were in Paris in 1851-52; he shared with EBB an interest in spiritualism.
1440] *Longfellow* Henry Wadsworth Longfellow (1807-82), American poet, was a close friend of W. W. Story, a member of the B circle in Rome; both of the Bs were familiar with his work. Longfellow had attended séances in the 1850s.
1441] *Hawthorne* B first met the American novelist Nathanial Hawthorne (1804-64) in 1858 in Rome; he discussed spiritualism with the Bs and seems to have been sceptical (Porter, *op. cit.* above, 54-76). According to Hawthorne, when B told the tale of the Ealing séance, he avowed his conviction that Home was a fake (P-C, 5.315; see *Composition and Sources* above).
1450-1452] *Lizard Age . . . Jerome Napoleon* Only some of these references illustrating types of historical writing are specific; the *Lizard Age* was a Victorian term for the paleontological age when dinosaurs lived (fossils are alluded to in l. 1454 below); Jerome Bonaparte (1784-1860) had a falling-out with his brother Napoleon, over Jerome's marriage to an American girl. Jerome's wife settled in Camberwell, the part of London where B was raised, and gave birth to a son. A decree from Napoleon annulled the marriage; Jerome's son Jerome (1805-70) returned with his mother to Baltimore and was the sire of the American branch of the Bonaparte family. Claims by various members of the Bo-

naparte family (several named Jerome) to be the rightful heir to the throne of Napoleon were commonplace through the 19th century.
1455] *fire into fog* M. Millhauser argues persuasively that this refers to a cosmological concept in Chambers's *Vestiges* ("Robert Browning, Robert Chambers, and Mr. Home, the Medium," *VN* [1971], 15-19); see also "Caliban upon Setebos," *Composition and Sources,* above.
1457] *thread . . . labyrinth* A reference to the Greek myth in which Ariadne provides Theseus with a thread to be followed back out of the labyrinth of Minos after killing the Minotaur within.
1466] *Golden City . . . Thebes* The ancient Greeks gave the name Thebes to a city in Egypt where Luxor now stands; it became the capital of Egypt and was alluded to by Homer as place of great wealth (*Odyssey,* 4.127).
1472] *Lady Jane Grey* For nine days in 1553 Lady Jane Grey (c. 1537-54) was crowned Queen of England, diverting the succession from Mary and Elizabeth, daughters of Henry VIII. Mary gathered her supporters and Jane Grey was deposed.
1474] *Queen Elizabeth* As the second of Henry VIII's daughters to reign, Elizabeth I (1533-1603) ruled from 1558 to 1603, in what has been called England's Golden Age.
1479] *arnica* An herb (genus *Arnica*) distilled into a healing salve.
1493-94] *Twenty V-notes more . . . Greeley* See l. 65n. and l. 54n. above.
1523] *herring-pond* The Atlantic ocean.

APPARENT FAILURE

Date] References in the opening lines of the poem establish the year of composition as 1863; B visited Paris in March, and Paris and Brittany during the summer and early autumn of that year.
3] *baptism of your Prince* The Bs spent many months in Paris in 1855 and 1856; they were there in the spring of 1856 at the time of the birth and baptism of the Prince Imperial, Eugène Louis Jean Joseph, the son of Napoleon III and the Empress Eugénie.
7-8] *Congress . . . Buol's replies* Napoleon III (1808-73) hosted an Imperial Congress in February and March 1856 to conclude a peace ending the Crimean War. One of the Russian diplomats at this conference was Prince Alexander Gorchakov (1798-1883), who ostentatiously refused to add his signature to the peace treaty. In a brilliant stroke of diplomacy, Count Camillo Cavour (1810-61) got the Congress of Paris to treat the Piedmont district of Italy (then under Austrian control) as

an equal partner in the peace because 15,000 Piedmontese troops had been sent to the Crimea. Thus Cavour took a step towards liberating Italy from Austria, whose representative Count Karl Buol-Schauenstein (1797-1865) strongly opposed this element of the treaty.

10] *Doric little morgue* The old Paris Morgue, with a columned portico typical of the Doric style of architecture, was located at the SE end of the Isle de la Cité, near the cathedral of Notre Dame. It was the depository for the bodies of unknown people who died in the river Seine or elsewhere in the city. In B's day, the public could view the corpses in the morgue for purposes of identification. According to Mrs. Orr (307), B visited the morgue and saw three bodies in 1856. The building was slated for demolition in 1863, but the plan was soon dropped.

12] *Petrarch's . . . Sorgue* Throughout the second half of his life, the Italian poet Francesco Petrarca (1304-1374) sought solitude in the Vaucluse valley, near Avignon in SE France. At the head of this valley is a cave in which a spring flows from a large depression to form the source of the river Sorgue. In poem 281 of his *Le Rime* (also identified as Sonnet 240), Petrarch compares the welling up of his recollection of his lost Laura to the flow of this spring (*Rime e Trionfi,* ed. M. Apollonio and L. Ferro [Brescia, 1972], 535-36). The Bs owned a complete edition of Petrarch (*Reconstruction,* A1480) and knew the poetry well.

38-39] *Buonaparte . . . Tuileries* Napoleon Bonaparte (1769-1821), as emperor of France, lived in the royal palace in the Tuileries gardens in Paris.

42-43] *red . . . Republic* The color red was associated with various types of political radicalism, including socialism, and *leveller* was a contemptuous term for those who, like socialists, opposed the class system. The two French Republics (1792-95 and 1848-52) both failed, to be followed by Empires (the first, 1804-14, and the second, 1852-70).

46-47] *red . . . black* The colors are those of the roulette table, where the gambler had his bad luck.

60] *after Last, returns the First* Adapted from Luke 13:30.

EPILOGUE

Date and Sources] There is general agreement that this poem was, as its title suggests, written as a late addition to the *Dramatis Personæ* collection. It comments broadly on the volume's religious and spiritual issues and follows directly from B's reading of Ernest Renan's influential *La Vie de Jésus,* published on 23 June 1863. B announced on 19 November: "I have just read Renan's book, and find it weaker and less honest than I was led to expect. I am glad it is written: if he thinks he can prove what he says, he has fewer doubts on the subject than I—but mine are none of his" (McAleer, 180). Interestingly, Renan (1823-92) was an acquaintance of B's close friend Joseph Milsand; B had Milsand ask Renan about a matter of interest to Isa Blagden (McAleer, 146-52). There is no indication of any direct contact between B and Renan, however.

B has taken some of the events referred to by "First Speaker, as David" from the biblical books 1 Kings and 2 Chronicles; David was a favorite figure of B's and is celebrated in "Saul," see above.

1-4] *Feast of Feasts . . . Altar in robed array* At the dedication of the temple, Solomon held a great feast (1 Kings 8:65 and 2 Chron. 7:10). At the dedication the Levites assisted the priests in bringing to the altar the Ark of the Covenant and the Tabernacle (1 Kings 8:3-4 and 2 Chron. 5:2-5); see also "Saul," l. 60 n. above.

6] *van* The front of a large group of people; a shortening of "vanguard."

7-21] *one accord . . . Lord* This entire passage derives from 2 Chron. 5:13-14 and 1 Kings 8:10-11.

21-22] *Renan* See *Date and Sources* above.

24] *star* Presumably the star of Bethlehem, which "came and stood over where the young child was" (Matt. 2:9).

26] *Face* B said that the "Face" referred to here and later in the poem is the face of Jesus (DeVane, *Hbk.*, 315); he had used the same figure in "Saul," ll. 309-10 (in *Men and Women II*, above).

PREFATORY NOTE TO "SELECTION" (1865)

Composition and publication] B not only wrote this note, but also read proof for *A Selection from the Works of Robert Browning* (London: Edward Moxon, 1865); the volume was the second in the "Moxon's Miniature Poets" series. On the textual authority of the *Selection*, see *Men and Women II, Text* n. in the present volume. A draft and a corrected proof of the prefatory note (see *Reconstruction*, E433) are in the Humanities Research Center at the University of Texas at Austin.

my old publishers] Moxon was B's fourth publisher, producing all of his works from *Sordello* (1840) through the end of the *Bells and Pomegranates* series (1846).

the Selection] That is, *Selections from the Poetical Works of Robert Browning*, edited by B's old friends J. Forster and B. W. Procter and published by Chapman and Hall in 1862. B's involvement in the 1862 volume was minimal.

my illustrious . . . friend] This cryptic passage makes an indirect bow to Tennyson, who was B's "predecessor" in that he had provided a selection from his works for the inaugural volume of Moxon's Miniature Poets earlier in 1865. B inscribed a copy of the Tennyson selection to his son on 28 January 1865 (*Reconstruction,* A2287).

PREFACE TO "SELECTION" FROM EBB (1866)

Composition and publication] Contributing to the sudden stream of volumes of selected poems in the 1860s was Chapman and Hall's *A Selection from the Poetry of Elizabeth Barrett Browning,* published in 1866 with this preface by B. He had written to Isa Blagden in October 1865 that he had "just been making a selection of Ba's poems" (McAleer, 227). The proofs of this volume, corrected by B, are now housed in the Humanities Research Center at the University of Texas at Austin (see *Reconstruction,* E512).

POETICAL WORKS (1868)

Prefatory Note] As this note indicates, circumstances forced B to acknowledge and include *Pauline* among his works in 1868; his effort to suppress the poem had not quite succeeded. The claim that "no syllable" was changed in his 1868 revisions is nearly true, for in the main B confined himself to changes in punctuation. In 1888 he went through the poem again, making more extensive revisions (see Volume I of the present edition).

Note to Volume III] Apparently B included this comment to explain why the contents of Volumes III, IV, and V of the 1868 edition did not follow the plan laid out in his prefatory note to Volume I: these poems are not arranged in "the order of their publication," but in the categories he had set up in 1863. B's tone may seem a bit disingenuous, since it would have been no great trouble to "disturb this arrangement" during the resetting of his text for the 1868 *Poetical Works;* but he was deep in the composition of *The Ring and The Book* at the time, and perhaps did not wish to rethink his categorization of his earlier works.

DEAF AND DUMB: A GROUP BY WOOLNER

Composition and Date] The poem was composed by 24 April 1862, when B hand-delivered it to Woolner's house (see Amy Woolner, *Thomas Woolner, R. A., Sculptor and Poet: His Life and Letters* [New York, 1917], 216). The letter containing the untitled lines is preserved in the ABL (*Reconstruction,* E78). Its subject was a sculpture by Woolner (1825-92) entitle "Brother and Sister, or Deaf and Dumb." Woolner was a member of the Pre-Raphaelite circle and had achieved fame with a bust of Tennyson. The lines were intended to appear in the catalogue of the International Exhibition of 1862, where Woolner's piece was shown, but were omitted. They were first published in the *Poetical Works* of 1868, as part of *Dramatis Personæ*. B and Woolner had been acquainted since at least September 1855, when both men were present at a gathering of poets and Pre-Raphaelites (D. Thomas, *Robert Browning, A Life Within Life* [New York, 1982], 159).

Cumulative Index of Titles

(Titles of long poems or of collections of short poems are capitalized.)

Abt Vogler VI.220
After VI.18
Andrea del Sarto VI.7
Another Way of Love VI.136
Any Wife To Any Husband V.213
Apparent Failure VI.352
Artemis Prologizes III.224
Before VI.16
Ben Karshook's Wisdom VI.151
Bishop Blougram's Apology V.293
Bishop Orders His Tomb at Saint Praxed's Church, The IV.189
BLOT IN THE 'SCUTCHEON, A IV.3
Boot and Saddle III.200
Boy and the Angel, The IV.239
By the Fireside V.200
Caliban upon Setebos VI.259
Cavalier Tunes III.197
"Childe Roland to the Dark Tower Came" V.248
CHRISTMAS-EVE AND EASTER-DAY V.49
Christmas-Eve V.53
Claret IV.244
Cleon VI.105
COLOMBE'S BIRTHDAY IV.63
Confessional, The IV.203
Confessions VI.271
Count Gismond III.203
Cristina III.239
Deaf and Dumb VI.373
Death in the Desert, A VI.235
"De Gustibus—" VI.90
Dîs Aliter Visum; or, Le Byron de Nos Jours VI.206

DRAMATIC LYRIC III.181
DRAMATIC ROMANCES AND LYRICS IV.147
DRAMATIS PERSONÆ VI.171
Earth's Immortalities IV.237
Easter-Day V.97
Englishman in Italy, The IV.173
Epilogue VI.355
Epistle Containing the Strange Medical Experience of Karshish, the Arab Physician, An V.219
Eurydice to Orpheus VI.167
ESSAY ON CHATTERTON III.159
ESSAY ON SHELLEY V.135
Evelyn Hope V.174
"Eyes Calm Beside Thee" I.53
Face, A VI.280
Flight of the Duchess, The IV.207
Flower's Name, The IV.194
Fra Lippo Lippi V.183
France and Spain IV.200
Garden Fancies IV.194
Give a Rouse III.199
Glove, The IV.264
Gold Hair: a Story of Pornic VI.193
Grammarian's Funeral, A VI.130
Guardian-Angel, The VI.102
"Here's to Nelson's Memory!" IV.245
Heretic's Tragedy, The VI.122
Holy-Cross Day VI.96
Home Thoughts from Abroad IV.187
Home Thoughts from the Sea IV.188
How It Strikes a Contemporary V.274
"How They Brought the Good News from Ghent to Aix" IV.161
In a Balcony VI.37
In a Gondola III.214
In a Year VI.21
Incident of the French Camp III.209
Instans Tyrannus V.241
In Three Days VI.19
Italian in England, The IV.167

James Lee's Wife VI.175
Johannes Agricola in Meditation III.242
KING VICTOR AND KING CHARLES III.83
Laboratory, The IV.200
Last Ride Together, The V.278
Life in a Love V.273
Light Woman, A V.258
Likeness, A VI.282
Lost Leader, The IV.183
Lost Mistress, The IV.186
Love Among the Ruins V.163
Love in a Life V.272
Lover's Quarrel, A V.167
LURIA IV.281
Marching Along III.197
Master Hugues of Saxe-Gotha V.285
May and Death VI.273
Meeting at Night IV.243
Memorabilia V.331
MEN AND WOMEN, VOLUME I V.153
MEN AND WOMEN, VOLUME II VI.3
Mesmerism V.230
Misconceptions VI.140
Mr. Sludge, "The Medium" VI.285
My Last Duchess III.201
My Star V.240
Nationality in Drinks IV.244
Old Pictures in Florence VI.24
One Way of Love VI.135
One Word More VI.141
PARACELSUS I.59
PAULINE I.3
Parting at Morning IV.243
Patriot, The V.283
Pictor Ignotus IV.164
Pied Piper of Hamelin, The III.249
PIPPA PASSES III.5
Popularity VI.119
Porphyria's Lover III.245

Pretty Woman, A V.244
Prospice VI.275
Protus VI.94
Rabbi Ben Ezra VI.226
Respectability V.257
RETURN OF THE DRUSES, THE III.263
Rudel to the Lady of Tripoli III.237
Saul IV.246, VI.72
Serenade at the Villa, A V.237
Sibrandus Schafnaburgensis IV.196
Soliloquy of the Spanish Cloister III.211
Song IV.388
SORDELLO II.119
SOUL'S TRAGEDY, A V.3
Statue and the Bust, The V.261
STRAFFORD II.3
Through the Metidja to Abd-el-Kadr III.247
Time's Revenges IV.261
Toccata of Galuppi's, A V.197
Tokay IV.244
Too Late VI.214
"Transcendentalism: a Poem in Twelve Books" VI.138
Twins, The VI.117
Two in the Campagna VI.127
Up at a Villa—Down in the City V.177
Waring III.228
Woman's Last Word, A V.181
Women and Roses VI.92
Worst of It, The VI.201
Youth and Art VI.276